CAPITAL PUNISHMENT

ISSN 2332-3787

CAPITAL PUNISHMENT

Kim Masters Evans

INFORMATION PLUS® REFERENCE SERIES
Formerly Published by Information Plus, Wylie, Texas

GALE
CENGAGE Learning·

Farmington Hills, Mich • San Francisco • New York • Waterville, Maine
Meriden, Conn • Mason, Ohio • Chicago

Capital Punishment

Kim Masters Evans

Kepos Media, Inc.: Steven Long and Janice Jorgensen, Series Editors

Project Editors: Kimberley A. McGrath, Kathleen J. Edgar, Elizabeth Manar

Rights Acquisition and Management: Sheila R. Spencer, Lynn Vagg

Composition: Evi Abou-El-Seoud, Mary Beth Trimper

Manufacturing: Rita Wimberley

Cover photograph: © Brandon Bourdages/Shutterstock.com.

Gale
27500 Drake Rd.
Farmington Hills, MI 48331-3535

ISBN-13: 978-0-7876-5103-9 (set)
ISBN-13: 978-1-56995-796-7

ISSN 2332-3787

This title is also available as an e-book.
ISBN-13: 978-1-56995-839-1 (set)
Contact your Gale sales representative for ordering information.

Printed in the United States of America
1 2 3 4 5 6 7 18 17 16 15 14

TABLE OF CONTENTS

penalty. National polls show majority support for capital punishment; opinions differ, however, based on respondent demographic factors, such as age, gender, and political affiliation and ideology. The various moral and practical reasons that people cite to support their opinions on capital punishment are also examined.

An international consideration of the death penalty is offered in this chapter. Information includes United Nations resolutions regarding capital punishment, statistics on countries that have retained capital punishment and those that have abolished it, rulings on U.S. death penalty cases by the International Court of Justice, and international public opinion polls on the death penalty.

This chapter contains statements that have been made in support of capital punishment by Lewis K. Smith (a district attorney), Don Kleine (a district attorney), Kevin Kane (Chief State's Attorney for Connecticut), Kimberly Sundquist (the niece of a murder victim), Robert Blecker (a law professor), and Justice Clarence Thomas of the U.S. Supreme Court.

This chapter contains statements that have been made in favor of abolishing capital punishment by Stanley L. Garnett (a district attorney), Jim Cunningham (Executive Director of the Nebraska Catholic Bishops Conference), Susan O. Storey (Chief Public Defender for Connecticut), Anne Stone (the mother of a murder victim), Ray Krone (a former death row inmate exonerated of murder), and Justice John Paul Stevens of the U.S. Supreme Court.

PREFACE

Capital Punishment is part of the *Information Plus Reference Series*. The purpose of each volume of the series is to present the latest facts on a topic of pressing concern in modern American life. These topics include the most controversial and studied social issues of the 21st century: abortion, care for senior citizens, education, the environment, health care, immigration, national security, social welfare, sports, women, youth, and many more. Although this series is written especially for high school and undergraduate students, it is an excellent resource for anyone in need of factual information on current affairs.

By presenting the facts, it is the intention of Gale, Cengage Learning to provide its readers with everything they need to reach an informed opinion on current issues. To that end, there is a particular emphasis in this series on the presentation of scientific studies, surveys, and statistics. These data are generally presented in the form of tables, charts, and other graphics placed within the text of each book. Every graphic is directly referred to and carefully explained in the text. The source of each graphic is presented within the graphic itself. The data used in these graphics are drawn from the most reputable and reliable sources, such as from the various branches of the U.S. government and from private organizations and associations. Every effort has been made to secure the most recent information available. Readers should bear in mind that many major studies take years to conduct and that additional years often pass before the data from these studies are made available to the public. Therefore, in many cases the most recent information available in 2014 is dated from 2010 or 2011. Older statistics are sometimes presented as well if they are landmark studies or of particular interest and no more-recent information exists.

Although statistics are a major focus of the *Information Plus Reference Series*, they are by no means its only content. Each book also presents the widely held positions and important ideas that shape how the book's subject is discussed in the United States. These positions are explained in detail and, where possible, in the words of their proponents. Some of the other material to be found in these books includes historical background, descriptions of major events related to the subject, relevant laws and court cases, and examples of how these issues play out in American life. Some books also feature primary documents or have pro and con debate sections that provide the words and opinions of prominent Americans on both sides of a controversial topic. All material is presented in an evenhanded and unbiased manner; readers will never be encouraged to accept one view of an issue over another.

HOW TO USE THIS BOOK

Few topics are as controversial as capital punishment. Capital punishment has been debated in the United States since the colonial period and is currently a worldwide issue. This book includes the history of capital punishment plus discussions of numerous court cases, legal decisions, and historical statistics. Also included is information about execution methods, minors and the death penalty, public attitudes, and capital punishment around the world.

Capital Punishment consists of 12 chapters and three appendixes. Each chapter is devoted to a particular aspect of capital punishment. For a summary of the information that is covered in each chapter, please see the synopses that are provided in the Table of Contents. Chapters generally begin with an overview of the basic facts and background information on the chapter's topic, then proceed to examine subtopics of particular interest. For example, Chapter 6: Statistics: Death Sentences, Capital Case Costs, and Executions presents statistics from government agencies and private organizations regarding inmates who have been sentenced to death and those who have been executed. It includes demographic data, such as age, gender, race, Hispanic origin, educational background, marital status, and criminal history. Time spent on death row and execution methods are also examined. The chapter provides a summary breakdown of the outcomes for all death row inmates and explains the various reasons that inmates are removed from under sentence of death. Jurisdictional and regional differences in numbers of death row inmates and numbers of executions are highlighted. In addition, recent statistical studies on the financial costs associated with capital punishment are reviewed, and the reasons that such studies are controversial are explained. Readers can find their way through a chapter by looking for the section and subsection headings, which are clearly set off from the text. They can also refer to the book's extensive Index if they already know what they are looking for.

Statistical Information

The tables and figures featured throughout *Capital Punishment* will be of particular use to readers in learning about this issue. The tables and figures represent an extensive collection of the most recent and important statistics on capital punishment and related issues—for example, graphics cover jurisdictions with and without the death penalty; public opinion concerning capital punishment; capital offenses by state; federal laws that provide for the death penalty; demographic characteristics of prisoners under the sentence of death; and the number of executions and the methods of execution used by each state. Gale, Cengage Learning believes that making this information available to readers is the most important way to fulfill the goal of this book: to help readers understand the issues and controversies surrounding capital punishment in the United States and to reach their own conclusions about them.

Each table or figure has a unique identifier appearing above it for ease of identification and reference. Titles for the tables and figures explain their purpose. At the end of each table or figure, the original source of the data is provided.

To help readers understand these often complicated statistics, all tables and figures are explained in the text. References in the text direct readers to the relevant statistics. Furthermore, the contents of all tables and figures are fully indexed. Please see the opening section of the Index at the back of this volume for a description of how to find tables and figures within it.

Appendixes

Besides the main body text and images, *Capital Punishment* has three appendixes. The first is the Important Names and Addresses directory. Here, readers will find contact information for a number of government and private organizations that can provide further information on aspects of capital punishment. The second appendix is the Resources section, which can also assist readers in conducting their own research. In this section the author and editors of *Capital Punishment* describe some of the sources that were most useful during the compilation of this book. The final appendix is the detailed Index. It has been greatly expanded from previous editions and should make it even easier to find specific topics in this book.

COMMENTS AND SUGGESTIONS

The editors of the *Information Plus Reference Series* welcome your feedback on *Capital Punishment*. Please direct all correspondence to:

Editors
Information Plus Reference Series
27500 Drake Rd.
Farmington Hills, MI 48331-3535

CHAPTER 1
A CONTINUING CONFLICT: A HISTORY OF CAPITAL PUNISHMENT IN THE UNITED STATES

Capital punishment is the ultimate punishment—death—administered by the government for the commission of serious crimes. The word *capital* comes from the Latin word *capitalis*, meaning "of the head." Throughout history societies have considered some crimes so appalling that the death penalty has been prescribed for them. Over time, changing moral values and ideas about government power have limited the number and types of offenses deemed worthy of death. Many countries have eliminated capital punishment completely, dismissing it as an inhumane response to criminal behavior. The United States is one of only a handful of modern societies that still administers the death penalty. This distinction from the United States' peers is not easily explainable. It arises from a complicated mix of social, legal, and political factors that shape American ideas about justice and the role of government in matters of law and order.

Capital punishment enjoys popular support in the United States. The Gallup Organization conducts an annual poll concerning the death penalty. In *U.S. Death Penalty Support Stable at 63%* (January 9, 2013, http://www.gallup.com/poll/159770/death-penalty-support-stable.aspx), Lydia Saad of the Gallup Organization indicates that 63% of those polled in December 2012 were in favor of capital punishment for persons convicted of murder. The level of approval has dropped since 1994 when it peaked at 80%. In spite of the strong support, capital punishment is rife with controversy.

Proponents and opponents of the death penalty are passionate in their beliefs. People on both sides of the debate often use philosophical, moral, and religious reasoning to justify their positions. Some view capital punishment as retribution (a justly deserved penalty for wrongdoing). Retributionists may rely on historical moral teachings, such as the Bible. One often quoted biblical phrase is "an eye for an eye," which comes from the book of Exodus (or Sh'mot in the Torah) and is part of

the religious laws that existed at the time the Bible was composed that clearly prescribed execution for murder. Death penalty opponents typically take an opposite moral viewpoint arguing that execution is wrong and is more about revenge than retribution. Furthermore, they believe the capital punishment process is flawed by discrimination against the poor and people of color and that it has captured innocent people in its web. There are also purely practical issues associated with capital punishment—its financial costs and its effectiveness (or lack thereof) at deterring others from murdering. Both opponents and advocates of the death penalty complain about the legal appeals process that follows a death sentence. Opponents say the so-called safeguards are inadequate and mistake-prone; advocates say the process takes too long and delays the administration of just punishment for heinous crimes.

The U.S. system of governance is based on the separation of federal and state powers. This means that individual states decide for themselves if they want to practice capital punishment. States with laws (or statutes) that allow death penalty sentences are said to have capital punishment by legislative authority. In other words, the state legislatures have enacted laws that permit the death penalty to be carried out under particular circumstances. However, laws are subject to court challenges regarding their constitutionality, their adherence to the strictures laid out in the U.S. Constitution. Capital punishment laws are often challenged in court. Those laws ruled unconstitutional cannot be enforced until they are changed to be constitutional. In some cases, state legislatures have been unable or unwilling to pass revised statutes. As a result, a state can have death penalty laws on its books that are actually unenforceable. As of October 2013, the federal government (including the U.S. military) and 32 states had death penalty statutes that were in force. (See Table 1.1.) The other 18 states (plus the District of Columbia) that did not have enforceable death penalty laws are listed in Table 1.2. Note that three states that have

TABLE 1.1

Jurisdictions with enforceable death penalty laws as of September 2013

State

Alabama	Mississippi	Tennessee
Arizona	Missouri	Texas
Arkansas	Montana	Utah
California	Nebraska	Virginia
Colorado	Nevada	Washington
Delaware	New Hampshire	Wyoming
Florida	North Carolina	U.S. government
Georgia	Ohio	U.S. military
Idaho	Oklahoma	
Indiana	Oregon	
Kansas	Pennsylvania	
Kentucky	South Carolina	
Louisiana	South Dakota	

SOURCE: Adapted from Tracy L. Snell, "Prisoners Executed under Civil Authority in the United States, by Year, Region, and Jurisdiction, 1977–2012," in *Prisoners Executed*, U.S. Department of Justice, Office of Justice Programs, Bureau of Justice Statistics, March 11, 2013, http://www.bjs.gov/content/data/exest.csv (accessed September 3, 2013)

TABLE 1.2

Jurisdictions without death penalty laws in force as of September 2013

State

Alaska	Maryland	North Dakota
Connecticut	Massachusetts	Rhode Island
District of Columbia	Michigan	Vermont
Hawaii	Minnesota	West Virginia
Illinois	New Jersey	Wisconsin
Iowa	New Mexico	
Maine	New York	

SOURCE: Adapted from Tracy L. Snell, "Prisoners Executed under Civil Authority in the United States, by Year, Region, and Jurisdiction, 1977–2012," in *Prisoners Executed*, U.S. Department of Justice, Office of Justice Programs, Bureau of Justice Statistics, March 11, 2013, http://www.bjs.gov/content/data/exest.csv (accessed September 3, 2013)

FIGURE 1.1

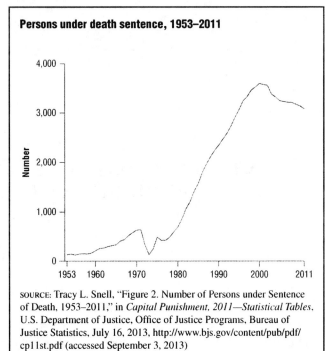

Persons under death sentence, 1953–2011

SOURCE: Tracy L. Snell, "Figure 2. Number of Persons under Sentence of Death, 1953–2011," in *Capital Punishment, 2011—Statistical Tables*, U.S. Department of Justice, Office of Justice Programs, Bureau of Justice Statistics, July 16, 2013, http://www.bjs.gov/content/pub/pdf/cp11st.pdf (accessed September 3, 2013)

abolished capital punishment—New Mexico (2009), Connecticut (2012), and Maryland (2013)—did so for future cases only. Already condemned prisoners remain under sentence of death.

Figure 1.1 shows the number of inmates under sentence of death in the United States between 1953 and 2011. The number skyrocketed during the 1980s and 1990s before leveling off around the turn of the 21st century and then declining. Just over 3,000 inmates were under sentence of death at the end of 2011. Table 1.3 lists the number of inmates under sentence of death that year in the 15 states with the most death row inmates and in the federal prison system.

The constitutionality of capital punishment has historically hinged on court interpretation of the short, but monumental, statement that composes the Eighth Amendment to the U.S. Constitution: "Excessive bail shall not be required, nor excessive fines imposed, nor cruel and unusual punishments inflicted." Is capital punishment cruel and unusual or not? American society has struggled with this question since the founding of the nation and continues to do so in the 21st century.

THE COLONIAL PERIOD

Since the first European settlers arrived in North America, the death penalty has been accepted as just punishment for a variety of offenses. In fact, the earliest recorded execution occurred in 1608, only a year after the English constructed their first settlement in Jamestown, Virginia. Captain George Kendall, one of the original leaders of the Virginia colony, was convicted of mutiny by a jury of his peers and sentenced to death by shooting in Jamestown. In 1632 Jane Champion, a slave, became the first woman to be put to death in the new colonies. She was hanged in James City, Virginia, for the murders of her master's children.

According to *Society's Final Solution: A History and Discussion of the Death Penalty* (Laura E. Randa, ed., 1997), capital law in the early colonies was based on English law, which prescribed the death penalty for hundreds of crimes by the 1700s. Actual practice, however, varied from colony to colony. The Quakers, who settled in the mid-Atlantic region, initially adopted much milder laws than those who settled in the Massachusetts, New York, and Virginia colonies.

TABLE 1.3

Persons under death sentence, by jurisdiction, as of December 31, 2011

California	705
Florida	393
Texas	301
Pennsylvania	207
Alabama	196
North Carolina	158
Ohio	142
Arizona	130
Georgia	96
Louisiana	87
Tennessee	87
Nevada	81
Oklahoma	63
Mississippi	57
Federal Bureau of Prisons	56
21 other jurisdictions*	323
Total	**3,082**

*New Mexico repealed the death penalty for offenses committed after July 1, 2009. As of December 31, 2011, two men were under previously imposed death sentences.

SOURCE: Adapted from Tracy L. Snell, "Figure 1. Status of the Death Penalty, December 31, 2011," in *Capital Punishment, 2011—Statistical Tables*, U.S. Department of Justice, Office of Justice Programs, Bureau of Justice Statistics, July 16, 2013, http://www.bjs.gov/content/pub/pdf/cp11st.pdf (accessed September 3, 2013)

The methods of execution in the fledgling North American colonies could be especially brutal. M. Watt Espy and John Ortiz Smykla note in *Executions in the United States, 1608–2002: The ESPY File* (2005) that even though hanging was the preferred method, some criminals were burned alive or pressed to death by heavy stones. Probably the cruelest punishment was known as "breaking at the wheel," wherein the executioner would snap all the offender's arm and leg joints with a chisel and then weave the extremities through the spokes of a large wheel like meaty ribbons. The prisoner would then be left outside to die of blood loss and exposure.

These executions were held in public as a warning to others, and often a festival atmosphere prevailed. Crowds of onlookers gathered near the gallows, and merchants sold souvenirs. Some spectators got drunk, turning unruly and sometimes violent. After the execution, the body of the convict was sometimes left hanging above the square in a metal cage.

David G. Chardavoyne describes a typical 19th-century execution scene in *A Hanging in Detroit: Stephen Gifford Simmons and the Last Execution under Michigan Law* (2003). One of only two executions in Michigan before the death penalty was outlawed there in 1846, Simmons was hanged in September 1830 for murdering his pregnant wife. Chardavoyne explains that at the time, "public executions owed much of their continuing legitimacy to the use of ritual." The associated rituals could last for hours and included parading the condemned prisoner through the crowd with a coffin by his side and a noose around his neck, speeches by public officials and religious leaders denouncing the crime, and in some cases a repentance speech by the prisoner.

Over time, the colonies phased out the crueler methods of execution, and almost all death sentences were carried out by hanging. The colonies also rewrote their death penalty statutes to cover only serious crimes involving willful acts of violence or thievery. By the late 1700s typical death penalty crimes included arson, piracy, treason, murder, and horse stealing. Southern colonies executed people for slave stealing or aiding in a slave revolt. After the American Revolution (1775–1783), some states went further by adopting death penalty statutes similar to those of Pennsylvania, which in 1682 had limited its death penalty to treason and murder. New York built its first penitentiary in 1796. With a place to house burglars and nonviolent criminals, the state reduced its capital offenses from 13 to two. Other states followed suit by constructing large jails and cutting their capital offenses to just a few of the worst crimes.

THE DEATH PENALTY ABOLITION MOVEMENT

Even though the founders of the United States generally accepted the death penalty, many early Americans did oppose capital punishment. During the late 18th century Benjamin Rush (1746–1813), a physician who helped establish the slavery abolition movement, decried capital punishment. He attracted the support of Benjamin Franklin (1706–1790), and it was at Franklin's home in Philadelphia, Pennsylvania, that Rush became one of the first Americans to propose a "House of Reform," a prison where criminals could be detained until they changed their antisocial behavior. Consequently, in 1790 the Walnut Street Jail, the primitive seed from which the U.S. penal system grew, was built in Philadelphia.

Rush published many pamphlets, the most notable of which was *Considerations on the Justice and Policy of Punishing Murder by Death* (1792). He argued that the biblical support given to capital punishment was questionable and that the threat of hanging did not deter crime. Influenced by the philosophy of the Enlightenment (an intellectual movement during the 17th and 18th centuries), Rush believed the state exceeded its granted powers when it executed a citizen. Besides Franklin, Rush attracted many other Pennsylvanians to his cause, including William Bradford (1755–1795), the attorney general of Pennsylvania. Bradford suggested the idea of different degrees of murder, some of which did not warrant the death penalty. As a result, in 1794 Pennsylvania repealed the death penalty for all crimes except for first-degree murder, which was defined as "willful, deliberate, and premeditated killing or murder committed during arson, rape, robbery, or burglary."

The 19th Century

Rush's proposals attracted many followers, and petitions aiming to abolish all capital punishment were presented in New Jersey, New York, Massachusetts, and Ohio. No state reversed its laws, but the number of crimes punishable by death was often reduced.

The second quarter of the 19th century was a time of reform in the United States. Capital punishment opponents rode the tide of righteousness and indignation created by antisaloon and antislavery advocates. Abolitionist societies (organizations against the death penalty) sprang up, especially along the East Coast. In 1845 the American Society for the Abolition of Capital Punishment was founded.

PUBLIC EXECUTIONS ARE PHASED OUT. Prior to the 1830s, executions were mostly public (and festive) events that attracted large and sometimes unruly crowds. Maine outlawed public executions and in 1835 put into effect a temporary moratorium (suspension) of executions after one public execution brought in 10,000 people, many of whom became violent after the execution and had to be restrained by the police. Other states followed suit. According to *Society's Final Solution: A History and Discussion of the Death Penalty*, many capital punishment abolitionists were opposed to these measures. They believed that executions conducted in public would eventually arouse the revulsion of American society against capital punishment.

During the late 1840s Horace Greeley (1811–1872), the founder and editor of the *New York Tribune* and a leading advocate of most abolitionist causes, led the crusade against the death penalty. In 1846 Michigan became the first state to abolish the death penalty for all crimes except treason (until 1963), making it the first English-speaking jurisdiction in the world to abolish the death penalty for common crimes. Common crimes, also called ordinary crimes, are crimes committed during peacetime. Ordinary crimes that could lead to the death penalty include murder, rape, and, in some countries, robbery or embezzlement of large sums of money. In comparison, exceptional crimes are military crimes committed during exceptional times, mainly wartime. Examples are treason, spying, or desertion (leaving the armed services without permission). The Michigan law took effect in March 1847. In 1852 and 1853 Rhode Island and Wisconsin, respectively, became the first two states to outlaw the death penalty for all crimes. Most states began limiting the number of capital crimes. Outside the South, murder and treason became the only acts punishable by death.

As the Civil War (1861–1865) neared, concern about the death penalty was lost amid the growing antislavery movement. It was not until after the Civil War that Maine and Iowa abolished the death penalty. Almost immediately, however, their legislatures reversed themselves and reinstated the death penalty. In 1887 Maine again reversed itself and abolished capital punishment. It has remained an abolitionist state ever since. Colorado abolished capital punishment in 1897, a decision that was apparently against the will of many of its citizens. In 1901 the state restored the death penalty. Meanwhile, the federal government, following considerable debate in Congress, reduced the number of federal crimes punishable by death to treason, murder, and rape.

INTRODUCTION OF ELECTROCUTION AS A METHOD OF EXECUTION. Around the end of the 19th century the use of electricity came into favor as a new means of execution. According to *Society's Final Solution: A History and Discussion of the Death Penalty*, the Edison Company electrocuted animals in public demonstrations. In 1888 New York became the first state to tear down its gallows and erect an electric chair. Two years later the chair was first used on a convict named William Kemmler. Even though electrocution was described as "clumsy, at best," other states quickly embraced the electric chair for carrying out capital punishment.

THE ANTI–DEATH PENALTY MOVEMENT

At the start of the 20th century, death penalty abolitionists again benefited from American reformism as the Progressives (liberal reformers) worked to correct perceived problems in the U.S. legal system. *Society's Final Solution: A History and Discussion of the Death Penalty* reports that by 1917 capital punishment had been abolished or limited to only a handful of serious crimes in nine states. However, many of these states reversed their decisions in the following decades. The Prohibition era (1920–1933), which was characterized by frequent disdain for law and order, almost destroyed the abolitionist movement, as many Americans began to believe that the death penalty was the only proper punishment for gangsters who committed murder.

The movement's complete collapse was prevented by the determined efforts of Clarence Darrow (1857–1938), the "attorney for the damned"; Lewis Edward Lawes (1883–1947), the abolitionist warden of Sing Sing Prison in New York; and the American League to Abolish Capital Punishment (founded in 1927). Nonetheless, between 1917 and 1957 no state abolished the death penalty.

Society's Final Solution: A History and Discussion of the Death Penalty reports that the abolitionist movement made a mild comeback during the mid-1950s. In 1957 the U.S. territories of Alaska and Hawaii abolished the death penalty. In the states, however, the movement's singular success in Delaware (1958) was reversed three years later (1961), a major disappointment for death penalty opponents. In 1963 Michigan, which in 1847 had abolished capital punishment for all crimes except treason, finally outlawed the death penalty for that crime as well. Oregon (1964), Iowa (1965), New York (1965), Vermont (1965), West Virginia (1965), and New Mexico (1969) all abolished capital punishment, whereas many other states sharply reduced the number of crimes punishable by death.

RESOLVING THE CONSTITUTIONAL ISSUES

Until the mid-20th century there was legally no question that the death penalty was acceptable under the U.S. Constitution. In 1958, however, the U.S. Supreme Court opened up the death penalty for reinterpretation when it ruled in *Trop v. Dulles* (356 U.S. 86) that the language of the Eighth Amendment (which states that criminals cannot be subjected to a cruel and unusual punishment) held the "evolving standards of decency that mark the progress of a maturing society." Opponents of capital punishment believed the death penalty should be declared unconstitutional in light of the *Trop* decision (which did not specifically address capital punishment). The abolitionists claimed that society had evolved to a point where the death penalty was cruel and unusual by the established "standards of decency." As such, the death penalty violated the Eighth Amendment of the Constitution.

In 1963 Justice Arthur J. Goldberg (1908–1990) dissented in *Rudolph v. Alabama* (375 U.S. 889), a rape case in which the defendant had been sentenced to death. Joined by Justices William O. Douglas (1898–1980) and William J. Brennan (1906–1997), Justice Goldberg raised the question of the legality of the death penalty. The filing of many lawsuits during the late 1960s led to an implied moratorium on executions until the court could decide whether the death penalty was constitutional.

In 1972 the high court finally handed down a landmark decision in *Furman v. Georgia* (408 U.S. 238), when it ruled that the death penalty violated the Eighth and 14th Amendments (the right to due process) because of the arbitrary nature with which the death penalty was administered across the United States. The court also laid down some guidelines for states to follow, declaring that a punishment was cruel and unusual if it was too severe, arbitrary, or offended society's sense of justice.

Before the late 1960s U.S. death penalty laws varied considerably from state to state and from region to region. Few national standards existed on how a murder trial should be conducted or which types of crimes deserved the death penalty. Specifically, *Furman* brought into question the laws of Georgia and a number of other states that allowed juries complete discretion in delivering a sentence. Critics feared the punishments such juries meted out were arbitrary and discriminatory against minorities.

CREATING A UNIFORM DEATH PENALTY SYSTEM ACROSS THE UNITED STATES

Within a year of the Supreme Court's ruling in *Furman*, most states had updated their laws regarding the death penalty. Many of these new statutes were brought before the high court during the mid-1970s. By issuing rulings on the constitutionality of these state statutes, the court created a uniform death penalty system for the United States. Table 1.4 provides a summary of the major cases decided by the court dealing with the death penalty between 1972 and 2008.

States amended their laws once again after the Supreme Court issued the new rulings. Every state switched to a bifurcated (two-part) trial system, where the first trial is used to determine a defendant's guilt, and the second trial determines the sentence of a guilty defendant. Generally, only those convicted of first-degree murder were eligible for the death penalty. Most states also required the jury or judge in the sentencing phase of the trial to identify one or more aggravating factors (circumstances that may increase responsibility for a crime) beyond a reasonable doubt before they could sentence a person to death. State legislatures drafted lists of aggravating factors that could result in a penalty of death. Typical aggravating factors included murders committed during robberies, the murder of a pregnant woman, murder committed after a rape, and the murder of an on-duty firefighter or police officer. The long appeals process for capital cases was also established during the mid-1970s.

THE END OF THE NATIONWIDE MORATORIUM

With the Supreme Court–approved laws in place, the states resumed executions. In January 1977 the nationwide moratorium ended when the state of Utah executed Gary Gilmore (1940–1977). Gilmore had been convicted of killing Ben Bushnell, a motel manager in Provo, Utah, on July 20, 1976. Authorities had also charged him with the July 19 murder of Max Jensen, a gas station attendant, in Orem, Utah. Gilmore received the death penalty for the Bushnell murder. He refused to appeal his case, demanding that his sentence be carried out swiftly. Gilmore requested the state supreme court to grant his wish because he did not want to spend his life on death row. The court granted his wish, but interventions by Gilmore's mother, as well as by anti–death penalty organizations, resulted in several stays (postponements) of execution. These organizations were concerned that the defendant's refusal to appeal his case and the court's agreement to carry out his wish might establish a precedent that would hurt the causes of other inmates. After several suicide attempts, Gilmore was finally executed by firing squad in January 1977.

TABLE 1.4

Major U.S. Supreme Court decisions involving the death penalty, selected years 1972–2008

Case	Year decided	Decision	Major effect
Furman v. Georgia	1972	5 to 4	The death penalty as administered by states at the time was deemed cruel and unusual punishment in violation of the Eighth and Fourteenth Amendments.
Gregg v. Georgia Proffit v. Florida Jurek v. Texas	1976	7 to 2	New death penalty statutes in Georgia, Florida, and Texas ruled constitutional.
Woodson v. North Carolina	1976	5 to 4	Mandatory death sentences ruled unconstitutional.
Coker v. Georgia	1977	5 to 4	The death penalty may not be imposed for raping an adult woman if the victim does not die.
Godfrey v. Georgia	1980	6 to 3	State statutes must clearly define the circumstances that qualify a crime as a capital crime.
Spaziano v. Florida	1984	5 to 3	Upheld as constitutional a judge's decision to impose a death sentence despite jury's recommendation of life in prison.
Ford v. Wainwright	1986	5 to 4	Inflicting the death penalty upon the insane ruled unconstitutional.
Murray v. Giarratamo	1989	5 to 4	Defendants under sentence of death do not have a constitutional right to counsel during postconviction proceedings.
Ring v. Arizona	2002	7 to 2	Only juries, not judges, can determine the presence of aggravating circumstances that warrant a death sentence.
Atkins v. Virginia	2002	6 to 3	Inflicting the death penalty upon the mentally retarded ruled unconstitutional.
Roper v. Simmons	2005	5 to 4	Death sentences imposed against minors (i.e., those less than 18 years of age when crime committed) ruled unconstitutional.
Baze and Bowling v. Rees	2008	7 to 2	Found that Kentucky's lethal injection "cocktail" (which was widely used in other death penalty states) did not violate the Eighth Amendment.
Kennedy v. Louisiana	2008	5 to 4	The death penalty may not be imposed for raping a child if the crime was not intended to cause, nor resulted in, the child's death.

SOURCE: Created by Kim Masters Evans for Gale, 2011

Several other states reinstated the death penalty after the Supreme Court declared it constitutional. Oregon brought back the death penalty in 1978. In 1995 New York became the 38th state to reinstate the death penalty, ending its 30-year ban on capital punishment.

After the nationwide moratorium ended in 1977, the number of executions per year began to rise. (See Figure 1.2.) As shown in Table 1.5, executions hit the double digits in 1984, when 21 inmates were put to death in the United States, and peaked in 1999, when 98 inmates were executed. The number of inmates put to death then dipped to 37 in 2008—the lowest level in about a decade and a half—before rising to 52 in 2009 and falling to 46 in 2010 and 43 each in 2011 and 2012. Of course, these numbers were much smaller than the number of executions that occurred during the early part of the 20th century. In 1938 alone, for instance, 190 people were executed. Overall, between 1977 and 2012, 1,320 people were put to death.

As shown in Figure 1.3, more than 400 people were on death row in 1977. The number climbed dramatically over the following decades, peaking at just over 3,600 in 2000. It then began a downward trend, dropping to 3,082 in 2011. Figure 1.3 clearly shows the rarity with which executions are carried out in the United States, compared with the large number of people under the sentence of death. Between 2002 and 2011 the United States executed an average of 53 people per year, whereas the number on death row averaged around 3,255 per year. (See Table 1.5.) This constitutes an execution rate of less than 2% per year.

THE HOMICIDE RATE CONNECTION

Figure 1.4 compares the homicide (murder) rate and the number of executions that were conducted in the United States each year between 1950 and 2011. The increasing usage of capital punishment during the 1980s and early 1990s was in part a response to rising homicide rates in the country. Between 1960 and 1980 the homicide rate doubled from 5.1 cases per 100,000 population to 10.2 cases per 100,000 population. After falling slightly during the early 1980s, it surged again, reaching its penultimate (second-highest) level in 1991, when 9.8 homicides occurred for every 100,000 people. Since that time the rate has generally declined. By 2000 it was 5.5 cases per 100,000 population. It remained around that level through 2007 and then declined sharply through 2011, when it was 4.7 homicides per 100,000 population.

The United States also experienced a surge of homicides in the early 1930s, during the Prohibition era. As mentioned earlier, this was a time when support for the

FIGURE 1.2

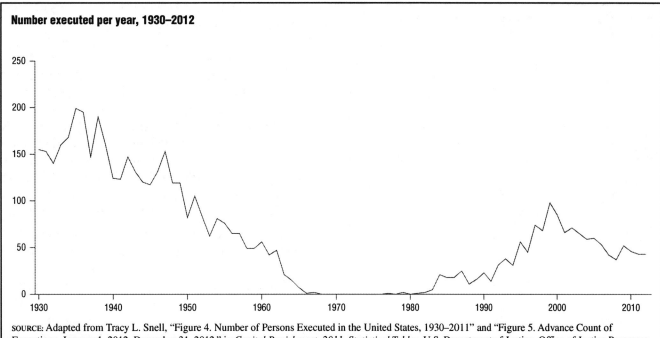

Number executed per year, 1930–2012

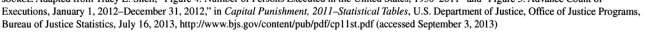

SOURCE: Adapted from Tracy L. Snell, "Figure 4. Number of Persons Executed in the United States, 1930–2011" and "Figure 5. Advance Count of Executions, January 1, 2012–December 31, 2012," in *Capital Punishment, 2011–Statistical Tables*, U.S. Department of Justice, Office of Justice Programs, Bureau of Justice Statistics, July 16, 2013, http://www.bjs.gov/content/pub/pdf/cp11st.pdf (accessed September 3, 2013)

death penalty strengthened around the country. As shown in Figure 1.2, the number of executions was historically high at that time.

NEW RULES IN THE MODERN DEATH PENALTY ERA

U.S. Supreme Court decisions continued to redefine state death penalty laws well after the *Furman* opinion. In particular, the court has ruled the death penalty to be unconstitutional for three groups of defendants: the insane, the mentally retarded, and juveniles.

Executing the Insane

In *Ford v. Wainwright* (477 U.S. 399 [1986]), the U.S. Supreme Court ruled that executing an insane person constituted a cruel and unusual punishment and was thus in violation of the Eighth Amendment. Because a precedent did not exist in U.S. legal history about executing the insane, the justices looked to English common law to make this ruling. English law expressly forbade the execution of insane people. The English jurist Sir Edward Coke (1552–1634) observed that even though the execution of a criminal was to serve as an example, the execution of a madman was considered "of extream inhumanity and cruelty, and can be no example to others."

Executing Mentally Retarded People

In 1989 the Supreme Court held in *Penry v. Lynaugh* (492 U.S. 302) that it was not unconstitutional to execute a mentally retarded person found guilty of a capital crime. According to the court, there was no emerging national consensus against such execution. Just two death penalty states—Georgia and Maryland—banned putting mentally retarded people to death. In 1988 Georgia became the first state to prohibit the execution of murderers found "guilty but mentally retarded." The legislation resulted from the 1986 execution of Jerome Bowden, who had an intelligence quotient (IQ) of 65. It is generally accepted that an IQ below 70 is evidence of mental retardation. (Normal IQ is considered 90 and above.) In 1988 Maryland passed similar legislation, which took effect in July 1989.

Between 1989 and 2001, 18 states outlawed the execution of offenders with mental retardation. The federal government also forbids the execution of mentally retarded inmates. In the Anti-Drug Abuse Act of 1988 the government permits the death penalty for any person working "in furtherance of a continuing criminal enterprise or any person engaging in a drug-related felony offense, who intentionally kills or counsels, commands, or causes the intentional killing of an individual," but forbids the imposition of the death penalty against anyone who is mentally retarded who commits such a crime. In 1994, when Congress enacted the Federal Death Penalty Act, which added more than 50 crimes punishable by death, it also exempted people with mental retardation from the death sentence.

Even though the Supreme Court had agreed to review the case of the North Carolina death row inmate Ernest

TABLE 1.5

Number of persons under sentence of death and executed, by year, 1977–2011

Year	Under sentence of death	Executed
1977	423	1
1978	482	0
1979	593	2
1980	692	0
1981	860	1
1982	1,066	2
1983	1,209	5
1984	1,420	21
1985	1,575	18
1986	1,800	18
1987	1,967	25
1988	2,117	11
1989	2,243	16
1990	2,346	23
1991	2,465	14
1992	2,580	31
1993	2,727	38
1994	2,905	31
1995	3,064	56
1996	3,242	45
1997	3,328	74
1998	3,465	68
1999	3,527	98
2000	3,601	85
2001	3,577	66
2002	3,562	71
2003	3,377	65
2004	3,320	59
2005	3,245	60
2006	3,228	53
2007	3,215	42
2008	3,210	37
2009	3,173	52
2010	3,139	46
2011	3,082	43
2012	Not available	43

SOURCE: Adapted from Tracy L. Snell, "Figure 4. Number of Persons Executed in the United States, 1930–2011" and "Figure 5. Advance Count of Executions, January 1, 2012–December 31, 2012," in *Capital Punishment, 2011—Statistical Tables*, U.S. Department of Justice, Office of Justice Programs, Bureau of Justice Statistics, July 16, 2013, http://www.bjs.gov/content/pub/pdf/cp11st.pdf (accessed September 3, 2013)

McCarver in 2001 to consider whether it is unconstitutional to execute inmates with mental retardation, the case was rendered moot when a state bill was passed that banned such executions. In June 2002 the Supreme Court finally ruled on a case involving the execution of mentally retarded convicts. In *Atkins v. Virginia* (536 U.S. 304), the court ruled 6–3 that executing the mentally retarded violates the Eighth Amendment ban against a cruel and unusual punishment. The court did not say what mental retardation consists of, leaving it to the states to set their own definitions.

Juveniles

The term *juvenile* varies under state criminal statutes. For example, some states consider people aged 17 years and younger to be juveniles, whereas other states define juveniles as those aged 16 years and younger. Literature on the death penalty typically considers "juvenile

offenders" as people who were under the age of 18 years when they committed their crimes. According to Victor L. Streib of Ohio Northern University, in *The Juvenile Death Penalty Today: Death Sentences and Executions for Juvenile Crimes, January 1, 1973–February 28, 2005* (2005, http://www.deathpenaltyinfo.org/juvdeath streib.pdf), the first execution of a juvenile in the United States took place in Plymouth Colony, Massachusetts, in 1642. Streib estimates that between 1642 and 2003, 366 inmates who were juveniles during the commission of their crimes were executed in the United States. In "Executing Female Juveniles" (*Connecticut Law Review*, vol. 22, no. 1, Fall 1989), Victor L. Streib and Lynn Sametz note that only 10 of the executed juveniles were females.

According to the Death Penalty Information Center (DPIC), 22 inmates who were juveniles at the time of their crimes were executed between 1973 and 2003, that is, within the modern death penalty era. Texas executed 13 juvenile offenders, followed by Virginia (3) and Oklahoma (2). Georgia, Louisiana, Missouri, and South Carolina each executed one juvenile offender. One of the executed juveniles was 16 years old when he committed a capital crime; the other 21 juveniles were aged 17 years when they committed capital crimes.

In *Roper v. Simmons* (543 U.S. 551 [2005]), the court decided that executing Donald Roper was cruel and unusual based on the fact that Roper was younger than age 18 when he committed murder. The majority reasoned that adolescents do not have the emotional maturity or understanding of lasting consequences that adults have and therefore should not be held to an adult standard or punished with a sentence of death. All states with the death penalty subsequently changed their laws to prohibit death sentences for people under the age of 18 years.

DNA TAKES THE STAND

During the 1980s and 1990s deoxyribonucleic acid (DNA) testing procedures advanced to the point where such evidence could be used in criminal cases. Across the United States, police suddenly had the ability to identify a suspect and place him or her squarely at the scene of a crime with a small sample of hair, blood, or other biological material. Because of the accuracy of DNA testing, DNA evidence could hold as much sway in a courtroom as an eyewitness or camera footage. States started collecting biological samples, such as blood and saliva, from criminal offenders and storing these DNA profiles in databases.

In 1994 Virginia became the first state to execute a person who was convicted as a result of DNA evidence. The defendant, Timothy Spencer, was convicted in 1988 and sentenced to death for the rapes and murders of four women: Debbie Davis, Susan Hellams, Diane Cho, and Susan Tucker. Spencer was also suspected of killing at

FIGURE 1.3

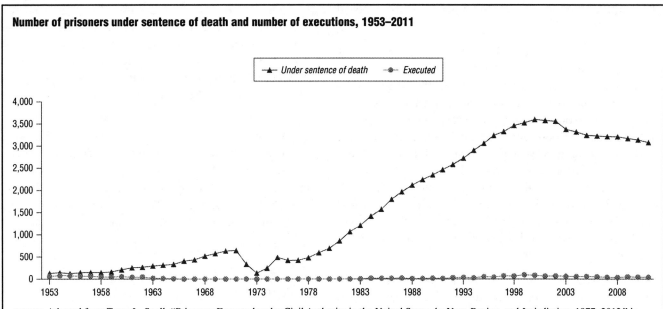

Number of prisoners under sentence of death and number of executions, 1953–2011

SOURCE: Adapted from Tracy L. Snell, "Prisoners Executed under Civil Authority in the United States, by Year, Region, and Jurisdiction, 1977–2012," in *Prisoners Executed*, U.S. Department of Justice, Office of Justice Programs, Bureau of Justice Statistics, March 11, 2013, http://www.bjs.gov/content/data/ exest.csv (accessed September 3, 2013), and Tracy L. Snell, "Figure 2. Number of Persons under Sentence of Death, 1953–2011," in *Capital Punishment, 2011—Statistical Tables*, U.S. Department of Justice, Office of Justice Programs, Bureau of Justice Statistics, July 16, 2013, http://www.bjs.gov/content/ pub/pdf/cp11st.pdf (accessed September 3, 2013)

FIGURE 1.4

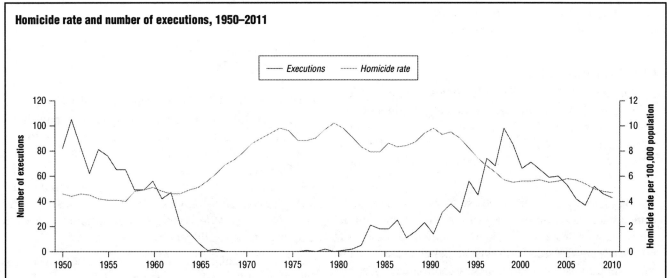

Homicide rate and number of executions, 1950–2011

SOURCE: Adapted from Alexia Cooper and Erica L. Smith, "Figure 1. Homicide Victimization Rates, 1950–2010," in *Homicide Trends in the United States, 1980–2008*, U.S. Department of Justice, Office of Justice Programs, Bureau of Justice Statistics, November 2011, http://www.bjs.gov/content/pub/sheets/ htus8008.zip (accessed September 3, 2013); "Table 1. Crime in the United States by Volume and Rate per 100,000 Inhabitants, 1992–2011," in *Crime in the United States 2011*, U.S. Department of Justice, Federal Bureau of Investigation, September 2012, http://www.fbi.gov/about-us/cjis/ucr/crime-in-the- u.s/2011/crime-in-the-u.s.-2011/tables/table-1 (accessed September 3, 2013); and Tracy L. Snell, "Figure 4. Number of Persons Executed in the United States, 1930–2011" and "Figure 5. Advance Count of Executions, January 1, 2012–December 31, 2012," in *Capital Punishment, 2011—Statistical Tables*, U.S. Department of Justice, Office of Justice Programs, Bureau of Justice Statistics, July 16, 2013, http://www.bjs.gov/content/pub/pdf/cp11st.pdf (accessed September 3, 2013)

least one other woman. In 2002 Virginia became the first state to execute someone based on a DNA "cold hit" when it executed James Earl Patterson in March 2002. (A cold hit is when DNA evidence collected at a crime scene matches a DNA sample already in a database.) In 1999 Patterson was in prison on a rape conviction when DNA from the 1987 rape and murder of Joyce Aldridge was found to match his DNA in the database. He confessed to the Aldridge crime in 2000 and was sentenced to death. Patterson waived his appeals to let his execution proceed as scheduled.

Not only has DNA evidence been useful in convicting felons but also it has been crucial in proving the innocence of falsely convicted individuals. Kirk Bloodsworth of Maryland was the nation's first death row inmate to be exonerated (cleared) based on post-conviction DNA testing. Bloodsworth was convicted for the rape and murder of nine-year-old Dawn Hamilton in 1984. He was sentenced to death in 1985. On retrial, Bloodsworth received two life terms. DNA testing in 1992 excluded him from the crime. In 1993 Bloodsworth was released from prison. In 1999 the state paid Bloodsworth $300,000 for wrongful conviction and imprisonment, including time on death row.

The use of DNA as an evidentiary tool is a relatively new phenomenon. Many inmates on death rows around the country in 2013 were convicted and sentenced decades ago, before DNA testing was common. The Bloodsworth case made clear that legal mechanisms needed to be established to allow post-conviction DNA testing, but change was slow in coming. The federal government did not pass such a law—the Innocence Protection Act—until 2004. All 50 states have also enacted legislation permitting post-conviction DNA testing; however, critics claim that the laws are too narrow in scope and erect legal hurdles that are difficult to overcome.

EXECUTIONS DECLINE

During the 1980s and early 1990s public opinion polls showed strong support for capital punishment. As noted earlier, annual polling conducted by the Gallup Organization found support reached its highest level in 1994, when 80% of Americans favored use of the death penalty for murderers.

Beginning in the mid-1990s support for capital punishment decreased for a variety of reasons. The advent of DNA testing resulted in highly publicized cases of inmates being released from prison, and even from death row. Abolitionists seized on these opportunities as proof that the U.S. capital punishment system was flawed. In addition, studies were released indicating that racial biases were occurring in death penalty cases and raising questions about the fairness of the system.

Another factor in the decline of death sentences is that the number of jurisdictions where it is possible to sentence a criminal to life in prison without the possibility of parole increased. According to the DPIC, in "Year That States Adopted Life without Parole (LWOP) Sentencing" (2013, http://www.deathpenaltyinfo.org/year-states-adopted-life-without-parole-lwop-sentencing), prior to the 1990s, 25 jurisdictions had life without parole sentences. They were joined by 22 additional jurisdictions during the 1990s and six more during the first decade of the 21st century. Texas, the most active state to carry out executions, added a life without parole option in 2005. As of October 2013, the federal and U.S. military justice systems, the District of Columbia, and all states except Alaska (which did not allow capital punishment) had life without parole sentences.

As shown in Figure 1.5, the annual number of death sentences issued nationwide decreased dramatically from a peak of 330 in 1994 to 80 sentences in 2011. Table 1.6 lists executions by jurisdiction and by year for 1977 through 2012. Of the 1,320 executions conducted, the largest numbers occurred in the following states:

- Texas (492)
- Virginia (109)
- Florida (74)
- Missouri (68)
- Alabama (55)
- Georgia (52)
- Ohio (49)
- North Carolina (43)
- South Carolina (43)
- Arizona (34)

Together, these 10 states accounted for 1,019 executions or 77.2% of the total.

CAPITAL PUNISHMENT RECONSIDERED

By the turn of the 21st century capital punishment had been abolished in Canada and in nearly all of Europe, which led to intense criticism in the international press of the United States' reliance on the death penalty. Pope John Paul II (1920–2005) also condemned capital punishment. Two popular movies—*Dead Man Walking* (1995) and *The Green Mile* (1999)—raised questions about the morality of the death penalty.

Two particular death penalty cases also aroused passion about the morality of capital punishment. Karla Faye Tucker became a born-again Christian while on death row in Texas for the brutal 1983 slayings of Jerry Lynn Dean and Deborah Thornton. In the months leading up to her execution in 1998, Tucker received widespread media attention and garnered support nationally and internationally for commutation of her sentence to life in prison. Her supporters included some unlikely allies: a handful of conservative-minded religious and political figures who believed that Tucker's religious conversion merited clemency (an act of leniency by a convening authority to reduce a sentence). Nevertheless, George W. Bush (1946–), the Texas governor, signed her death warrant.

FIGURE 1.5

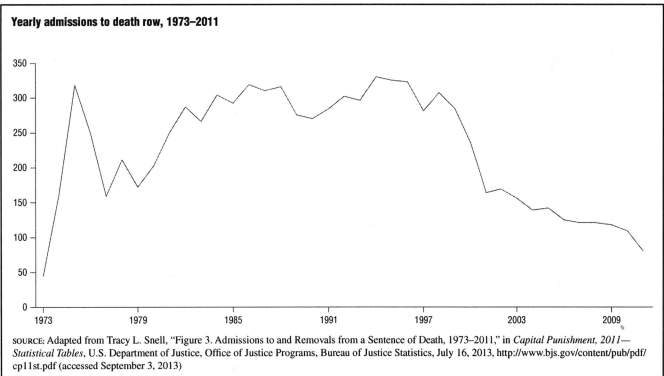

Yearly admissions to death row, 1973–2011

SOURCE: Adapted from Tracy L. Snell, "Figure 3. Admissions to and Removals from a Sentence of Death, 1973–2011," in *Capital Punishment, 2011—Statistical Tables*, U.S. Department of Justice, Office of Justice Programs, Bureau of Justice Statistics, July 16, 2013, http://www.bjs.gov/content/pub/pdf/cp11st.pdf (accessed September 3, 2013)

In 2005 the execution of Stanley "Tookie" Williams also garnered considerable public attention. Williams received a death sentence for the 1979 killings of four people during robberies: Albert Owens, Yen-I Yang, Tasi-Shai Yang, and Yee-Chen Lin. At the time of the murders, he was a leading figure in the notorious and violent Crips gang in Los Angeles, California. During his decades on death row Williams became an outspoken critic of gangs and wrote books encouraging children to avoid gangs and violence. For his work he received nominations for the Nobel Peace Prize. His supporters included Hollywood celebrities who lobbied the California governor Arnold Schwarzenegger (1947–) for clemency, arguing that Williams had redeemed himself while in prison. The governor refused, noting that Williams had never expressed remorse for his crimes.

The Great Recession of 2007 to 2009 spurred some states to reconsider the financial costs that are associated with administering the death penalty, as described in Chapter 6. In general, capital cases are more costly than noncapital homicide cases because they take much longer to proceed through the court system. Legal safeguards, such as automatic appeals, mean that judges, prosecutors, and defense attorneys spend more time on capital cases. Because the vast majority of capital defendants cannot afford to pay for their attorneys, these litigation costs are largely paid through tax dollars. In addition, there are extra expenses associated with housing death row inmates, because they are kept in specially designed facilities and receive much more intense supervision than non-death row inmates.

In 2007 New Jersey abolished capital punishment and changed all existing death sentences to life sentences. In 2009 New Mexico eliminated the death penalty for new capital crimes; however, inmates already under sentence of death retained those sentences. The state's governor abolished capital punishment due to concerns about racial bias in its administration and the growing number of exonerations. In 2011 Illinois abandoned the death penalty and resentenced all death row inmates to life in prison without the possibility of parole. Again, concerns about capital punishment's fairness and accuracy were driving factors. Connecticut (2012) and Maryland (2013) also abolished the death penalty for new crimes, but already condemned prisoners remained under sentence of death.

The 2011 execution of Troy Davis, a Georgia death row inmate, captured widespread public attention and spurred anti-death penalty demonstrations around the world. Davis was convicted for the 1989 murder of Mark MacPhail, an off-duty police officer. Davis's conviction was based almost entirely on the testimony of seven eyewitnesses to the crime and two people who claimed that Davis confessed to them afterward. However, over subsequent years seven of these individuals issued recantations (official denials) of portions or all of their original statements. The details of this case are examined in Chapter 8.

TABLE 1.6

Inmates executed under civil authority by year, region, and jurisdiction, 1977–2012

Region and jurisdiction	Total	1977	1978	1979	1980	1981	1982	1983	1984	1985	1986	1987	1988	1989	1990	1991	1992	1993	1994	1995	1996	1997	1998	1999	2000	2001	2002	2003	2004	2005	2006	2007	2008	2009	2010	2011	2012
U.S. total	**1,320**	1	0	2	0	1	2	5	21	18	18	25	11	16	23	14	31	38	31	56	45	74	68	98	85	66	71	65	59	60	53	42	37	52	46	43	43
Federal	3	0	0	0	0	0	0	0	0	0	0	0	0	0	0	0	0	0	0	0	0	0	0	0	0	2	0	1	0	0	0	0	0	0	0	0	0
State	1,317	1	0	2	0	1	2	5	21	18	18	25	11	16	23	14	31	38	31	56	45	74	68	98	85	64	71	64	59	60	53	42	37	52	46	43	43
Northeast	**4**	0	0	0	0	0	0	0	0	0	0	0	0	0	0	0	0	0	0	2	0	0	0	1	0	0	0	0	0	1	0	0	0	0	0	0	0
Connecticut	1	0	0	0	0	0	0	0	0	0	0	0	0	0	0	0	0	0	0	0	0	0	0	0	0	0	0	0	0	1	0	0	0	0	0	0	0
Maine	0	0	0	0	0	0	0	0	0	0	0	0	0	0	0	0	0	0	0	0	0	0	0	0	0	0	0	0	0	0	0	0	0	0	0	0	0
Massachusetts	0	0	0	0	0	0	0	0	0	0	0	0	0	0	0	0	0	0	0	0	0	0	0	0	0	0	0	0	0	0	0	0	0	0	0	0	0
New Hampshire	0	0	0	0	0	0	0	0	0	0	0	0	0	0	0	0	0	0	0	0	0	0	0	0	0	0	0	0	0	0	0	0	0	0	0	0	0
New Jersey	0	0	0	0	0	0	0	0	0	0	0	0	0	0	0	0	0	0	0	0	0	0	0	0	0	0	0	0	0	0	0	0	0	0	0	0	0
New York	0	0	0	0	0	0	0	0	0	0	0	0	0	0	0	0	0	0	0	0	0	0	0	0	0	0	0	0	0	0	0	0	0	0	0	0	0
Pennsylvania	3	0	0	0	0	0	0	0	0	0	0	0	0	0	0	0	0	0	0	2	0	0	0	1	0	0	0	0	0	0	0	0	0	0	0	0	0
Rhode Island	0	0	0	0	0	0	0	0	0	0	0	0	0	0	0	0	0	0	0	0	0	0	0	0	0	0	0	0	0	0	0	0	0	0	0	0	0
Vermont	0	0	0	0	0	0	0	0	0	0	0	0	0	0	0	0	0	0	0	0	0	0	0	0	0	0	0	0	0	0	0	0	0	0	0	0	0
Midwest	**155**	0	0	0	0	1	0	0	0	1	0	0	0	1	5	1	1	4	3	11	9	10	5	12	5	10	9	7	7	14	6	5	2	7	8	6	5
Illinois	12	0	0	0	0	0	0	0	0	0	0	0	0	0	1	0	0	0	1	5	1	2	1	1	0	0	0	0	0	0	0	0	0	0	0	0	0
Indiana	20	0	0	0	0	1	0	0	0	0	0	0	0	0	0	0	0	0	1	0	1	1	0	1	0	3	1	2	1	5	1	1	0	1	0	0	0
Iowa	0	0	0	0	0	0	0	0	0	0	0	0	0	0	0	0	0	0	0	0	0	0	0	0	0	0	0	0	0	0	0	0	0	0	0	0	0
Kansas	0	0	0	0	0	0	0	0	0	0	0	0	0	0	0	0	0	0	0	0	0	0	0	0	0	0	0	0	0	0	0	0	0	0	0	0	0
Michigan	0	0	0	0	0	0	0	0	0	0	0	0	0	0	0	0	0	0	0	0	0	0	0	0	0	0	0	0	0	0	0	0	0	0	0	0	0
Minnesota	0	0	0	0	0	0	0	0	0	0	0	0	0	0	0	0	0	0	0	0	0	0	0	0	0	0	0	0	0	0	0	0	0	0	0	0	0
Missouri	68	0	0	0	0	0	0	0	0	0	0	0	0	1	1	0	1	4	0	6	6	6	3	9	5	7	6	2	0	5	0	0	0	1	0	1	0
Nebraska	3	0	0	0	0	0	0	0	0	0	0	0	0	0	0	0	0	0	1	0	1	1	0	0	0	0	0	0	0	0	0	0	0	0	0	0	0
North Dakota	0	0	0	0	0	0	0	0	0	0	0	0	0	0	0	0	0	0	0	0	0	0	0	0	0	0	0	0	0	0	0	0	0	0	0	0	0
Ohio	49	0	0	0	0	0	0	0	0	0	0	0	0	0	0	0	0	0	0	0	0	0	0	1	0	1	3	3	7	4	5	2	2	5	8	5	3
South Dakota	3	0	0	0	0	0	0	0	0	0	0	0	0	0	0	0	0	0	0	0	0	0	0	0	0	0	0	0	0	0	0	1	0	0	0	0	2
Wisconsin	0	0	0	0	0	0	0	0	0	0	0	0	0	0	0	0	0	0	0	0	0	0	0	0	0	0	0	0	0	0	0	0	0	0	0	0	0
South	**1,076**	0	0	1	0	0	2	5	21	16	18	24	10	13	17	13	26	30	26	41	29	60	55	74	76	50	61	57	50	43	44	36	35	45	35	32	31
Alabama	55	0	0	0	0	0	0	1	0	0	0	0	0	4	1	0	2	0	5	2	1	3	1	2	4	0	2	3	2	4	1	3	0	6	5	6	0
Arkansas	27	0	0	0	0	0	0	0	0	0	0	0	0	0	2	0	2	2	5	2	1	4	1	4	2	1	0	0	1	0	0	0	0	0	0	0	0
Delaware	16	0	0	0	0	0	0	0	0	0	0	0	0	0	0	0	1	2	1	3	0	0	0	1	1	2	0	3	0	1	0	1	0	0	0	0	0
Dist. of Col.	0	0	0	0	0	0	0	0	0	0	0	0	0	0	0	0	0	0	0	0	0	0	0	0	0	0	0	0	0	0	0	0	0	0	0	0	0
Florida	74	0	0	1	0	0	0	1	8	3	3	1	2	1	4	2	2	3	1	3	2	1	4	1	6	0	0	3	2	2	1	4	0	2	2	1	3
Georgia	52	0	0	0	0	0	0	1	2	3	1	5	1	0	0	0	2	2	1	2	2	0	1	3	0	0	4	3	1	3	0	0	1	3	2	4	0
Kentucky	3	0	0	0	0	0	0	0	0	0	0	0	0	0	0	0	0	0	0	0	0	1	0	1	0	0	0	0	0	0	0	0	1	0	0	0	0
Louisiana	28	0	0	0	0	0	0	1	5	1	0	8	3	0	1	1	0	2	0	0	1	1	1	0	1	0	0	1	0	0	0	0	0	1	0	0	0
Maryland	5	0	0	0	0	0	0	0	0	0	0	0	0	0	0	0	0	0	1	0	0	1	1	0	0	0	0	0	1	1	0	0	0	0	0	0	0
Mississippi	21	0	0	0	0	0	0	1	0	0	0	2	0	1	0	0	0	0	0	0	0	0	0	0	0	0	1	0	0	0	1	0	0	2	3	2	6
North Carolina	43	0	0	0	0	0	0	0	2	0	0	0	0	0	1	1	0	1	3	2	1	3	4	0	5	2	7	4	4	4	0	0	0	0	2	0	0
Oklahoma	102	0	0	0	0	0	0	0	0	0	0	0	0	0	1	0	1	0	0	3	2	1	4	6	11	18	7	14	6	4	4	3	2	3	3	2	6
South Carolina	43	0	0	0	0	0	0	0	0	1	1	0	0	0	1	1	0	0	1	1	6	2	7	4	1	0	3	0	4	3	1	1	0	3	2	1	0
Tennessee	6	0	0	0	0	0	0	0	0	0	0	0	0	0	0	0	0	0	0	0	0	0	0	0	1	0	0	0	0	0	1	2	0	2	0	0	0
Texas	492	0	0	0	0	0	1	0	3	6	10	6	3	4	4	5	12	17	14	19	3	37	20	35	40	17	33	24	23	19	24	26	18	24	17	13	15
Virginia	109	0	0	0	0	0	1	0	1	1	1	1	0	1	3	2	4	5	2	5	8	9	13	14	8	2	4	2	5	0	4	0	4	3	3	1	0
West Virginia	0	0	0	0	0	0	0	0	0	0	0	0	0	0	0	0	0	0	0	0	0	0	0	0	0	0	0	0	0	0	0	0	0	0	0	0	0

TABLE 1.6

Inmates executed under civil authority by year, region, and jurisdiction, 1977–2012 [CONTINUED]

Region and jurisdiction	Total	1977	1978	1979	1980	1981	1982	1983	1984	1985	1986	1987	1988	1989	1990	1991	1992	1993	1994	1995	1996	1997	1998	1999	2000	2001	2002	2003	2004	2005	2006	2007	2008	2009	2010	2011	2012
West	82	1	0	1	0	0	0	0	0	1	0	1	1	2	1	0	4	4	2	2	7	4	8	11	4	4	1	0	2	2	3	1	0	0	3	5	7
Alaska	0	0	0	0	0	0	0	0	0	0	0	0	0	0	0	0	0	0	0	0	0	0	0	0	0	0	0	0	0	0	0	0	0	0	0	0	0
Arizona	34	0	0	0	0	0	0	0	0	0	0	0	0	0	0	0	1	2	0	1	2	2	4	7	3	0	0	0	0	0	0	1	0	0	1	4	6
California	13	0	0	0	0	0	0	0	0	0	0	0	0	0	0	0	1	1	0	0	2	0	1	2	1	1	1	0	0	2	1	0	0	0	0	0	0
Colorado	1	0	0	0	0	0	0	0	0	0	0	0	0	0	0	0	0	0	0	0	0	1	0	0	0	0	0	0	0	0	0	0	0	0	0	0	0
Hawaii	0	0	0	0	0	0	0	0	0	0	0	0	0	0	0	0	0	0	0	0	0	0	0	0	0	0	0	0	0	0	0	0	0	0	0	0	0
Idaho	3	0	0	0	0	0	0	0	0	0	0	0	0	0	0	0	0	0	1	0	0	0	0	0	0	0	0	0	0	0	0	0	0	0	0	1	1
Montana	3	0	0	0	0	0	0	0	0	0	0	0	0	0	0	0	0	0	0	1	0	0	1	0	0	0	0	0	0	0	1	0	0	0	0	0	0
Nevada	12	0	0	1	0	0	0	0	0	1	0	0	0	2	1	0	0	0	0	0	1	0	1	1	0	1	0	0	2	0	1	0	0	0	0	0	0
New Mexico	1	0	0	0	0	0	0	0	0	0	0	0	0	0	0	0	0	0	0	0	0	0	0	0	0	1	0	0	0	0	0	0	0	0	0	0	0
Oregon	2	0	0	0	0	0	0	0	0	0	0	0	0	0	0	0	0	0	0	0	1	1	0	0	0	0	0	0	0	0	0	0	0	0	0	0	0
Utah	7	1	0	0	0	0	0	0	0	0	0	1	1	0	0	0	1	0	0	0	1	0	0	1	0	0	0	0	0	0	0	0	0	0	1	0	0
Washington	5	0	0	0	0	0	0	0	0	0	0	0	0	0	0	0	0	1	1	0	0	0	1	0	0	1	0	0	0	0	0	0	0	0	1	0	0
Wyoming	1	0	0	0	0	0	0	0	0	0	0	0	0	0	0	0	1	0	0	0	0	0	0	0	0	0	0	0	0	0	0	0	0	0	0	0	0

Note: Preliminary counts for 2012 based on publicly available data.

SOURCE: Tracy L. Snell, "Prisoners Executed under Civil Authority in the United States, by Year, Region, and Jurisdiction, 1977–2012," in *Prisoners Executed*, U.S. Department of Justice, Office of Justice Programs, Bureau of Justice Statistics, March 11, 2013, http://www.bjs.gov/content/data/exest.csv (accessed September 3, 2013)

Human rights groups and prominent public figures, including former president Jimmy Carter (1924–), advocated for Davis to receive a new trial. In 2009 the U.S. Supreme Court ordered a U.S. district court to hold an evidentiary hearing on the case. At the 2010 hearing the district court discounted the authenticity and evidentiary importance of the recantations and allowed the death sentence to stand. Davis exhausted his remaining appeals. As his execution date approached, hundreds of thousands of people signed petitions calling for him to be pardoned, but the request was denied by the Georgia State Board of Pardons and Paroles. Davis was executed in September 2011.

Davis's supporters believe that he was innocent or that sufficient doubt existed to justify overturning his death sentence. To them the case epitomizes the tragic shortcomings and irreversible nature of capital punishment. Death penalty advocates argue that Davis's claims of innocence were carefully considered by the legal system and ultimately rejected for lack of merit. They believe that his execution was just punishment for the horrific crime for which he was convicted.

WORLDWIDE TREND

The moratorium on the death penalty in the United States between 1967 and 1976 paralleled a general worldwide movement, especially among Western nations, toward the abolition of capital punishment. Even though the United States resumed executions in 1977, most of the Western world either formally or informally abolished capital punishment.

As of October 2013, among the Western democratic nations (with which the United States traditionally compares itself), only the United States imposed the death penalty. There are technical exceptions: for example, Israel maintains the death penalty in its statute books for "crimes against mankind" but has executed only Adolf Eichmann (1906–1962). As a Schutzstaffel (SS) officer, Eichmann was responsible for the murder of millions of Jews in Nazi-occupied Europe during the Holocaust and World War II (1939–1945). Some countries still maintain the death penalty for treason— although no Western democracy has actually imposed it. One of the first acts of the parliaments of many of the east European countries after the fall of communism was to abolish capital punishment.

Amnesty International states in "Abolitionist and Retentionist Countries" (http://www.amnesty.org/en/death-penalty/abolitionist-and-retentionist-countries) that 58 countries and territories around the world continued to maintain and use the death penalty for ordinary crimes in 2013. However, some of these countries had not actually implemented a death sentence for many years. Amnesty International reports in *Death Sentences and Executions, 2012* (April 9, 2013, http://www.amnestyusa.org/research/reports/death-sentences-and-executions-2012) that there were at least 682 executions (excluding China) carried out in 21 countries in 2012. China is believed to have conducted thousands more executions that year, but the exact number is a state secret. According to Amnesty International, the six countries with the highest number of executions in 2012 were China (1,000s), Iran (314+), Iraq (129+), Saudi Arabia (79+), and the United States (43).

CHAPTER 2

SUPREME COURT RULINGS I: CONSTITUTIONALITY OF THE DEATH PENALTY, GUIDELINES FOR JUDGES AND JURIES, JURY SELECTION, AND SENTENCING PROCEDURES

In 1967 a coalition of anti–death penalty groups sued Florida and California, the states with the most inmates on death row at that time, challenging the constitutionality of state capital punishment laws. An unofficial moratorium (temporary suspension) of executions resulted, pending U.S. Supreme Court decisions on several cases on appeal. The defendants in these cases claimed that the death penalty is a cruel and unusual punishment in violation of the Eighth Amendment to the U.S. Constitution. Moreover, they alleged that the death penalty also violates the 14th Amendment, which prevents states from denying anyone equal protection of the laws. This moratorium lasted until January 17, 1977, when the convicted murderer Gary Gilmore (1940–1977) was executed by the state of Utah for killing Bennie Bushnell and Max Jensen during robberies in 1976.

IS THE DEATH PENALTY CONSTITUTIONAL?

On June 29, 1972, a split 5–4 Supreme Court reached a landmark decision in *Furman v. Georgia* (408 U.S. 238, which included *Jackson v. Georgia* and *Branch v. Texas*), holding that "as the statutes before us are now administered . . . [the] imposition and carrying out of [the] death penalty in these cases [is] held to constitute cruel and unusual punishment in violation of [the] Eighth and Fourteenth Amendments." In other words, the justices did not address whether capital punishment as a whole is unconstitutional. Rather, they considered capital punishment in the context of its application in state statutes (laws created by state legislatures). The justices, whether they were of the majority opinion or of the dissenting opinion, could not agree on the arguments explaining why they opposed or supported the death penalty. As a result, the decision consisted of nine separate opinions.

Majority Opinions in *Furman*

Justice William O. Douglas (1898–1980), in his concurring majority opinion, quoted the observation of the former U.S. attorney general Ramsey Clark (1927–) in his book *Crime in America: Observations on Its Nature, Causes, Prevention, and Control* (1970): "It is the poor, the sick, the ignorant, the powerless and the hated who are executed." Douglas added, "We deal with a system of law and of justice that leaves to the uncontrolled discretion of judges or juries the determination whether defendants committing these crimes should die or be imprisoned. Under these laws no standards govern the selection of the penalty. People live or die, dependent on the whim of one man or of 12 . . . . Thus, these discretionary statutes are unconstitutional in their operation. They are pregnant with discrimination and discrimination is an ingredient not compatible with the idea of equal protection of the laws that is implicit in the ban on 'cruel and unusual' punishments."

Justice William J. Brennan (1906–1997) stated, "At bottom, then, the Cruel and Unusual Punishments Clause prohibits the infliction of uncivilized and inhuman punishments. The State, even as it punishes, must treat its members with respect for their intrinsic worth as human beings. A punishment is 'cruel and unusual,' therefore, if it does not comport with human dignity."

Justice Potter J. Stewart (1915–1985) stressed another point, saying, "These death sentences are cruel and unusual in the same way that being struck by lightning is cruel and unusual. For, of all the people convicted of rapes and murders in 1967 and 1968, many just as reprehensible as these, the petitioners are among a capriciously selected random handful upon whom the sentence of death has in fact been imposed."

This did not mean that Justice Stewart would rule out the death penalty. He believed that the death penalty was justified, but he wanted to see a more equitable system of determining who should be executed. He explained, "I cannot agree that retribution is a constitutionally impermissible ingredient in the imposition of punishment. The instinct for retribution is part of the nature of man, and channeling that instinct in the administration of criminal justice serves an important purpose in promoting the stability of a society governed by law. When people begin to believe that organized society is unwilling or unable to impose upon criminal offenders the punishment they 'deserve,' then there are sown the seeds of anarchy—of self-help, vigilante justice, and lynch law."

Justice Byron R. White (1917–2002), believing that the death penalty was so seldom imposed that executions were ineffective deterrents to crime, chose instead to address the role of juries and judges in imposing the death penalty. He concluded that the cases before the courts violated the Eighth Amendment because the state legislatures, having authorized the application of the death penalty, left it to the discretion of juries and judges whether or not to impose the punishment.

Justice Thurgood Marshall (1908–1993) thought that "the death penalty is an excessive and unnecessary punishment that violates the Eighth Amendment." He added that "even if capital punishment is not excessive, it nonetheless violates the Eighth Amendment because it is morally unacceptable to the people of the United States at this time in their history." Justice Marshall also noted that the death penalty was applied with discrimination against certain classes of people (the poor, the uneducated, and members of minority groups) and that innocent people had been executed before they could prove their innocence. He also believed that it hindered the reform of the treatment of criminals and that it promoted sensationalism during trials.

Dissenting Opinions

Chief Justice Warren Burger (1907–1995), disagreeing with the majority, observed that "the constitutional prohibition against 'cruel and unusual punishments' cannot be construed to bar the imposition of the punishment of death." Justice Harry A. Blackmun (1908–1999) was disturbed by Justices Stewart's and White's remarks that as long as capital punishment was mandated for specific crimes, it could not be considered unconstitutional. He feared "that statutes struck down today will be re-enacted by state legislatures to prescribe the death penalty for specified crimes without any alternative for the imposition of a lesser punishment in the discretion of the judge or jury, as the case may be."

Justice Lewis F. Powell Jr. (1907–1998) declared, "I find no support—in the language of the Constitution, in its history, or in the cases arising under it—for the view that this Court may invalidate a category of penalties because we deem less severe penalties adequate to serve the ends of penology.... This Court has long held that legislative decisions in this area, which lie within the special competency of that branch, are entitled to a pre-

sumption of validity." In other words, he believed that the court should not question the validity of a government entity properly doing its job unless its actions were way out of line.

Justice William H. Rehnquist (1924–2005) agreed with Justice Powell, adding, "How can government by the elected representatives of the people co-exist with the power of the federal judiciary, whose members are constitutionally insulated from responsiveness to the popular will, to declare invalid laws duly enacted by the popular branches of government?"

Summary of Court Decision

Only Justices Brennan and Marshall concluded that the Eighth Amendment prohibited the death penalty for all crimes and under all circumstances. Justice Douglas, while ruling that the death penalty statutes reviewed by the high court were unconstitutional, did not necessarily require the final abolition of the death penalty. Justices Stewart and White also did not rule on the validity of the death penalty, noting instead that, because of the capricious (unpredictable) imposition of the sentence, the death penalty violated the Eighth Amendment. However, Justices Rehnquist, Burger, Powell, and Blackmun concluded that the Constitution allows capital punishment.

Consequently, most state legislatures went to work to revise their capital punishment laws. They strove to make these laws more equitable to swing the votes of Justices Stewart and White (and later that of Justice John Paul Stevens [1920–], who replaced the retired Justice Douglas).

PROPER IMPOSITION OF THE DEATH PENALTY

Four years later, on July 2, 1976, the Supreme Court ruled decisively on a series of cases. In *Gregg v. Georgia* (428 U.S. 153), perhaps the most significant of these cases, the justices concluded 7–2 that the death penalty was, indeed, constitutional as presented in some new state laws. With Justices Brennan and Marshall dissenting, the court stressed (just in case *Furman* had been misunderstood) that "the death penalty is not a form of punishment that may never be imposed, regardless of the circumstances of the offense, regardless of the character of the offender, and regardless of the procedure followed in reaching the decision to impose it." Furthermore, "the infliction of death as a punishment for murder is not without justification and thus is not unconstitutionally severe."

The court upheld death penalty statutes in Georgia (*Gregg v. Georgia*), Florida (*Proffitt v. Florida*, 428 U.S. 242 [1976]), and Texas (*Jurek v. Texas*, 428 U.S. 262 [1976]), but struck down laws in North Carolina (*Woodson v. North Carolina*, 428 U.S. 280 [1976]) and Louisiana (*Roberts v. Louisiana*, 428 U.S. 325 [1976]). It ruled that laws in the latter two states were too rigid in imposing mandatory death sentences for certain types of murder.

Citing the new Georgia laws in *Gregg*, Justice Stewart supported the bifurcated (two-part) trial system, in which the accused is first tried to determine his or her guilt. Then, in a separate trial, the jury considers whether the convicted person deserves the death penalty or whether mitigating factors (circumstances that may lessen responsibility for a crime) warrant a lesser sentence, usually life imprisonment without parole. He believed that this system meets the requirements demanded by *Furman*. Noting how the Georgia statutes fulfilled these demands, Justice Stewart observed:

> These procedures require the jury to consider the circumstances of the crime and the criminal before it recommends sentence. No longer can a Georgia jury do as Furman's jury did: reach a finding of the defendant's guilt and then, without guidance or direction, decide whether he should live or die. Instead, the jury's attention is directed to the specific circumstances of the crime: Was it committed in the course of another capital felony? Was it committed for money? Was it committed upon a peace officer or judicial officer? Was it committed in a particularly heinous way or in a manner that endangered the lives of many persons? In addition, the jury's attention is focused on the characteristics of the person who committed the crime: Does he have a record of prior convictions for capital offenses? Are there any special facts about this defendant that mitigate against imposing capital punishment (e. g., his youth, the extent of his cooperation with the police, his emotional state at the time of the crime). As a result, while some jury discretion still exists, "the discretion to be exercised is controlled by clear and objective standards so as to produce non-discriminatory application."

In addition, the Georgia law required that all death sentences be automatically appealed to the state supreme court, an "important additional safeguard against arbitrariness and caprice." The bifurcated trial system has since been adopted in the trials of all capital murder cases.

In *Proffitt v. Florida*, the high court upheld Florida's death penalty law that separated the conviction and sentencing phases of a capital trial. In Florida the sentence is determined by the trial judge rather than by the jury, who has an advisory role during the sentencing phase. (This is often referred to as a trifurcated trial system, because there are three levels of decision-making involved.) The court found Florida's sentencing guidelines adequate in preventing unfair imposition of the death sentence.

In *Jurek v. Texas*, the revised death penalty law of Texas was found constitutional. One sentencing practice that was at issue concerned predicting future dangerousness. The Texas statute requires that during the sentencing phase of a trial, after the defendant had been found guilty, the jury determines whether it is probable the defendant will commit future criminal acts of violence that would threaten society. The U.S. Supreme Court upheld this practice as constitutional.

In *Woodson v. North Carolina*, the Supreme Court invalidated North Carolina's new capital law, which basically called for mandatory death sentences for all first-degree murders. The justices held that as a whole the American public had rejected the idea of mandatory death sentences long ago. In addition, the court noted that the state law did not include standards to guide juries in their decision making and did not let the jury consider the convicted defendant's character, criminal record, or the circumstances of the crime before the imposition of the death sentence.

The Louisiana mandatory death sentence for first-degree murder suffered from similar inadequacies. It did, however, permit the jury to consider lesser offenses such as second-degree murder. In *Roberts v. Louisiana*, the Supreme Court rejected the Louisiana law because it forced the jury to find the defendant guilty of a lesser crime to avoid imposing the death penalty. In other words, if the crime was not heinous enough to warrant the death penalty, then the jury was forced to convict the defendant of second-degree murder or a lesser charge. The jury did not have the option of first determining if the accused was indeed guilty of first-degree murder for the crime he or she had actually committed and then recommending a lesser sentence if there were mitigating circumstances to support it.

JURY MAY CONSIDER A LESSER CHARGE

In 1977 Gilbert Franklin Beck was convicted of robbing and murdering 80-year-old Roy Malone. According to Beck, he and an accomplice entered Malone's home and were tying up the victim to rob him when Beck's accomplice unexpectedly struck and killed Malone. Beck admitted to the robbery but claimed the murder was not part of the plan. Beck was tried under an Alabama statute for "robbery or attempts thereof when the victim is intentionally killed by the defendant."

Under Alabama law the judge was specifically prohibited from giving the jury the option of convicting the defendant of a lesser, included offense. Instead, the jury was given the choice of either convicting the defendant of the capital crime, in which case he possibly faced the death penalty, or acquitting him, thus allowing him to escape all penalties for his alleged participation in the crime. The judge could not have offered the jury the lesser alternative of felony murder, for example.

Beck appealed, claiming this law created a situation in which the jury was more likely to convict. The Supreme Court, in *Beck v. Alabama* (447 U.S. 625 [1980]), agreed and reversed the lower court's ruling, thus vacating (annulling) his death sentence. The high court observed that, while not a matter of due process, it was virtually universally accepted in lesser offenses that a third alternative be offered. *Beck* did not require a jury to consider a lesser charge in every case, but only where the consideration would be justified. Beck was subsequently retried and given a lesser sentence. As of October 2013, his name did not appear on a list of inmates kept by the Alabama Department of Corrections.

EXCLUSION FROM JURIES OF THOSE AGAINST CAPITAL PUNISHMENT

In *Witherspoon v. Illinois* (391 U.S. 510 [1968]), the Supreme Court held that a death sentence cannot be carried out if the jury that imposed or recommended such punishment was selected by excluding prospective jurors simply because they have qualms against the death penalty or reservations against its infliction. The court found that the prosecution excluded those who opposed the death penalty without determining whether their beliefs would compel them to reject capital punishment out of hand. The defendant argued that this selective process had resulted in a jury that was not representative of the community.

The justices could not definitively conclude that the exclusion of jurors opposed to the death penalty results in an unrepresentative jury. However, they believed that a person who opposes the death penalty can still abide by his or her duty as a juror and consider the facts presented at trial before making his or her decision about the defendant's punishment.

The court specifically noted that its findings in *Witherspoon* did not prevent the infliction of the death sentence when the prospective jurors excluded had made it "unmistakably clear" that they would automatically vote against the death sentence without considering the evidence presented during the trial or that their attitudes toward capital punishment would keep them from making a fair decision about the defendant's guilt. Consequently, based on *Witherspoon*, it has become the practice to exclude prospective jurors who indicate that they could not possibly in good conscience return a death sentence.

In *Lockett v. Ohio* (438 U.S. 586 [1978]), the U.S. Supreme Court ruled against a defendant who claimed that juror exclusions made during her trial violated *Witherspoon*. The prospective jurors had told the prosecutor that they were so against the death penalty they could not be impartial about the case. They had also admitted that they would not take an oath saying they would consider the evidence before making a judgment of innocence or guilt. The defendant—Sandra Lockett—had her death sentence overturned because of a separate issue related to mitigating circumstances, as described in Chapter 4.

In *Uttecht v. Brown* (551 U.S. ___ [2007]), the Supreme Court considered another case based on *Witherspoon*. During a capital trial the judge had dismissed a juror (designated "Juror Z") who had indicated that he would impose capital punishment only if the crime was "severe." The defendant, Cal Coburn Brown, was subsequently convicted and sentenced to death for the robbery, rape, torture, and murder of 22-year-old Holly Washa in 1991 in Washington state. On appeal, Brown's lawyers argued that the dismissal of Juror Z constituted unfair jury selection. The U.S. Court of Appeals for the Ninth Circuit agreed. However, the Supreme Court in its 5 to 4 decision reversed the appeals court ruling noting that the trial court had "acted well within its discretion in granting the State's motion to excuse Juror Z." Further, the Supreme Court stated that the trial court "is entitled to deference because it had an opportunity to observe the demeanor of Juror Z." In 2010 Brown was executed by the State of Washington.

A Special Selection Process Is Not Required When Selecting Jurors in Capital Cases

In *Wainwright v. Witt* (469 U.S. 412 [1985]), a 7–2 Supreme Court decision eased the strict requirements of *Witherspoon*. Writing for the majority, Justice Rehnquist declared that the new capital punishment procedures left less discretion to jurors. Rehnquist indicated that potential jurors in capital cases should be excluded from jury duty in a manner similar to how they were excluded in noncapital cases. (In a noncapital case, the prospective jurors typically go through a selection process in which the prosecution and the defense question them about their attitudes toward the crime and the people and issues related to it to determine if they are too biased to be fair.)

No longer would a juror's "automatic" bias against imposing the death penalty have to be proved with "unmistakable clarity." A prosecutor could not be expected to ask all the questions necessary to determine if a juror would automatically rule against the death penalty or fail to convict a defendant if he or she were likely to face execution. Fundamentally, the question of exclusion from a jury should be determined by the interplay of the prosecutor and the defense lawyer and by the decision of the judge based on his or her initial observations of the prospective juror. Judges can see firsthand whether prospective jurors' beliefs would bias their ability to impose the death penalty.

In his dissent, Justice Brennan claimed that making it easier to eliminate those who opposed capital punishment from the jury created a jury not only more likely to impose the death sentence but also more likely to convict. He also attacked the majority interpretation that now treated exclusion from a capital case as being similar to exclusion from any other case.

It Does Not Matter if "Death-Qualified" Juries Are More Likely to Convict

In *Lockhart v. McCree* (476 U.S. 162 [1986]), the Supreme Court firmly resolved the issue presented in *Witherspoon* regarding a fair trial with a death-qualified jury. (A death-qualified jury is another name for a jury that is willing to sentence a person to death after hearing the evidence of the case.)

Ardia V. McCree was convicted of murdering Evelyn Boughton while robbing her gift shop and service station in Camden, Arkansas, in February 1978. In accordance with Arkansas law, the trial judge removed eight prospective jurors because they indicated they could not, under any circumstances, vote for the imposition of the death sentence. The resulting jury then convicted McCree and, even though the state sought the death penalty, sentenced the defendant to life imprisonment without parole.

McCree appealed, claiming that the removal of the so-called *Witherspoon* excludables violated his right to a fair trial under the Sixth and 14th Amendments. These amendments guaranteed that his innocence or guilt would be determined by an impartial jury selected from a representative cross-section of the community, which would include people strongly opposed to the death penalty. McCree cited several studies, revealing that death-qualified juries were more likely to convict. Both the federal district court and the federal court of appeals agreed with McCree, but in a 6–3 decision, the Supreme Court disagreed.

The high court majority did not accept the validity of the studies. Speaking for the majority, Justice Rehnquist argued that, even if the justices did accept the validity of these studies, "the Constitution does not prohibit the States from 'death qualifying' juries in capital cases." Justice Rehnquist further observed:

> The exclusion from jury service of large groups of individuals not on the basis of their inability to serve as jurors, but on the basis of some immutable characteristic such as race, gender, or ethnic background, undeniably gave rise to an "appearance of unfairness."
>
> [Nevertheless], unlike blacks, women, and Mexican-Americans, "*Witherspoon*-excludables" are singled out for exclusion in capital cases on the basis of an attribute that is within the individual's control. It is important to remember that not all who oppose the death penalty are subject to removal for cause in capital cases; those who firmly believe that the death penalty is unjust may nevertheless serve as jurors in capital cases so long as they state clearly that they are willing to temporarily set aside their own beliefs in deference to the rule of law. Because the group of "*Witherspoon*-excludables" includes only those who cannot and will not conscientiously obey the law with respect to one of

the issues in a capital case, "death qualification" hardly can be said to create an "appearance of unfairness."

Writing in dissent, Justice Marshall observed that if the high court thought in *Witherspoon* that excluding those who opposed the death penalty meant that a convicted murderer would not get a fair hearing during the sentencing part of the trial, it would also logically mean that he or she would not get a fair hearing during the initial trial part. The dissenting justices generally accepted the studies showing "that 'death qualification' in fact produces juries somewhat more 'conviction-prone' than 'non-death-qualified' juries."

As of October 2013, McCree's name did not appear on a list of inmates kept by the Arkansas Department of Corrections, nor was he listed on an execution database maintained by the Death Penalty Information Center (http://www.deathpenaltyinfo.org/views-executions).

DOES THE BUCK STOP WITH THE JURY?

During the course of a robbery in October 1980 Bobby Caldwell shot and killed Elizabeth Faulkner, the owner of a Mississippi grocery store. Caldwell was tried and found guilty. In the sentencing phase of the trial his attorney pleaded for mercy, concluding his summation by emphasizing to the jury, "I implore you to think deeply about this matter.... You are the judges and you will have to decide his fate. It is an awesome responsibility, I know—an awesome responsibility."

Responding to the defense attorney's plea, the prosecutor played down the responsibility of the jury, stressing that a life sentence would be reviewed by a higher court: "[The defense] would have you believe that you're going to kill this man and they know—they know that your decision is not the final decision.... Your job is reviewable.... They know, as I know, and as Judge Baker has told you, that the decision you render is automatically reviewable by the Supreme Court."

The jury sentenced Caldwell to death, and the case was automatically appealed. The Mississippi Supreme Court upheld the conviction, but split 4–4 on the validity of the death sentence, thereby upholding the death sentence by an equally divided court. Caldwell appealed to the U.S. Supreme Court.

In a 5–3 decision (Justice Powell took no part in the decision), the Supreme Court, in *Caldwell v. Mississippi* (472 U.S. 320 [1985]), vacated (annulled) the death sentence. Writing for the majority, Justice Marshall noted, "It is constitutionally impermissible to rest a death sentence on a determination made by a sentencer who has been led to believe, as the jury was in this case, that the responsibility for determining the appropriateness of the defendant's death rests elsewhere.... [This Court] has taken as a given that capital sentencers would view their task as the serious one of determining whether a specific human being should die at the hands of the State."

Furthermore, the high court pointed out that the appeals court was not the place to make this life-or-death decision. Most appellate courts would presume that the sentencing was correctly done, which would leave the defendant at a distinct disadvantage. The jurors, expecting to be reversed by an appeals court, might choose to "send a message" of extreme disapproval of the defendant's acts and sentence him or her to death to show they will not tolerate such actions. Should the appeals court fail to reverse the decision, the defendant might be executed when the jury only intended to "send a message."

The three dissenting judges believed "the Court has overstated the seriousness of the prosecutor's comments" and that it was "highly unlikely that the jury's sense of responsibility was diminished."

Caldwell was subsequently sentenced to life in prison, and as of October 2013 was incarcerated in Mississippi.

KEEPING PAROLE INFORMATION FROM THE JURY

In 1990 Jonathan Dale Simmons beat an elderly woman, Josie Lamb, to death in her home in Columbia, South Carolina. The week before his capital murder trial began, he pleaded guilty to first-degree burglary and two counts of criminal sexual conduct in connection with two prior assaults on elderly women. These guilty pleas resulted in convictions for violent offenses, which made him ineligible for parole if convicted of any other violent crime.

At the capital murder trial, over the defense counsel's objection, the court did not allow the defense to ask prospective jurors if they understood the meaning of a "life" sentence as it applied to the defendant. Under South Carolina law a defendant who was deemed a future threat to society and receiving a life sentence was ineligible for parole. The prosecution also asked the judge not to mention parole.

During deliberation, the jurors asked the judge if the imposition of a life sentence carried with it the possibility of parole. The judge told the jury, "You are instructed not to consider parole or parole eligibility in reaching your verdict.... The terms life imprisonment and death sentence are to be understood in their plan [sic] and ordinary meaning."

The jury convicted Simmons of murder, sentencing him to death. On appeal the South Carolina Supreme Court upheld the sentence. The case was brought before the U.S. Supreme Court. In *Simmons v. South Carolina* (512 U.S. 154 [1994]), the high court overruled the South Carolina Supreme Court in a 6–2 decision, concluding:

Where a defendant's future dangerousness is at issue, and state law prohibits his release on parole, due process requires that the sentencing jury be informed that the defendant is parole ineligible. An individual cannot be executed on the basis of information which he had no opportunity to deny or explain. Petitioner's jury reasonably may have believed that he could be released on parole if he were not executed. To the extent that this misunderstanding pervaded [the jury's] deliberations, it had the effect of creating a false choice between sentencing him to death and sentencing him to a limited period of incarceration. The trial court's refusal to apprise the jury of information so crucial to its determination, particularly when the State alluded to the defendant's future dangerousness in its argument, cannot be reconciled with this Court's well established precedents interpreting the Due Process Clause.

Simmons was subsequently sentenced to life in prison, and as of October 2013 was incarcerated in South Carolina.

JUDGE SENTENCING

As explained in Chapter 5, as of October 2013 three states—Alabama, Delaware, and Florida—allowed trial judges to override jury-imposed sentences in capital cases. The constitutionality of the Alabama and Florida laws has been considered by the U.S. Supreme Court.

Florida

Under Florida's trifurcated trial system for capital cases, the jury decides the innocence or guilt of the accused. If the jury finds the defendant guilty, it recommends an advisory sentence of either life imprisonment or death. The trial judge considers mitigating and aggravating circumstances, weighs them against the jury recommendation, and then sentences the convicted murderer to either life or death. (Mitigating circumstances may lessen the responsibility for a crime, whereas aggravating circumstances may increase the responsibility for a crime.)

In 1975 a Florida jury convicted Joseph Spaziano of torturing and murdering Laura Lynn Harberts. The jury recommended that Spaziano be sentenced to life imprisonment, but the trial judge, after considering the mitigating and aggravating circumstances, sentenced the defendant to death. In his appeal, Spaziano claimed the judge's overriding of the jury's recommendation of life imprisonment violated the Eighth Amendment's prohibition against a cruel and unusual punishment. The Supreme Court, in a 5–3 decision in *Spaziano v. Florida* (468 U.S. 447 [1984]), did not agree.

Spaziano's lawyers claimed juries, not judges, were better equipped to make reliable capital-sentencing decisions and that a jury's decision of life imprisonment should not be superseded. They reasoned that the death penalty was unlike any other sentence and required that the jury have the ultimate word. This belief had been upheld, Spaziano claimed, because 30 out of 37 states with capital punishment had the jury decide the prisoner's fate. Furthermore, the primary justification for the death penalty was retribution and an expression of community outrage. The jury served as the voice of the community and knew best whether a particular crime was so terrible that the community's response must be the death sentence.

The high court indicated that even though Spaziano's argument had some appeal, it contained two fundamental flaws. First, retribution played a role in all sentences, not just death sentences. Second, a jury was not the only source of community input: "The community's voice is heard at least as clearly in the legislature when the death penalty is authorized and the particular circumstances in which death is appropriate are defined." That trial judges imposed sentences was a normal part of the judicial system. The Supreme Court continued, "In light of the facts that the Sixth Amendment does not require jury sentencing, that the demands of fairness and reliability in capital cases do not require it, and that neither the nature of, nor the purpose behind, the death penalty requires jury sentencing, we cannot conclude that placing responsibility on the trial judge to impose the sentence in a capital case is unconstitutional."

The court added that just because 30 out of 37 states let the jury make the sentencing decision did not mean states that let a judge decide were wrong. The court pointed out that there is no one right way for a state to establish its method of capital sentencing.

Writing for the dissenters, Justice Stevens indicated, "Because of its severity and irrevocability, the death penalty is qualitatively different from any other punishment, and hence must be accompanied by unique safeguards to ensure that it is a justified response to a given offense.... I am convinced that the danger of an excessive response can only be avoided if the decision to impose the death penalty is made by a jury rather than by a single governmental official [because a jury] is best able to 'express the conscience of the community on the ultimate question of life or death.'"

Justice Stevens also gave weight to the fact that 30 out of 37 states had the jury make the decision, attesting to the high "level of consensus" that communities strongly believe life-or-death decisions should remain with the people—as represented by the jury—rather than relegated to a single government official.

Spaziano was subsequently sentenced to life in prison and as of October 2013 was incarcerated in the state of Florida.

Alabama

In March 1988 Louise Harris asked a coworker, Lorenzo McCarter, with whom she was having an affair, to find someone to kill her husband, Isaiah Harris. McCarter paid two accomplices $100, with a promise of more money after they killed the husband. McCarter testified against Harris in exchange for the prosecutor's promise that he would not seek the death penalty against McCarter. McCarter testified that Harris had asked him to kill her husband so they could share in his death benefits. An Alabama jury convicted Harris of capital murder. At the sentencing hearing, witnesses testified to her good background and strong character. She was rearing seven children, held three jobs simultaneously, and was active in her church.

Alabama law gives capital sentencing authority to the trial judge but requires the judge to "consider" an advisory jury verdict. The jury voted 7–5 to give Harris life imprisonment without parole. The trial judge then considered her sentence. He found one aggravating circumstance (the murder was committed for monetary gain), one statutory mitigating circumstance (Harris had no prior criminal record), and one nonstatutory mitigating circumstance (Harris was a hardworking, respected member of her church).

Noting that she had planned the crime, financed it, and stood to benefit from the murder, the judge felt that the aggravating circumstance outweighed the other mitigating circumstances and sentenced her to death. On appeal, the Alabama Supreme Court affirmed the conviction and sentence. It rejected Harris's arguments that the procedure was unconstitutional because Alabama state law did "not specify the weight the judge must give to the jury's recommendation and thus permits the arbitrary imposition of the death penalty."

On appeal, the U.S. Supreme Court upheld in *Harris v. Alabama* (513 U.S. 504 [1995]) the Alabama Supreme Court's decision. Alabama's capital-sentencing process is similar to Florida's. Both require jury participation during sentencing but give the trial judge the ultimate sentencing authority. Nevertheless, even though the Florida statute requires that a trial judge must give "great weight" to the jury recommendation, the Alabama statute requires only that the judge "consider" the jury's recommendation.

As in the *Spaziano* case, the high court ruled that the Eighth Amendment does not require the state "to define the weight the sentencing judge must give to an advisory jury verdict." The court stated, "Because the Constitution permits the trial judge, acting alone, to impose a capital sentence... it is not offended when a State further requires the judge to consider a jury recommendation and trusts the judge to give it the proper weight."

Harris was subsequently sentenced to life without parole and as of October 2013 was incarcerated in Alabama.

JURY SENTENCING

In 2002 the Supreme Court decided a case concerning death sentencing in Arizona involving the Sixth Amendment right to an impartial jury (as opposed to the Eighth Amendment, which bars a cruel and unusual punishment). Timothy Stuart Ring was convicted of murder in the armed robbery of armored-car driver John Magoch in 1994. According to Arizona law, Ring's offense was punishable by life imprisonment or death. He would only be eligible for the death penalty if the trial judge held a separate hearing and found that aggravating factors warranted the death penalty.

One of Ring's accomplices, who negotiated a plea bargain in return for a second-degree murder charge, testified against him at a separate sentencing hearing without a jury present. The same judge who had presided at Ring's trial concluded that Ring committed the murder and that the crime was committed "in an especially heinous, cruel or depraved manner." Weighing the two aggravating circumstances against the mitigating evidence of Ring's minimal criminal record, the judge sentenced Ring to death.

Ring appealed to the Arizona Supreme Court, claiming that the state's capital sentencing law violated his Sixth and 14th Amendment rights because it allowed a judge, rather than a jury, to make the factual findings that made him eligible for a death sentence. The court put aside Ring's argument against Arizona's judge-sentencing system in light of the U.S. Supreme Court's ruling in *Walton v. Arizona* (497 U.S. 639 [1990]). The court held in *Walton* that Arizona's sentencing procedure was constitutional because "the additional facts found by the judge qualified as sentencing considerations, not as 'element[s] of the offense of capital murder.'" Next, the Arizona Supreme Court threw out the trial judge's finding of the heinous nature of the crime but concluded that Ring's minimal criminal record was not enough to outweigh the aggravating evidence of "planned, ruthless robbery and killing." The court affirmed the death sentence.

Ring took his case to the U.S. Supreme Court. On June 24, 2002, by a 7–2 vote, the court ruled in *Ring v. Arizona* (536 U.S. 584) that only juries and not judges can determine the presence of aggravating circumstances that warrant the death sentence. This case differs from the *Harris* and *Spaziano* cases in which the court ruled simply that a judge could sentence a person to death after hearing a jury's recommendation. In the *Ring* opinion the court included a discussion of *Apprendi v. New Jersey* (530 U.S. 466 [2000]), in which it held that "the Sixth Amendment does not permit a defendant to be 'expose[d]...to a penalty exceeding the maximum he would receive if punished according to the facts reflected in the jury verdict alone.'" *Apprendi* involved a defendant in a noncapital case who received a prison term beyond the maximum sentence. This occurred because New Jersey law allowed sentencing judges to increase the penalty if they found that a crime was racially motivated. In *Apprendi*, the court held that any fact other than a prior conviction that increases the punishment for a crime beyond the maximum allowed by law must be found by a jury beyond a reasonable doubt. The court found *Walton* and *Apprendi* irreconcilable. The court overruled *Walton* "to the extent that it allows a sentencing judge, sitting without a jury, to find an aggravating circumstance necessary for imposition of the death penalty." Justice Ruth Bader Ginsburg (1933–), who delivered the opinion of the court, wrote, "The right to trial by jury guaranteed by the Sixth Amendment would be senselessly diminished if it encompassed the factfinding necessary to increase a defendant's sentence by two years [referring to *Apprendi*], but not the factfinding necessary to put him to death. We hold that the Sixth Amendment applies to both."

However, Justice Antonin Scalia (1936–), joined by Justice Clarence Thomas (1948–), pointed out in a separate concurring opinion that under *Ring*, states that let judges impose the death sentence may continue to do so by requiring the finding of aggravating factors necessary to the imposition of the death penalty during the trial phase.

Justice Sandra Day O'Connor (1930–), in her dissenting opinion, joined by Chief Justice Rehnquist, claimed that just as the *Apprendi* decision has overburdened the appeals courts, the *Ring* decision will cause more federal appeals. O'Connor observed that *Ring v. Arizona* also invalidates the capital sentencing procedure of four other states. These included Idaho and Montana, where a judge had the sole sentencing authority, as well as Colorado and Nebraska, where a three-judge panel made the sentencing decisions. The court ruling also potentially affected Alabama, Delaware, Florida, and Indiana, where the jury rendered an advisory verdict, but the judge had the ultimate sentencing authority.

Ring was subsequently sentenced to life in prison and as of October 2013 was incarcerated in Arizona.

The *Ring* Decision Does Not Retroactively Apply to Those Already Sentenced for Murder

The Arizona death row inmate Warren Summerlin was convicted of brutally crushing the skull of bill collector Brenna Bailey and then sexually assaulting her. Summerlin was convicted by a jury, and an Arizona trial judge sentenced him to death in 1982. After the *Ring* decision was handed down, the U.S. Court of Appeals for the Ninth Circuit ruled 8–3 in *Summerlin v. Stewart* (309 F.3d 1193 [9th Cir., 2003]) that in light of *Ring v. Arizona*, Summerlin's death sentence should be vacated. The appellate court held that the Supreme Court's ruling should apply retroactively, even to those inmates who have exhausted their appeals. The prosecution brought the case to the U.S. Supreme Court.

In *Schriro v. Summerlin* (No. 03-526 [2004]), the Supreme Court reversed the appellate court's decision in a 5–4 vote. The nation's highest court concluded that the *Ring* ruling changed only the procedures involved in a sentencing trial for capital punishment cases and did not alter those fundamental legal guidelines judges and juries follow when sentencing a person to death. As such, the *Ring* ruling does not call into question the accuracy of past convictions and should not be retroactive. Speaking for the majority, Justice Scalia wrote, "[We] give retroactive effect to only a small set of 'watershed rules of criminal procedure' implicating the fundamental fairness and accuracy of the criminal proceeding.... That a new procedural rule is 'fundamental' in some abstract sense is not enough; the rule must be one 'without which the likelihood of an accurate conviction is seriously diminished.'"

Summerlin was subsequently sentenced to life in prison and as of October 2013 was incarcerated in Arizona.

SENTENCING PROCEDURES

On July 5, 1978, in Mira Mesa, California, Robert Alton Harris and his brother, Daniel Marcus Harris, decided to steal a car they would need for a getaway in a planned bank robbery. Robert Harris approached two 16-year-old boys—John Mayeski and Michael Baker—eating hamburgers in a car. He forced them at gunpoint to drive to a nearby wooded area. The teenagers offered to delay telling the police of the car robbery and even to give the authorities misleading descriptions of the two robbers. When one of the boys appeared to be fleeing, Robert Harris shot both of them. He and his brother later committed the robbery, were soon caught, and confessed to the robbery and murders.

Both brothers were found guilty. In California, a convicted murderer could be sentenced to death or life imprisonment without parole only if "special circumstances" existed and the murder had been "willful, deliberate, premeditated, and committed during the commission of kidnapping and robbery." This had to be proven during a separate sentencing hearing.

The state showed that Robert Harris was convicted of manslaughter in 1975; he was found in possession of a makeshift knife and garrote (an instrument used for strangulation) while in prison; he and other inmates sodomized another inmate; and he threatened that inmate's life. Harris testified that he had an unhappy childhood, had little education, and his father had sexually molested his sisters. Based, in part, on his brother's testimony, Robert Harris was sentenced by a jury to death, and the judge concurred.

Harris claimed the U.S. Constitution, as interpreted in previous capital punishment rulings, required the state of California to give his case comparative proportionality review to determine if his death sentence was not out of line with that of others convicted of similar crimes. In comparative proportionality review, a court considers the seriousness of the offense, the severity of the penalty, the sentences imposed for other crimes, and the sentencing in other jurisdictions for the same crime. Courts have occasionally struck down punishments that were inherently disproportionate and, therefore, cruel and unusual. Georgia, by law, and Florida, by practice, had incorporated such reviews in their procedures. Other states, such as Texas and California, had not.

When the case reached the U.S. Court of Appeals for the Ninth Circuit, the court agreed with Harris and ordered California to establish proportionality or lift the death sentence. In *Pulley v. Harris* (465 U.S. 37 [1984]), the U.S. Supreme Court, in a 7–2 decision, did not agree. The court noted that the California procedure contained enough safeguards to guarantee a defendant a fair trial and those convicted a fair sentence. The high court added, "That some [state statutes] providing proportionality review are constitutional does not mean that such review is indispensable.... To endorse the statute as a whole is not to say that anything different is unacceptable.... Examination of our 1976 cases makes clear that they do not establish proportionality review as a constitutional requirement."

Justice Brennan, joined by Justice Marshall, dissented. He noted that the Supreme Court had thrown out the existing death penalty procedures during the 1970s because they were deemed arbitrary (subject to individual judgment) and capricious. He believed they still were, but the introduction of proportionality might "eliminate some, if only a small part, of the irrationality that currently infects imposition of the death penalty by the various States."

In 1992, Robert Harris was executed in the gas chamber in California. His brother served time in prison for kidnapping the two boys and was released in 1983.

CHAPTER 3

SUPREME COURT RULINGS II: CIRCUMSTANCES THAT DO AND DO NOT WARRANT THE DEATH PENALTY, RIGHT TO EFFECTIVE COUNSEL, APPEALS BASED ON NEW EVIDENCE, AND CONSTITUTIONALITY OF EXECUTION METHODS

CIRCUMSTANCES FOUND NOT TO WARRANT THE DEATH PENALTY

Rape of Adult Women and Kidnapping

On June 29, 1977, a 5–4 divided U.S. Supreme Court ruled in *Coker v. Georgia* (433 U.S. 584) that the death penalty may not be imposed for the crime of raping an adult woman that does not result in death. The court stated in *Coker*: "Rape is without doubt deserving of serious punishment; but in terms of moral depravity and of the injury to the person and to the public, it does not compare with murder, which does involve the unjustified taking of human life."

The court also held that kidnapping did not warrant the death penalty. Even though the victims usually suffered tremendously, they had not lost their lives. (If the kidnapped victim was killed, then the kidnapper could be tried for murder.)

Child Rape

The Supreme Court's ruling regarding rape was interpreted to apply only to the rape of adult women. The constitutionality of the death penalty for child rape remained untested. In 2008 the issue was resolved when the court ruled in *Kennedy v. Louisiana* (554 U.S. ___ [2008]) that a statute in Louisiana that allowed the death penalty for child rape violated the Eighth Amendment of the U.S. Constitution. The Eighth Amendment bars "cruel and unusual punishments."

In 2003 Patrick Kennedy was convicted of raping his eight-year-old stepdaughter in 1998. The girl was severely injured by the intercourse and required emergency surgery to stem excessive bleeding and repair internal injuries. At that time, Louisiana law allowed the death penalty for aggravated rape of a child under the age of 12 years. In 2007 the state supreme court upheld the sentence, noting that four other states—Georgia, Montana, Oklahoma, and South Carolina—had similar

laws and that "children are a class that need special protection." However, Chief Justice Pascal Frank Calogero Jr. (1931–) of the Louisiana Supreme Court dissented with the ruling, arguing that the U.S. Supreme Court had "set out a bright-line and easily administered rule" that forbids capital punishment for crimes in which the victim survives.

In June 2008 the U.S. Supreme Court overturned the death sentence in a narrow 5–4 decision. Justice Anthony M. Kennedy (1936–) acknowledged the heinous nature of the crime, determining: "Petitioner's crime was one that cannot be recounted in these pages in a way sufficient to capture in full the hurt and horror inflicted on his victim or to convey the revulsion society, and the jury that represents it, sought to express by sentencing petitioner to death." Nevertheless, the majority of the justices held that there was no national consensus on the imposition of capital punishment for child rape. Only a handful of states had or were attempting to pass similar laws. In addition, Louisiana was the only state at the time with people on death row for child rape. (Another man, Richard Davis, had been sentenced to die for raping a five-year-old girl in 2006.)

The court's decision was extremely controversial and received harsh criticism from the Louisiana governor Bobby Jindal (1971–) and then–presidential candidates Senator John McCain (1936–) and Senator Barack Obama (1961–). In October 2008 Louisiana asked the court to reconsider its ruling after it came to light that the military penal code also allowed the death penalty for child rape—a fact not mentioned or apparently considered by the court in its original deliberations over the existence of a "national consensus" on the issue. The court refused to reopen the case. It did issue a modified opinion (October 2008, http://www.scotusblog.com/wp/wp-content/uploads/2008/10/07-343.pdf) that stated, "We find that the military penalty does not affect our reasoning or conclusions."

CRIMINAL INTENT

On April 1, 1975, Sampson Armstrong and Jeanette Armstrong, on the pretext of requesting water for their overheated car, tried to rob Thomas Kersey at his home. Earl Enmund waited in the getaway car. Kersey called for his wife, Eunice Kersey, who tried to shoot Jeanette Armstrong. Sampson Armstrong then killed the Kerseys, an elderly couple. Sampson Armstrong was convicted of robbery-murder and received the death penalty. Enmund was tried for aiding and abetting in the robbery-murder and also sentenced to death.

In *Enmund v. Florida* (458 U.S. 782 [1982]), the Supreme Court ruled 5–4 that, in this case, the death penalty violated the Eighth and 14th Amendments to the U.S. Constitution. The majority noted that only nine of the 36 states with capital punishment permitted its use on a criminal who was not actually present at the scene of the crime. The exception was the case where someone paid a hit man to murder the victim.

Furthermore, over the years juries had tended not to sentence to death criminals who had not actually been at the scene of the crime. Certainly, Enmund was guilty of planning and participating in a robbery, but murder had not been part of the plan. Statistically, because someone is killed in 1 out of 200 robberies, Enmund could not have expected that the Kerseys would be murdered during the robbery attempt. The court concluded that, because Enmund did not kill or plan to kill, he should be tried only for his participation in the robbery. The court observed, "We have no doubt that robbery is a serious crime deserving serious punishment. It is not, however, a crime 'so grievous an affront to humanity that the only adequate response may be the penalty of death.' It does not compare with murder, which does involve the unjustified taking of human life.... The murderer kills; the [robber], if no more than that, does not. Life is over for the victim of the murderer; for the [robbery] victim, life...is not over and normally is not beyond repair."

Writing for the minority, Justice Sandra Day O'Connor (1930–) concluded that intent is a complex issue. It should be left to the judge and jury trying the accused to decide intent, not a federal court far removed from the actual trial.

The sentences of Sampson Armstrong and Earl Enmund were subsequently changed to life in prison. As of October 2013 they were incarcerated in Florida.

Enmund Revisited

Just because a person had no intent to kill does not mean that he or she cannot be sentenced to death. In the early morning of September 22, 1978, Crawford Bullock and his friend Ricky Tucker had been drinking at a bar in Jackson, Mississippi, and were offered a ride home by Mark Dickson, an acquaintance.

During the drive an argument ensued over money that Dickson owed Tucker, and Dickson stopped the car. The argument escalated into a fistfight, and, outside the car, Bullock held Dickson while Tucker punched Dickson and hit him in the face with a whiskey bottle. When Dickson fell, Tucker smashed his head with a concrete block, killing him. Tucker and Bullock disposed of the body. The next day police spotted Bullock driving the victim's car. After his arrest Bullock confessed.

Under Mississippi law a person involved in a robbery that results in murder may be convicted of capital murder regardless of "the defendant's own lack of intent that any killing take place." The jury was never asked to consider whether Bullock in fact killed, attempted to kill, or intended to kill. He was convicted and sentenced to death as an accomplice to the crime. During the appeals process the Mississippi Supreme Court confirmed that Bullock was indeed a participant in the murder.

In January 1986 a divided U.S. Supreme Court modified the *Enmund* decision with a 5–4 ruling in *Cabana v. Bullock* (474 U.S. 376). The court indicated that even though *Enmund* had to be considered at some point during the judicial process, the initial jury trying the accused did not necessarily have to consider the *Enmund* ruling. The high court ruled that even though the jury had not been made aware of the issue of intent, the Mississippi Supreme Court had considered this question. Because *Enmund* did not require that intent be presented at the initial jury trial, only that it be considered at some time during the judicial process, the state of Mississippi had met that requirement.

The four dissenting justices claimed that it was difficult for any appeals court to determine intent from reading a typed transcript of a trial. Seeing the accused and others involved was important in helping determine who was telling the truth and who was not. This was why *Enmund* must be raised to the jury so it could consider the question of intent in light of what it had seen and heard directly.

As of October 2013, the names of Bullock and Tucker did not appear on a list of inmates kept by the Mississippi Department of Corrections, nor were they listed on an execution database maintained by the Death Penalty Information Center (http://www.deathpenaltyinfo.org/views-executions).

"Reckless Indifference to the Value of Human Life"

Gary Tison was a convicted criminal who had been sentenced to life imprisonment for murdering a prison guard during an escape from the Arizona State Prison in Florence, Arizona. Tison's three sons—Donald, Ricky,

and Raymond—his wife, his brother, and other relatives planned a prison escape involving Tison and a fellow prisoner, Randy Greenawalt, also a convicted murderer.

On the day of the planned escape in July 1978, Tison's sons smuggled guns into the prison's visitation area. After locking up the guards and visitors, the five men fled in a car. They later transferred to another car and waited in an abandoned house for a plane to take them to Mexico. When the plane did not come, the men got back on the road. The car soon had flat tires. One son flagged down a passing car. It contained a young married couple, John and Donnelda Lyons, their infant son Christopher, and 15-year-old niece Teresa Tyson.

Gary Tison then told his sons to go get some water from the motorist's car, which was going to be left with the family they planned to abandon in the desert. While the sons were gone, Tison and Greenawalt shot and killed the family. The gang encountered and killed two more people—James and Margene Judge—before police engaged them in a shoot-out at a road block. Ricky and Raymond Tison and Greenawalt were captured. Donald Tyson was killed, and Gary Tison escaped into the desert, where he later died of exposure.

The surviving Tisons and Greenawalt were found guilty and sentenced to death. Ricky and Raymond Tison citing *Enmund*, appealed, claiming that they had neither pulled the triggers nor intended the deaths of the family who had stopped to help them. In *Tison v. Arizona* (481 U.S. 137 [1987]), the Supreme Court ruled 5–4 to uphold the death sentence, indicating that the Tison sons had shown a "reckless indifference to the value of human life [which] may be every bit as shocking to the moral sense as an 'intent to kill.'"

The Tisons may not have pulled the triggers (and the court fully accepted the premise that they did not do the shootings or directly intend them to happen), but they released and then assisted two convicted murderers. They should have realized that freeing two killers and giving them guns could very well put innocent people in great danger. Moreover, they continued to help the escapees even after the family was killed.

"These facts," concluded Justice O'Connor for the majority, "not only indicate that the Tison brothers' participation in the crime was anything but minor; they also would clearly support a finding that they both subjectively appreciated that their acts were likely to result in the taking of innocent life." Unlike the situation in the *Enmund* case, they were not sitting in a car far from the murder scene. They were direct participants in the whole event. The death sentence would stand.

Writing for the minority, Justice Brennan observed that had a prison guard been murdered (Gary Tison had murdered a prison guard in a previous escape attempt),

then the court's argument would have made sense. The murder of the family, however, made no sense and was not even necessary for the escape. The Tison sons were away from the murder scene getting water for the victims and could have done nothing to save them. Even though they were guilty of planning and carrying out an escape, the murder of the family who stopped to help them was an unexpected outcome of the escape.

Furthermore, the father had promised his sons that he would not kill during the escape, a promise he had kept despite several opportunities to kill during the actual prison escape. Therefore, it was not unreasonable for the sons to believe that their father would not kill in a situation that did not appear to warrant it. Justice Brennan concluded that "like Enmund, the Tisons neither killed nor attempted or intended to kill anyone. Like Enmund, the Tisons have been sentenced to death for the intentional acts of others which the Tisons did not expect, which were not essential to the felony, and over which they had no control."

In 1992 the Arizona Supreme Court overturned the death penalty sentences for Ricky and Raymond Tison because they were under the age of 20 at the time of the crimes. They were subsequently sentenced to life in prison, and as of October 2013 were incarcerated in Arizona. Greenawalt was executed in 1997.

RIGHT TO EFFECTIVE COUNSEL

In 1989 Kevin Eugene Wiggins received a death sentence for the 1988 drowning of Florence Lacs, an elderly Maryland woman, in her home. The Maryland Court of Appeals affirmed his sentence in 1991. With the help of new counsel, Wiggins sought post-conviction relief, challenging the quality of his initial lawyers. Wiggins claimed his lawyers failed to investigate and present mitigating evidence (evidence that may lessen responsibility for a crime) that he was physically and sexually abused as a child. The sentencing jury never heard that he was starved, that his mother punished him by burning his hand on the stove, and that after the state put him in foster care at age six, he suffered more physical and sexual abuse.

In 2001 a federal district court concluded that Wiggins's first lawyers should have conducted a more thorough investigation into his childhood abuse, which would have kept the jury from imposing a death sentence. However, the U.S. Court of Appeals for the Fourth Circuit reversed the district court decision, ruling that the original attorneys had made a "reasonable strategic decision" to concentrate their defense on raising doubts about Wiggins's guilt instead.

On June 26, 2003, the U.S. Supreme Court threw out the death sentence. In *Wiggins v. Smith* (539 U.S. 510), the court ruled 7–2 that Wiggins's lawyers violated his Sixth Amendment right to effective assistance of counsel. The court noted, "Counsel's investigation into Wiggins' background did not reflect reasonable professional judgment.... Given the nature and extent of the abuse, there is a reasonable probability that a competent attorney, aware of this history, would have introduced it at sentencing, and that a jury confronted with such mitigating evidence would have returned with a different sentence."

Wiggins was subsequently sentenced to life in prison with the chance for parole. As of October 2013 he was incarcerated in Maryland.

When Does the Right to State-Paid Counsel End?

Joseph M. Giarratano was sent to Virginia's death row for the 1979 murder of Barbara Kline and the rape and murder of her 15-year-old daughter Michelle Kline. He received full counsel for his trial and for his initial appeal. Afterward, Virginia would no longer provide him with his own lawyer. He went to court, complaining that because he was poor the state of Virginia should provide him with counsel to help prepare post-conviction appeals. Virginia permitted the condemned prisoner the right to use the prison libraries to prepare an appeal, but it did not provide the condemned with his own personal attorney.

Virginia had unit attorneys, who were assigned to help prisoners with prison-related legal matters. A unit attorney could give guidance to death row inmates but could not act as the personal attorney for any one particular inmate. This case became a class action in which the federal district court certified a class made up of "all current and future Virginia inmates awaiting execution who do not have and cannot afford counsel to pursue postconviction proceedings."

The federal district court and the federal court of appeals agreed with Giarratano, but the Supreme Court, in *Murray v. Giarratano* (492 U.S. 1 [1989]), disagreed. Writing for the majority, Chief Justice Rehnquist concluded that even though the Sixth and 14th Amendments to the Constitution ensure an impoverished defendant the right to counsel at the trial stage of a criminal proceeding, they do not provide for counsel for post-conviction proceedings, as the court ruled in *Pennsylvania v. Finley* (481 U.S. 551 [1987]). Because *Finley* had not specifically considered prisoners on death row, but all prisoners in general, the majority did not believe the decision needed to be reconsidered just because death row prisoners had more at stake.

Chief Justice Rehnquist agreed that those facing the death penalty have a right to counsel for the trial and during the initial appeal. During these periods the defendant needs a heightened measure of protection because the death penalty is involved. Later appeals, however, involve more procedural matters that "serve a different and more limited purpose than either the trial or appeal."

In dissent, Justice John Paul Stevens (1920–), who was joined by Justices Brennan, Marshall, and Harry A. Blackmun (1908–1999), indicated that he thought condemned prisoners in Virginia faced three critical differences from those considered in *Finley*. First, the Virginia prisoners had been sentenced to death, which made their condition different from a sentence of life imprisonment. Second, Virginia's particular judicial decision forbids certain issues to be raised during the direct review or appeals process and forces them to be considered only during later post-conviction appeals. This means that important issues may be considered without the benefit of counsel. Finally, "unlike the ordinary inmate, who presumably has ample time to use and reuse the prison library and to seek guidance from other prisoners experienced in preparing...petitions...a grim deadline imposes a finite limit on the condemned person's capacity for useful research."

He continued, quoting from the district court's decision on the matter, an "inmate preparing himself and his family for impending death is incapable of performing the mental functions necessary to adequately pursue his claims."

In 1991 Giarratano's sentence was commuted to life in prison only days before his scheduled electrocution. As of October 2013 he was incarcerated in the State of Virginia.

Federal Judges Can Delay Executions to Allow Habeas Corpus Reviews

In 1988 Congress passed the Anti-Drug Abuse Act, which guaranteed qualified legal representation for poor death row defendants wanting to file for habeas corpus (a prisoner's petition to be heard in federal court) so that the counsel could assist in the preparation of the appeal. In 1994 this law was brought to question before the Supreme Court by the death row inmate Frank McFarland.

In November 1989 a Texas jury found McFarland guilty of stabbing to death Terri Lynn Hokanson, a woman he had met in a bar. He was sentenced to death. The state appellate court upheld his conviction, and two lower federal courts refused his request for a stay (postponement) of execution. The federal courts ruled that they did not have jurisdiction to stop the execution until McFarland filed a habeas corpus. The inmate argued that without the stay, he would be executed before he could obtain a lawyer to prepare the petition.

The Supreme Court granted a stay of execution. In *McFarland v. Scott* (512 U.S. 849 [1994]), the court ruled 5–4 to uphold the 1988 federal law. Once a defendant requested counsel, the federal court could postpone execution so the lawyer would have time to prepare an appeal. Justice Blackmun stated that "by providing indigent [poor] capital defendants with a mandatory right to qualified legal counsel in these proceedings, Congress has recognized that Federal habeas corpus has a particularly important role to play in promoting fundamental fairness in the imposition of the death penalty."

McFarland was executed in Texas in 1998.

APPEALS BASED ON NEW EVIDENCE
Newly Discovered Evidence Does Not Stop Execution

On an evening in late September 1981, the body of Officer David Rucker of the Texas Department of Public Safety was found lying beside his patrol car. He had been shot in the head. At about the same time, Officer Enrique Carrisalez saw a vehicle speeding away from the area where Rucker's body had been found. Carrisalez and his partner chased the vehicle and pulled it over. Carrisalez walked to the car. The driver opened his door and exchanged a few words with the police officer before firing at least one shot into Carrisalez's chest. The officer died nine days later.

Leonel Torres Herrera was arrested a few days after the shootings and charged with capital murder. In January 1982 he was tried and found guilty of murdering Carrisalez. In July 1982 he pleaded guilty to Rucker's murder.

At the trial Officer Carrisalez's partner identified Herrera as the person who fired the gun. He also testified that there was only one person in the car. In a statement by Carrisalez before he died, he also identified Herrera. The speeding car belonged to Herrera's girlfriend, and Herrera had the car keys in his pocket when he was arrested. Splatters of blood on the car and on Herrera's clothes were the same type as Rucker's. Strands of hair found in the car also belonged to Rucker. Finally, a handwritten letter, which strongly implied that he had killed Rucker, was found on Herrera when he was arrested.

In 1992, 10 years after the initial trial, Herrera appealed to the federal courts, alleging that he was innocent of the murders of Rucker and Carrisalez and that his execution would violate the Eighth and 14th Amendments. He presented affidavits (sworn statements) claiming that he had not killed the officers but that his now dead brother had. The brother's attorney, one of Herrera's cellmates, and a school friend all swore that the brother had killed the police officers. The dead brother's son also said that he had witnessed his father killing the police officers.

In *Herrera v. Collins* (506 U.S. 390 [1993]), the U.S. Supreme Court ruled 6–3 that executing Herrera would not violate the Eighth and 14th Amendments. The high court said that the trial—not the appeals process—judges a defendant's innocence or guilt. Appeals courts determine only the fairness of the proceedings.

Writing for the majority, Chief Justice Rehnquist stated:

> A person when first charged with a crime is entitled to a presumption of innocence, and may insist that his guilt be established beyond a reasonable doubt.... Once a defendant has been afforded a fair trial and convicted of the offense for which he was charged, the presumption of innocence disappears.... Here, it is not disputed that the State met its burden of proving at trial that petitioner was guilty of the capital murder of Officer Carrisalez beyond a reasonable doubt. Thus, in the eyes of the law, petitioner does not come before the Court as one who is "innocent," but on the contrary, as one who has been convicted by due process of law of two brutal murders.
>
> Based on affidavits here filed, petitioner claims that evidence never presented to the trial court proves him innocent....
>
> Claims of actual innocence based on newly discovered evidence have never been held to state a ground for [court] relief absent an independent constitutional violation occurring in the underlying state criminal proceeding....
>
> This rule is grounded in the principle that [appeals] courts sit to ensure that individuals are not imprisoned in violation of the Constitution—not to correct errors of fact.

Rehnquist continued that states all allow the introduction of new evidence. Texas was one of 17 states that require a new trial motion based on new evidence within 60 days. Herrera's appeal came 10 years later. The chief justice, however, emphasized that Herrera still had options, saying, "For under Texas law, petitioner may file a request for executive clemency.... Executive clemency has provided the 'fail-safe' in our criminal justice system.... It is an unalterable fact that our judicial system, like the human beings who administer it, is fallible. But history is replete with examples of wrongfully convicted persons who have been pardoned in the wake of after-discovered evidence establishing their innocence."

The majority opinion found the information presented in the affidavits inconsistent with the other evidence. The justices questioned why the affidavits were produced at the very last minute. The justices also wondered why Herrera had pleaded guilty to Rucker's murder if he had been innocent. They did note that some of the information in the affidavits might have been important to the jury, "but coming 10 years after petitioner's trial, this showing of innocence falls far short of that which would have to be made in order to trigger the sort of constitutional claim [to decide for a retrial]."

Speaking for the minority, Justice Blackmun wrote:

We really are being asked to decide whether the Constitution forbids the execution of a person who has been validly convicted and sentenced, but who, nonetheless, can prove his innocence with newly discovered evidence. Despite the State of Texas' astonishing protestation to the contrary... I do not see how the answer can be anything but "yes."

The Eighth Amendment prohibits "cruel and unusual punishments." This proscription is not static, but rather reflects evolving standards of decency. I think it is crystal clear that the execution of an innocent person is "at odds with contemporary standards of fairness and decency." ... The protection of the Eighth Amendment does not end once a defendant has been validly convicted and sentenced.

Herrera was executed in Texas in 1993.

Claim of Miscarriage of Justice

Lloyd E. Schlup Jr., a Missouri prisoner, was convicted of participating in the murder of a fellow inmate—Arthur Dade—in 1984 and sentenced to death. He had filed one petition for habeas corpus, arguing that he had inadequate counsel. He claimed the counsel did not call fellow inmates and other witnesses to testify that could prove his innocence. He filed a second petition, alleging that constitutional error at his trial deprived the jury of crucial evidence that would again have established his innocence.

Using a previous U.S. Supreme Court ruling (*Sawyer v. Whitley*, 505 U.S. 333 [1992]), the district court claimed that Schlup had not shown "by clear and convincing evidence that but for a constitutional error no reasonable jury would have found him guilty." Schlup's lawyers argued that the district court should have used another ruling (*Murray v. Carrier*, 477 U.S. 478 [1986]), in which a petitioner need only to show that "a constitutional violation has probably resulted in the conviction of one who is actually innocent." The appellate court affirmed the district court's ruling, noting that Schlup's guilt, which had been proven at the trial, barred any consideration of his constitutional claim.

The U.S. Supreme Court, on appeal, reviewed the case to determine whether the *Sawyer* standard provides enough protection from a miscarriage of justice that would result from the execution of an innocent person. In *Schlup v. Delo* (513 U.S. 298 [1995]), the court observed, "If a petitioner such as Schlup presents evidence of innocence so strong that a court cannot have confidence in the outcome of the trial... the petitioner should be allowed to... argue the merits of his underlying claims."

The justices concluded that the less stringent *Carrier* standard, as opposed to the rigid *Sawyer* standard, focuses the investigation on the actual innocence, allow-

ing the court to review relevant evidence that might have been excluded or unavailable during the trial. The court noted "because both the Court of Appeals and the District Court evaluated the record under an improper standard, further proceedings are necessary." The case was remanded back to the district court. In 1999 Schlup was being retried when he pleaded guilty to noncapital murder as part of a plea deal and was given a life sentence with a chance for parole. As of September 2013, no information could be determined on Schlup's status; he was not found in a website search of the list of inmates incarcerated by the Missouri Department of Correction (https://web.mo.gov/doc/offSearchWeb/search Offender.do).

Schlup v. Delo Revisited in *House v. Bell*

In 2006 the Supreme Court heard a case involving the Tennessee prisoner Paul House, who had been convicted in 1985 of murdering Carolyn Muncey. The prosecution alleged that House, a paroled sex offender, murdered Muncey during an attempted rape. He was convicted based on circumstantial evidence and forensics tests that showed semen stains on Muncey's clothing were of House's blood type. More incriminating were small blood stains found on House's blue jeans that matched Muncey's blood type.

In 1996 House's lawyers filed a habeas corpus petition in the U.S. District Court and presented new evidence, including deoxyribonucleic acid tests showing that the semen on Muncey's clothing was from her husband, not House. Several witnesses testified that Hubert Muncey Jr. had confessed to them while he was drunk that he did commit the murder. They also testified that he had a history of beating his wife. In addition, the original blood evidence came into question, due to allegations of the mishandling of blood that was collected during the autopsy. The defense attorneys argued that some of the autopsy blood spilled on House's pants before they were tested at the FBI laboratory in Washington, D.C. The state admitted that the autopsy blood was improperly sealed and transported and spilled, but argued that the spill occurred after the pants were tested. The district court ruled that the new evidence did not demonstrate actual innocence as required under *Schlup v. Delo* and failed to show that House was ineligible for the death penalty under *Sawyer v. Whitley*. The ruling was eventually upheld on appeal.

In *House v. Bell* (No. 04-8990 [2006]), the U.S. Supreme Court ruled 5–3 that House's habeas petition should proceed, because the new evidence constituted a "stringent showing" under *Schlup v. Delo*. (Note that only eight justices, rather than the usual nine justices, decided this case, because of its timing. The case was argued on January 11, 2006, and decided on June 12, 2006.

Neither Justice O'Connor nor Justice Samuel A. Alito Jr. [1950–], her successor, participated in the case because Alito replaced O'Connor on January 31, 2006.) The court concluded:

> This is not a case of conclusive exoneration. Some aspects of the State's evidence—Lora Muncey's memory of a deep voice, House's bizarre evening walk, his lie to law enforcement, his appearance near the body, and the blood on his pants—still support an inference of guilt. Yet the central forensic proof connecting House to the crime—the blood and the semen—has been called into question, and House has put forward substantial evidence pointing to a different suspect. Accordingly, and although the issue is close, we conclude that this is the rare case where—had the jury heard all the conflicting testimony—it is more likely than not that no reasonable juror viewing the record as a whole would lack reasonable doubt.

Supporters of House's innocence, including members of the state legislature, petitioned the governor for a pardon. Eventually, in 2008 the U.S. Supreme Court determined that the jury that convicted House did not hear testimony at the time that could have cleared him of the murder. During the spring of 2009 prosecutors dropped their charges against House, who had contracted multiple sclerosis and was confined to a wheelchair. Shortly thereafter he was released from prison and moved in with his mother.

Suppressed Evidence Means a New Trial

Curtis Lee Kyles was convicted by a Louisiana jury of the first-degree murder of Dolores Dye in a grocery store parking lot in 1984. Kyles was sentenced to death. It was revealed on review that the prosecutor had never disclosed certain evidence favorable to the defendant. Among the evidence were conflicting statements by an informant who, the defense believed, wanted to get rid of Kyles to get his girlfriend. The state supreme court, the federal district court, and the Fifth Circuit Court denied Kyles's appeals. The U.S. Supreme Court, in *Kyles v. Whitley* (514 U.S. 419 [1995]), reversed the lower courts' decisions. The high court ruled, "Favorable evidence is material, and constitutional error results from its suppression by the government, if there is a 'reasonable probability' that, had the evidence been disclosed to the defense, the result of the proceeding would have been different.... [The] net effect of the state-suppressed evidence favoring Kyles raises a reasonable probability that its disclosure would have produced a different result at trial."

The conviction was overturned. Four mistrials followed. On February 18, 1998, after his fifth and final trial ended with a hung jury, Kyles was released from prison. He had spent 14 years on death row.

CHALLENGING THE ANTITERRORISM AND EFFECTIVE DEATH PENALTY ACT OF 1996

The Antiterrorism and Effective Death Penalty Act (AEDPA) became law in April 1996, shortly after the first anniversary of the Oklahoma City bombing. The AEDPA aims in part to "provide for an effective death penalty." After passage of the law the lower courts differed in their interpretations of certain core provisions. For the first time, on April 18, 2000, the U.S. Supreme Court addressed these problems.

Federal Habeas Corpus Relief and the AEDPA

The AEDPA restricts the power of federal courts to grant habeas corpus relief to state inmates who have exhausted their state appeals. Through the writ of habeas corpus, an inmate could have a court review his or her conviction or sentencing. The AEDPA bars a federal court from granting an application for a writ of habeas corpus unless the state court's decision "was contrary to, or involved an unreasonable application of, clearly established federal law, as determined by the Supreme Court of the United States." The idea was to curtail the amount of habeas reviews filed by convicts and thus save the overbooked federal courts time and money.

In 1986 Terry Williams, while incarcerated in a Danville, Virginia, city jail, wrote to the police that he had killed and robbed an elderly man named Harris Thomas Stone. Williams was subsequently convicted of robbery and capital murder. During the sentencing hearing the prosecutor presented many crimes Williams had committed previously. Two state witnesses also testified to the defendant's future dangerousness.

Williams's lawyer, however, called on his mother to testify to his being a nonviolent person. The defense also played a taped portion of a psychiatrist's statement, who said that Williams admitted to him that during a previous robbery he had removed bullets from a gun so as not to harm anyone. During his closing statement, however, the lawyer noted that the jury would probably find it hard to give his client mercy because he did not show mercy to his victims. The jury sentenced Williams to death, and the trial judge imposed the sentence.

In 1988 Williams filed a state habeas corpus petition. The Danville Circuit Court found Williams's conviction valid. The court found, however, that the defense lawyer's failure to present several mitigating factors at the sentencing phase violated Williams's right to effective assistance of counsel as prescribed by *Strickland v. Washington* (466 U.S. 668 [1984]). The mitigating circumstances included early childhood abuse and borderline mental retardation. The habeas corpus hearing further revealed that the state expert witnesses had testified that if Williams were kept in a "structured environment," he would not be a threat to society. The circuit court recommended a new sentencing hearing.

In 1997 the Virginia Supreme Court rejected the circuit court's recommendation for a new sentencing hearing, concluding that the omitted evidence would not have affected the sentence. In making its ruling, the state supreme court relied on what it considered to be an established U.S. Supreme Court precedent.

Next, Williams filed a federal habeas corpus petition. The federal trial judge ruled not only that the death sentence was "constitutionally infirm" but also that defense counsel was ineffective. However, the U.S. Court of Appeals for the Fourth Circuit reversed the federal trial judge's decision, holding that the AEDPA prohibits a federal court from granting habeas corpus relief unless the state court's decision "was contrary to, or involved an unreasonable application of, clearly established federal law, as determined by the Supreme Court of the United States."

On April 18, 2000, the U.S. Supreme Court, in *Williams v. Taylor* (529 U.S. 362 [2000]), reversed the Fourth Circuit Court's ruling by a 6–3 decision. The court concluded that the Virginia Supreme Court's decision rejecting Williams's claim of ineffective assistance was contrary to a Supreme Court–established precedent (*Strickland v. Washington*), as well as an unreasonable application of that precedent. This was the first time the Supreme Court had granted relief on such a claim.

In November 2000, during a court hearing, Williams accepted a plea agreement of a life sentence without parole after prosecutors agreed not to seek the death penalty. As of October 2013, he was incarcerated in Virginia.

Federal Evidentiary Hearings for Constitutional Claims

Under an AEDPA provision, if the petitioner has failed to develop the facts of his or her challenges of a constitutional claim in state court proceedings, the federal court shall not hold a hearing on the claim unless the facts involve an exception listed by the AEDPA.

In 1993, three men were arrested in connection with a crime spree in Virginia that left six people dead. Two of the defendants—Michael Wayne Williams and his friend Jeffrey Alan Cruse—were the subject of a case heard before the U.S. Supreme Court. After robbing the home of Morris Keller Jr. and his wife, Mary Elizabeth, Williams and Cruse raped the woman and then killed the couple. In exchange for the state's promise not to seek capital punishment, Cruse described details of the crimes. Williams received the death sentence for the capital murders. The prosecution told the jury about the plea agreement with Cruse. The state later revoked the plea

agreement after discovering that Cruse had also raped the wife and failed to disclose it. After Cruse's court testimony against Williams, however, the state gave Cruse a life sentence, which Williams alleged amounted to a second, informal plea agreement.

Williams filed a habeas petition in state court, claiming he was not told of the second plea agreement between the state and his codefendant. The Virginia Supreme Court dismissed the petition (1994) and the U.S. Supreme Court refused to review the case (1995).

In 1996, on appeal, a federal district court agreed to an evidentiary hearing of Williams's claims of the undisclosed second plea agreement. The defendant had also claimed that a psychiatric report about Cruse, which was not revealed by the prosecution, could have shown that Cruse was not credible. Moreover, a certain juror might have had possible bias, which the prosecution failed to disclose. Before the hearing could be held, the state concluded that the AEDPA prohibited such a hearing. Consequently, the federal district court dismissed Williams's petition.

When the case was brought before the U.S. Court of Appeals for the Fourth Circuit, the court, interpreting the AEDPA, concluded that the defendant had failed to develop the facts of his claims. On April 18, 2000, in *Williams v. Taylor* (529 U.S. 420), a unanimous U.S. Supreme Court did not address Williams's claim of the undisclosed plea agreement between Cruse and the state. Instead, the high court held that the defendant was entitled to a federal district court evidentiary hearing regarding his other claims. According to the court, "Under the [AEDPA], a failure to develop the factual basis of a claim is not established unless there is lack of diligence, or some greater fault, attributable to the prisoner or the prisoner's counsel.... We conclude petitioner has met the burden of showing he was diligent in efforts to develop the facts supporting his juror bias and prosecutorial misconduct claims in collateral proceedings before the Virginia Supreme Court."

As of October 2013 the name Michael Wayne Williams did not appear on a list maintained by the DPIC of persons executed in Virginia.

High Court Upholds Restriction on Federal Appeals

Even though the Supreme Court ruled in favor of new resentencing hearings for Terry Williams and Michael Williams, it stressed that the AEDPA places a new restriction on federal courts with respect to granting habeas relief to state inmates. The court noted in *Williams v. Taylor* (529 U.S. 362) that under the AEDPA:

> The writ may issue only if one of the following two conditions is satisfied—the state-court adjudication resulted in a decision that (1) "was contrary to... clearly established Federal law, as determined by the

Supreme Court of the United States," or (2) "involved an unreasonable application of . . . clearly established Federal law, as determined by the Supreme Court of the United States." Under the "contrary to" clause, a federal habeas court may grant the writ if the state court arrives at a conclusion opposite to that reached by this court on a question of law or if the state court decides a case differently than this court has on a set of materially indistinguishable facts. Under the "unreasonable application" clause, a federal habeas court may grant the writ if the state court identifies the correct governing legal principle from this court's decisions but unreasonably applies that principle to the facts of the prisoner's case.

METHODS OF EXECUTION
The Role of the U.S. Food and Drug Administration

The injection of a deadly combination of drugs has become the method of execution in most states permitting capital punishment. Condemned prisoners from Texas and Oklahoma, two of the first states to introduce this method, brought suit claiming that even though the drugs used had been approved by the U.S. Food and Drug Administration (FDA) for medical purposes, they had never been approved for use in or tested for human executions.

The FDA commissioner refused to act, claiming serious questions whether the agency had jurisdiction in the area. The U.S. District Court for the District of Columbia disagreed with the condemned prisoners that the FDA had a responsibility to determine if the lethal mixture used during execution was safe and effective. The court noted that decisions by a federal agency not to take action were not reviewable in court.

A divided U.S. Court of Appeals for the District of Columbia reversed the lower court ruling. A generally irritated U.S. Supreme Court agreed to hear the case "to review the implausible result that the FDA is required to exercise its enforcement power to ensure that States only use drugs that are 'safe and effective' for human execution."

In *Heckler v. Chaney* (470 U.S. 821 [1985]), the unanimous court agreed that, in this case, the FDA did not have jurisdiction.

Is Execution by Hanging Constitutional?

Washington state law imposes capital punishment either by "hanging by the neck" or, if the condemned chooses, by lethal injection. Charles Rodham Campbell was convicted in 1982 of murdering Ranae Wicklund, her eight-year-old daughter Shannah, and a neighbor, Barbara Hendrickson, and was sentenced to death. Campbell, in challenging the constitutionality of hanging under the Washington statute, claimed that execution by hanging violated his Eighth Amendment right because it was a cruel and unusual punishment. Furthermore, the direction

that he be hanged unless he chose lethal injection was a cruel and unusual punishment. He claimed that such instruction further violated his First Amendment right by forcing him to participate in his own execution to avoid hanging.

In *Campbell v. Wood* (18 F.3d. 662 [9th Cir. 1994]), the U.S. Court of Appeals for the Ninth Circuit noted, "We do not consider hanging to be cruel and unusual simply because it causes death, or because there may be some pain associated with death . . . . As used in the Constitution, 'cruel' implies 'something inhuman and barbarous, something more than the mere extinguishment of life.' . . . Campbell is entitled to an execution free only of 'the unnecessary and wanton infliction of pain.'"

According to the court, just because the defendant was given a choice of method of execution did not mean that he was being subjected to a cruel and unusual punishment: "We believe that benefits to prisoners who may choose to exercise the option and who may feel relieved that they can elect lethal injection outweigh the emotional costs to those who find the mere existence of an option objectionable."

Campbell argued that the state was infringing on his First Amendment right of free exercise of his religion. He claimed that it was against his religion to participate in his own execution by being allowed to elect lethal injection over hanging.

The court contended that Campbell did not have to choose an execution method or participate in his own execution. "He may remain absolutely silent and refuse to participate in any election. The statute provides for imposition of the death penalty by hanging, and does not require him to choose the method of his execution." On appeal (*Campbell v. Wood*, No. 93-8931 [1994]), the U.S. Supreme Court decided not to hear the case. In 1994 Campbell was executed by hanging. He refused to cooperate during the execution and had to be pepper sprayed and strapped to a board to carry out the hanging.

Is Execution by Lethal Gas Constitutional?

On April 17, 1992, three California death row inmates—David Rey Fierro, Alejandro Gilbert Ruiz, and Robert Alton Harris—filed a suit on behalf of themselves and all others under sentence of execution by lethal gas. In *Fierro v. Gomez* (790 F. Supp. 966 [N.D. Cal. 1992]), the inmates alleged that California's method of execution by lethal gas violated the Eighth and 14th Amendments. Harris was scheduled to be executed four days later, on April 21—an execution that was carried out.

The district court prohibited James Gomez, the director of the California Department of Corrections, and

Arthur Calderon, the warden of San Quentin Prison, from executing any inmate until a hearing was held. On appeal from Gomez and Calderon, the U.S. Court of Appeals for the Ninth Circuit vacated (annulled) the district court's ruling. On his execution day Harris had filed a habeas corpus petition with the California Supreme Court, challenging the constitutionality of the gas chamber. The court declined to review the case, and Harris was put to death that day. In the aftermath of Harris's execution, the California legislature amended in 1993 its death penalty statute, providing that, if lethal gas "is held invalid, the punishment of death shall be imposed by the alternative means," lethal injection.

In October 1994 a federal district judge, Marilyn Hall Patel (1938–), ruled that execution by lethal gas "is inhumane and has no place in civilized society" (865 F. Supp. at 1415). She then ordered California's gas chamber closed and that lethal injection be used instead. This was the first time a federal judge had ruled that any method of execution violated the Eighth and 14th Amendments. Even though the state of California maintained that cyanide gas caused almost instant unconsciousness, the judge referred to doctors' reports and witnesses' accounts of gas chamber executions, which indicated that the dying inmates stayed conscious for 15 seconds to a minute or longer and suffered "intense physical pain."

Gomez and Calderon appealed Judge Patel's ruling on the unconstitutionality of the gas chamber before the U.S. Court of Appeals for the Ninth Circuit. The court also appealed the permanent injunction against the use of lethal gas as a method of execution. In February 1996, in *Fierro v. Gomez* (77 F.3d. 301 [9th Cir.]), the appellate court affirmed Judge Patel's ruling.

Gomez and Calderon appealed the case to the U.S. Supreme Court. In October 1996 a 7–2 Supreme Court, in *Gomez v. Fierro* (519 U.S. 918), vacated the appellate court's ruling and returned the case to the appellate court for additional proceedings, citing the death penalty statute amended in 1993 (lethal injection as an alternative to lethal gas). As of October 2013, Fierro remained on death row. Ruiz died of natural causes in early 2007.

Does Electrocution Constitute a Cruel and Unusual Punishment?

During the 1990s, even though Florida had three botched executions using the electric chair, the state supreme court ruled each time that electrocution does not constitute a cruel and unusual punishment. In 1990 and 1997 flames shot out from the headpiece worn by the condemned inmate. On July 8, 1999, Allen Lee Davis developed a nosebleed during his execution in the electric chair.

Thomas Provenzano, who was scheduled to be electrocuted after Davis, challenged the use of the electric chair as Florida's sole method of execution. In *Provenzano v. Moore* (No. 95973 [1999]), the Florida Supreme Court ruled 4–3 that the electric chair was not a cruel and unusual punishment. The court further reported that Davis's nosebleed occurred before the execution and did not result from the electrocution.

Subsequently, the court, as it routinely does with all its rulings, posted the *Provenzano* decision on the Internet. Three photographs of Davis covered with blood were posted as part of the dissenting opinion of Justice Leander J. Shaw Jr. (1930–). The photographs brought public outcry worldwide. Justice Shaw claimed that Davis was "brutally tortured to death."

In October 1999, for the first time, the U.S. Supreme Court agreed to consider the constitutionality of electrocution. The death row inmate Anthony Braden Bryan asked the court to review his case, based on the unreliability of the electric chair. Bryan was on death row for kidnapping, robbing, and murdering George Wilson. Before the high court could hear the case, however, the Florida legislature voted in a special session to replace electrocution with lethal injection as the primary method of execution, but allowed a condemned person to choose the electric chair as an alternative. On January 24, 2000, the Supreme Court dismissed *Bryan v. Moore* (No. 99-6723) as moot (irrelevant), based on Florida's new legislation. Bryan was executed by lethal injection the following month.

In 2001 the Georgia Supreme Court held that electrocution was a cruel and unusual punishment in violation of the state constitution. It was the first appellate court to rule a method of execution unconstitutional. Throughout the first decade of the 21st century all other death penalty states made lethal injection their primary (and sometimes only) method of execution. Nebraska was the last state to do so. In 2008 the Nebraska Supreme Court ruled that execution by electrocution was unconstitutional. The following year the Nebraska legislature passed legislation that established lethal injection as the state's only method of execution. As explained in Chapter 5, some other states still authorize alternative means of execution (i.e., electrocution, lethal gas, hanging, or firing squad) under certain circumstances.

Challenges to Lethal Injection

In April 2006 the U.S. Supreme Court considered a case in which the Florida inmate Clarence E. Hill challenged the state's form of lethal injection as unnecessarily painful and thus a violation of his Eighth Amendment rights. Hill was convicted in 1983 for the capital murder of Officer Stephen Taylor and sentenced to death. After exhausting his state appeals, he filed for a federal writ of habeas corpus, which was denied. As Hill's execution loomed in January 2006, his lawyers filed a new challenge, this time against the lethal injection procedure itself. A trial court dismissed the claim, because Hill had already exhausted his federal habeas corpus appeals. Federal law prohibits multiple appeals of this type. The ruling was upheld by the Florida Supreme Court.

In *Hill v. McDonough* (No. 05-8794 [2006]), the U.S. Supreme Court issued a unanimous 9–0 opinion that Hill's challenge of the form of execution did not constitute a second habeas corpus appeal, but was a new action of a different type. The decision came only minutes before Hill was to be executed. He was already strapped to a gurney and hooked up to intravenous lines. However, the reprieve proved to be temporary. Florida courts refused to hear Hill's challenge, arguing that it was presented too late. His execution date was reset, and the Supreme Court denied a second appeal. In September 2006 Hill was executed by lethal injection.

In September 2007 the U.S. Supreme Court agreed to hear another case pertaining to lethal injection. Two Kentucky death row inmates—Ralph Baze and Thomas Bowling—petitioned the court after lower courts rejected their challenges to the three-drug protocol used for lethal injection in Kentucky. Neither of the men, who had been convicted in separate double murders, had execution dates set at that time. Because the lethal injection protocol in question was widely used by other death penalty states, the court's agreement to hear the case triggered a national moratorium (suspension) on pending executions. In April 2008 the court issued its opinion in *Baze v. Rees* (553 U.S. ___). The court ruled 7–2 that Kentucky's three-drug protocol for lethal injection did not violate the Eighth Amendment's ban on cruel and unusual punishment.

The protocol included the administration of sodium thiopental (to render the prisoner unconscious) followed by pancuronium bromide (a paralyzing agent) and potassium chloride, which causes cardiac arrest resulting in death. Even though the court acknowledged that improper administration of the drugs (particularly the sodium thiopental) could result in a painful death, it rejected the petitioners' claim that there was a "significant risk" that the protocol would not be properly followed. The court also refused to consider the petitioners' claim that an alternative single-drug protocol for lethal injection offered far less risk of pain. It noted that pursuing such claims in numerous death row cases "would embroil the courts in ongoing scientific controversies beyond their expertise, and would substantially intrude on the role of state legislatures in implementing execution procedures." However, the court warned that states that refused to adopt suitable alternative protocols in the future might violate the Eighth Amendment. The court

noted that an alternative protocol would be considered suitable if it was "feasible, readily implemented, and in fact significantly reduced a substantial risk of severe pain." As of October 2013, Baze and Bowling remained on death row in Kentucky.

The U.S. Supreme Court's decision in *Baze* spurred states to reexamine their lethal injection protocols. Problems related to the protocols and to acquiring the needed drugs are described in Chapter 5.

DOES EXTENDED STAY ON DEATH ROW CONSTITUTE A CRUEL AND UNUSUAL PUNISHMENT?

In 2002 Charles Kenneth Foster, a Florida inmate, asked the U.S. Supreme Court to consider whether his long wait for execution constitutes a cruel and unusual punishment prohibited by the Eighth Amendment. Foster had been on death row since 1975 for the murder of Julian Lanier, who was beaten and stabbed to death. In 1981 and 1984 the defendant was granted stays of execution to allow his federal habeas corpus petition to be filed.

Justice Stephen G. Breyer (1938–) dissented from the court's refusal to hear the case (*Foster v. Florida*, No. 01-10868 [2002]). Justice Breyer pointed out that the defendant's long wait on death row resulted partly from Florida's repeated errors in proceedings. The justice added, "Death row's inevitable anxieties and uncertainties have been sharpened by the issuance of two death warrants and three judicial reprieves. If executed, Foster, now 55, will have been punished both by death and also by more than a generation spent in death row's twilight. It is fairly asked whether such punishment is both unusual and cruel."

Concurring with the court opinion not to hear Foster's case, Justice Clarence Thomas (1948–) observed that the defendant could have ended the "anxieties and uncertainties" of death row had he submitted to execution, which the people of Florida believe he deserves. As of October 2013, Foster remained on death row in Florida.

In *Thompson v. McNeil* (No. 08-7369 [2009]) the Supreme Court refused to hear a similar case involving a Florida man who had been on death row for 32 years. William Thompson was sentenced to death for the kidnapping, torture, and murder of Sally Ivester in 1976. Justices Breyer and Stevens expressed their displeasure with the court's decision. Breyer noted that the state of Florida "was in significant part responsible" for Thompson's long stay on death row due to judicial errors during his sentencing trial. Stevens described "the especially severe conditions of confinement" in which Thompson had been held on death row and remarked on the psychological toll that an impending execution takes when a prisoner experiences a long wait for the execution to be administered. He concluded, "Executing defendants after such long delays is unacceptably cruel." However, Justice Thomas noted that Thompson had taken advantage of the many appeals processes allowed under the law and was now complaining about a delayed execution. Thomas recounted the gruesome details of Thompson's crime and the brutal manner in which Ivester was tortured to death.

He notes, "Three juries recommended that petitioner receive the death penalty for this heinous murder, and petitioner has received judicial review of his sentence on at least 17 occasions." He concluded, "It is the crime—and not the punishment imposed by the jury or the delay in petitioner's execution—that was 'unacceptably cruel.'" As of October 2013, Thompson was still on death row in Florida.

CHAPTER 4
SUPREME COURT RULINGS III: MITIGATING CIRCUMSTANCES, YOUTH, INSANITY, MENTAL RETARDATION, THE ADMISSIBILITY OF VICTIM IMPACT STATEMENTS, AND THE INFLUENCE OF RACE IN CAPITAL CASES

MITIGATING CIRCUMSTANCES

Mitigating circumstances may lessen the responsibility for a crime, whereas aggravating circumstances may add to the responsibility for a crime. In 1978 an Ohio case highlighted the issue of mitigating circumstances before the U.S. Supreme Court after Sandra Lockett was convicted of capital murder for her role in a pawnshop robbery that resulted in the shooting death of the storeowner, Sydney Cohen. Lockett helped plan the robbery, drove the getaway car, and hid her accomplices in her home, but she was not present in the store at the time the storeowner was shot. According to the Ohio death penalty statute, capital punishment had to be imposed on Lockett unless "(1) the victim induced or facilitated the offense; (2) it is unlikely that the offense would have been committed but for the fact that the offender was under duress, coercion, or strong provocation; or (3) the offense was primarily the product of the offender's psychosis or mental deficiency." Lockett was found guilty and sentenced to die.

Lockett appealed, claiming that the Ohio law did not give the sentencing judge the chance to consider the circumstances of the crime, the defendant's criminal record, and the defendant's character as mitigating factors, lessening her responsibility for the crime. In July 1978 the Supreme Court, in *Lockett v. Ohio* (438 U.S. 586), upheld Lockett's contention. Chief Justice Warren Burger (1907–1995) observed, "A statute that prevents the sentencer in capital cases from giving independent mitigating weight to aspects of the defendant's character and record and to the circumstances of the offense proffered in mitigation creates the risk that the death penalty will be imposed in spite of factors that may call for a less severe penalty, and when the choice is between life and death, such risk is unacceptable and incompatible with the commands of the Eighth and Fourteenth Amendments."

Lockett's death sentence was overturned and she was given a lesser sentence. In 1993 Lockett was released from prison.

Mitigating Circumstances Must Always Be Considered

In *Hitchcock v. Dugger* (481 U.S. 393 [1987]), a unanimous Supreme Court further emphasized that all mitigating circumstances had to be considered before the convicted murderer could be sentenced. A Florida judge had instructed the jury not to consider evidence of mitigating factors that were not specifically indicated in the Florida death penalty law. Writing for the court, Justice Antonin Scalia (1936–) stressed that a convicted person had the right "to present any and all relevant mitigating evidence that is available."

ENDING CAPITAL PUNISHMENT FOR MINORS

As described in Chapter 1, during the modern death penalty era in the United States (from 1973 onward) 22 individuals were executed for murders they committed when they were minors. All were 17 years of age at the times of their crimes except one was aged 16 years. The U.S. Supreme Court heard several cases during the late 20th and early 21st centuries involving juvenile defendants who had been sentenced to death.

Not at 15 Years Old

In January 1983, together with three adults, William Thompson brutally murdered his former brother-in-law, Charles Keene, in Oklahoma. Thompson was 15 at the time of the murder, but the state determined that Thompson, who had a long history of violent assault, had "virtually no reasonable prospects for rehabilitation . . . within the juvenile system and . . . should be held accountable for his acts as if he were an adult and should be certified to stand trial as an adult." Thompson was tried as an adult and found guilty. Thompson's age was considered a mitigating circumstance, but the jury still sentenced him to death.

Thompson appealed, and even though the Court of Criminal Appeals of Oklahoma upheld the decision, the U.S. Supreme Court did not in *Thompson v. Oklahoma* (487 U.S. 815 [1988]). In a 5–3 majority vote, with Justice Sandra Day O'Connor (1930–) agreeing to vacate (annul) the sentence but not agreeing with the majority reasoning, the case was reversed. (Justice Anthony M. Kennedy [1936–] took no part in the decision.)

Writing for the majority, Justice John Paul Stevens (1920–) observed that "inexperience, less education, and less intelligence make the teenager less able to evaluate the consequences of his or her conduct while at the same time he or she is much more apt to be motivated by mere emotion or peer pressure than is an adult. The reasons why juveniles are not trusted with the privileges and responsibilities of an adult also explain why their irresponsible conduct is not as morally reprehensible as that of an adult."

Justice Stevens noted that 18 states required the age of at least 16 years before the death penalty could be considered. Counting the 14 states prohibiting capital punishment, a total of 32 states did not execute people under the age of 16 years.

Justice O'Connor agreed with the judgment of the court that the appellate court's ruling should be reversed. O'Connor pointed out, however, that even though most 15-year-old criminals are generally less blameworthy than adults who commit the same crimes, some may fully understand the horrible deeds they have done. Individuals, after all, have different characteristics, including their capability to distinguish right from wrong.

Writing for the minority, Justice Scalia found no national consensus forbidding the execution of a person who was 16 years old at the commission of the murder. The justice could not understand the majority's calculations establishing a "contemporary standard" that forbade the execution of young minors. He reasoned that abolitionist states (states with no death penalty) should not be considered in the issue of executing minors because they did not have executions in the first place. Rather, the 18 states that prohibited the execution of offenders who were younger than 16 when they murdered should be compared with the 19 states that applied the death penalty to young offenders.

For a Number of Years Minors Could Be Sentenced to Death at Age 16 or 17

The Supreme Court, in two jointly considered cases, *Stanford v. Kentucky* and *Wilkins v. Missouri* (492 U.S. 361 [1989]), ruled that inmates who committed their crimes at ages 16 or 17 could be executed for murder.

In January 1981, 17-year-old Kevin Stanford and an accomplice raped Barbel Poore, an attendant at a Kentucky gas station they were robbing. They then took the woman to a secluded area near the station, where Stanford shot her in the face and in the back of the head. Stressing the seriousness of the offense and Stanford's long history of criminal behavior, the court certified him as an adult. He was tried, found guilty, and sentenced to death.

In July 1985, 16-year-old Heath Wilkins stabbed Nancy Allen to death while he was robbing the convenience store where she worked. Wilkins indicated he murdered Allen because "a dead person can't talk." Based on his long history of juvenile delinquency, a Missouri court ordered Wilkins to be tried as an adult. He was found guilty and sentenced to death.

Writing for the majority, Justice Scalia could find no national consensus that executing minors aged 16 and 17 years constituted a cruel and unusual punishment. Scalia observed that of the 37 states whose statutes allowed the death penalty, just 15 states refused to impose it on 16-year-old offenders and only 12 states refused to impose it on 17-year-old offenders. Thus, overall, 22 out of 37 states allowed the death penalty for 16-year-old offenders, and 25 out of 37 states allowed the death penalty for 17-year-old offenders.

Furthermore, Justice Scalia saw no connection between the defendant's argument that those under the age of 18 years were denied the right to drive, drink, or vote because they were not considered mature enough to do so responsibly and whether this standard of maturity should be applied to a minor's understanding that murder is terribly wrong. Scalia added, "Even if the requisite degrees of maturity were comparable, the age statutes in question would still not be relevant.... These laws set the appropriate ages for the operation of a system that makes its determinations in gross, and that does not conduct individualized maturity tests for each driver, drinker, or voter.... In the realm of capital punishment in particular, 'individualized consideration [is] a constitutional requirement,'... and one of the individualized mitigating factors that sentencers must be permitted to consider is the defendant's age."

Writing for the minority, Justice William J. Brennan (1906–1997) found a national consensus among 30 states when he added the 15 states forbidding the execution of a person who was 16 years old during the commission of the crime to those with no capital punishment, and the states that, in practice if not in law, did not execute minors. Justice Brennan, taking serious exception to the majority's observation that they had to find a national consensus in the laws passed by the state legislatures, stated, "Our judgment about the constitutionality of a punishment under the Eighth Amendment is informed, though not determined ... by an examination of contemporary attitudes toward the punishment, as evidenced in the actions of legislatures and of juries. The views of organizations with expertise in relevant fields and the choices of governments elsewhere in the world also merit our attention as indicators whether a punishment is acceptable in a civilized society."

In 1996 Wilkins was retried in Missouri and sentenced to three life terms. Stanford remained on Kentucky's death row until 2003, when his sentence was commuted to life without parole by Governor Paul E. Patton (1937–).

The Supreme Court Reverses Its Decision Regarding Minors

Until 2005 the nation's highest court held fast on its decision to allow for the execution of minors aged 16 or 17 who committed capital crimes. The Supreme Court even rejected another appeal by Stanford in 2002. In *Roper v. Simmons* (543 U.S. 551 [2005]), however, the court reversed its earlier opinion when it ruled that executing Christopher Simmons was cruel and unusual based on the fact that Simmons was a minor when he committed murder.

In 1993, 17-year-old Simmons and two friends, John Tessmer (aged 16 years) and Charles Benjamin (aged 15 years), planned the elaborate burglary and murder of Shirley Cook, who lived in Fenton, Missouri. The three teenagers wanted to experience the thrill of the crime, reasoning that they would not be held accountable because they were under the age of 18 years. On the night of the murder, Benjamin and Simmons broke into Cook's house. (Tessmer backed out.) When Cook identified who the boys were, they covered her eyes and mouth with duct tape and bound her hands. The teenagers drove Cook to a state park, wrapped more duct tape over her entire face, tied her hands and feet with electrical wire, and threw her off a railroad trestle into a river.

The next day Simmons began bragging about the murder at school and was picked up by the police along with the two other teenagers. Benjamin was convicted and sentenced to life in prison. Simmons confessed on videotape and was tried and sentenced to death. He made a number of unsuccessful appeals and pleas for habeas corpus (a petition to be heard in federal court). Just weeks before he was scheduled to die, the Missouri Supreme Court called off the execution and reopened the debate in light of the U.S. Supreme Court's *Atkins* decision. (In *Atkins v. Virginia* [536 U.S. 304 (2002)], the court ruled that executing mentally retarded criminals was a violation of the Eighth Amendment because the mentally retarded do not have as strong a sense of lasting consequences or of right and wrong as normal adults.) The state court overturned Simmons's death sentence 6–3,

stating that a national consensus had developed against executing minors since *Stanford* and *Wilkins* were decided. Simmons was resentenced to life in prison without parole, and remained incarcerated in October 2013.

The U.S. Supreme Court upheld the Missouri court's decision in a 5–4 vote, reversing *Stanford*. The majority reasoned that adolescents do not have the emotional maturity and understanding of lasting consequences that adults have. As such, they cannot be held to as high of a standard and should not be sentenced to death. The majority also agreed with the Missouri court in that a national and international consensus had changed over the past 15 years. The court noted, "To implement this framework we have established the propriety and affirmed the necessity of referring to 'the evolving standards of decency that mark the progress of a maturing society.'"

Justices O'Connor, Scalia, Rehnquist, and Clarence Thomas (1948–) dissented, claiming that the guidelines for executing minors should not be inflexible and that a great many U.S. citizens still favor the death penalty for teenagers who commit especially heinous crimes. Scalia stated that the majority was bowing to international pressures. In his dissent, he wrote, "Though the views of our own citizens are essentially irrelevant to the Court's decision today, the views of other countries and the so-called international community take center stage."

Youth: A Mitigating Circumstance Even for Those over the Age of 18 Years

On March 23, 1986, Dorsie Lee Johnson Jr. and an accomplice staked out a convenience store in Snyder, Texas, with the intention of robbing it. They learned that only one employee worked during the predawn hours. Agreeing to leave no witnesses to the crime, the 19-year-old Johnson shot and killed the clerk, Jack Huddleston. They then emptied the cash register and stole some cigarettes.

The following month Johnson was arrested and subsequently confessed to the robbery and murder. During jury selection the defense attorneys asked potential jurors whether they believed that people were capable of change and whether they, the potential jurors, had ever done things in their youth that they would not now do.

The only witness the defense called was Johnson's father, who told of his son's drug use, grief over the death of his mother two years before the crime, and the murder of his sister the following year. He spoke of his son's youth and the fact that, at age 19, he did not evaluate things the way a person of 30 or 35 would.

Johnson was tried and convicted of capital murder. Under Texas law the homicide qualified as a capital offense because Johnson intentionally or knowingly caused Huddleston's death. Moreover, the murder was carried out in the course of committing a robbery.

In the sentencing phase of the trial, the judge instructed the jury to answer two questions: (1) whether Johnson's actions were deliberate and intended to kill, and (2) whether there was a possibility that he would continue to commit violent crimes and be a threat to society. If the jury answered "yes" to both questions, Johnson would be sentenced to death. If the jury returned a "no" answer to either question, the defendant would be sentenced to life in prison. The jury was not to consider or discuss the possibility of parole.

Of equal importance was the instruction that the jury could consider all the evidence, both aggravating and mitigating, in either phase of the trial. The jury unanimously answered yes to both questions, and Johnson was sentenced to death.

Five days after the state appellate court denied Johnson's motions for a rehearing, the U.S. Supreme Court issued its opinion in *Penry v. Lynaugh* (492 U.S. 302 [1989]), in which it held that the jury should have been instructed that it could consider mental retardation as a mitigating factor during the penalty phase. Based on the *Penry* ruling, Johnson appealed once more, claiming that a separate instruction should have been given to the jurors that would have allowed them to consider his youth. Again, the appellate court rejected his petition.

Affirming the Texas appellate court decision, Justice Kennedy delivered the opinion of the Supreme Court in *Johnson v. Texas* (509 U.S. 350 [1993]). He was joined by Justices Rehnquist, White, Scalia, and Thomas. Kennedy noted that the Texas special-issues system (two questions asked of the jury and instruction to consider all evidence) allowed for adequate consideration of Johnson's youth. Justice Kennedy stated:

> Even on a cold record, one cannot be unmoved by the testimony of petitioner's father urging that his son's actions were due in large part to his youth. It strains credulity to suppose that the jury would have viewed the evidence of petitioner's youth as outside its effective reach in answering the second special issue. The relevance of youth as a mitigating factor derives from the fact that the signature qualities of youth are transient; as individuals mature, the impetuousness and recklessness that may dominate in younger years can subside.... As long as the mitigating evidence is within "the effective reach of the sentencer," the requirements of the Eighth Amendment are satisfied.

Justice O'Connor, in a dissenting opinion joined by Justices Blackmun, Stevens, and David H. Souter (1939–), stated that the jurors were not allowed to give full effect to his strongest mitigating circumstance: his youth. Hearing of his less than exemplary youth, a jury might

easily conclude, as Johnson's did, that he would continue to be a threat to society.

In 1997 Johnson was executed by lethal injection in the state of Texas.

INSANITY AND EXECUTION
Can an Insane Person Be Executed?

In 1974 Alvin Bernard Ford was convicted of murdering police officer Walter Illyankoff during a restaurant robbery and sentenced to death in Florida. There was no question that he was completely sane at the time of his crime, at his trial, and at his sentencing. Eight years later Ford began to show signs of delusion—from thinking that people were conspiring to force him to commit suicide to believing that family members were being held hostage in prison.

Ford's lawyers had a psychiatrist examine their client. After 14 months of evaluation and investigation, the doctor concluded that Ford suffered from a severe mental disorder that would preclude him from assisting in the defense of his life. A second psychiatrist concluded that Ford did not understand why he was on death row.

Florida law required the governor to appoint a panel of three psychiatrists to determine whether Ford was mentally capable of understanding the death penalty and the reasons he was being sentenced to death. The three state-appointed doctors met with Ford once for about 30 minutes and then filed separate reports. Ford's lawyers were present but were ordered by the judge not to participate in the examination in "any adversarial manner."

The three psychiatrists submitted different diagnoses, but all agreed that Ford was sane enough to be executed. Ford's lawyers attempted to submit to the governor the reports of the first two psychiatrists along with other materials. However, the governor refused to inform the lawyers whether he would consider these reports. He eventually signed Ford's death warrant.

Ford's appeals were denied in state and federal courts, but a 7–2 Supreme Court, in *Ford v. Wainwright* (477 U.S. 399 [1986]), reversed the earlier judgments. In light of the fact that there had been no precedent formed for such a case in U.S. history, the justices turned to English law. Writing for the majority, Justice Thurgood Marshall (1908–1993) observed that even though the reasons appear unclear, English common law forbade the execution of the insane. The English jurist William Blackstone (1723–1780) had labeled such a practice "savage and inhuman." Likewise, the other noted English judicial resource, Sir Edward Coke (1552–1634), observed that even though the execution of a criminal was to serve as an example, the execution of a madman was considered "of extream inhumanity and cruelty, and can be no example to others." Consequently, because the

Eighth Amendment forbidding a cruel and unusual punishment was prepared by men who accepted English common law, there could be no question that the Eighth Amendment prohibited the execution of the insane.

The issue then became the method the state used to determine Ford's insanity. The high court noted that Florida did not allow the submission of materials that might be relevant to the decision whether or not to execute the condemned man. In addition, Ford's lawyers were not given the chance to question the state-appointed psychiatrists about the basis for finding their client competent. Questions the defense could have asked included the possibility of personal bias on the doctors' part toward the death penalty, any history of error in their judgment, and their degree of certainty in reaching their conclusions. Finally, the justices pointed out that the greatest defect in Florida's practice is its entrusting the ultimate decision about the execution entirely to the executive branch. The high court observed, "Under this procedure, the person who appoints the experts and ultimately decides whether the State will be able to carry out the sentence that it has long sought is the Governor, whose subordinates have been responsible for initiating every stage of the prosecution of the condemned from arrest through sentencing. The commander of the State's corps of prosecutors cannot be said to have the neutrality that is necessary for reliability in the factfinding proceeding."

The high court further observed that even though a prisoner has been sentenced to death, he is still protected by the Constitution. Therefore, ascertaining his sanity as a basis for a legal execution is as important as other proceedings in a capital case.

In dissent, Justice Rehnquist, joined by Chief Justice Burger, thought the Florida procedure was consistent with English common law, which had left the decision to the executive branch. Rehnquist warned, "A claim of insanity may be made at any time before sentence and, once rejected, may be raised again; a prisoner found sane two days before execution might claim to have lost his sanity the next day, thus necessitating another judicial determination of his sanity and presumably another stay of his execution."

Ford remained on Florida's death row until 1991, when he died of natural causes.

Can an Insane Person Stabilized by Drugs Be Executed?

In 1979 Charles Singleton stabbed Mary Lou York twice in the neck after robbing her grocery store in Hamburg, Arkansas. He was tried, convicted, and sentenced to death. He was sane during the murder and throughout the trial.

However, Singleton developed schizophrenia while in prison. At one point during his incarceration, Singleton claimed his prison cell was possessed by demons. When given antipsychotic medication, however, Singleton regained his sanity. Fearing a psychotic outburst from Singleton, the prison forced medication on him when he refused to take it. Singleton filed several habeas corpus petitions in state and federal courts, claiming that in light of *Ford*, he was not competent enough to be executed. He also argued that the forcible administration of antipsychotic medication was a violation of the Eighth Amendment, which forbids a cruel and unusual punishment.

The case was taken up by the U.S. Court of Appeals for the Eighth Circuit. In *Singleton v. Norris* (319 F.3d 1018 [8th Cir., 2003]), the appellate court upheld the death penalty for Singleton in a 5–4 decision. The majority felt that as long as Singleton was on medication and in full control of his faculties, his execution was not a violation of the Eighth Amendment. Singleton appealed to the U.S. Supreme Court, but the high court turned the case down, effectively endorsing the decision of the appellate court. Singleton was executed by the state of Arkansas in 2004.

CAN A MENTALLY RETARDED PERSON BE EXECUTED?
Penry I

In 1979 Pamela Carpenter was brutally raped, beaten, and stabbed with a pair of scissors in Livingston, Texas. Before she died, she was able to describe her attacker, and as a result, Johnny Paul Penry was arrested for, and later confessed to, the crime. At the time of the crime, Penry was out on parole for another rape. He was found guilty for the murder of Carpenter and sentenced to death.

Among the issues considered in his appeal was whether the state of Texas could execute a mentally retarded person. At Penry's competency hearing a psychiatrist testified that the defendant had an intelligence quotient (IQ) of 54. Penry had been tested in the past as having an IQ between 50 and 63, indicating mild to moderate retardation. (It is generally accepted that an IQ below 70 is evidence of mental retardation. Normal IQ is considered 90 and above.) According to the psychiatrist, during the commission of the crime the 22-year-old Penry had the mental age of a child six-and-a-half years old and the social maturity of someone who was nine to 10 years old. Penry's attorneys argued, "Because of their mental disabilities, mentally retarded people do not possess the level of moral culpability to justify imposing the death sentence.... There is an emerging national consensus against executing the mentally retarded."

Writing for the majority regarding the execution of mentally retarded people, Justice O'Connor, in *Penry v. Lynaugh* (492 U.S. 302 [1989]), found no emerging national consensus against such executions. Furthermore, even though profoundly retarded people had not been executed for murder historically, Penry did not fall into this group.

Justice O'Connor noted that Penry was found competent to stand trial. He was able to consult rationally with his lawyer and understood the proceedings against him. She thought that the defense was guilty of lumping all mentally retarded people together, ascribing, among other things, a lack of moral capacity to be culpable for actions that call for the death punishment. O'Connor wrote:

> Mentally retarded persons are individuals whose abilities and experiences can vary greatly. [If the mentally retarded were not treated as individuals, but as an undifferentiated group,] a mildly mentally retarded person could be denied the opportunity to enter into contracts or to marry by virtue of the fact that he had a "mental age" of a young child.... In light of the diverse capacities and life experiences of mentally retarded persons, it cannot be said on the record before us today that all mentally retarded people, by definition, can never act with the level of culpability associated with the death penalty.

Furthermore, the majority could find no national movement toward any type of consensus on this issue. Even though *Penry* produced several public opinion polls that indicated strong public opposition to executing the retarded, almost none of this public opinion was reflected in death penalty legislation. Only the federal Anti-Drug Abuse Act of 1988 and the states of Georgia and Maryland at the time banned the execution of retarded people found guilty of a capital crime.

Justice Brennan disagreed. Even though he agreed that lumping mentally retarded people together might result in stereotyping and discrimination, he believed there are characteristics that fall under the clinical definition of mental retardation. Citing the amicus curiae brief prepared by the American Association on Mental Retardation, he noted, "'Every individual who has mental retardation'—irrespective of his or her precise capacities or experiences—has 'a substantial disability in cognitive ability and adaptive behavior.'... Though individuals, particularly those who are mildly retarded, may be quite capable of overcoming these limitations to the extent of being able to 'maintain themselves independently or semi-independently in the community,' nevertheless, the mentally retarded by definition 'have a reduced ability to cope with and function in the everyday world.'"

Justice Brennan did not believe that executing a person not fully responsible for his or her actions would serve the "penal goals of deterrence or retribution." What is the point of executing someone who did not fully recognize the terrible evil that he or she had done? Furthermore, he argued, executing a mentally retarded person would not deter non-retarded people, those who would be aware of the possibility of an execution.

Even though the Supreme Court held that executing people with mental retardation was not a violation of the Eighth Amendment, it ruled that Penry's Eighth Amendment right was violated because the jury was not instructed that it could consider mental retardation as a mitigating factor during sentencing. The case was sent back to the lower court. In 1990 Texas retried Penry, and he was again found guilty of capital murder. During the sentencing phase the prosecution used a specific portion of a psychiatric report to point out the doctor's opinion that, if released from custody, Penry would be a threat to society. Penry appealed his case all the way to the Supreme Court. Ten years later, in November 2000, with Penry less than three hours from being put to death, the Supreme Court granted a stay of execution to hear Penry's claims.

Penry II

Penry once again appealed to the Supreme Court after his case was retried. In his appeal to the Supreme Court, Penry argued that the use of a portion of an old psychiatric report at his 1990 retrial violated his Fifth Amendment right against self-incrimination. In 1977 Penry was arrested in connection with another rape. During this rape case the state of Texas provided Penry with a psychiatrist at the request of his lawyer. The psychiatrist was to determine the defendant's competency to stand trial. In 2000 Penry argued that the psychiatrist was an "agent of the State" and that the prosecution's use of his report in the 1990 retrial for murder violated Penry's right against self-incrimination. Penry also claimed jury instructions were inadequate.

On June 4, 2001, the Supreme Court ruled 6–3 in *Penry v. Johnson* (532 U.S. 782) that the admission of the psychiatrist's report did not violate Penry's Fifth Amendment right. The court held that this case was different from *Estelle v. Smith*, in which the justices found that the psychiatrist's testimony about the defendant's future dangerousness based on the defendant's statements without his lawyer present violated his Fifth Amendment right. The justices emphasized that *Estelle* was restricted to that particular case.

The justices, however, sent the case back to the trial court for resentencing because, as in the original *Penry* case, the state did not give the sentencing jury adequate instructions about how to weigh mental retardation as a mitigating factor.

The Court Revisits Mental Retardation

Daryl Renard Atkins was convicted and sentenced to death for the 1996 abduction, armed robbery, and capital murder of Eric Michael Nesbitt. On appeal to the Virginia Supreme Court, Atkins argued that he could not be executed because he was mentally retarded. Relying on *Penry v. Lynaugh*, the court affirmed the conviction. The court ordered a sentencing retrial because the trial court had used the wrong verdict form. As with the first penalty trial, a psychologist testified that Atkins was "mildly mentally retarded," having an IQ of 59. The jury sentenced Atkins to death for a second time. Atkins again appealed to the Virginia Supreme Court, which upheld the trial court ruling.

The U.S. Supreme Court unanimously agreed to hear Atkins's case. Thirteen years after ruling that executing the mentally retarded does not violate the Constitution, the Supreme Court, in a 6–3 decision, reversed its 1989 *Penry* decision. On June 20, 2002, in *Atkins v. Virginia* (536 U.S. 304), most of the court held that "executions of mentally retarded criminals are 'cruel and unusual punishments' prohibited by the Eighth Amendment."

Justice Stevens delivered the opinion of the court. Justices O'Connor, Kennedy, Souter, Ruth Bader Ginsburg (1933–), and Stephen G. Breyer (1938–) joined the opinion. According to the court, since *Penry*, many states had concluded that death is not a suitable punishment for mentally retarded offenders, reflecting society's sentiments that these individuals are less culpable than average offenders. The court observed, "Mentally retarded persons... have diminished capacities to understand and process information, to communicate, to abstract from mistakes and learn from experience, to engage in logical reasoning, to control impulses, and to understand the reactions of others.... Their deficiencies do not warrant an exemption from criminal sanctions, but they do diminish their personal culpability."

The justices also noted that even though the theory is that capital punishment would serve as deterrence to those contemplating murder, this theory does not apply to the mentally retarded because their diminished mental capacities prevent them from appreciating the possibility of execution as punishment. Moreover, the lesser culpability of mentally retarded criminals does not warrant the severe punishment of death.

Justice Scalia disagreed with the ruling that a person who is slightly mentally retarded does not possess the culpability to be sentenced to death. He claimed that the ruling finds "no support in the text or history of the Eighth Amendment." The justice also noted that current social attitudes do not support the majority decision. He pointed out that the state laws that the majority claimed reflect society's attitudes against executing the mentally

retarded are still in their infancy and have not undergone the test of time.

On the relationship between a criminal's culpability and the deserved punishment, Justice Scalia stated:

> Surely culpability, and deservedness of the most severe retribution, depends not merely (if at all) upon the mental capacity of the criminal (above the level where he is able to distinguish right from wrong) but also upon the depravity of the crime—which is precisely why this sort of question has traditionally been thought answerable not by a categorical rule of the sort the Court today imposes upon all trials, but rather by the sentencer's weighing of the circumstances (both degree of retardation and depravity of crime) in the particular case. The fact that juries continue to sentence mentally retarded offenders to death for extreme crimes shows that society's moral outrage sometimes demands execution of retarded offenders. By what principle of law, science, or logic can the Court pronounce that this is wrong? There is none. Once the Court admits (as it does) that mental retardation does not render the offender morally blameless... there is no basis for saying that the death penalty is never appropriate retribution, no matter how heinous the crime.

Atkins was resentenced by the State of Virginia to several life terms in prison, where he remained as of October 2013.

Penry's Sentence Revisited

On July 3, 2002, about two weeks after the Supreme Court ruled that it is unconstitutional to execute a mentally retarded person, a Texas jury concluded that Penry was not mentally retarded. He was resentenced to death. Three years later the Texas Court of Criminal Appeals ruled that the jury had not fully considered Penry's claim of mental retardation and ordered a new sentencing hearing. The Texas attorney general appealed the decision. In 2008 Penry's sentence was converted to three life terms in prison without the chance of parole. As part of a plea deal agreement, Penry had to apologize to the victim's family and concede that he was not mentally retarded. Penry remained in prison as of October 2013.

COMPETENCY STANDARD

In Las Vegas, Nevada, on August 2, 1984, Richard Allen Moran fatally shot Sandra Devere and Russell Rhodes four times each in a Las Vegas barroom. Several days later he went to the home of his former wife, Linda Vandervoort, and fatally shot her, then turned the gun on himself. However, his suicide attempt failed, and Moran confessed to his crimes. Later, he pleaded not guilty to three counts of first-degree murder. Two psychiatrists examined Moran and concluded that he was competent to stand trial. Approximately 10 weeks after the evaluations, Moran decided to dismiss his attorneys and change his plea to guilty. After review of the psychiatric reports, the trial court accepted the waiver for counsel and the guilty plea. Moran was later sentenced to death.

Seven months later Moran appealed his case, claiming that he had been "mentally incompetent to represent himself." The appellate court reversed the conviction, ruling that "competency to waive constitutional rights requires a higher level of mental functioning than that required to stand trial." A defendant is considered competent to stand trial if he can understand the proceedings and help in his defense. Yet, for a defendant to be considered competent to waive counsel or to plead guilty, he has to be capable of "'reasoned choice' among the alternatives available to him." The appellate court found Moran mentally incapable of the reasoned choice needed to be in a position to waive his constitutional rights.

The Supreme Court ruled 7–2 in *Godinez v. Moran* (509 U.S. 389 [1993]) to reverse the judgment of the court of appeals, holding that the standard for measuring a criminal defendant's competency to plead guilty or to waive his right to counsel is not higher than the standard for standing trial. The high court then sent the case back to the lower courts for further proceedings. Moran was executed in March 1996.

VICTIM IMPACT STATEMENTS
First, They Are Not Constitutional

In 1983 John Booth and Willie Reid stole money from Booth's elderly neighbors, Irvin and Rose Bronstein, to buy heroin. Booth, knowing his neighbors could identify him, tied up the elderly couple and then repeatedly stabbed them in the chest with a kitchen knife. The couple's son found their bodies two days later. Booth and Reid were found guilty.

The state of Maryland required a victim impact statement and permitted it to be read to the jury during the sentencing phase of the trial. The victim impact statement prepared in this case explained the tremendous pain caused by the murder of the parents and grandparents to the family. A 5–4 Supreme Court, in *Booth v. Maryland* (482 U.S. 496 [1987]), while recognizing the agony caused to the victims' family, ruled that victim impact statements, as required by Maryland's statute, were unconstitutional and could not be used during the sentencing phase of a capital murder trial.

Writing for the majority, Justice Lewis F. Powell Jr. (1907–1998) indicated that a jury must determine whether the defendant should be executed, based on the circumstances of the crime and the character of the offender. These factors had nothing to do with the victim. The high court noted that it is the crime and the criminal that are at issue. Had Booth and Reid viciously murdered a homeless man, the crime would have been just as horrible. Furthermore, some families could express the pain and disruption they suffered as a result of the murder better than other families, and a sentencing should not depend on how well a family could express its grief.

Reid's sentence was later converted to two life terms. As of October 2013, Booth, who has since unofficially changed his last name to Booth-el, remained on Maryland's death row.

... And Then They Are

Pervis Tyrone Payne of Tennessee spent the morning and early afternoon of June 27, 1987, injecting cocaine and drinking beer. Later, he drove around the town with a friend, each of them taking turns looking at a pornographic magazine. In mid-afternoon, Payne went to the apartment of his girlfriend, who was away visiting her mother in Arkansas. Charisse Christopher lived across the hall from the apartment. Payne entered Christopher's apartment and made sexual advances toward Christopher, who resisted. Payne became violent.

When the police arrived, they found Christopher on the floor with 42 direct knife wounds and 42 defensive wounds on her arms and hands. Her two-year-old daughter had suffered stab wounds to the chest, abdomen, back, and head. The murder weapon, a butcher knife, was found at her feet. Christopher's three-year-old son, despite several stab wounds that went completely through his body, was still alive. Payne was arrested, and a Tennessee jury convicted him of the first-degree murders of Christopher and her daughter and of the first-degree assault, with intent to murder, of Christopher's son, Nicholas.

During the sentencing phase of the trial, Payne called his parents, his girlfriend, and a clinical psychologist to testify about the mitigating aspects of his background and character. The prosecutor, however, called Nicholas's grandmother, who testified how much the child missed his mother and baby sister. In arguing for the death penalty, the prosecutor commented on the continuing effects the crime was having on Nicholas and his family. The jury sentenced Payne to death on each of the murder counts. The state supreme court agreed, rejecting Payne's claim that the admission of the grandmother's testimony and the state's closing argument violated his Eighth Amendment rights under *Booth v. Maryland*.

On hearing the appeal, the U.S. Supreme Court ruled 6–3 in *Payne v. Tennessee* (501 U.S. 808 [1991]) to uphold the death penalty and overturned *Booth v. Maryland*. In *Payne*, the court ruled that the Eighth Amendment does not prohibit a jury from considering, at the sentencing phase of a capital trial, victim impact evidence relating to a victim's personal characteristics and the emotional impact of the murder on the victim's family. The Eighth Amendment also does not bar a prosecutor from arguing such evidence at the sentencing phase.

The court reasoned that the assessment of harm caused by a defendant as a result of a crime has long been an important concern of criminal law in determining both the elements of the offense and the appropriate punishment. Victim impact evidence is simply another form or method of informing the sentencing jury or judge about the specific harm caused by the crime in question.

The *Booth* case unfairly weighted the scales in a capital trial. No limits were placed on the mitigating evidence the defendant introduced relating to his own circumstances. The state, however, was potentially barred from offering a glimpse of the life of the victim or from showing the loss to the victim's family or to society. *Booth* was decided by narrow margins, the court continued, and had been questioned by members of the Supreme Court as well as by the lower courts.

Dissenting, Justice Stevens stated that a victim impact statement "sheds no light on the defendant's guilt or moral culpability, and thus serves no purpose other than to encourage jurors to decide in favor of death rather than life on the basis of their emotions rather than their reason."

As of October 2013, Payne remained on Tennessee's death row.

THE ISSUE OF RACE IN CAPITAL CASES

In 1978 Willie Lloyd Turner, an African American, robbed a jewelry store in Franklin, Virginia. Angered because the owner had set off a silent alarm, Turner first shot the owner—W. Jack Smith—in the head, wounding him, and then shot him twice in the chest, killing him for "snitching." Turner's lawyer submitted to the judge the following question for the jurors: "The defendant, Willie Lloyd Turner, is a member of the Negro race. The victim, W. Jack Smith, Jr., was a white Caucasian. Will these facts prejudice you against Willie Lloyd Turner or affect your ability to render a fair and impartial verdict based solely on the evidence?"

The judge refused to allow this question to be asked. A jury of eight whites and four African Americans convicted Turner and then, in a separate sentencing hearing, recommended the death sentence, which the judge imposed.

Turner appealed his conviction, claiming that the judge's refusal to ask prospective jurors about their racial attitudes deprived him of his right to a fair trial. Even though his argument failed to persuade state and federal appeals courts, the U.S. Supreme Court heard his case. The high court ruled 7–2 in *Turner v. Murray* (476 U.S. 28 [1986]) to overturn Turner's death sentence, but not his conviction.

Writing for the majority, Justice White noted that, in considering a death sentence, every juror makes a subjective decision that is uniquely his or her own regarding what punishment should be meted out to the offender. White further stated:

> Because of the range of discretion entrusted to a jury in a capital sentencing hearing, there is a unique opportunity for racial prejudice to operate but remain undetected. On the facts of this case, a juror who believes that blacks are violence prone or morally inferior might well be influenced by that belief in deciding whether petitioner's crime involved the aggravating factors specified under Virginia law. Such a juror might also be less favorably inclined toward petitioner's evidence of mental disturbance as a mitigating circumstance. More subtle, less consciously held racial attitudes could also influence a juror's decision in this case. Fear of blacks, which could easily be stirred up by the violent facts of petitioner's crime, might incline a juror to favor the death penalty.

The high court recognized that the death sentence differs from all other punishments and, therefore, requires a more comprehensive examination of how it is imposed. The lower court judge, by not asking prospective jurors about their racial attitudes, had not exercised this thorough examination. Consequently, the Supreme Court reversed Turner's death sentence. Justice Powell, in his dissent, observed that the court ruling seemed to be "based on what amounts to a constitutional presumption that jurors in capital cases are racially biased. Such presumption unjustifiably suggests that criminal justice in our courts of law is meted out on racial grounds."

In 1987 a Virginia court resentenced Turner to death. After completing the appeals process he was executed in 1995.

Limits to Consideration of Racial Attitudes

On May 13, 1978, Warren McCleskey and three armed men robbed a furniture store in Georgia. A police officer, Frank Schlatt, responding to a silent alarm, entered the store, was shot twice, and died. McCleskey was African American; the officer was white. McCleskey admitted taking part in the robbery but denied shooting the police officer. The state proved that at least one shot came from the weapon McCleskey was carrying and produced two witnesses who had heard McCleskey admit to the shooting. A jury found him guilty, and McCleskey, offering no mitigating circumstances during the sentencing phase, received the death penalty.

McCleskey eventually appealed his case all the way to the U.S. Supreme Court. Part of his appeal was based on two major statistical studies of more than 2,000 Georgia murder cases that occurred during the 1970s. Prepared by David C. Baldus, Charles A. Pulanski Jr., and George Woodworth, the statistical analyses were referred to as the Baldus study. (The two studies were "Comparative Review of Death Sentences: An Empirical Study of the Georgia Experience" [*Journal of Criminal Law and Criminology*, vol. 74, no. 3, Autumn 1983] and "Monitoring and Evaluating Contemporary Death Sentencing Systems: Lessons from Georgia" [*University of California Davis Law Review*, vol. 18, no. 1375, 1985].)

The Baldus study found that defendants charged with killing white people received the death penalty in 11% of cases, but defendants charged with killing African Americans received the death penalty in only 1% of the cases. The study also found a reverse racial difference, based on the defendant's race—4% of the African American defendants received the death penalty, as opposed to 7% of the white defendants.

Furthermore, the Baldus study reported on the cases based on the combination of the defendant's race and that of the victim. The death penalty was imposed in 22% of the cases involving African American defendants and white victims, in 8% of the cases involving white defendants and white victims, in 3% of the cases involving white defendants and African American victims, and in 1% of the cases involving African American defendants and African American victims.

The Baldus study also found that prosecutors sought the death penalty in 70% of the cases involving African American defendants and white victims, in 32% of the cases involving white defendants and white victims, in 19% of the cases involving white defendants and African American victims, and in 15% of the cases involving African American defendants and African American victims.

Finally, after taking account of variables that could have explained the differences on nonracial grounds, the study concluded that defendants charged with killing white victims were 4.3 times as likely to receive the death penalty as defendants charged with killing African Americans. In addition, African American defendants were 1.1 times as likely to get a death sentence as other defendants were. Therefore, McCleskey, who was African American and killed a white victim, had the greatest likelihood of being sentenced to death.

In court testimony, Baldus testified that, in particularly brutal cases when support for the death penalty is especially strong, racial discrimination on the part of the jurors tends to disappear. The racial factors usually come into play in midrange cases, such as McCleskey's, where the jurors were faced with choices.

Even though the federal district court did not accept the Baldus study, both the court of appeals and the U.S. Supreme Court accepted the study as valid. However, a 5–4 Supreme Court, in *McCleskey v. Kemp* (481 U.S. 279 [1987]), rejected McCleskey's appeal. McCleskey had to show that the state of Georgia had acted in a discriminatory manner in his case, and the Baldus study was not enough to support the defendant's claim that any of the jurors had acted with discrimination.

Justice Powell noted that statistics, at most, may show that a certain factor might likely enter some decision-making processes. The court recognized that a jury's decision could be influenced by racial prejudice, but the majority believed previous rulings had built in enough safeguards to guarantee equal protection for every defendant. The court declared, "At most, the Baldus study indicates a discrepancy that appears to correlate with race. Apparent disparities in sentencing are an inevitable part of our criminal justice system . . . . We hold that the Baldus study does not demonstrate a constitutionally significant risk of racial bias affecting the Georgia capital sentencing process."

The court expressed concern that if it ruled that Baldus's findings did represent a risk, the findings might well be applied to lesser cases. It further noted that it is the job of the legislative branch to consider these findings and incorporate them into the laws to guarantee equal protection in courts of law.

Justice Brennan, who, along with Justice Marshall, believed capital punishment constitutes a cruel and unusual punishment and, therefore, is unconstitutional, thought the Baldus study powerfully demonstrated that it is impossible to eliminate arbitrariness in the imposition of the death penalty. Therefore, he argued, the death penalty must be abolished altogether because the court cannot rely on legal safeguards to guarantee an African American defendant a fair sentencing. Even though the Baldus study did not show that racism necessarily led to McCleskey's death sentence, it had surely shown that McCleskey faced a considerably greater likelihood of being sentenced to death because he was an African American man convicted of killing a white man.

Also writing in dissent, Justice Blackmun thought the court majority had concentrated too much on the potential racial attitudes of the jury. As important, he thought, were the racial attitudes of the prosecutor's office, which the Baldus study found to be much more likely to seek the death penalty for an African American person who had killed a white person than for other categories.

The district attorney for Fulton County had testified that no county policy existed on how to prosecute capital cases. Decisions to seek the death penalty were left to the judgment of the assistant district attorneys who handled the cases. Blackmun thought that such a system was certainly open to abuse. Without guidelines, the prosecutors could let their racial prejudices influence their decisions.

Blackmun also noted that the court majority had totally dismissed Georgia's history of racial prejudice as past history. Even though it should not be the overriding factor, this bias should be considered in any case presented to the high court, he thought. Justice Blackmun found most disturbing the court's concern that, if the Baldus findings were upheld, they might be applied to other cases, leading to constitutional challenges. Blackmun thought that a closer scrutiny of the effects of racial discrimination would benefit the criminal justice system and, ultimately, society.

In 1991 McCleskey was executed in the electric chair by the state of Georgia.

Race, Ethnicity, and Future Dangerousness

On June 5, 2000, the U.S. Supreme Court, in a summary disposition, ordered the Texas Court of Criminal Appeals to hold a new sentencing hearing for Victor Saldano, an Argentine national on death row. In a summary disposition, the court decides a case in a simple proceeding without a jury. Generally, a summary disposition is rare in criminal cases. In this instance, the crime was committed by a foreign national and thus fell outside of a trial jury's mandate. In *Saldano v. Texas* (No. 99-8119), the court cited the confession of error by the Texas attorney general John Cornyn (1952–) regarding the use of race as a factor in sentencing the defendant.

Texas death penalty statutes require that the jury consider a defendant's future dangerousness to determine whether or not to impose the death penalty. At the sentencing hearing Walter Quijano, the court-appointed psychologist, testified that Saldano was "a continuing threat to society" because he is Hispanic. Quijano told the jury that because Hispanics are "over-represented" in prisons they are more likely to be dangerous. Following this decision, other death row inmates whose cases reflected similar circumstances were granted new sentencing hearings. Saldano's own case continued in the courts; in March 2004 the U.S. Court of Appeals for the Fifth Circuit refused to reinstate Saldano's death sentence. As of October 2013, Saldano remained on Texas's death row.

BIASED PEREMPTORY STRIKES IN JURY SELECTION

During the jury selection process both the prosecution and the defense can strike (dismiss) potential jurors from serving on the jury for a variety of reasons. These are called peremptory strikes (or peremptory challenges), and the number allowed per trial is determined by the laws of the jurisdiction involved. The U.S. Supreme Court has made several rulings in cases in which African American defendants charged that prosecutors used peremptory strikes to dismiss most or all African Americans

from jury pools. The defendants alleged that these actions amounted to violations of the equal protection clause under the 14th Amendment to the U.S. Constitution.

In 1965 the U.S. Supreme Court ruled on such a claim in *Swain v. Alabama* (380 U.S. 202 [1965]). This is an Alabama case in which an African American man, Robert Swain, had been convicted of raping a white woman and sentenced to death by an all-white jury. (At that time rape was a capital crime under Alabama law.) Although the original jury pool included eight African Americans, all were dismissed—two by the judge and six by peremptory challenges from the prosecution. Upon appeal, the U.S. Supreme Court refused to overturn Swain's conviction, arguing that there was no evidence that the prosecutor's actions were racially motivated. Neither prosecutors nor defense attorneys had to provide reasons for their peremptory challenges. The court agreed with this practice, noting "it would be an unreasonable burden to require an attorney for either side to justify his use of peremptory challenges."

However, two decades later in *Batson v. Kentucky* (476 U.S. 79 [1986]) the U.S. Supreme Court superseded *Swain* by ruling that a defendant could make a case claiming the denial of equal protection of the laws based solely on evidence that the prosecutor had used peremptory challenges to exclude members of the defendant's race from the jury. Although the court ruled that a defendant is not guaranteed that a jury will contain members of his or her race, the State cannot exclude potential jurors because of their race "or on the false assumption that members of [the defendant's] race as a group are not qualified to serve as jurors."

In 1991 in *Powers v. Ohio* (499 U.S. 400 [1991]) the U.S. Supreme Court extended its prohibitions against using peremptory challenges based on race to apply regardless of the defendant's race. In other words, a white defendant could contest peremptory challenges used to strike African American jurors and vice versa. In 1992 the so-called *Batson* rule was further extended in *Georgia v. McCollum* (505 U.S. 42 [1992]) to apply to the defense as well as the prosecution. In 1994 the Supreme Court, in *J. E. B. v. Alabama* (511 U.S. 127 [1994]) ruled that peremptory strikes based on juror gender are also unconstitutional. Note that various state supreme courts have extended the protected categories beyond race and gender to religion, sexual orientation, and other juror qualities. However, in capital cases, race has been the primary factor that has triggered claims of unconstitutional jury selection.

In 2005 the U.S. Supreme Court made a decision that was seen as a reprimand to a lower court for not upholding the Batson rule more stringently. In *Miller-El v. Dretke* the court ordered the Fifth Circuit Court of Appeals to reconsider its rejection of a *Batson* claim by Thomas Joe Miller-El of Texas. The African American defendant had been convicted of murdering a hotel clerk, Douglas Walker, in 1985 and had been sentenced to death. His attorneys contended that prosecutors struck 10 of the 11 African Americans in the jury pool in accordance with a long-standing policy in the Dallas County prosecutor's office to bar minorities from juries. The latter accusation was based on a controversial jury selection manual that had once been used by the office. In "Dallas Jury Selection under Scrutiny in Death Penalty Appeal" (Associated Press, February 17, 2002), April Castro reports that "prosecutors who have worked in the office readily acknowledge the memo-turned-training guide, which urged prosecutors not to select 'Jews, Negroes, Dagos, Mexicans or a member of any minority race on a jury, no matter how rich or how well educated.'"

The Fifth Circuit Court of Appeals at first refused to hear Miller-El's *Batson* claim, but was ordered to do so by the U.S. Supreme Court in 2002 in *Miller-El v. Cockrell* (545 U.S. ___ [2005]). The appeals court then considered the claim, but rejected it. In *Miller-El v. Dretke* the U.S. Supreme Court reversed the lower court's decision and ruled that the defendant's *Batson* claim was valid and he was due a new trial. The U.S. Supreme Court concluded that the jury selection process during his trial "was replete with evidence that prosecutors were selecting and rejecting potential jurors because of race." In addition, the court found fault with the jury selection manual that had once been used by the prosecutor's office. Miller-El was subsequently sentenced to life in prison.

CHAPTER 5
DEATH PENALTY LAWS: STATE, FEDERAL, AND U.S. MILITARY

In essence there are three separate capital punishment systems in the United States: state, federal, and military. Although each jurisdiction that practices capital punishment has its own laws, the laws share many common elements. This is due in large part to U.S. Supreme Court rulings (some of which are described in Chapters 2, 3, and 4) that have shaped death penalty laws to ensure their adherence with the U.S. Constitution and to provide some legal consistency across the country.

As of September 2013, 18 states and the District of Columbia had either outlawed capital punishment or did not have valid state laws allowing the death penalty to be carried out. (See Table 5.1.) New Mexico (in 2009), Connecticut (in 2012), and Maryland (in 2013) abolished capital punishment prospectively (i.e., for future cases); however, already condemned inmates remain under sentence of death. Michigan and Vermont only permit capital punishment for the crime of treason, a crime that is so unusual that these states are considered to have effectively abolished the death penalty. The vast majority of the jurisdictions listed in Table 5.1 have not carried out an execution since 1977, which is considered the dawn of the modern death penalty age in the United States.

The federal government and the U.S. military operate their own judicial systems, both of which have long allowed the use of capital punishment for certain crimes. However, the federal government has executed only three people since 1977 and the U.S. military has executed none. (See Table 1.6 in Chapter 1.)

STATE DEATH PENALTY LAWS

Before the 1970s U.S. death penalty laws varied considerably from state to state. Few national standards existed on how a murder trial should be conducted or which types of crimes deserved the death penalty. In South Carolina, for instance, a person could be executed for rape or robbery. In Georgia and in a number of other states, juries were given complete discretion in delivering a sentence along with the conviction. Although verdicts were swift, the punishments such juries meted out could be arbitrary and discriminatory.

During the late 1960s and early 1970s the U.S. Supreme Court undertook a series of cases that questioned the constitutionality of state capital punishment laws. In *Furman v. Georgia* (408 U.S. 238 [1972]), the court ruled that the death penalty, as it was then being administered, constituted a cruel and unusual punishment in violation of the Eighth and 14th Amendments to the U.S. Constitution. According to the court the state laws that were then in effect led to arbitrary sentencing of the death penalty. As a result, many states changed their laws to conform to standards set by the *Furman* decision. Since *Furman*, review of individual state statutes has continued as appeals of capital sentences reach state courts or the U.S. Supreme Court. In particular, the use of capital punishment against the insane (*Ford v. Wainwright*, 477 U.S. 399 [1986]), the mentally retarded (*Atkins v. Virginia*, 536 U.S. 304 [2002]), and juveniles (*Roper v. Simmons*, 543 U.S. 551 [2005]) has been found to be unconstitutional by the U.S. Supreme Court.

Court decisions have also affected state trial and sentencing procedures. Under revised laws, most states now use a bifurcated (two-part) trial system, where the first trial is used to determine a defendant's guilt, and the second trial determines the sentence of a guilty defendant. In most trials jurors are usually only given the option of either sentencing a convicted felon to life in prison or to death. During a sentencing hearing, juries must consider all the aggravating circumstances presented by the prosecution and the mitigating circumstances presented by the defense. Aggravating circumstances may lessen the responsibility for a crime, whereas mitigating circumstances may add to the responsibility for a crime.

TABLE 5.1

States that have abolished the death penalty or do not have valid death penalty laws, 2013

State	Most recent year of abolishment	Note	Number of executions (1977–2012)	Last execution year (1977–2012)
Alaska	1957	Alaska Territory abolished death penalty before becoming a state in 1959.	0	None
Connecticut	2012	Already condemned prisoners remained under sentence of death.	1	2005
District of Columbia	1981		0	None
Hawaii	1957	Hawaii Territory abolished death penalty before becoming a state in 1959.	0	None
Illinois	2011	All existing death sentences were changed to life sentences with no parole.	12	1999
Iowa	1965		0	None
Maine	1887		0	None
Maryland	2013	Already condemned prisoners remained under sentence of death.	5	2005
Massachusetts	See note:	Court rulings, most recently in 1984, invalidated state death penalty laws.	0	None
Michigan	1963	In 1846 banned death penalty except for treason against the state.	0	None
Minnesota	1911		0	None
New Jersey	2007	All existing death sentences were changed to life sentences.	0	None
New Mexico	2009	Already condemned prisoners remained under sentence of death.	1	2001
New York	See note:	Court rulings, most recently in 2007, invalidated state death penalty laws.	0	None
North Dakota	1973		0	None
Rhode Island	1984		0	None
Vermont	1987	Death penalty for treason still allowed under state law.	0	None
West Virginia	1965		0	None
Wisconsin	1853		0	None

SOURCE: Adapted from "Prisoners Executed under Civil Authority in the United States, by Year, Region, and Jurisdiction, 1977–2012," in *Prisoners Executed*, U.S. Department of Justice, Office of Justice Programs, Bureau of Justice Statistics, March 11, 2013, http://www.bjs.gov/content/data/exest.csv (accessed September 3, 2013)

Capital Offenses under State Laws

State laws, statutes, and criminal codes specifically lay out which crimes are to be handled as capital cases. Table 5.2 lists capital offenses by state in 2011, according to the U.S. Department of Justice's Bureau of Justice Statistics (BJS). Note that while Connecticut and Maryland eliminated the death penalty (in 2012 and 2013, respectively) for future crimes, already condemned inmates remained under sentence of death. In addition, New York's capital punishment law has been found, in part, to be unconstitutional, as is described in Chapter 8.

Different types of capital murder are specified by legal definition. Even though varying somewhat from one jurisdiction to another, the types of homicide most commonly specified are murder carried out during the commission of a felony (serious offenses such as rape, robbery, or arson); murder of a law officer, corrections employee, or firefighter engaged in the performance of official duties; murder by an inmate serving a life sentence; and murder for hire (contract murder). Different statutory terminology may be used in different states to designate essentially similar crimes. Terms such as *capital murder*, *first-degree murder*, *capital felony*, or *murder Class 1 felony* may indicate the same offense in different states.

The laws of each state lay out specific aggravating and mitigating factors in capital cases. Examples of aggravating factors include a previous conviction of the defendant for another capital offense, murder committed for pecuniary (monetary) gain, and murder committed in an especially heinous, atrocious, or cruel manner. Mitigating factors may relate to the defendant personally (e.g., youth, a history of being abused as a child, or having no prior criminal record) or to the circumstances of the crime (e.g., there was no intent to kill the victim or the victim was a criminal accomplice).

NONHOMICIDE CRIMES. As described in Chapter 3, the imposition of the death penalty for some nonhomicide crimes has been ruled unconstitutional by the courts. The notable examples are rape and kidnapping. As shown in Table 5.2, some state laws still list these crimes as capital offenses; however, such prosecutions are not legal under existing Supreme Court decisions. Other nonhomicide crimes (such as treason and air piracy or hijacking) that carry the death penalty under state laws have not yet had their constitutionality tested.

Under Texas law a person who is party to, but does not actually commit, a murder can receive the death penalty. Section 7.02 of the Texas Penal Code took effect in 1974 and allows prosecutors to charge an accomplice with capital murder if the accomplice should have anticipated that the murder was going to occur. This is known informally as "the law of parties."

The Texas law of parties aroused controversy in 1997, when it was used to impose a death sentence against Kenneth Foster for his role as the getaway driver in a robbery in which one of his passengers left the car and killed Michael LaHood Jr. during an altercation. Foster garnered the support of abolitionists (people against the death penalty), who argued that a death

TABLE 5.2

Capital offenses by state, 2011

State	Offense
Alabama	Intentional murder with 18 aggravating factors (Ala. Stat. Ann. 13A-5-40(a)(1)-(18)).
Arizona	First-degree murder, including pre-meditated murder and felony murder, accompanied by at least 1 of 14 aggravating factors (A.R.S. § 13-703(F)).
Arkansas	Capital murder (Ark. Code Ann. 5-10-101) with a finding of at least 1 of 10 aggravating circumstances; treason.
California	First-degree murder with special circumstances; sabotage; train wrecking causing death; treason; perjury in a capital case causing execution of an innocent person; fatal assault by a prisoner serving a life sentence.
Colorado	First-degree murder with at least 1 of 17 aggravating factors; first-degree kidnapping resulting in death; treason.
Connecticut	Capital felony with 8 forms of aggravated homicide (C.G.S. § 53a-54b).
Delaware	First-degree murder (11 Del. C. § 636) with at least 1 statutory aggravating circumstance (11 Del. C. § 4209).
Florida	First-degree murder; felony murder; capital drug trafficking; capital sexual battery.
Georgia	Murder with aggravating circumstances; kidnapping with bodily injury or ransom when the victim dies; aircraft hijacking; treason.
Idaho	First-degree murder with aggravating factors; first-degree kidnapping; perjury resulting in the execution of an innocent person.
Indiana	Murder with 16 aggravating circumstances (IC 35-50-2-9).
Kansas	Capital murder (KSA 21-5401) with 8 aggravating circumstances (KSA 21-6617, KSA 21-6624).
Kentucky	Capital murder with the presence of at least one statutory aggravating circumstance; capital kidnapping (KRS 532.025).
Louisiana	First-degree murder; treason (La. R.S. 14:30 and 14:113).
Maryland	First-degree murder, either premeditated or during the commission of a felony, provided that certain death eligibility requirements are satisfied.
Mississippi	Capital murder (Miss. Code Ann. § 97-3-19(2)); aircraft piracy (Miss. Code Ann. § 97-25-55(1)).
Missouri	First-degree murder (565.020 RSMO 2000).
Montana	Capital murder with 1 of 9 aggravating circumstances (Mont. Code Ann. § 46-18-303); aggravated kidnapping; felony murder; aggravated sexual intercourse without consent (Mont. Code Ann. § 45-5-503).
Nebraska	First-degree murder with a finding of at least 1 statutorily-defined aggravating circumstance.
Nevada	First-degree murder with at least 1 of 15 aggravating circumstances (NRS 200.030, 200.033, 200.035).
New Hampshire	Murder committed in the course of rape, kidnapping, drug crimes, or burglary; killing of a police officer, judge, or prosecutor; murder for hire; murder by an inmate while serving a sentence of life without parole (RSA 630:1, RSA 630:5).
New Mexico[a]	First-degree murder with at least 1 of 7 aggravating factors (NMSA 1978 § 31-20A-5).
New York[b]	First-degree murder with 1 of 13 aggravating factors (NY Penal Law §125.27).
North Carolina	First-degree murder (NCGS §14-17) with the finding of at least 1 of 11 statutory aggravating circumstances (NCGS§ 15A-2000).
Ohio	Aggravated murder with at least 1 of 10 aggravating circumstances (O.R.C. secs. 2903.01, 2929.02, and 2929.04).
Oklahoma	First-degree murder in conjunction with a finding of at least 1 of 8 statutorily-defined aggravating circumstances.
Oregon	Aggravated murder (ORS 163.095).
Pennsylvania	First-degree murder with 18 aggravating circumstances.
South Carolina	Murder with at least 1 of 12 aggravating circumstances (§ 16-3-20(C)(a)).
South Dakota	First-degree murder with 1 of 10 aggravating circumstances.
Tennessee	First-degree murder (Tenn. Code Ann. § 39-13-202) with 1 of 16 aggravating circumstances (Tenn. Code Ann. § 39-13-204).
Texas	Criminal homicide with 1 of 9 aggravating circumstances (Tex. Penal Code § 19.03).
Utah	Aggravated murder (76-5-202, Utah Code Annotated).
Virginia	First-degree murder with 1 of 15 aggravating circumstances (VA Code § 18.2-31).
Washington	Aggravated first-degree murder.
Wyoming	First-degree murder; murder during the commission of sexual assault, sexual abuse of a minor, arson, robbery, burglary, escape, resisting arrest, kidnapping or abuse of a minor under 16 (W.S.A. § 6-2-101(a)).

[a]New Mexico enacted a prospective repeal of its capital statute as of July 1, 2009. Offenders who committed their offenses prior to that date are eligible for the death penalty.
[b]The New York Court of Appeals held that a portion of New York's death penalty sentencing statute (CPL 400.27) was unconstitutional (*People v. Taylor*, 9 N.Y3d 129 (2007)). As a result, no defendants can be sentenced to death until the legislature corrects the errors in this statute.
Note: Connecticut (2012) and Maryland (2013) have since abolished the death penalty for future crimes.

SOURCE: Tracy L. Snell, "Table 1. Capital Offenses, by State, 2011," in *Capital Punishment, 2011—Statistical Tables*, U.S. Department of Justice, Office of Justice Programs, Bureau of Justice Statistics, July 16, 2013, http://www.bjs.gov/content/pub/pdf/cp11st.pdf (accessed September 3, 2013)

sentence was too harsh a penalty for his crime. After exhausting all appeals Foster faced execution on August 31, 2007. Just hours before the scheduled execution, the Texas governor Rick Perry (1950–) granted clemency—a very rare occurrence in the state. Foster's sentence was changed to life imprisonment with a possibility for parole. In September 2013 Texas executed Robert Gene Garza for his role in the 2002 ambush killings of four women: Dantizene Lizeth Vasquez Beltran, Celina Linares Sanchez, Lourdes Yesenia Araujo Torres, and Maria De La Luz Bazaldua Cobbarubias. Although Garza was not one of the triggermen, he set up the ambush and was in the car with the shooters, who were fellow gang members.

FETAL HOMICIDE. Fetal homicide is the murder of a fetus, that is, a baby developing within the womb. In

"Governor Allows Fetal Homicide Bill to Become Law" (BigforkEagle.com, May 24, 2013,), Caleb M. Soptelean indicates that in May 2013 Montana became the 39th state to pass a fetal homicide (or feticide) law. The Montana law allows the death penalty as a sentence for intentionally killing a fetus. In "Fetal Homicide Laws" (2013, http://www.ncsl.org/issues-research/health/fetal-homicide-state-laws.aspx), the National Conference of State Legislatures provides a summary listing of state feticide laws around the country. The laws do not apply in cases of legal abortions.

Feticide laws became the focus of public attention during 2013 due to a high-profile case. In May 2013 Ariel Castro (1960–2013) was arrested in Ohio and charged with keeping three women (Michelle Knight, Georgina DeJesus, and Amanda Berry) in captivity in his home for at least a decade. Prosecutors announced they were considering charging him with feticide because one of the women said he beat and starved her while she was pregnant, causing five miscarriages. Fetal homicide is eligible for the death penalty under Ohio law. If Castro had been convicted of feticide and sentenced to death, he would have been the first person to face capital punishment for feticide in the United States. However, Castro pleaded guilty and was sentenced to life in prison with no chance of parole plus 1,000 years. Castro died in prison in September 2013.

ACTS OF TERRORISM. In the aftermath of the September 11, 2001, attacks on the World Trade Center and the Pentagon, several states expanded their death penalty statutes to apply to acts of terrorism. Because acts of terrorism generally include "regular" criminal offenses already defined by state law, terrorism statutes include additional criteria to define terrorist acts.

As of October 2013, no one has been prosecuted under state capital terrorism statutes. The individuals accused of terrorist acts related to the September 11, 2001, attacks and in relation to the subsequent U.S. war on terrorism have been prosecuted under federal or military law instead. Another prominent terrorist act, the April 2013 bombing of the Boston Marathon, resulted in the death of three people—Krystle Campbell, Martin Richard, and Lu Lingzi—and injuries to hundreds of others. Dzhokhar Tsarnaev (1993–) faced both federal and state charges in late 2013 in relation to the bombing and also the murder of Sean A. Collier after the bombing. (Tamerlan Tsarnaev [1987?–2013], Dzhokhar's brother, was also implicated in the bombings but was killed in a shoot-out following the bombings.) However, as shown in Table 5.1, Massachusetts's capital punishment law was unenforceable as of 2013, so if Tsarnaev faces capital charges it will only be under federal law. Federal prosecutors expected to announce in early 2014 if they would pursue the death penalty for Tsarnaev.

2013 State Legislature Actions

The Death Penalty Information Center (DPIC) is a private nonprofit organization that is opposed to the death penalty. The DPIC tracks capital punishment legislation across the country and lists proposed and passed bills, by year and state, at "Recent Legislative Activity" (http://www.deathpenaltyinfo.org/recent-legislative-activity). The list for 2013 (as of October 2013) indicates that legislatures in dozens of states had considered bills related to the death penalty.

Sixteen states—Alabama, Arizona, Arkansas, Colorado, Delaware, Florida, Indiana, Kansas, Kentucky, Maryland, Missouri, Montana, Nebraska, Oregon, Texas, and Washington—considered bills abolishing capital punishment. In May 2013 Maryland did repeal its death

penalty statute, but only for future cases. Already condemned prisoners remained under sentence of death. In all other states, proposed repeal measures failed to pass or were considered by the DPIC unlikely to pass before yearend 2013. Legislative actions in Delaware and Nebraska were watched closely, because death penalty opponents thought there was some chance that repeal bills would be successful. The Delaware state senate passed a repeal bill in March 2013, but the bill was tabled (removed from consideration) by the state house. In March 2013 Nebraska's judiciary committee passed a bill to abolish the death penalty; however, it failed to pass the legislature as a whole.

The DPIC notes that during 2013, four states without the death penalty—Iowa, Massachusetts, New Jersey, and West Virginia—considered bills to reinstate capital punishment. None of the proposed measures had passed as of October 2013, nor did the DPIC expect them to pass before the end of the year.

According to the DPIC, two states expanded their capital punishment statutes during 2013. Under its expanded law, Alabama considers defendants eligible for the death penalty if they committed murders in which their victims had previously obtained protective orders against them. Mississippi added terroristic acts as an aggravating factor in death penalty cases.

In Ohio a bill was introduced in 2013 to allow the death penalty for rape and other sexual crimes against minors; however, the DPIC notes that, if passed, such a law would likely be considered unconstitutional in light of the U.S. Supreme Court decision in *Kennedy v. Louisiana* (554 U.S. ___ [2008]), which is described in Chapter 3. Georgia legislators considered, but did not pass, a bill that would have made gang membership an aggravating factor in death penalty cases. As of October 2013, the Kansas House had passed a bill expanding the use of capital punishment to murders in which the perpetrators were fleeing after committing other felonies. The state senate had not yet voted on the measure. In addition, Texas legislators were considering a bill to make the murder of a district attorney automatically eligible for the death penalty.

Several states considered measures that would limit the circumstances in which the death penalty could be applied, some of which were enacted. For example, a Florida Senate committee heard testimony regarding a bill that would require a unanimous jury decision for capital punishment, as opposed to the simple majority (i.e., at least seven votes for the death penalty from twelve jurors) required under existing law. In addition, the committee considered limiting death penalty cases to those in which a confession or scientific evidence of guilt was obtained. As of October 2013, these measures had not passed, nor had reform measures proposed in other states with two exceptions. Oklahoma revised its law so that judges could no longer authorize capital punishment for convicted murderers even when that penalty had not been sought by prosecutors. Texas passed a new law requiring that "all" DNA evidence related to a death penalty case be tested prior to trial.

The DPIC indicates that legislatures in two states—California and Florida—considered bills during 2013 to speed up the capital punishment appeals process. The California bill did not pass. Florida did put into law its Timely Justice Act, which is described later in this chapter.

Hybrid Systems

In most death penalty states the sentencing decision is made by juries. As of 2013 Alabama, Delaware, and Florida allowed trial judges to override jury-imposed sentences in capital cases. In these states the jury recommends a sentence and the trial judge can accept the recommendation or override it. This system is variously called a hybrid, judicial override, or jury override system. As described in Chapter 2, the constitutionality of judicial override in Florida and Alabama was upheld by the U.S. Supreme Court in *Spaziano v. Florida* (468 U.S. 447 [1984]) and *Harris v. Alabama* (513 U.S. 504 [1995]), respectively. Delaware's system has not faced a court test.

The Equal Justice Institute (EJI) is a private nonprofit legal organization based in Alabama that is opposed to capital punishment. In *The Death Penalty in Alabama: Judge Override* (July 2011, http://eji.org/eji/files/Override _Report.pdf), the EJI notes that Florida law has long required a judge to give "great weight" to a jury's recommendation and strictly limits judicial override of a life sentence with a death sentence. Delaware law is based on Florida law in this respect. As a result, judicial overrides in these two states have been rare. According to the EJI, Alabama law, by contrast, only requires that the trial judge "consider" the jury's recommendation. This distinction has meant that between 1976 and March 2011, 98 jury recommendations for life sentences in Alabama were overridden by judges imposing death sentences. Only nine jury recommendations for death sentences were overridden by judges to life sentences.

The Appeals Process in State Capital Cases

Criminal convictions and sentences can be appealed to higher courts by either the prosecutor or the defendant, but the vast majority of appeals are initiated by defendants. Appeal proceedings are not the same as retrials. Appeals courts review the original trial proceedings and records to determine if any legal errors or problems occurred. According to Justia.com (2013, http://www.justia.com/criminal/criminal-appeals/), "Potential grounds

for appeal in a criminal case include legal error, juror misconduct and ineffective assistance of counsel. Legal errors may result from improperly admitted evidence, incorrect jury instructions, or lack of sufficient evidence to support a guilty verdict."

Appeals courts traditionally give deference (benefit of the doubt) to trial courts. In other words, appeals courts are reluctant to second-guess decisions and actions made by trial courts. In addition, even if an appeals court finds that legal errors occurred, this does not necessarily mean that the appeals court will overturn or modify the original conviction or sentence. The errors must reach a certain level of significance to trigger such a response. In legal terminology the errors must not be "harmless errors." Appeals courts can affirm (uphold) or reverse (overturn) an original conviction or sentence. They also have the power to modify a conviction or sentence, or to remand (send back) the case to the trial court for it to retry, resentence, or release the defendant.

The appeals process in capital cases varies slightly from state to state but generally includes the steps shown in Figure 5.1.

The appeals process in every state begins with the automatic direct appeal. In *Gregg v. Georgia* (428 U.S. 153 [1976]), the U.S. Supreme Court ruled that any death sentence must be appealed from the trial court directly to the highest court in the state with criminal jurisdiction. The highest court of the state may be either the state supreme court or the highest court of criminal appeals. The state high court evaluates the trial court records for constitutional or legal errors. If the high court upholds the conviction and sentence, the defendant can appeal directly to the U.S. Supreme Court using a writ of certiorari. A writ of certiorari is a petition to the Supreme Court to review only the issues brought up in the direct appeal in the state's high court. If the Supreme Court denies certiorari, the trial court's ruling stands.

If the direct appeals fail, the inmate may then pursue a state appeals process. This second round of appeals differs from the direct appeal in that the condemned may raise issues that were not and could not have been raised during the direct appeal. These issues include the incompetence of the defense lawyer, jury bias, or the suppression of evidence by police or the prosecution. This appeal is also the time that the inmate's attorney can present any newly discovered exculpatory evidence (evidence that is favorable to the inmate) that was not available during the original trial. Some states call this process the collateral appeal, because it does not directly challenge the original conviction or sentence, but raises collateral issues. Other states call it a state habeas corpus procedure. Habeas corpus is a Latin phrase that literally means "have the body." The rest of the phrase "brought before me" is

FIGURE 5.1

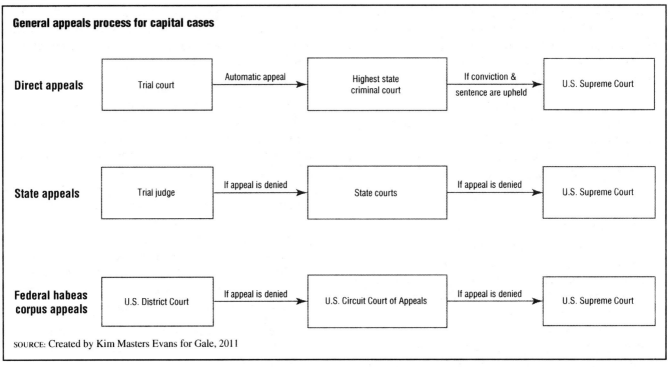

General appeals process for capital cases

Direct appeals	Trial court	→ Automatic appeal →	Highest state criminal court	→ If conviction & sentence are upheld →	U.S. Supreme Court
State appeals	Trial judge	→ If appeal is denied →	State courts	→ If appeal is denied →	U.S. Supreme Court
Federal habeas corpus appeals	U.S. District Court	→ If appeal is denied →	U.S. Circuit Court of Appeals	→ If appeal is denied →	U.S. Supreme Court

SOURCE: Created by Kim Masters Evans for Gale, 2011

implied. A writ (or order) of habeas corpus is a command from one court to another court (or to a lesser authority, such as a prison warden) to produce an inmate and explain why that inmate is being detained. Whatever the name, the scope of the state appeals process is limited to collateral issues and typically begins with the trial judge. If turned down by the trial judge, the convict may petition the first level of state appellate courts and finally the state's highest court. If the state review is denied, the condemned can again appeal directly to the U.S. Supreme Court.

A death row inmate who has exhausted all state appeals can then file a petition for a federal habeas corpus review on grounds of violation of his or her constitutional rights. These petitions typically allege violations of the Sixth Amendment to the U.S. Constitution (the right to have the assistance of counsel for defense), the Eighth Amendment (the ban against a cruel and unusual punishment), or the 14th Amendment (the right to due process). The inmate files the appeal with the district court with jurisdiction over the city or county in which he or she was convicted. If the district court denies the appeal, the inmate can proceed to the U.S. Circuit Court of Appeals in the region. As of 2013, there were 94 federal judicial districts and 12 U.S. Circuit Courts of Appeal in the United States. (See Figure 5.2; note that the 12th circuit is the District of Columbia.) Finally, if the circuit court denies the appeal, the condemned can for a third time ask the U.S. Supreme Court for a certiorari review.

POST-CONVICTION COUNSEL. In capital punishment terminology *post-conviction counsel* refers to legal counsel provided for free to indigent (poor) defendants following their convictions and direct appeals. As described in Chapter 3, in 1989 the U.S. Supreme Court found in *Murray v. Giarratano* (492 U.S. 1 [1989]) that inmates sentenced to death are not constitutionally guaranteed a right to post-conviction counsel. Sarah L. Thomas notes in "A Legislative Challenge: A Proposed Model Statute to Provide for the Appointment of Counsel in State Habeas Corpus Proceedings for Indigent Petitioners" (*Emory Law Journal*, vol. 54, no. 2, Spring 2005) that "the U.S. Supreme Court and most state supreme courts do not require that counsel be provided as a matter of constitutional right to indigent petitioners in habeas corpus cases. Most courts have rejected a constitutional right to counsel because of the belief that the writ of habeas corpus is technically a civil matter." Nevertheless, some states appoint post-conviction legal counsel for indigent capital defendants in capital cases. For example, in "Post-conviction Proceedings in Capital Cases" (January 1, 2010, http://www.judges.org/capitalcasesresources/bookpdf/Chapter%209%20Post-Conviction%20Proceedings%20in%20Capital%20Cases.pdf), Judge Kevin M. Emas explains that laws in Arizona, Florida, Nevada, and Oklahoma require post-conviction legal counsel for defendants sentenced to death.

The DPIC (2013, http://www.deathpenaltyinfo.org/death-penalty-representation#post_conviction) maintains a listing of organizations that represent or provide

FIGURE 5.2

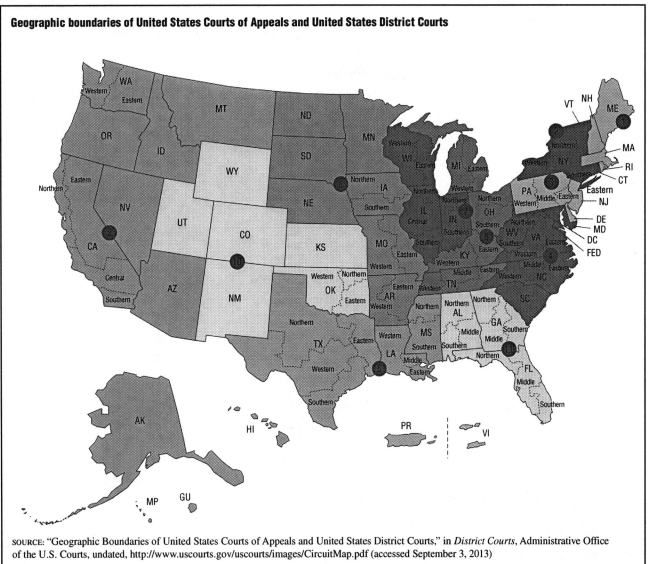

Geographic boundaries of United States Courts of Appeals and United States District Courts

SOURCE: "Geographic Boundaries of United States Courts of Appeals and United States District Courts," in *District Courts*, Administrative Office of the U.S. Courts, undated, http://www.uscourts.gov/uscourts/images/CircuitMap.pdf (accessed September 3, 2013)

assistance to condemned inmates after their direct appeals are completed.

APPEALS ARE TIME CONSUMING. The appeals process for capital cases can take years and even decades to complete. This is evident in statistics collected about death row inmates by the BJS. Tracy L. Snell of the BJS examines in *Capital Punishment, 2011—Statistical Tables* (July 2013, http://www.bjs.gov/content/pub/pdf/cp11st.pdf) the status of the 8,300 inmates who were sentenced to death between 1973 and 2011. Nearly all (8,231) of the inmates were sentenced under state law. Another 69 were sentenced under federal law. As shown in Table 5.3, 1,277 inmates (1,274 under state law and three under federal law) were executed over this period. An inmate executed in 1984 had spent an average of 74 months (6 years and 2 months) on death row. By 1999 that time had nearly doubled to 143 months (11 years and 11 months). An inmate executed in 2011 had spent an average of 198 months (16 years and 6

months) on death row. Thus, the typical inmate executed in 2011 had been sentenced in 1995.

Snell also examines the average length of time spent under sentence of death by the 3,082 inmates who were on death row at yearend 2011. (See Table 5.4.) Note that averages were not calculated for states with fewer than 10 death row inmates. The overall average was 13.7 years. The highest averages were for Nevada (16.8 years), Tennessee (16.1 years), and Kentucky (15.9 years). However, these states had relatively small numbers of death row inmates. For the five jurisdictions with the most death row inmates at yearend 2011, the averages were: California (15.3 years), Florida (15.2 years), Texas (12 years), Pennsylvania (14.9 years), and Alabama (11.1 years).

Table 5.5 shows the sentencing dates for the 3,082 inmates on death row at yearend 2011. Nearly 5% (139) of the inmates had been sentenced between 1974 and

TABLE 5.3

Average time between sentencing and execution, 1977–2011

Year	Number of inmates executed	Average elapsed time from sentence to execution for all inmates
Total	1,277	134 mo.
1977	1	—
1979	2	—
1981	1	—
1982	2	—
1983	5	—
1984	21	74
1985	18	71
1986	18	87
1987	25	86
1988	11	80
1989	16	95
1990	23	95
1991	14	116
1992	31	114
1993	38	113
1994	31	122
1995	56	134
1996	45	125
1997	74	133
1998	68	130
1999	98	143
2000	85	137
2001	66	142
2002	71	127
2003	65	131
2004	59	132
2005	60	147
2006	53	145
2007	42	153
2008	37	139
2009	52	169
2010	46	178
2011	43	198

—Not calculated. A reliable average could not be generated from fewer than 10 cases.
Note: In 1972, the U.S. Supreme Court invalidated capital punishment statutes in several states (*Furman v. Georgia*, 408 U.S. 238 (1972)), effecting a moratorium on executions. Executions resumed in 1977 when the Supreme Court found that revisions to several state statutes had effectively addressed the issues previously held unconstitutional (*Gregg v. Georgia*, 428 U.S. 153 (1976) and its companion cases). Average time was calculated from the most recent sentencing date.

SOURCE: Tracy L. Snell, "Table 10. Average Time between Sentencing and Execution, 1977–2011," in *Capital Punishment, 2011—Statistical Tables*, U.S. Department of Justice, Office of Justice Programs, Bureau of Justice Statistics, July 16, 2013, http://www.bjs.gov/content/pub/pdf/cp11st.pdf (accessed September 3, 2013)

TABLE 5.4

Prisoners on death row by jurisdiction and average number of years on death row, December 31, 2011

Jurisdiction	Under sentence of death, 12/31/11	Average number of years under sentence of death as of 12/31/11
Total	3,082	13.7
California	705	15.3
Florida	393	15.2
Texas	301	12.0
Nevada	81	16.8
Tennessee	87	16.1
Arizona	130	11.9
Pennsylvania	207	14.9
Georgia	96	14.3
Alabama	196	11.1
Kentucky	34	15.9
Ohio	142	14.8
Mississippi	57	12.6
Missouri	46	12.2
Idaho	13	15.1
South Carolina	52	10.1
Arkansas	39	13.0
Montana	2	—
Maryland	5	—
Louisiana	87	12.4
Oklahoma	63	10.6
Utah	8	—
North Carolina	158	13.3
Nebraska	11	9.3
Connecticut	10	10.6
Indiana	12	11.3
Washington	8	—
Oregon	36	10.3
Federal System	56	7.6
Delaware	18	8.3
South Dakota	4	—
New Mexico	2	—
Colorado	3	—
Virginia	9	—
Kansas	9	—
Wyoming	1	—
New Hampshire	1	—

—Not calculated. A reliable average could not be generated from fewer than 10 cases.
Note: For persons sentenced to death more than once, the numbers are based on the most recent death sentence.

SOURCE: Adapted from Tracy L. Snell, "Table 15. Prisoners under Sentence of Death on December 31, 2011, by Jurisdiction and Year of Sentencing," in *Capital Punishment, 2011—Statistical Tables*, U.S. Department of Justice, Office of Justice Programs, Bureau of Justice Statistics, July 16, 2013, http://www.bjs.gov/content/pub/pdf/cp11st.pdf (accessed September 3, 2013)

1983. They had spent 28 to 37 years on death row. California had the largest contingent (48) of these "long-timers," followed by Florida (36) and Texas (11). Hundreds of other death row inmates had sentencing dates within the 1984 to 1991 range, indicating they had spent 20 to 28 years on death row. In total, 678 (22%) of all the inmates had been on death row for at least two decades at yearend 2011.

The *Justice System Journal* is a periodical published by the National Center for State Courts. In "Why So Long? Explaining Processing Time in Capital Appeals" (*Justice System Journal*, vol. 29, no. 3, 2008), James N. G. Cauthen and Barry Latzer describe the factors that con-

tribute to the lengthy appeals process for capital cases. One factor is the complexity of capital trials; they typically last longer and are more complicated than noncapital trials. During the appeals, numerous constitutional issues that have been ruled on by supreme courts at the state and federal level have to be considered. Another factor is the bifurcated (two-part) trial system. Having two distinct trials, rather than just one trial that incorporates both guilt determination and sentencing, provides many more opportunities for legal errors and other appeal-worthy problems to occur. This adds to the appeals processing time.

SPEEDING UP APPEALS. Table 5.4 indicates that appeal times vary by jurisdiction. Some states have made

TABLE 5.5

Prisoners on death row by jurisdiction and year of sentencing, December 31, 2011

Jurisdiction	Year of sentence for prisoners under sentence of death, 12/31/2011																Under sentence of death, 12/31/11
	1974–1983	1984–1985	1986–1987	1988–1989	1990–1991	1992–1993	1994–1995	1996–1997	1998–1999	2000–2001	2002–2003	2004–2005	2006–2007	2008–2009	2010	2011	
Total	139	92	119	160	168	232	257	297	318	228	226	233	206	220	108	79	3,082
California	48	26	30	57	44	65	57	74	68	58	34	33	26	49	26	10	705
Florida	36	15	18	25	33	33	36	16	36	24	14	21	29	29	14	14	393
Texas	11	3	7	8	11	19	17	20	35	30	46	33	24	21	8	8	301
Nevada	8	7	3	7	6	1	10	14	5	4	2	3	3	4	4	0	81
Tennessee	8	6	6	7	7	2	4	10	7	7	10	3	2	4	1	3	87
Arizona	5	4	3	8	11	14	6	6	5	1	6	14	12	17	10	8	130
Pennsylvania	4	6	18	16	13	18	25	17	18	14	15	12	12	13	2	4	207
Georgia	4	0	6	5	5	8	6	15	16	5	3	9	6	7	0	1	96
Alabama	3	2	5	5	5	9	21	17	26	12	14	19	23	18	8	9	196
Kentucky	3	1	4	1	2	3	2	2	5	4	0	1	3	0	2	1	34
Ohio	2	9	11	9	10	7	15	12	18	6	13	10	7	4	7	2	142
Mississippi	2	0	0	0	7	5	5	5	5	6	9	1	5	2	4	1	57
Missouri	1	2	1	1	3	2	2	7	5	3	2	5	4	8	0	0	46
Idaho	1	1	1	1	1	1	1	1	0	0	0	2	1	0	2	0	13
South Carolina	1	1	0	3	0	0	2	5	6	3	9	7	7	6	2	0	52
Arkansas	1	0	0	1	0	7	3	8	4	4	1	3	2	4	1	0	39
Montana	1	0	0	0	0	1	0	0	0	0	0	0	0	0	0	0	2
Maryland	0	3	0	0	0	0	0	1	1	0	0	0	0	0	0	0	5
Louisiana	0	2	4	1	2	3	9	16	16	7	5	8	2	5	2	5	87
Oklahoma	0	2	1	2	0	1	2	5	9	8	10	9	6	8	0	0	63
Utah	0	1	0	2	1	0	0	2	1	0	0	0	0	1	0	0	8
North Carolina	0	1	0	0	4	22	29	29	23	15	10	8	7	3	4	3	158
Nebraska	0	0	1	0	0	0	1	1	0	0	1	4	1	1	1	0	11
Connecticut	0	0	0	1	2	0	1	0	0	0	0	2	2	1	1	0	10
Indiana	0	0	0	1	1	1	0	1	1	1	3	2	0	1	0	0	12
Washington	0	0	0	0	0	0	1	2	1	1	1	0	0	0	1	0	8
Oregon	0	0	0	0	0	5	1	4	5	5	3	3	4	0	3	3	36
Federal System	0	0	0	0	0	2	0	4	1	6	7	15	11	7	3	3	56
Delaware	0	0	0	0	0	2	0	1	0	3	4	1	3	1	1	2	18
South Dakota	0	0	0	0	0	1	1	0	0	0	0	0	0	0	0	2	4
New Mexico	0	0	0	0	0	0	1	0	0	0	1	0	0	0	0	0	2
Colorado	0	0	0	0	0	0	0	0	0	0	0	2	0	0	1	0	3
Virginia	0	0	0	0	0	0	0	0	0	1	3	1	1	3	0	0	9
Kansas	0	0	0	0	0	0	0	0	0	0	3	1	3	2	0	0	9
Wyoming	0	0	0	0	0	0	0	0	0	0	0	1	0	0	0	0	1
New Hampshire	0	0	0	0	0	0	0	0	0	0	0	0	0	1	0	0	1

Note: For persons sentenced to death more than once, the numbers are based on the most recent death sentence.

SOURCE: Adapted from Tracy L. Snell, "Table 15. Prisoners under Sentence of Death on December 31, 2011, by Jurisdiction and Year of Sentencing," in *Capital Punishment, 2011—Statistical Tables,* U.S. Department of Justice, Office of Justice Programs, Bureau of Justice Statistics, July 16, 2013, http://www.bjs.gov/content/pub/pdf/cp11st.pdf (accessed September 3, 2013)

concerted efforts to speed up appeals in capital cases, such as by establishing deadlines for the filing of post-conviction motions. Virginia is considered to have the most streamlined death penalty process in the country. An average death row time for condemned inmates at yearend 2011 was not calculated for Virginia in Table 5.4, because the state had fewer than 10 death row inmates at that time. However, Virginia has been a very active death penalty state. Table 5.6 shows the top 20 states in terms of the number of death sentences meted out between 1973 and 2011. Virginia ranked 17th. The state carried out 109 executions during this period, the second-highest number for any state. Only Texas (477) conducted more executions. As of yearend 2011, Virginia had executed 72% of its inmates condemned to death since 1973. This percentage is much higher than that of any other state, including Texas (45%).

Frank Green indicates in "Path to Execution Swifter, More Certain in Va." (TimesDispatch.com, December 31, 2012) that Virginia inmates spend on average 7.1 years on death row from time of sentencing to execution. This value is far lower than the averages shown in Table 5.4 for states with more than 10 inmates on death row at yearend 2011. Capital appeals are processed much faster in Virginia than in other states for a variety of reasons. According to Green, Virginia law allows state habeas petitions to be filed directly with the state supreme court. As shown in Figure 5.1, other death penalty states begin the state appeals process with trial judges. Thus, Virginia skips an appeals step that is followed by other states. In addition, Green explains that Virginia, "unlike most other states," has a deadline for the filing of the petitions. State appeals rules are laid out in state laws. In "Capital Offense Conviction Appeals Process in Virginia" (2013, http://www.pro deathpenalty.com/virginia/capitalappeals.html), ProDeath Penalty.com notes that "in Virginia, the range of claims available to be raised in the state habeas process is quite limited." All these factors combine to speed up capital case appeals in Virginia.

In an effort to lessen the time between capital sentencing and execution, Florida passed the Timely Justice Act in 2013. According to the article "Attorneys Challenge Timely Justice Act" (Associated Press, June 27, 2013), the law "creates tighter timeframes for appeals, post-conviction motions and imposes reporting requirements on case progress. It also re-establishes a separate agency for north Florida to provide appellate-level legal representation to inmates sentenced to death, and requires them to 'pursue all possible remedies in state court.'" The law was challenged in court as unconstitutional only weeks after it went into effect. Attorneys from the Capital Collateral Regional Counsel (the source of appointed lawyers during post-conviction proceedings) filed a lawsuit on behalf of more than 100 death row inmates in Florida. As of October 2013, the lawsuit had not been heard in court.

TABLE 5.6

Top 20 states in terms of death sentences, 1973–2011

State	Number sentenced to death, 1973–2011	State death sentence rank	Number executed, 1973–2011	State execution rank	Percent of condemned inmates executed
All states	**8,231**		**1,274**		**15%**
Texas	1,057	1	477	1	45%
Florida	1,005	2	71	4	7%
California	962	3	13	17	1%
North Carolina	535	4	43	9	8%
Alabama	429	5	55	6	13%
Ohio	412	6	46	8	11%
Pennsylvania	405	7	3	24	1%
Oklahoma	350	8	96	3	27%
Georgia	323	9	52	7	16%
Illinois	307	10	12	18	4%
Arizona	302	11	28	11	9%
Louisiana	244	12	28	12	11%
Tennessee	225	13	6	21	3%
South Carolina	205	14	43	10	21%
Mississippi	193	15	15	15	8%
Missouri	182	16	68	5	37%
Virginia	152	17	109	2	72%
Nevada	152	18	12	19	8%
Arkansas	113	19	27	13	24%
Indiana	100	20	20	14	20%

Note: Illinois abolished the death penalty in 2011 and all inmates then on death row were given life sentences.

SOURCE: Adapted from Tracy L. Snell, "Table 17. Number Sentenced to Death and Number of Removals, by Jurisdiction and Reason for Removal, 1973–2011," in *Capital Punishment, 2011—Statistical Tables*, U.S. Department of Justice, Office of Justice Programs, Bureau of Justice Statistics, July 16, 2013, http://www.bjs.gov/content/pub/pdf/cp11st.pdf (accessed September 3, 2013)

Execution of "Volunteers"

Death row inmates can choose to waive their appeals to speed their execution date. These so-called volunteers often pursue appeals on first being condemned and then abandon their efforts at a later point, typically after spending many years on death row. As a result, the mental competency of execution volunteers is hotly debated.

In 2004 John Blume of the Cornell Law School published a study on the volunteer phenomena. In "Killing the Willing: 'Volunteers,' Suicide and Competency" (*Michigan Law Review*, vol. 103, no. 5, March 2005), Blume notes that 106 of the 885 executions that took place in the United States between 1977 and 2003 involved volunteers. He presents data indicating that at least 93 (88% of the total) of the volunteers suffered from "documented mental illness or severe substance-abuse disorders."

The DPIC lists in "Information on Defendants Who Were Executed since 1976 and Designated as 'Volunteers'" (July 29, 2013, http://www.deathpenaltyinfo.org/information-defendants-who-were-executed-1976-and-designated-volunteers) that 151 inmates executed between 1976 and July 2013 had reportedly waived their appeals rights. Texas had the highest number (27), followed by Nevada (11), Florida (9), and South Carolina (8).

In "Death Row Inmates' Desire to Die Renews Debate" (LATimes.com, November 25, 2011), Carol J. Williams relates the story of the California death row inmate Gerald Frank Stanley, who was sentenced to death in 1984 for the 1980 murder of his fourth wife, Cindy Stanley. At the time, he was on parole for the 1975 murder of his second wife, Kathy Stanley. Gerald Stanley is also suspected, but was never charged, in the 1980 disappearance of his third wife, Dianna Stanley, and the 1980 murder of Cheryl Renee Wright, whom he allegedly picked up on a highway after she had a flat tire. Williams states that Gerald Stanley has long sought to end his appeals in order to hasten his execution. Stanley has offered to tell authorities the burial site of his third wife (Dianna) in exchange for a set execution date. Williams notes that Stanley is in poor physical health and has told authorities he deserves the death penalty for his crimes. Stanley's attorneys argue that he is "severely mentally disordered"; however, he was found mentally competent by a court in 2011. As of October 2013, Stanley remained on California's death row.

Clemency

If a convict exhausts all appeals and is still on death row, the only way the sentence can be altered is through the power of clemency. The power of clemency may rest solely with a state's governor, with a clemency board, or with the governor and a board of advisers. All states provide for clemency, which may take the form of a reprieve, a commutation, or a pardon. A reprieve, which typically involves a stay of execution, is just a temporary measure to allow further investigation of a case. A commutation involves the reduction of a criminal sentence after a criminal conviction. In the context of capital punishment, a commutation typically means replacing the death sentence with a lesser sentence, such as life without parole. As shown in Table 5.7, the BJS reports that 388 state and federal death penalty sentences were commuted between 1973 and 2011. Illinois had the most commutations (171), followed by Texas (55) and Ohio (20). Table 5.8 shows the number of commutations by year of sentencing. Most inmates who had their sentences commuted were sentenced to death from the 1970s through the 1990s.

Neither a reprieve nor a commutation removes a person's responsibility for the crime. A pardon, however, frees from punishment a person who has been convicted of a crime and removes his or her criminal record as if the conviction never happened. Pardons are generally only given if investigators can prove beyond any doubt that a death row inmate did not commit the crime of which he or she was convicted.

In "Clemency" (2013, http://www.deathpenaltyinfo.org/clemency), the DPIC reports that 273 clemencies were granted by states and the federal government "for humanitarian reasons" between 1976 and 2012.

The DPIC notes that humanitarian reasons include "doubts about the defendant's guilt or conclusions of the governor regarding the death penalty process." The vast majority (187) of the humanitarian-based clemencies occurred in Illinois. In 2003 the Illinois governor George Ryan (1934–) commuted the death sentences or pardoned all of the state's death row prisoners. However, capital punishment remained legal in Illinois and death sentences continued to be given out until 2011. That year, Illinois abolished the death penalty and commuted the sentences of its death row inmates to life in prison with no possibility of parole.

The DPIC reports that there were four humanitarian-reason clemencies in 2012: two in Ohio and one each in Delaware and Georgia.

It should be noted that death penalty sentences have also been commuted on technical or legal grounds, particularly following U.S. Supreme Court decisions ruling that certain practices are unconstitutional, namely the execution of the mentally retarded (2002) and minors (2005). The DPIC explains that commutations to lower sentences have also been granted by states for "judicial expediency," for example, to avoid capital case retrials following the overturning of death sentences by appeals

TABLE 5.7

Number of sentences commuted by jurisdiction, 1973–2011

Jurisdiction	Number of removals, 1973–2011
	Sentence commuted
U.S. total	**388**
Federal	1
Alabama	2
Arizona	7
Arkansas	2
California	15
Colorado	1
Connecticut	0
Delaware	0
Florida	18
Georgia	9
Idaho	3
Illinois	171
Indiana	6
Kansas	0
Kentucky	2
Louisiana	7
Maryland	4
Massachusetts	2
Mississippi	0
Missouri	3
Montana	2
Nebraska	2
Nevada	4
New Hampshire	0
New Jersey	8
New Mexico	5
New York	0
North Carolina	8
Ohio	20
Oklahoma	4
Oregon	0
Pennsylvania	6
Rhode Island	0
South Carolina	3
South Dakota	0
Tennessee	6
Texas	55
Utah	1
Virginia	11
Washington	0
Wyoming	0

Note: In 1972, the U.S. Supreme Court invalidated capital punishment statutes in several states (*Furman v. Georgia*, 408 U.S. 238 (1972)), effecting a moratorium on executions. Executions resumed in 1977 when the Supreme Court found that revisions to several state statutes had effectively addressed the issues previously held unconstitutional (*Gregg v. Georgia*, 428 U.S. 153 (1976) and its companion cases). Some inmates executed since 1977 or currently under sentence of death were sentenced prior to 1977. For persons sentenced to death more than once, the numbers are based on the most recent death sentence.

SOURCE: Adapted from Tracy L. Snell, "Table 17. Number Sentenced to Death and Number of Removals, by Jurisdiction and Reason for Removal, 1973–2011," in *Capital Punishment, 2011—Statistical Tables*, U.S. Department of Justice, Office of Justice Programs, Bureau of Justice Statistics, July 16, 2013, http://www.bjs.gov/content/pub/pdf/cp11st.pdf (accessed September 3, 2013)

TABLE 5.8

Number of sentences commuted by year of sentencing, 1973–2011

Year of sentence	Number of prisoners removed from under sentence of death
	Appeal or higher courts overturned
	Sentence commuted
Total, 1973–2011	**388**
1973	9
1974	22
1975	21
1976	15
1977	7
1978	8
1979	6
1980	12
1981	12
1982	12
1983	15
1984	13
1985	14
1986	14
1987	9
1988	14
1989	13
1990	18
1991	11
1992	21
1993	15
1994	15
1995	14
1996	15
1997	11
1998	9
1999	10
2000	9
2001	2
2002	5
2003	1
2004	5
2005	1
2006	3
2007	2
2008	3
2009	1
2010	1
2011	0

Note: In 1972, the U.S. Supreme Court invalidated capital punishment statutes in several states (*Furman v. Georgia*, 408 U.S. 238 (1972)), effecting a moratorium on executions. Executions resumed in 1977 when the Supreme Court found that revisions to several state statutes had effectively addressed the issues previously held unconstitutional (*Gregg v. Georgia*, 428 U.S. 153 (1976) and its companion cases). Some inmates executed since 1977 or currently under sentence of death were sentenced prior to 1977. For persons sentenced to death more than once, the numbers are based on the most recent death sentence.

SOURCE: Adapted from Tracy L. Snell, "Table 16. Prisoners Sentenced to Death and the Outcome of Sentence, by Year of Sentencing, 1973–2011," in *Capital Punishment, 2011—Statistical Tables*, U.S. Department of Justice, Office of Justice Programs, Bureau of Justice Statistics, July 16, 2013, http://www.bjs.gov/content/pub/pdf/cp11st.pdf (accessed September 3, 2013)

courts. The DPIC describes these commutations as being for the "state's convenience."

State Death Penalty Methods

Snell indicates in *Capital Punishment, 2011—Statistical Tables* that 36 states used lethal injection as the primary method of execution in 2011. (See Table 5.9.) Some states also authorized one or more alternative methods: electrocution, lethal gas, hanging, or death by firing squad. According to Snell, the choice of method is generally left up to the condemned, depending on when the sentence was imposed. Note that Connecticut and Maryland abolished capital sentencing in 2012 and 2013, respectively, but already condemned inmates remain under sentence of death.

As explained in Chapter 3, a national moratorium (suspension) of executions was triggered in 2007, when

TABLE 5.9

Execution methods by state, 2011

Jurisdiction	Lethal injection	Electrocution	Lethal gas	Hanging	Firing squad
Total	**36**	**8**	**3**	**3**	**2**
Alabama	X	X			
Arizona[a]	X		X		
Arkansas[b]	X	X			
California	X				
Colorado	X				
Connecticut	X				
Delaware[c]	X			X	
Florida	X	X			
Georgia	X				
Idaho	X				
Indiana	X				
Kansas	X				
Kentucky[d]	X	X			
Louisiana	X				
Maryland	X				
Mississippi	X				
Missouri	X		X		
Montana	X				
Nebraska	X				
Nevada	X				
New Hampshire[e]	X			X	
New Mexico[f]	X				
New York	X				
North Carolina	X				
Ohio	X				
Oklahoma[g]	X	X			X
Oregon	X				
Pennsylvania	X				
South Carolina	X	X			
South Dakota	X				
Tennessee[h]	X	X			
Texas	X				
Utah[i]	X				X
Virginia	X	X			
Washington	X			X	
Wyoming[j]	X		X		

[a]Authorizes lethal injection for persons sentenced after November 15, 1992; inmates sentenced before that date may select lethal injection or gas.
[b]Authorizes lethal injection for inmates whose offense occurred on or after July 4, 1983; inmates whose offense occurred before that date may select lethal injection or electrocution.
[c]Authorizes hanging if lethal injection is held to be unconstitutional by a court of competent jurisdiction.
[d]Authorizes lethal injection for persons sentenced on or after March 31, 1998; inmates sentenced before that date may select lethal injection or electrocution.
[e]Authorizes hanging only if lethal injection cannot be given.
[f]Authorizes lethal injection for inmates whose capital offense occurred prior to July 1, 2009.
[g]Authorizes electrocution if lethal injection is held to be unconstitutional, and firing squad if both lethal injection and electrocution are held to be unconstitutional.
[h]Authorizes lethal injection for inmates whose capital offense occurred after December 31, 1998; inmates whose offense occurred before that date may select electrocution by written waiver.
[i]Authorizes firing squad if lethal injection is held unconstitutional. Inmates who selected execution by firing squad prior to May 3, 2004, may still be entitled to execution by that method.
[j]Authorizes lethal gas if lethal injection is held to be unconstitutional.
CFR = Code of Federal Regulations.
USC = United States Code.
Note: The method of execution of federal prisoners is lethal injection, pursuant to 28 CFR, Part 26. For offenses prosecuted under the federal Violent Crime Control and Law Enforcement Act of 1994, the execution method is that of the state in which the conviction took place (18 U.S.C. 3596).

SOURCE: Tracy L. Snell, "Table 2. Method of Execution, by State, 2011," in *Capital Punishment, 2011—Statistical Tables*, U.S. Department of Justice, Office of Justice Programs, Bureau of Justice Statistics, July 16, 2013, http://www.bjs.gov/content/pub/pdf/cp11st.pdf (accessed September 3, 2013)

the U.S. Supreme Court agreed to hear a case challenging the constitutionality of the three-drug protocol that was used for lethal injection in Kentucky. In 2008 the court ruled in *Baze v. Rees* (553 U.S. ___ [2008]) that the protocol is constitutional. At that time the protocol used by Kentucky, and by many other states, was sodium thiopental (a sedative), followed by pancuronium bromide (a paralyzing agent) and potassium chloride (to stop the heart).

In May 2008 executions resumed. According to Snell, 37 inmates were executed throughout the remain-

der of that year. Another 52 executions were carried out in 2009, 46 in 2010, and 43 in 2011. As shown in Figure 5.3, 43 executions during 2012 took place in nine states: Texas (15), Mississippi (6), Oklahoma (6), Arizona (6), Ohio (3), Florida (3), South Dakota (2), Delaware (1), and Idaho (1).

Since 2009 a series of events have forced death penalty states to reconsider their lethal injection drug protocols. First, the producer of sodium thiopental, Hospira Inc., stopped producing the drug. Kevin Sack reports in "Executions in Doubt in Fallout over Drug"

FIGURE 5.3

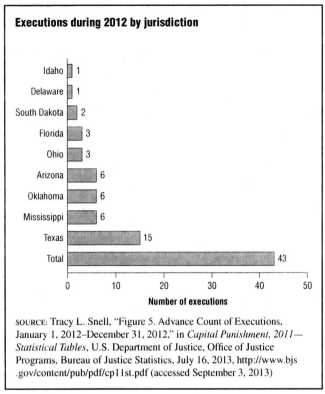

Executions during 2012 by jurisdiction

Jurisdiction	Number of executions
Idaho	1
Delaware	1
South Dakota	2
Florida	3
Ohio	3
Arizona	6
Oklahoma	6
Mississippi	6
Texas	15
Total	43

Number of executions

SOURCE: Tracy L. Snell, "Figure 5. Advance Count of Executions, January 1, 2012–December 31, 2012," in *Capital Punishment, 2011—Statistical Tables*, U.S. Department of Justice, Office of Justice Programs, Bureau of Justice Statistics, July 16, 2013, http://www.bjs.gov/content/pub/pdf/cp11st.pdf (accessed September 3, 2013)

(NYTimes.com, March 16, 2011) that the company ceased production because it was unable to obtain one of the ingredients used to produce the drug. Also in 2009, the execution of the convicted murderer Romell Broom (1956–) went awry. Ohio executioners tried and failed 18 times, over a period of two hours, to find a suitable vein in which to deliver lethal drugs to Broom. Governor Ted Strickland (1941–) halted the execution and imposed a temporary moratorium on further executions in Ohio until alternative injection protocols could be developed. Broom remained on death row in October 2013. In "Capital Punishment in Ohio" (May 1, 2013, http://drc.ohio .gov/Public/capital.htm), the Ohio Department of Rehabilitation and Correction notes that in November 2009 Ohio "became the first state in the country to adopt a one-drug protocol for lethal injections." Sodium thiopental alone was used that month to execute Kenneth Biros (1958–2009), a man on death row for the 1991 murder of Tami L. Engstrom.

In January 2011 Hospira announced in the press release "Hospira Statement Regarding Pentothal (Sodium Thiopental) Market Exit" http://phx.cor porate-ir.net/phoenix.zhtml?c=175550&p=irol-news Article&ID=1518610&highlight=) that it would not resume production of sodium thiopental. The company noted that it had intended to produce the drug at a plant in Italy; however, Italian authorities disapproved of the drug's use in capital punishment in the United States. Fearing liability issues, the company decided to exit the

market completely. By this time state correctional officials were running low on supplies of sodium thiopental. According to Sack, the typical shelf life of the drug is approximately two years.

In March 2011 the Drug Enforcement Administration (DEA) seized a shipment of sodium thiopental that Georgia correctional officials had imported from a distributor in England. Sack notes that the seizure was "presumably" spurred by a complaint that was filed with the U.S. attorney general Eric Holder (1951–) the previous month by John T. Bentivoglio, a lawyer representing an inmate on Georgia's death row. Bentivoglio alleged that Georgia did not have a federal license to import controlled substances. In "Seeking Execution Drug, States Cut Legal Corners" (NYTimes.com, April 13, 2011), John Schwartz reports that by 2011 lawsuits had been filed "in many states" over concerns about how correctional officials were obtaining the drug. According to Schwartz, death penalty states had established a "legally questionable swap club," in which states with ample supplies of the drug shared it with states that were running low. Meanwhile, some states allegedly continued to import the drug from foreign distributors.

Katie Zezima indicates in "2 More States Turn over a Drug Used in Executions" (NYTimes.com, April 1, 2011) that in April 2011 Tennessee and Kentucky relinquished their supplies of sodium thiopental to the DEA. Zezima notes that both states, along with California and Arizona, were believed to have obtained the drug from foreign suppliers. She also reports that the British government had instituted a ban on exporting drugs to the United States that will be used in executions.

As supplies of sodium thiopental dwindled in late 2010 and early 2011 some states turned to an alternative sedative: pentobarbital. According to the Ohio Department of Rehabilitation and Correction, the state announced in January 2011 a new one-drug protocol for executions using pentobarbital. That drug was subsequently used in March 2011 to execute Johnnie Baston for the 1994 murder of Chong-Hoon Mah. Baston is believed to be the first death row inmate executed using a single dose of pentobarbital.

In July 2011 the Danish pharmaceutical company Lundbeck announced distribution restrictions in the United States for its sodium pentobarbital drug Nembutal. In "Danish Company Blocks Sale of Drug for U.S. Executions" (NYTimes.com, July 1, 2011), David Jolly reports that the company issued a statement saying that it "adamantly opposes the distressing misuse of our product in capital punishment." Lundbeck said it will implement ordering and delivery restrictions that are intended to prevent prisons in death penalty states from obtaining the drug.

The DPIC indicates in "Execution List 2013" (http://www.deathpenaltyinfo.org/execution-list-2013) that between January and September 2013, 25 inmates were executed. One, in Virginia, was electrocuted. The other 24 inmates were executed using lethal injection—15 with pentobarbital only and nine with a 3-drug cocktail including pentobarbital.

In "Europe Pushes to Keep Lethal Injection Drugs from U.S. Prisons" (BusinessWeek.com, February 7, 2013), Makkiko Kitamura and Adi Narayan indicate that Missouri decided in 2012 to use a different sedative, propofol, for its future executions. However, the health care company Fresenius Kabi announced that it would not sell the drug to U.S. departments of correction. Allen Nicklasson, who was sentenced to death for the 1994 murder of Richard Drummond, was scheduled for execution in October 2013. In early October 2013 the Missouri governor Jay Nixon (1956–) delayed Nicklasson's execution due to concerns about the state's lethal injection protocol. According to the article "New Execution Date Set for Mo. Inmate Allen Nicklasson" (Associated Press, November 8, 2013), the European producers of propofol had threatened to cut off supplies to the United States of the widely used anesthetic if there was a chance it would be used in executions. In response, the Missouri Department of Corrections switched its execution protocol to pentobarbital and rescheduled Nicklasson's execution for December 11, 2013.

In "Death Penalty in Flux" (2013, http://www.death penaltyinfo.org/death-penalty-flux), the DPIC notes that as of October 2013, several states, including California, were delaying executions due to drug shortages, court challenges to new drug protocols, or related lethal injection issues.

One area of contention has been the use of compounding pharmacies to prepare the needed drugs. The U.S. Food and Drug Administration (FDA) explains in "Pharmacy Compounding" (November 11, 2013, http://www.fda.gov/drugs/GuidanceComplianceRegula toryInformation/PharmacyCompounding/) that "pharmacy compounding is a practice in which a licensed pharmacist combines, mixes, or alters ingredients in response to a prescription to create a medication tailored to the medical needs of an individual patient. Pharmacy compounding, if done properly, can serve an important public health need if a patient cannot be treated with an FDA-approved medication." In "Texas Refuses to Give Back Lethal Drugs, Plans to Proceed with Execution" (FOXNews.com, October 9, 2013), Barnini Chakraborty notes that in 2013 Texas purchased pentobarbital from a compounding pharmacy within the state to use in upcoming executions. The pharmacy owner complained that his business' role was leaked by state officials, and he was subjected to protests, media attention, and "hate

calls." The owner requested the drugs be returned, but the state refused to do so. In October 2013 compounded pentobarbital was used to execute Michael Yowell, who had been sentenced to death in 1998 for killing his parents, John and Carol Yowell, and blowing up their house. His grandmother, Viola Davis, was killed by injuries she received during the blast.

In May 2013 Georgia (http://www.legis.ga.gov/Legis lation/en-US/display/20132014/HB/122) enacted a new law making confidential any "identifying information" of persons or entities that participate in executions or manufacture, supply, compound, or prescribe "the drugs, medical supplies, or medical equipment utilized in the execution of a death sentence." The law states "such information shall be classified as a confidential state secret." In July 2013 lawyers for condemned inmate Warren Lee Hill convinced a Georgia appeals court to delay his pending execution over concerns about the new law. Hill was sentenced to death for murdering fellow inmate Joseph Handspike in 1990. At the time, Hill was serving a life sentence for the 1985 murder of his girlfriend, Myra Wright. Claire Simms notes in "State Appeal Delayed in Hill Execution" (GPB.org, July 19, 2013) that the state acknowledges that it obtained pentobarbital from a compounding pharmacy, but refuses to divulge the source. Hill's lawyer argued successfully to an appeals court that "without information about who produced the drug, there is no way for Hill to research potential problems with the lab or the process used to create the pentobarbital." According to Simms, Hill's lawyer also claims that the new Georgia law violates the state's separation of powers, because one branch of government—the executive branch, acting through the department of corrections—is concealing information from the judicial branch. As of October 2013, the challenges to the new law had not been heard in court.

Capital punishment advocates complain that the controversy over lethal injection drugs is a stalling tactic by abolitionists. In "Death Row Improvises, Lacking Lethal Mix" (NYTimes.com, August 18, 2013), Rick Lyman quotes Kent Scheideggar of the Criminal Justice Legal Foundation (an organization that supports capital punishment) as saying, "It's an artificially created problem. There is no difficultly in using a sedative such as pentobarbital. It's done every day in animal shelters throughout the country. But what we have is a conspiracy to choke off capital punishment by limiting the availability of drugs."

Witnesses to State Executions

Death penalty states have statutes or policies (or both) that specify which witnesses may be present during an execution. Witnesses usually include prison officials, physicians, the condemned inmate's relatives, the vic-

TABLE 5.10

Federal capital offenses, 2011

Statute	Description
8 U.S.C. 1342	Murder related to the smuggling of aliens.
18 U.S.C. 32–34	Destruction of aircraft, motor vehicles, or related facilities resulting in death.
18 U.S.C. 36	Murder committed during a drug-related drive-by shooting.
18 U.S.C. 37	Murder committed at an airport serving international civil aviation.
18 U.S.C. 115(b)(3) [by cross-reference to 18 U.S.C. 1111]	Retaliatory murder of a member of the immediate family of law enforcement officials.
18 U.S.C. 241, 242, 245, 247	Civil rights offenses resulting in death.
18 U.S.C. 351 [by cross-reference to 18 U.S.C. 1111]	Murder of a member of Congress, an important executive official, or a Supreme Court Justice.
18 U.S.C. 794	Espionage.
18 U.S.C. 844(d), (f), (i)	Death resulting from offenses involving transportation of explosives, destruction of government property, or destruction of property related to foreign or interstate commerce.
18 U.S.C. 924(i)	Murder committed by the use of a firearm during a crime of violence or a drug-trafficking crime.
18 U.S.C. 930	Murder committed in a federal government facility.
18 U.S.C. 1091	Genocide.
18 U.S.C. 1111	First-degree murder.
18 U.S.C. 1114	Murder of a federal judge or law enforcement official.
18 U.S.C. 1116	Murder of a foreign official.
18 U.S.C. 1118	Murder by a federal prisoner.
18 U.S.C. 1119	Murder of a U.S. national in a foreign country.
18 U.S.C. 1120	Murder by an escaped federal prisoner already sentenced to life imprisonment.
18 U.S.C. 1121	Murder of a state or local law enforcement official or other person aiding in a federal investigation; murder of a state correctional officer.
18 U.S.C. 1201	Murder during a kidnapping.
18 U.S.C. 1203	Murder during a hostage taking.
18 U.S.C. 1503	Murder of a court officer or juror.
18 U.S.C. 1512	Murder with the intent of preventing testimony by a witness, victim, or informant.
18 U.S.C. 1513	Retaliatory murder of a witness, victim, or informant.
18 U.S.C. 1716	Mailing of injurious articles with intent to kill or resulting in death.
18 U.S.C. 1751 [by cross-reference to 18 U.S.C. 1111]	Assassination or kidnapping resulting in the death of the president or vice president.
18 U.S.C. 1958	Murder for hire.
18 U.S.C. 1959	Murder involved in a racketeering offense.
18 U.S.C. 1992	Willful wrecking of a train resulting in death.
18 U.S.C. 2113	Bank robbery-related murder or kidnapping.
18 U.S.C. 2119	Murder related to a carjacking.
18 U.S.C. 2245	Murder related to rape or child molestation.
18 U.S.C. 2251	Murder related to sexual exploitation of children.
18 U.S.C. 2280	Murder committed during an offense against maritime navigation.
18 U.S.C. 2281	Murder committed during an offense against a maritime fixed platform.
18 U.S.C. 2332	Terrorist murder of a U.S. national in another country.
18 U.S.C. 2332a	Murder by the use of a weapon of mass destruction.
18 U.S.C. 2340	Murder involving torture.
18 U.S.C. 2381	Treason.
21 U.S.C. 848(e)	Murder related to a continuing criminal enterprise or related murder of a federal, state, or local law enforcement officer.
49 U.S.C. 1472–1473	Death resulting from aircraft hijacking.

Note: U.S.C = United States Code.

SOURCE: Tracy L. Snell, "Table 3. Federal Capital Offenses, 2011," in *Capital Punishment, 2011—Statistical Tables*, U.S. Department of Justice, Office of Justice Programs, Bureau of Justice Statistics, July 16, 2013, http://www.bjs.gov/content/pub/pdf/cp11st.pdf (accessed September 3, 2013)

tim's relatives, spiritual advisers, selected state citizens, and reporters. In celebrated cases, however, such as that of Julius Rosenberg (1918–1953) and Ethel Rosenberg (1915–1953), who were convicted spies, the notorious California killer Caryl Chessman (1921–1960), and the convicted Oklahoma City bomber Timothy McVeigh (1968–2001), the witnesses made up a larger group.

FEDERAL DEATH PENALTY LAWS

In modern times, capital punishment has generally fallen under the states' purview. Each year, the federal government pursues the death penalty in far fewer cases than most states with death penalty statutes. The reason for this is simple: Most crimes are state crimes. Generally

speaking, the federal government is only involved in prosecuting a relatively small number of crimes—those that cross state boundaries, those that are committed on federal property, or those that affect federal officials or the working of the federal government. Table 5.10 lists federal capital offenses by law as of 2011.

The federal government, however, has been executing criminals almost since its formation. In 1790 Thomas Bird became the first inmate to be executed under the federal death penalty. He was hanged in Maine for murder. In "Federal Executions 1927–2003" (2013, http://www.deathpenaltyinfo.org/federal-executions-1927-2003), the DPIC reports that 34 people were executed by the federal government between 1927 and 1963. On March

15, 1963, Victor Feguer was hanged in Iowa for kidnapping and murder. This was the last execution by the federal government until nearly 40 years later.

In 1988 Congress enacted the first of several laws that broadened the scope of the federal death penalty:

- Anti-Drug Abuse Act (1988)

- Violent Crime Control and Law Enforcement Act (1994; also known as the Federal Death Penalty Act)

- Antiterrorism and Effective Death Penalty Act (1996)

- Terrorist Bombings Convention Implementation Act (2002)

In addition, the USA Patriot Act of 2001 and the USA Patriot Act Improvement and Reauthorization Act of 2005 expanded the list of terrorist acts deemed federal crimes that could be subject to the death penalty.

In 2001 the federal government carried out its first execution in decades. Timothy McVeigh was sentenced to death for conspiracy and murder in 1997 for the bombing of the Alfred P. Murrah Federal Building in Oklahoma City, Oklahoma, on April 19, 1995, which killed 168 people. On June 11, 2001, his execution was carried out. Eight days later, on June 19, 2001, the Texas drug boss Juan Raul Garza became the second federal prisoner to be executed since 1963. He was the first person to be executed under the Anti-Drug Abuse Act of 1988, for murders resulting from a drug enterprise. Garza received the death sentence in 1993 for the 1990 murders of three associates: Thomas Rumbo, Erasmo de la Fuente, and Gilberto Matos.

Louis Jones Jr., a retired soldier, was executed by the U.S. government on March 18, 2003. In 1995 Jones was convicted of killing a female soldier. He admitted to kidnapping Tracie Joy McBride from an air force base in Texas. The federal government prosecuted Jones because his crime originally occurred at a U.S. military facility.

As of October 2013, Jones was the last person to have been executed by the federal government. All three of the federal executions that took place after 1963 occurred during President George W. Bush's (1946–) first administration (January 2001 to January 2005). No executions were carried out during Bush's second administration (January 2005 to January 2009). Likewise, as of October 2013, no executions had been conducted under the first or second administrations of Barack Obama (1961–), who first took office in January 2009.

The federal government's death row and execution chamber are located in Terre Haute, Indiana. According to the DPIC in "Federal Death Row Prisoners" (http://www.deathpenaltyinfo.org/federal-death-row-prisoners),

59 inmates were on federal death row as of September 18, 2013.

Federal Capital Punishment in Non–death Penalty States

The federal government has sought the death penalty for defendants who committed federal crimes in states that do not use capital punishment. According to the DPIC, in "Federal Death Row Prisoners" as of September 18, 2013, seven of the inmates on federal death row had been sentenced for crimes that occurred in states that did not have the death penalty: two in Iowa and one each in Massachusetts, Michigan, New York, North Dakota, and Vermont.

In 2011 the Rhode Island governor Lincoln D. Chafee (1953–) made national headlines when he refused to turn over to federal authorities a defendant who was charged with killing a man at a Rhode Island bank. Federal authorities have jurisdiction over crimes at federally insured banks. In "R.I. Aims to Block Death-Penalty Trial" (Boston.com, July 28, 2011), Milton J. Valencia reports that Jason W. Pleau murdered David M. Main in September 2010 and agreed to plead guilty to the murder in state court in exchange for a life sentence without parole. Rhode Island does not have the death penalty. In June 2011 Chafee refused to relinquish custody of Pleau to federal authorities to face possible capital charges for the murder. In the editorial "Lincoln D. Chafee: My Pleau Stand Affirms Core R.I. Values" (ProvidenceJournal.com, August 24, 2011), Chafee acknowledges that Pleau is "a career criminal with an extensive record of deplorable acts," but argues that "this does not justify the abandonment of Rhode Island's long-standing abolition of capital punishment." In July 2013 the tug-of-war was finally resolved when the federal government accepted a guilty plea from Pleau in exchange for dropping its pursuit of the death penalty against him.

U.S. MILITARY DEATH PENALTY LAWS

The U.S. military has its own death penalty law: the Uniform Code of Military Justice (UCMJ) found under U.S. Code, Title 10, Chapter 47. Lethal injection is the method of execution. For crimes that occurred on or after November 17, 1997, the UCMJ provides the alternative sentence of life without the possibility of parole. As commander in chief, the president of the United States can write regulations and procedures to implement the UCMJ provisions. The military needs the president's approval to implement a death sentence.

The first U.S. soldier to be executed since the Civil War (1861–1865) was Private Edward Slovik of the U.S. Army. In 1944 he was charged with desertion while assigned to the European theater during World War II

(1939–45). Even though Slovik was just one of hundreds of U.S. soldiers who were convicted of desertion and sentenced to death, he was the only one executed. It is believed that, among other reasons, the military wanted to use his case as a deterrent to future desertions. Slovik died by firing squad on January 31, 1945, in France. Since then no other soldier has been executed for desertion. The last military execution occurred on April 13, 1961, when Private John A. Bennett of the U.S. Army was hanged for the 1955 rape and attempted murder of an 11-year-old girl in Austria.

The military death penalty received little notice until 2008, when President Bush signed a death warrant for Ronald Gray (1966–), a former army private convicted of conducting a murderous crime spree during the late 1980s. As explained by the article "Bush Approves Execution of American Soldier Ronald Gray" (TheTimes.co.uk, July 29, 2008), Gray was first convicted in North Carolina, because his crimes occurred in Fayetteville, near Fort Bragg, the army base at which Gray was stationed. He received eight life sentences in exchange for a guilty plea for raping and murdering Kimberly Anne Ruggles and Laura Lee Vickery Clay and raping and attempting to murder another woman. In 1988 Gray was found guilty in a court-martial (military trial) for the same crimes and was sentenced to death. Only days before his scheduled execution date in December 2008, he received a stay of execution from a federal judge to allow more time for appeals in the case. As of October 2013, a new execution date had not been set for Gray.

In "The U.S. Military Death Penalty" (2013, http://www.deathpenaltyinfo.org/us-military-death-penalty), the DPIC reports that there were five men under military sentence of death as of October 2013. The most recent addition was Nidal Malik Hasan (1970–), a U.S. Army major convicted of killing 13 people during a shooting rampage at Fort Hood, an army base near Killeen, Texas. As reported by NPR in "Fort Hood Shooter Sentenced to Death Penalty" (NPR.org, August 28, 2013), Hasan admitted to the murders, which he said he committed to protect Taliban fighters from U.S. forces in Afghanistan. Hasan was sentenced to death on August 28, 2013.

CHAPTER 6
STATISTICS: DEATH SENTENCES, CAPITAL CASE COSTS, AND EXECUTIONS

STATISTICAL SOURCES

On a nationwide basis there are three primary sources of statistical information regarding death sentences, inmates on death row, and executions. The first is the Bureau of Justice Statistics (BJS), a division of the Office of Justice Programs under the U.S. Department of Justice (DOJ). Since 1993 the BJS has published an annual report titled *Capital Punishment* (http://www.bjs.gov/index.cfm?ty=tp&tid=18) that summarizes data collected by the U.S. Census Bureau from state correctional offices as part of the National Prisoner Statistics program. The reports for 1993 through 2005 are available in both paper and electronic format and include detailed information and data analysis. The reports for 2006 through 2011 (the most recent available as of October 2013) are electronic versions only and include a limited number of statistical tables with no detailed analysis. *Capital Punishment, 2011—Statistical Tables* (July 2013, http://www.bjs.gov/content/pub/pdf/cp11st.pdf) by Tracy L. Snell of the BJS provides statistics on death row inmates and executions conducted through 2011 and preliminary information regarding executions performed during 2012. In some cases in this chapter, the BJS statistics are updated with data for 2012–13 that were collected from two other notable sources: the Death Penalty Information Center (DPIC) and the Criminal Justice Project of the National Association for the Advancement of Colored People's Legal Defense and Educational Fund Inc. (LDF). The DPIC and the LDF are opposed to capital punishment.

The DPIC is a private nonprofit organization that provides an array of news, statistics, and other information about capital punishment and the inmates on death row. Since 1996 the DPIC has published in December an annual report known as its yearend report (http://www.deathpenaltyinfo.org/reports#YER). As of September 2013, the most recent report available was *The Death Penalty in 2012: Year End Report* (December 2012, http://deathpenaltyinfo.org/documents/2012YearEnd.pdf).

On its website, the LDF (2013, http://naacpldf.org/about-ldf) calls itself "America's premier legal organization fighting for racial justice." Since 2000 the organization's Criminal Justice Project has published a series of reports titled *Death Row U.S.A* (http://naacpldf.org/death-row-usa) that list the names of all individuals known to be on death row or to have been executed. The race and gender of death row defendants is included. Information is also provided on the race and gender of executed defendants and their victims on a state-by-state basis. As of September 2013, the most recent report available was *Death Row U.S.A.: Winter 2013* (May 1, 2013, http://www.naacpldf.org/files/publications/DRUSA_Winter_2013.pdf) by Deborah Fins.

DEATH ROW

The number of inmates on death row is constantly changing. New death sentences increase the number, but existing death sentences may be overturned during the appeals process. Commutations (replacement of a death sentence with a lesser sentence), pardons, executions, and deaths due to causes other than execution also reduce the number of prisoners on death row in any given year.

Figure 6.1 provides the status of the 8,300 persons sentenced to death in the United States between 1973 and 2011. As shown in Figure 6.1, 37% of the total were still under sentence of death at yearend 2011. Fifteen percent had been executed and 6% had died of causes other than execution. A small percentage (5%) had their sentences commuted, while less than 1% had been removed from death row for other reasons. More than one-third (37%) had their sentence or conviction overturned by appeals courts or other higher courts. A breakdown of the latter cases by year of sentencing is provided in Table 6.1.

FIGURE 6.1

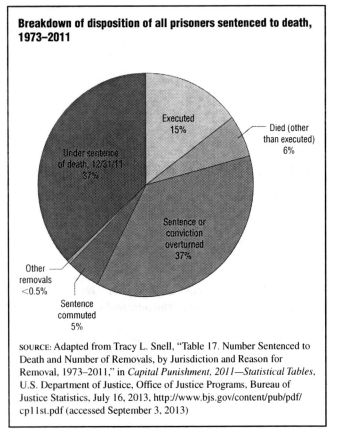

Breakdown of disposition of all prisoners sentenced to death, 1973–2011

Executed 15%

Died (other than executed) 6%

Under sentence of death, 12/31/11 37%

Sentence or conviction overturned 37%

Other removals <0.5%

Sentence commuted 5%

SOURCE: Adapted from Tracy L. Snell, "Table 17. Number Sentenced to Death and Number of Removals, by Jurisdiction and Reason for Removal, 1973–2011," in *Capital Punishment, 2011—Statistical Tables*, U.S. Department of Justice, Office of Justice Programs, Bureau of Justice Statistics, July 16, 2013, http://www.bjs.gov/content/pub/pdf/cp11st.pdf (accessed September 3, 2013)

TABLE 6.1

Prisoners removed from under sentence of death due to appeal or higher court decisions

| | Number of prisoners removed from under sentence of death | | |
| | Appeal or higher courts overturned— | | |
Year of sentence	Death penalty statute	Conviction	Sentence
Total, 1973–2011	522	863	1,674
1973	14	9	8
1974	65	15	30
1975	171	24	67
1976	136	17	42
1977	40	26	33
1978	21	36	65
1979	2	28	59
1980	4	30	52
1981	0	42	81
1982	0	40	84
1983	1	30	71
1984	2	46	75
1985	1	43	89
1986	1	51	69
1987	7	45	77
1988	1	35	74
1989	0	33	67
1990	2	36	57
1991	2	37	61
1992	0	27	55
1993	3	24	45
1994	10	35	56
1995	6	20	47
1996	4	21	63
1997	3	19	41
1998	4	22	46
1999	8	21	35
2000	4	12	32
2001	3	5	24
2002	3	3	18
2003	1	5	11
2004	1	5	13
2005	0	3	9
2006	0	7	5
2007	2	8	3
2008	0	3	8
2009	0	0	2
2010	0	0	0
2011	0	0	0

Note: In 1972, the U.S. Supreme Court invalidated capital punishment statutes in several states (*Furman v. Georgia*, 408 U.S. 238 (1972)), effecting a moratorium on executions. Executions resumed in 1977 when the Supreme Court found that revisions to several state statutes had effectively addressed the issues previously held unconstitutional (*Gregg v. Georgia*, 428 U.S. 153 (1976) and its companion cases). Some inmates executed since 1977 or currently under sentence of death were sentenced prior to 1977. For persons sentenced to death more than once, the numbers are based on the most recent death sentence.

SOURCE: Adapted from Tracy L. Snell, "Table 16. Prisoners Sentenced to Death and the Outcome of Sentence, by Year of Sentencing, 1973–2011," in *Capital Punishment, 2011—Statistical Tables*, U.S. Department of Justice, Office of Justice Programs, Bureau of Justice Statistics, July 16, 2013, http://www.bjs.gov/content/pub/pdf/cp11st.pdf (accessed September 3, 2013)

Overall, 522 removals were due to problematic death penalty statutes (laws). (See Table 6.1.) A flurry of U.S. Supreme Court cases during the 1970s and 1980s caused more than 400 prisoners sentenced during the 1970s to be removed from death row because the laws and procedures that resulted in their death sentences were found to be unconstitutional. Since that time few condemned inmates have left death row for this reason.

Table 6.1 shows that many more removals were the result of an appeals court overturning an individual's conviction (863) or sentence (1,674). A total of 2,537 inmates sentenced to death between 1973 and 2011 had their convictions or sentences overturned. The number of people removed from death row by judicial action is relatively low for people sentenced during the 21st century. This is likely due in part to the fact that the death penalty appeals process can take many years, even decades, to complete.

Death Row Demographics: Yearend 2011

As noted earlier, the BJS publication *Capital Punishment, 2011: Statistical Tables* provides statistics on death row inmates as of yearend 2011. Table 6.2 shows the breakdown of death row entries and exits during 2011 for the state and federal prison systems. At the end of 2010, 3,139 prisoners were under sentence of death. The vast majority of prisoners (3,082) were on state death rows.

Only 57 of the inmates were on federal death row. At that time there were 1,743 white inmates (55.5% of all death row inmates) on death row and 1,309 African American inmates (41.7%). The other 87 inmates on death row at that time were of other races (2.8%).

As shown in Table 6.2, 80 new prisoners under sentence of death were received by corrections officials during 2011. Another 94 prisoners were removed from

TABLE 6.2

Death row totals, yearend 2010 and yearend 2011

Region and jurisdiction	Prisoners under sentence of death, 12/31/10 Total[b]	Received under sentence of death, 2011 Total[b]	Removed from death row (excluding executions), 2011[a] Total[b]	Executed, 2011 Total[b]	Prisoners under sentence of death, 12/31/11 Total[b]
U.S. total	3,139	80	94	43	3,082
Federal[c]	57	0	1	0	56
State	3,082	80	93	43	3,026

[a]Includes 21 deaths from natural causes (4 in Florida; 3 in California; 2 each in Pennsylvania, Ohio, Alabama, North Carolina, and Oklahoma; and 1 each in Nebraska, Mississippi, Texas, and Arizona) and 3 deaths from suicide (1 each in Alabama, Florida, and California).
[b]Includes American Indians, Alaska Natives, Asians, Native Hawaiians, other Pacific Islanders, and Hispanic inmates for whom no other race was identified.
[c]Excludes persons held under armed forces jurisdiction with a military death sentence for murder.

SOURCE: Adapted from Tracy L. Snell, "Table 4. Prisoners under Sentence of Death, by Region, Jurisdiction, and Race, 2010 and 2011," in *Capital Punishment, 2011—Statistical Tables*, U.S. Department of Justice, Office of Justice Programs, Bureau of Justice Statistics, July 16, 2013, http://www.bjs.gov/content/pub/pdf/cp11st.pdf (accessed September 3, 2013)

death row for causes other than execution that year. Forty-three prisoners on death row were executed in 2011. As a result, there were 3,082 prisoners under sentence of death at yearend 2011. Nearly all (3,026) were on state death rows, while 56 were on federal death row. Overall, 1,703 (55.3%) of the condemned prisoners were white, and 1,288 (41.8%) were African American—a very similar ratio to that reported at the end of 2010. The other 91 (2.9%) death row prisoners at yearend 2011 were of other races.

ENTRIES DURING 2011. Table 6.3 provides additional details for the 80 inmates that entered death row during 2009. All of them were sentenced under state laws. The largest number (49 inmates, or 61.3% of the total) were sentenced in the South. The three southern states with the largest number of new death row entries were Florida (14 inmates), Alabama (nine inmates), and Texas (eight inmates). Each of the other regions sent far fewer numbers to death row in 2011. The West added 21 inmates, or 26.3% of the total. These prisoners were sentenced in California (10 inmates), Arizona (eight inmates), and Oregon (three inmates). The Midwest received six new inmates under sentence of death: three in Ohio, two in South Dakota, and one in Kansas. Only one northeastern state, Pennsylvania, added inmates to its death row during 2011, with four new entries.

REMOVALS DURING 2011. As shown in Table 6.4, in 2011 a total of 137 inmates were removed from death row. Of these inmates, 43 were executed. The largest numbers were in Texas (13), Alabama (6), and Ohio (5). Another 24 death row inmates died of causes other than execution in 2011. Overall, 70 people were removed from death row and remained alive. Courts overturned the death sentences of 43 people and the convictions of eight people. Nineteen inmates had their sentences commuted. Nearly all (15) of the inmates that received sentence commutations were in Illinois. As explained in Chapter 5, during 2011 the state abolished the death

penalty and changed the sentences of all of its death row inmates to life in prison with no parole.

Of the 70 inmates who were removed alive from death row in 2011, the largest number (29 inmates) were in the South, followed by 22 inmates in the Midwest, nine inmates in the Northeast (Pennsylvania only), nine inmates in the West, and one inmate in the federal system. (See Table 6.4.)

REGIONAL AND DEMOGRAPHIC CHARACTERISTICS. The BJS reports the regional makeup of the death row population at yearend 2011 in Table 6.5. The southern states had the largest number (1,595 prisoners, or 51.7% of the total), followed by the western states (989 prisoners, or 32.1% of the total), the Midwestern states (224 prisoners, or 7.3% of the total), the northeastern states (218 prisoners, or 7.1% of the total), and the federal system (56 prisoners or 1.8% of the total). Overall, the five states with the largest numbers of death row inmates at yearend 2011 were California (705 inmates), Florida (393 inmates), Texas (301 inmates), Pennsylvania (207 inmates), and Alabama (196 inmates).

Table 6.6 provides a summary of certain demographic information for the 3,082 state and federal prisoners under sentence of death at yearend 2011. Nearly all (98%) were male, whereas only 2% were female. Concerning the racial and ethnic background of the death row prisoners, 55.3% were white, 41.8% were African American, and 3% were of other races. A large majority (76.9%) of the inmates were non-Hispanic, while 12.6% were Hispanic. However, the Hispanic origin of 325 inmates on death row was unknown.

Table 6.6 also provides an age breakdown of condemned inmates at yearend 2011. The age category containing the largest percentage (17.9%) of inmates was 40 to 44 years old. The next two largest categories were inmates aged 45 to 49 years (16.8%) and inmates aged 35 to 39 years (14.8%). Overall, nearly half (49.5%) of

TABLE 6.3

Death sentences during 2011, by jurisdiction and race

Region and jurisdiction	Received under sentence of death, 2011		
	Total[a]	White[b]	Black[b]
U.S. total	80	39	37
Federal[c]	0	0	0
State	80	39	37
Northeast	4	2	2
Connecticut	0	0	0
New Hampshire	0	0	0
New York	0	0	0
Pennsylvania	4	2	2
Midwest	6	5	1
Illinois	0	0	0
Indiana	0	0	0
Kansas	1	1	0
Missouri	0	0	0
Nebraska	0	0	0
Ohio	3	2	1
South Dakota	2	2	0
South	49	19	29
Alabama	9	4	5
Arkansas	0	0	0
Delaware	2	0	2
Florida	14	4	9
Georgia	1	1	0
Kentucky	1	1	0
Louisiana	5	2	3
Maryland	0	0	0
Mississippi	1	0	1
North Carolina	3	1	2
Oklahoma	0	0	0
South Carolina	0	0	0
Tennessee	3	0	3
Texas	8	4	4
Virginia	2	2	0
West	21	13	5
Arizona	8	4	1
California	10	6	4
Colorado	0	0	0
Idaho	0	0	0
Montana	0	0	0
Nevada	0	0	0
New Mexico	0	0	0
Oregon	3	3	0
Utah	0	0	0
Washington	0	0	0
Wyoming	0	0	0

[a]Includes American Indians, Alaska Natives, Asians, Native Hawaiians, other Pacific Islanders, and Hispanic inmates for whom no other race was identified.

[b]Counts of white and black inmates include persons of Hispanic or Latino origin, which may differ from other tables in this report.

[c]Excludes persons held under armed forces jurisdiction with a military death sentence for murder.

SOURCE: Adapted from Tracy L. Snell, "Table 4. Prisoners under Sentence of Death, by Region, Jurisdiction, and Race, 2010 and 2011," in *Capital Punishment, 2011—Statistical Tables*, U.S. Department of Justice, Office of Justice Programs, Bureau of Justice Statistics, July 16, 2013, http://www.bjs.gov/content/pub/pdf/cp11st.pdf (accessed September 3, 2013)

all death row inmates were between the ages of 35 and 49 years. The mean (average) age of a death row inmate was 45 years.

The educational background of death row inmates at yearend 2011 is shown in Table 6.6. Only 7.6% of the prisoners had attended college. The largest percentage (34.6%) had graduated from high school or received a general equivalency diploma. Another 29.2% had attended at least some high school but had not graduated.

Roughly one out of 10 (11.3%) had no more than an eighth grade education. Note that the educational status of 534 death row inmates was unknown (17.3%).

Table 6.6 also provides information about the marital status of death row prisoners at yearend 2011. Nearly half (48.3%) had never been married. Less than one-fourth (19.7%) of the inmates on death row were married at the time. A slightly lower percentage (17.8%) were divorced or separated. Only 2.6% of the inmates were widowed. The BJS could not determine the marital status of 357 death row inmates (11.6%).

LENGTH OF TIME ON DEATH ROW. Table 5.5 in Chapter 5 and Figure 6.2 provides a breakdown of inmates sentenced to death by year of sentencing and by jurisdiction between 1974 and 2011. Out of the 3,082 total inmates on death row at yearend 2011, 139 inmates (4.5% of the total) had been sentenced to death between 1974 and 1983. The vast majority of these inmates were in California (48 inmates), Florida (36 inmates), and Texas (11 inmates). Another 371 inmates (12%) had been sentenced from 1984 through 1989, while 1,272 inmates (41.3%) had been sentenced to death during the 1990s, and 1,113 inmates (36.1%) entered death row during the first decade of the 21st century. The remaining 187 inmates (or 5.4% of the total) were sentenced to death in 2010 and 2011.

In comparing the two-year sentencing periods between 1974 and 2011, the largest addition of death row inmates occurred in 1998 and 1999, when 318 inmates were added. (See Figure 6.2.)

WOMEN ON DEATH ROW. According to the BJS, 62 women were on death row at yearend 2011. (See Table 6.7.) Forty-two (67.7%) of the women were white and 16 (25.8%) were African American. California (19) had the largest contingent of women under sentence of death, followed by Texas (9) and North Carolina (5).

HISPANICS ON DEATH ROW. As shown in Table 6.8, 387 Hispanics were on death row at yearend 2011. The largest number under state jurisdiction were in California (168), followed by Texas (89), Florida (33), Arizona (26), and Pennsylvania (20). Eight Hispanic inmates were reported on the federal death row.

CRIMINAL HISTORY. BJS statistics indicate that most prisoners on death row at yearend 2011 were already convicted felons when they were arrested for their capital crimes. (See Table 6.9.) Around two-thirds (66.6%) of the prisoners under sentence of death had prior felony convictions, and 8.4% of the death row inmates had prior homicide convictions. Over one-third of death row prisoners at yearend 2011 had committed their capital crime while they were in the criminal justice system in some manner: 16.1% were on parole, 10.9% were on probation, 8% had other charges pending, 3.4% committed their

TABLE 6.4

Prisoners removed from under sentence of death, by jurisdiction and method of removal, 2011

Region and jurisdiction	Total	Execution	Other death	Appeals or higher courts overturned Conviction	Appeals or higher courts overturned Sentence	Sentence commuted
U.S. total	**137**	**43**	**24**	**8**	**43**	**19**
Federal	1	0	0	0	1	0
State	136	43	24	8	42	19
Northeast	**11**	**0**	**2**	**0**	**9**	**0**
Pennsylvania	11	0	2	0	9	0
Midwest	**31**	**6**	**3**	**0**	**4**	**18**
Illinois	15	0	0	0	0	15
Indiana	1	0	0	0	1	0
Missouri	3	1	0	0	1	1
Nebraska	1	0	1	0	0	0
Ohio	11	5	2	0	2	2
South	**75**	**32**	**14**	**8**	**20**	**1**
Alabama	14	6	3	3	2	0
Arkansas	3	0	0	1	2	0
Delaware	2	1	0	1	0	0
Florida	12	2	5	0	5	0
Georgia	4	4	0	0	0	0
Kentucky	1	0	0	0	1	0
Louisiana	2	0	0	1	1	0
Mississippi	4	2	1	0	1	0
North Carolina	3	0	2	0	1	0
Oklahoma	7	2	2	1	2	0
South Carolina	3	1	0	0	2	0
Tennessee	2	0	0	0	1	1
Texas	16	13	1	0	2	0
Virginia	2	1	0	1	0	0
West	**19**	**5**	**5**	**0**	**9**	**0**
Arizona	11	4	1	0	6	0
California	5	0	4	0	1	0
Idaho	2	1	0	0	1	0
Oregon	1	0	0	0	1	0

SOURCE: Tracy L. Snell, "Table 9. Inmates Removed from under Sentence of Death, by Method of Removal, 2011," in *Capital Punishment, 2011—Statistical Tables*, U.S. Department of Justice, Office of Justice Programs, Bureau of Justice Statistics, July 16, 2013, http://www.bjs.gov/content/pub/pdf/cp11st.pdf (accessed September 3, 2013)

capital offenses while they were incarcerated, and 1.3% committed them after having escaped from incarceration. The remaining 59.9% had no particular legal status at the time they committed their capital crime. It should be noted that the legal history and status of 331 death row inmates at yearend 2011 could not be determined.

Historical Death Row Dispositions

As shown in Table 6.10, 8,300 inmates were under sentence of death at some time between 1973 and 2011 in the state and federal systems. The five jurisdictions with the largest numbers sentenced to death were:

- Texas—1,057 inmates (12.7% of the total)

- Florida—1,005 inmates (12.1% of the total)

- California—962 inmates (11.6% of the total)

- North Carolina—535 inmates (6.4% of the total)

- Alabama—429 inmates (5.2% of the total)

Together, these five states accounted for nearly half (48%, or 3,988) of the inmates sentenced to death during this period.

As shown in Table 6.10, 1,277 inmates were executed between 1973 and 2011. The jurisdictions with the largest numbers of inmates executed were:

- Texas—477 inmates (37.3% of the total)

- Virginia—109 inmates (8.5% of the total)

- Oklahoma—96 inmates (7.5% of the total)

- Florida—71 inmates (5.6% of the total)

- Missouri—68 inmates (5.3% of the total)

Together, these five states accounted for nearly two-thirds (64.3%, or 821) of the inmates executed.

A number of prisoners are removed from death row each year for reasons other than execution: resentencing, retrial, commutation, or death while awaiting execution (natural death, murder, or suicide). Of the 460 condemned inmate deaths due to reasons other than execution, the most deaths occurred in California (81), followed by Florida (63), Texas (42), Alabama (34), and Pennsylvania (28). (See Table 6.10.)

TABLE 6.5

Persons under sentence of death, by jurisdiction, December 31, 2011

Region and jurisdiction	Prisoners under sentence of death, 12/31/11		
	Total	White[a]	Black[a]
U.S. total	**3,082**	**1,703**	**1,288**
Federal[b]	56	28	27
State	3,026	1,675	1,261
Northeast	**218**	**81**	**128**
Connecticut	10	4	6
New Hampshire	1	0	1
New York	0	0	0
Pennsylvania	207	77	121
Midwest	**224**	**121**	**99**
Illinois	0	0	0
Indiana	12	9	3
Kansas	9	6	3
Missouri	46	26	20
Nebraska	11	7	2
Ohio	142	69	71
South Dakota	4	4	0
South	**1,595**	**853**	**717**
Alabama	196	99	96
Arkansas	39	14	24
Delaware	18	7	11
Florida	393	246	145
Georgia	96	50	46
Kentucky	34	29	5
Louisiana	87	31	55
Maryland	5	1	4
Mississippi	57	24	32
North Carolina	158	67	83
Oklahoma	63	33	26
South Carolina	52	22	30
Tennessee	87	49	36
Texas	301	176	120
Virginia	9	5	4
West	**989**	**620**	**317**
Arizona	130	100	17
California	705	413	257
Colorado	3	0	3
Idaho	13	13	0
Montana	2	2	0
Nevada	81	48	32
New Mexico	2	2	0
Oregon	36	30	4
Utah	8	6	1
Washington	8	5	3
Wyoming	1	1	0

[a]Counts of white and black inmates include persons of Hispanic or Latino origin, which may differ from other tables in this report.
[b]Excludes persons held under armed forces jurisdiction with a military death sentence for murder.

SOURCE: Adapted from Tracy L. Snell, "Table 4. Prisoners under Sentence of Death, by Region, Jurisdiction, and Race, 2010 and 2011," in *Capital Punishment, 2011—Statistical Tables*, U.S. Department of Justice, Office of Justice Programs, Bureau of Justice Statistics, July 16, 2013, http://www.bjs.gov/content/pub/pdf/cp11st.pdf (accessed September 3, 2013)

TABLE 6.6

Demographic characteristics of persons under sentence of death, December 31, 2011

Characteristic	Total yearend	%
Total inmates	**3,082**	**100%**
Sex		
Male	3,020	98.0%
Female	62	2.0%
Race[a]		
White	1,703	55.3%
Black	1,288	41.8%
All other races[b]	91	3.0%
Hispanic origin		
Hispanic	387	12.6%
Non-Hispanic	2,370	76.9%
Number unknown	325	10.5%
Age		
18–19	0	0%
20–24	28	0.9%
25–29	133	4.3%
30–34	338	11.0%
35–39	456	14.8%
40–44	553	17.9%
45–49	519	16.8%
50–54	454	14.7%
55–59	286	9.3%
60–64	197	6.4%
65 or older	118	3.8%
Mean age	45 yr	
Median age	45 yr	
Education		
8th grade or less	347	11.3%
9th–11th grade	899	29.2%
High school graduate/GED	1,067	34.6%
Any college	235	7.6%
Number unknown	534	17.3%
Marital status		
Married	608	19.7%
Divorced/separated	548	17.8%
Widowed	81	2.6%
Never married	1,488	48.3%
Number unknown	357	11.6%

[a]Counts for white and black inmates include persons of Hispanic or Latino origin, which may differ from other tables in this report.
[b]At yearend 2011, inmates in "all other races" consisted of 24 American Indians, 41 Asians, and 26 self-identified Hispanics.

SOURCE: Adapted from Tracy L. Snell, "Appendix Table 1. Number of Inmates under Sentence of Death, by Demographic Characteristics, 2011" and "Table 5. Demographic Characteristics of Prisoners under Sentence of Death, 2011," in *Capital Punishment, 2011—Statistical Tables*, U.S. Department of Justice, Office of Justice Programs, Bureau of Justice Statistics, July 16, 2013, http://www.bjs.gov/content/pub/pdf/cp11st.pdf (accessed September 3, 2013)

Table 6.10 notes that 3,059 death row inmates had their sentence or conviction overturned between 1973 and 2011. The largest numbers occurred in the following states:

- Florida—458 inmates (15% of the total)

- North Carolina—303 inmates (9.9% of the total)

- Ohio—182 inmates (5.9% of the total)

- Texas—181 inmates (5.9% of the total)

- Oklahoma—172 inmates (5.6% of the total)

Together, these five states accounted for 42.4% (1,296) of the total.

Also shown in Table 6.10 is a breakdown by jurisdiction of the 388 death sentences that were commuted between 1973 and 2011. Illinois had more than three times as many commutations (171) than any other single state, the result of commuting the sentences of all of its death row inmates in 2003 and again in 2011. Texas had

FIGURE 6.2

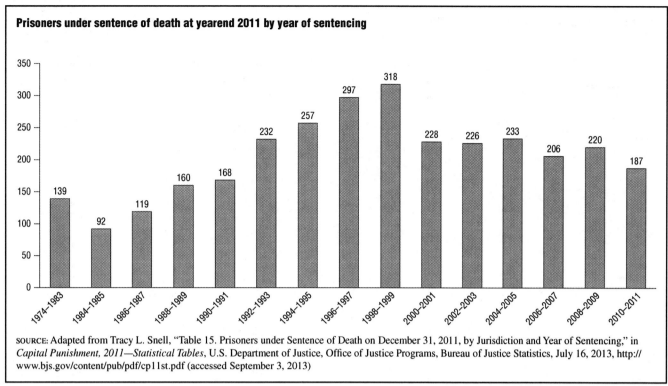

Prisoners under sentence of death at yearend 2011 by year of sentencing

SOURCE: Adapted from Tracy L. Snell, "Table 15. Prisoners under Sentence of Death on December 31, 2011, by Jurisdiction and Year of Sentencing," in *Capital Punishment, 2011—Statistical Tables*, U.S. Department of Justice, Office of Justice Programs, Bureau of Justice Statistics, July 16, 2013, http://www.bjs.gov/content/pub/pdf/cp11st.pdf (accessed September 3, 2013)

the next largest number of commutations, with 55, followed by Ohio (20), Florida (18), and California (15).

The overall breakdown by disposition of all 8,300 inmates sentenced to death between 1973 and 2011 is shown as of yearend 2011 in Figure 6.1:

- Executed—1,277 inmates (15.4%)

- Died due to causes other than execution—460 inmates (5.5%)

- Removed from death row due to appeals or higher court decisions—3,059 inmates (36.8%)

- Sentence commuted—388 inmates (4.7%)

- Other removals—34 inmates (less than 1%)

- Remained on death row—3,082 inmates (37%)

Death Row Population over Time

As shown in Figure 6.3, in 1953 the nation's death row population was only 131 inmates. By 1971 the number had grown to 642, before plummeting to 134 in 1973. This drop was due to the landmark 1972 decision by the U.S. Supreme Court, which ruled in *Furman v. Georgia* (408 U.S. 238) that the death penalty was unconstitutional as it had thus far been carried out. The ruling forced states to develop more uniform systems for applying capital punishment. During the late 1970s the death row population began to grow once more. It underwent a long and steady increase that persisted for more than two decades. In 2000 the number of prisoners under sentence

of death reached its highest level ever: 3,601 inmates. The number then dipped through 2011 to 3,082.

Death Row Demographics: January 2013

According to Fins, there were 3,125 inmates on death row as of January 1, 2013. The vast majority of the inmates (3,062, or 98% of the total) were male, whereas only 63 inmates (2% of the total) were female. Fins notes that 1,351 of the inmates (43.2% of the total) were white and 1,309 (41.9% of the total) were African American. Another 387 inmates (12.4% of the total) were Hispanic. Much smaller numbers were Asian American (44, or 1.4%) or Native American (33, or 1%). The race of one inmate was not known.

DEATH SENTENCES DECLINE AS HOMICIDES DECLINE

During the late 1990s the number of individuals sentenced to death each year began to decline. (See Figure 6.4.) In 1973 only 44 inmates entered death row in the United States. During the 1980s and early 1990s between 250 and 300 defendants per year were regularly admitted to death row. The number peaked in 1996 at 330 and then began a dramatic decline, dropping to 80 in 2011, the lowest number in more than three decades. In *The Death Penalty in 2012: Year End Report*, the DPIC estimates that 77 defendants were sentenced to death in 2012. The decline in death sentences beginning in the late 1990s may be linked to the corresponding decrease in the nation's homicide rate. As shown in Figure 1.4 in

TABLE 6.7

Women under sentence of death, by race and jurisdiction, yearend 2011

Region and jurisdiction	Under sentence of death, 12/31/11		
	Total[a]	White[b]	Black[b]
U.S. total	**62**	**42**	**16**
Federal	2	2	0
State	60	40	16
Northeast	**4**	**1**	**3**
Pennsylvania	4	1	3
Midwest	**2**	**1**	**1**
Indiana	1	0	1
Ohio	1	1	0
South	**30**	**19**	**10**
Alabama	4	3	1
Florida	4	2	2
Georgia	1	1	0
Kentucky	1	1	0
Louisiana	2	1	1
Mississippi	2	2	0
North Carolina	5	2	2
Oklahoma	1	1	0
Tennessee	1	1	0
Texas	9	5	4
West	**24**	**19**	**2**
Arizona	3	3	0
California	19	14	2
Idaho	1	1	0
Oregon	1	1	0

Note: No women were executed during 2011.

[a]Includes American Indians, Alaska Natives, Asians, Native Hawaiians, other Pacific Islanders, and Hispanic inmates for whom no other race was identified.

[b]Counts of white and black inmates include persons of Hispanic or Latino origin, which may differ from other tables in this report.

SOURCE: Adapted from Tracy L. Snell, "Table 6. Women under Sentence of Death, by Region, Jurisdiction, and Race, 2010 and 2011," in *Capital Punishment, 2011—Statistical Tables*, U.S. Department of Justice, Office of Justice Programs, Bureau of Justice Statistics, July 16, 2013, http://www.bjs.gov/content/pub/pdf/cp11st.pdf (accessed September 3, 2013)

TABLE 6.8

Hispanics under sentence of death, by jurisdiction, yearend 2011

Region and jurisdiction	Under sentence of death, 12/31/11
U.S. total	387
Federal	8
State	379
Northeast	**21**
Connecticut	1
Pennsylvania	20
Midwest	**9**
Illinois	0
Nebraska	5
Ohio	4
South	**139**
Alabama	2
Arkansas	1
Delaware	2
Florida	33
Georgia	2
Kentucky	0
Louisiana	2
North Carolina	4
Oklahoma	2
South Carolina	1
Tennessee	1
Texas	89
West	**210**
Arizona	26
California	168
Idaho	1
Nevada	8
New Mexico	1
Oregon	3
Utah	3

SOURCE: Adapted from Tracy L. Snell, "Table 7. Hispanics under Sentence of Death, by Region and Jurisdiction, 2010 and 2011," in *Capital Punishment, 2011—Statistical Tables*, U.S. Department of Justice, Office of Justice Programs, Bureau of Justice Statistics, July 16, 2013, http://www.bjs.gov/content/pub/pdf/cp11st.pdf (accessed September 3, 2013)

Chapter 1, the homicide rate dropped dramatically from 9.8 homicides per 100,000 population in 1991 to 4.7 homicides per 100,000 population in 2011.

FINANCIAL COSTS OF THE DEATH PENALTY

As noted in Chapter 1, capital cases are more expensive to litigate than noncapital cases. Capital cases typically require more lawyer preparation, expert witness testimony, jury selection time, and trial time than noncapital cases. In addition, there is the lengthy appeals process that is built in to the death penalty process. Another added expense is the cost of specialized housing and extra security provided on death rows. Death penalty opponents often point to the high costs of capital cases as a practical reason for abolishing capital punishment. They argue that imprisoning someone for life without the possibility of parole is less expensive than putting someone through the capital punishment process, and that the money saved by the justice system could be devoted elsewhere, for example, to investigating unsolved crimes.

However, death penalty advocates dispute the idea that life without parole sentencing is less expensive than capital punishment. Their reasoning is based on the high incarceration costs associated with imprisoning offenders for perhaps many decades until their natural deaths. One contributing factor is the high cost of health care of elderly inmates. Furthermore, death penalty advocates argue that the cost of capital punishment would be lower if not for the lengthy appeals process, which they believe should be dramatically shortened. They point to Virginia as a model in this respect. As described in Chapter 5, Virginia has a streamlined appeals process for capital cases that has provided a much shorter average time from sentencing to execution than in other jurisdictions.

The debate over capital punishment costs took on added emphasis after a severe economic recession enveloped the United States from 2007 to 2009. Pinched by declining budgets, state governments began looking for ways to reduce expenses. As a result, death penalty costs attracted greater scrutiny. Since 2007, five states have

TABLE 6.9

Criminal history profile of prisoners under sentence of death, 2011

Criminal history	Allª
U.S. total	100%
Prior felony convictions[b]	
Yes	66.6%
No	33.4
Prior homicide convictions[c]	
Yes	8.4%
No	91.6
Legal status at time of capital offense[d]	
Charges pending	8.0%
Probation	10.9
Parole	16.1
On escape	1.3
Incarcerated	3.4
Other status	0.3
None	59.9

[a]Includes American Indians, Alaska Natives, Asians, Native Hawaiians, and other Pacific Islanders.
[b]Data were not reported for 241 inmates.
[c]Data were not reported for 49 inmates.
[d]Data were not reported for 331 inmates.
Note: Percentages are based on offenders for whom data were reported. Detail may not sum to total because of rounding.

SOURCE: Adapted from Tracy L. Snell, "Table 8. Criminal History Profile of Prisoners under Sentence of Death, by Race and Hispanic Origin, 2011," in *Capital Punishment, 2011—Statistical Tables*, U.S. Department of Justice, Office of Justice Programs, Bureau of Justice Statistics, July 16, 2013, http://www.bjs.gov/content/pub/pdf/cp11st.pdf (accessed September 3, 2013)

abolished the death penalty: New Jersey (2007), New Mexico (2009; does not apply to already condemned prisoners), Illinois (2011), Connecticut (2012; does not apply to already condemned prisoners), and Maryland (2013; does not apply to already condemned prisoners). These decisions were based, in part, on financial considerations. This is an example of a utilitarian attitude, based on the practical issue of how much capital punishment was costing state government. However, many death penalty supporters have a retributionist viewpoint, meaning that they believe execution to be a just and deserved punishment. Retributionists are not swayed by financial arguments against capital punishment. For example, Mike Ward quotes in "Cost of Executions Skyrocketing in Texas, Other States" (Statesman.com, February 24, 2012) the death penalty advocate William "Rusty" Hubbarth as saying, "As for the rising cost, what price would you put on justice?"

Since 2006 several studies have been performed to analyze the financial costs associated with capital punishment systems in various jurisdictions. (See Table 6.11.) Quantifying costs in these cases is very difficult. Numerous parties participate in trials, and no single entity tracks all the expenses involved. As a result, researchers are forced to make certain assumptions and estimates as part of their cost analyses. These uncertainties open the studies to criticism, particularly from death penalty support-

ers. This is especially true when analysts attempt to compare costs between capital and noncapital cases. It is impossible to determine the costs for a capital and noncapital prosecution for the same offender for the same crime. As a result, researchers typically estimate this by using data to compare the costs of murder prosecutions that resulted in death sentences to murder prosecutions that resulted in life without parole sentences.

California

In June 2011 the Loyola Law School in Los Angeles published a study by Arthur L. Alarcón and Paula Mitchell. In "Executing the Will of the Voters?: A Roadmap to Mend or End the California Legislature's Multi-billion-Dollar Death Penalty Debacle" (*Loyola of Los Angeles Law Review*, vol. 44), the researchers estimate that between 1978 and 2011 California had spent more than $4 billion on its "dysfunctional" capital punishment system. Because only 13 executions took place during that time, the cost per execution was around $308 million. Alarcón and Mitchell complain that "billions of taxpayer dollars have been spent to create a bloated system, in which condemned inmates languish on death row for decades before dying of natural causes and in which executions rarely take place." The researchers put much of the blame for the delays on the state legislature, which they suggest had failed to fund programs to provide "adequate" legal counsel for death row inmates during the appeals process.

According to Alarcón and Mitchell, California spends an estimated $144 million annually on housing, medical care, and legal costs for death row inmates. At the time the report was written, the state had more than 700 death row inmates. The researchers estimate that it will take more than 20 years to resolve those cases unless reforms are implemented to eliminate the delays and backlog. They conclude that reforming the state's capital punishment system will require "tens of millions of dollars annually on a statewide basis" until the backlog is reduced. Limiting application of the death penalty to "the worst of the worst" offenders would provide "immediate" savings of millions of dollars to the state. So would abolishing the death penalty in favor of life sentences with no chance of parole. Alarcón and Mitchell estimate that this option would save "billions of dollars over the next 20 years."

The California Commission on the Fair Administration of Justice (CCFAJ; 2011, http://www.ccfaj.org/) was created in 2004 by the state legislature to examine California's criminal justice system and make recommendations to remedy any problems. The CCFAJ examined numerous issues that were associated with the state's capital punishment system, many of which had cost implications. In June 2008 its findings and recommendations

TABLE 6.10

Prisoners sentenced to death and outcome of the sentence, by year of sentencing, 1973–2011

Jurisdiction	Total sentenced to death, 1973–2011	Number of removals, 1973–2011					Under sentence of death, 12/31/11
		Executed	Died	Sentence or conviction overturned	Sentence commuted	Other removals	
U.S. total	8,300	1,277	460	3,059	388	34	3,082
Federal	69	3	0	9	1	0	56
Alabama	429	55	34	142	2	0	196
Arizona	302	28	17	119	7	1	130
Arkansas	113	27	3	42	2	0	39
California	962	13	81	148	15	0	705
Colorado	22	1	2	15	1	0	3
Connecticut	14	1	0	3	0	0	10
Delaware	59	15	0	26	0	0	18
Florida	1,005	71	63	458	18	2	393
Georgia	323	52	17	148	9	1	96
Idaho	42	2	3	21	3	0	13
Illinois	307	12	15	97	171	12	0
Indiana	100	20	4	56	6	2	12
Kansas	13	0	0	4	0	0	9
Kentucky	83	3	6	38	2	0	34
Louisiana	244	28	6	115	7	1	87
Maryland	53	5	3	36	4	0	5
Massachusetts	4	0	0	2	2	0	0
Mississippi	193	15	6	112	0	3	57
Missouri	182	68	10	55	3	0	46
Montana	15	3	2	6	2	0	2
Nebraska	33	3	5	12	2	0	11
Nevada	152	12	15	40	4	0	81
New Hampshire	1	0	0	0	0	0	1
New Jersey	52	0	3	33	8	8	0
New Mexico	28	1	1	19	5	0	2
New York	10	0	0	10	0	0	0
North Carolina	535	43	23	303	8	0	158
Ohio	412	46	22	182	20	0	142
Oklahoma	350	96	15	172	4	0	63
Oregon	63	2	2	23	0	0	36
Pennsylvania	405	3	28	161	6	0	207
Rhode Island	2	0	0	2	0	0	0
South Carolina	205	43	6	101	3	0	52
South Dakota	6	1	1	0	0	0	4
Tennessee	225	6	16	108	6	2	87
Texas	1,057	477	42	181	55	1	301
Utah	27	7	1	10	1	0	8
Virginia	152	109	6	16	11	1	9
Washington	39	5	1	25	0	0	8
Wyoming	12	1	1	9	0	0	1

Note: In 1972, the U.S. Supreme Court invalidated capital punishment statutes in several states (*Furman v. Georgia*, 408 U.S. 238 (1972)), effecting a moratorium on executions. Executions resumed in 1977 when the Supreme Court found that revisions to several state statutes had effectively addressed the issues previously held unconstitutional (*Gregg v. Georgia*, 428 U.S. 153 (1976) and its companion cases). Some inmates executed since 1977 or currently under sentence of death were sentenced prior to 1977. For persons sentenced to death more than once, the numbers are based on the most recent death sentence.

SOURCE: Adapted from Tracy L. Snell, "Table 17. Number Sentenced to Death and Number of Removals, by Jurisdiction and Reason for Removal, 1973–2011," in *Capital Punishment, 2011—Statistical Tables*, U.S. Department of Justice, Office of Justice Programs, Bureau of Justice Statistics, July 16, 2013, http://www.bjs.gov/content/pub/pdf/cp11st.pdf (accessed September 3, 2013)

were published in *California Commission on the Fair Administration of Justice: Report and Recommendations on the Administration of the Death Penalty in California* (http://www.ccfaj.org/documents/reports/dp/official/FINAL%20REPORT%20DEATH%20PENALTY.pdf).

The CCFAJ noted that one particularly expensive component of the state's capital punishment system is the lengthy amount of time that prisoners spend on death row. The average time between death sentence and execution in California is 20 to 25 years. This is about twice the national average for other death penalty states. The CCFAJ

complained, "Just to keep cases moving at this snail's pace, we spend large amounts of taxpayers' money each year: by conservative estimates, well over one hundred million dollars annually." Part of the problem, noted the CCFAJ, is a lack of funding for qualified attorneys to handle death sentence appeals and habeas corpus proceedings, which has resulted in a huge backlog of cases.

The CCFAJ made numerous recommendations to the California legislature for reform of the capital punishment system. However, Alarcón and Mitchell complain that the legislature failed to act on these recommendations. In "Death

FIGURE 6.3

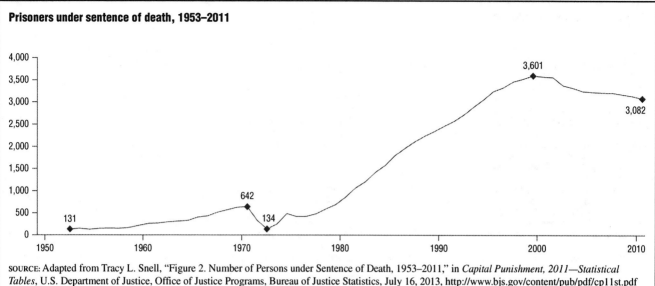

Prisoners under sentence of death, 1953–2011

SOURCE: Adapted from Tracy L. Snell, "Figure 2. Number of Persons under Sentence of Death, 1953–2011," in *Capital Punishment, 2011—Statistical Tables*, U.S. Department of Justice, Office of Justice Programs, Bureau of Justice Statistics, July 16, 2013, http://www.bjs.gov/content/pub/pdf/cp11st.pdf (accessed September 3, 2013)

FIGURE 6.4

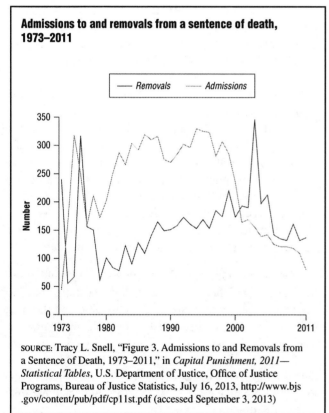

Admissions to and removals from a sentence of death, 1973–2011

SOURCE: Tracy L. Snell, "Figure 3. Admissions to and Removals from a Sentence of Death, 1973–2011," in *Capital Punishment, 2011—Statistical Tables*, U.S. Department of Justice, Office of Justice Programs, Bureau of Justice Statistics, July 16, 2013, http://www.bjs.gov/content/pub/pdf/cp11st.pdf (accessed September 3, 2013)

Penalty Costs California $184 Million a Year, Study Says" (LATimes.com, June 20, 2011), Carol J. Williams reports that "none of the remedies" described by the CCFAJ "has been adopted by lawmakers or put to the public for a vote."

Alarcón and Mitchell's report is generally regarded to be fair and unbiased, even by death penalty advocates. Williams notes that even though Mitchell has publicly voiced her opposition to capital punishment, Alarcón is not opposed to the death penalty and prosecuted capital cases earlier in his career. Debra J. Saunders, a conservative columnist who favors capital punishment, admits in "Death Penalty Foes' Self-Fulfilling Prophecies" (SFChronicle.com, July 17, 2011) that Alarcón and Mitchell did "a solid job quantifying how much taxpayers must pay for the death penalty." However, she suggests that they "gloss over the role of frivolous appeals and bonehead rulings by federal judges." The latter complaint relates to the Ninth Circuit of Appeals, which has reversed approximately 70% of the capital cases that have come before it and is widely criticized by death penalty advocates as having an anti-capital punishment bias. Saunders concludes that "for decades, capital punishment opponents have tried to thwart California's 1978 death-penalty law with frivolous appeals that clog courts, delay punishment and burn through taxpayers' dollars. They now have been so successful that they can argue that California's death penalty doesn't work and costs too much."

Colorado

In "The Cost of Colorado's Death Penalty" (*University of Denver Criminal Law Review*, vol. 3, Spring 2013), Justin F. Marceau and Hollis Whitson examine murder cases filed in Colorado from 1999 through 2010 and compare the number of days in court associated with capital and noncapital prosecutions for "the most serious of the first-degree murders." As shown in Table 6.10, Colorado has had few death penalty convictions in the modern era (i.e., since 1973). Only 22 people were sentenced to death in the state between 1973 and 2011. Marceau and Whitson limit their analysis to the six capital cases initiated after the U.S. Supreme Court ruling

TABLE 6.11

Capital punishment cost studies

Study title	Date	Author(s)	Publisher(s)/sponsor(s)	Jurisdiction
The cost of Colorado's death penalty	Spring 2013	Justin F. Marceau and Hollis A. Whitson	University of Denver Criminal Law Review	Colorado
Executing the Will of the Voters?: A Roadmap to Mend or End the California Legislature's Multi-billion-Dollar Death Penalty Debacle	June 2011	Arthur L. Alarcón and Paula Mitchell	Loyola Law School in Los Angeles	California
Final Report on HB 520, Chapter 284, Laws of 2009	December 2010	Commission to Study the Death Penalty in New Hampshire	New Hampshire legislature	New Hampshire
Report to the Committee on Defender Services, Judicial Conference of the United States: Update on the Cost and Quality of Defense Representation in Federal Death Penalty Cases	September 2010	Jon B. Gould and Lisa Greenman	Office of Defender Services of the Administrative Office of the U.S. Courts	Federal
California Commission on the Fair Administration of Justice: Report and Recommendations on the Administration of the Death Penalty in California	June 2008	California Commission on the Fair Administration of Justice	California legislature	California
The Cost of the Death Penalty in Maryland	March 2008	John Roman et al.	The Urban Institute	Maryland
New Jersey Death Penalty Study Commission Report	January 2007	New Jersey Death Penalty Study Commission	New Jersey governor	New Jersey
Final Report of the Death Penalty Subcommittee of the Committee on Public Defense	December 2006	Washington State Bar Assocation	Washington State Bar Assocation	Washington

SOURCE: Created by Kim Masters Evans for Gale, 2013

in *Ring v. Arizona* (536 U.S. 584 [2002]). As described in Chapter 2, in that case the court found unconstitutional the practice of allowing a judge, rather than a jury, to make certain capital sentencing decisions. The ruling invalidated Colorado's existing sentencing procedure and forced the state to change it. For comparison purposes, Marceau and Whitson use 148 first-degree aggravated murder cases initiated between 2005 and 2010 for their life without parole dataset. The defendants in these cases were eligible for the death penalty because their crimes included aggravating factors; however, prosecutors exercised their discretion not to seek the death penalty in these cases.

Of the six capital cases, only two resulted in death penalty sentences. Another defendant was acquitted and two defendants received life without parole sentences. The sixth case was ongoing at the time of the assessment. Overall, Marceau and Whitson find that the capital cases required, on average, 148 court days each. This total covers the period from the pretrial hearings through the sentencing proceedings. By comparison, the noncapital cases required, on average, 24.5 court days each. The researchers do not attempt to put a dollar figure on the respective court proceedings. Instead, they assume that more days in court translate to higher litigation costs for the capital cases than for the noncapital cases. Even so, they believe their findings to be conservative. They point out that "death penalty cases require more experienced lawyers, more experts, and likely cost considerably more per day than non-death cases." Marceau and Whitson limit their analysis to the time between charging and sentencing. They do not take into account the appeals process or the costs of incarceration.

Cost Studies in Other Jurisdictions

THE FEDERAL GOVERNMENT. In September 2010 the Office of Defender Services (ODS) of the Administrative Office of the U.S. Courts published its second-phase report *Report to the Committee on Defender Services, Judicial Conference of the United States: Update on the Cost and Quality of Defense Representation in Federal Death Penalty Cases* (http://www.deathpenaltyinfo.org/documents/FederalDPCost2010.pdf) by Jon B. Gould and Lisa Greenman. The report was an update of a 1998 study on the federal death penalty system that specifically examined funding for defense services provided to defendants in capital cases. Gould and Greenman analyze cost data for federal death penalty cases from 1998 to 2004 in which the government provided public defenders (at taxpayer expense) for the defendants.

Gould and Greenman's results included medians for total costs of defense representation, meaning that half the values were less than the median value and the other half of the values were greater than the median value. The median cost for a death-authorized case was $353,185. The median cost for a death-eligible but non-death-authorized case was $44,809. The researchers note that "the median cost of a case in which the Attorney General authorized seeking the death penalty was nearly eight times greater than the cost of a case that was eligible for capital prosecution but in which the death penalty was *not* authorized." The median cost of a death-authorized case that proceeded to trial was more than twice the cost of a death-authorized case that was resolved through a plea bargain agreement. Furthermore, Gould and Greenman report that the cost of defending federal capital cases "increased substantially" during the first decade of the 21st century for a number of reasons, including legal and forensic factors.

MARYLAND. In March 2008 the Urban Institute published *The Cost of the Death Penalty in Maryland* (http://www.urban.org/UploadedPDF/411625_md_death_penalty.pdf) by John Roman et al. The Urban Institute is a nonprofit organization based in Washington, D.C. According to the institute (2013, http://www.urban.org/about/), it "gathers data, conducts research, evaluates programs, offers technical assistance overseas, and educates Americans on social and economic issues—to foster sound public policy and effective government." Roman et al.'s research was funded by the Abell Foundation (2013, http://www.abell.org/aboutthefoundation/index.html) of Baltimore, Maryland, a private organization that is devoted to helping "the disadvantaged in the Baltimore community and the region."

Roman et al. examine the costs of adjudication (the process of judging) and incarceration for 1,136 cases that occurred between 1978 and 1999 in which the defendant was eligible for the death penalty. Note this does not mean that the prosecution sought a death sentence, only that the defendant was eligible for capital punishment under state law. Roman et al. conclude that an average case in which a death sentence was not sought cost more than $1.1 million. An average case in which a death sentence was sought, but not imposed, cost $1.8 million. An average case in which a death sentence was sought and imposed cost just over $3 million. The breakdown for the latter was about $1.7 million for adjudication costs and about $1.3 million for incarceration costs.

NEW HAMPSHIRE. In *Final Report on HB 520, Chapter 284, Laws of 2009* (2010, http://gencourt.state.nh.us/statstudcomm/reports/2009.pdf), the Commission to Study the Death Penalty in New Hampshire found that the cost of prosecuting and incarcerating inmates in New Hampshire capital cases was "significantly" higher than in noncapital murder cases. However, the commission concluded that "the death penalty is pursued sparingly in this state and those costs are necessary to provide both a high quality of prosecution and a vigorous defense." As shown in Table 6.10, New Hampshire had sentenced only one person to death between 1973 and 2011.

NEW JERSEY. In 2006 the governor of New Jersey appointed the New Jersey Death Penalty Study Commission (NJDPSC) to assess the state's capital punishment system and issue recommendations regarding its continued usage. At that time, New Jersey only had eight prisoners on death row and had not executed anyone in more than two decades. In January 2007 the NJDPSC published *New Jersey Death Penalty Study Commission Report* (http://www.njleg.state.nj.us/committees/dpsc_final.pdf), which recommended replacing the state's death sentence with a sentence of life imprisonment without the chance of

parole. The decision was based on a number of factors, including costs. The commission noted, "The costs of the death penalty are greater than the costs of life in prison without parole, but it is not possible to measure these costs with any degree of precision." However, estimates provided from state agencies indicated that eliminating the death penalty in favor of lifetime incarceration would save nearly $1.5 million per year in public defender costs for the 19 capital cases active at that time and would save approximately $1 million per death row inmate in incarceration costs. The potential cost savings in court-related expenses could not be estimated, and it was concluded that no cost savings would be achieved by prosecutor offices in the state.

In December 2007 New Jersey abolished the death penalty in the state and replaced it with lifetime incarceration without parole.

WASHINGTON. In December 2006 the Washington State Bar Association (WSBA) published *Final Report of the Death Penalty Subcommittee of the Committee on Public Defense*. At that time there had been 79 death penalty cases in Washington in the previous 25 years. However, only four executions had taken place, the most recent in 2001. The WSBA reviewed previous statistical reports on costs associated with the state's death penalty and surveyed prosecutors and defense attorneys who had been involved in capital cases regarding trial costs and attorney compensation. Data were also collected on state and federal costs during the appeals process.

The WSBA noted that quantifying and comparing costs between criminal cases is very difficult. It estimated that trying a death penalty case in Washington cost an average of $467,000 more than a comparable noncapital case. This figure includes the extra expenses incurred by the prosecutor and the defense. Fees and costs at the appellate level were estimated to be at least $100,000 more for a capital case than for a comparable noncapital case. The WSBA concluded that "it costs significantly more to try a capital case to final verdict than to try the same case as an aggravated murder case where the penalty sought is life without possibility of parole."

EXECUTIONS

Until 1930 the U.S. government did not keep any record of the number of people executed under the death penalty. As shown in Table 6.12, from 1930 through 2012 a total of 5,179 executions were conducted under civil authority in the United States. Military authorities carried out an additional 160 executions between 1930 and 1961, the date of the last military execution.

Between 1930 and 1939 a total of 1,667 inmates were executed, the highest number of people put to death in any decade. The number of executions generally declined between the 1930s and the 1960s. In 1930, 155 executes took place, reaching a high of 199 in 1935. (See Figure 1.2 in Chapter 1.) By 1950 executions were down to 82, further dropping to 49 each in 1958 and 1959, and then rising slightly to 56 in 1960. In 1967 a 10-year moratorium (temporary suspension) of the death penalty began as states waited for the U.S. Supreme Court to determine a constitutionally acceptable procedure for carrying out the death penalty.

The moratorium ended in 1976, but no executions occurred that year. The first execution following the moratorium occurred in Utah in January 1977. The number of executions each year during the 1980s remained relatively low, but increased sharply during the 1990s. In 1999, 98 inmates were put to death, the most in a one-year period after the death penalty was reinstated. (See Figure 6.5.) By 2012 the number had dropped to 43 executions. As shown in Table 6.12, between 1977 and the end of 2012, 1,320 people were put to death.

Executions by Jurisdiction

Table 6.12 shows the number of prisoners executed by jurisdiction between 1930 and 2012 and between 1977 and 2012. Texas, by far, had the most executions during both periods: 789 executions between 1930 and 2012 and 492 executions between 1977 and 2012.

Overall, 35 jurisdictions carried out executions between 1977 and 2012. (See Table 6.12.) The federal government executed three inmates. As mentioned previously, the largest number of executions in a single state occurred in Texas (492), followed by Virginia (109), Oklahoma (102), Florida (74), Missouri (68), Alabama (55), Georgia (52), and Ohio (49). Together, these eight states carried out just over three-quarters (76%, or 1,001) of all executions between 1977 and 2012. (See Figure 6.6.) The breakdown by state for executions conducted during 2012 is shown in Figure 5.3 in Chapter 5. In total, 43 executions took place. Texas conducted 15 executions, the most of any state.

Gender

The BJS does not provide state or yearly breakdowns of the number of women executed in the United States. However, Victor L. Streib of Ohio Northern University has been compiling information on female offenders and the death penalty in the United States since 1984. In *Death Penalty for Female Offenders: January 1, 1973, through December 31, 2011* (January 24, 2012, http://deathpenaltyinfo.org/documents/FemDeathDec2011.pdf), Streib notes that between 1632 and 2011, 571 executions of women in the United States had been documented. Of this total, 12 women were put to death between 1973 and 2011. In *Capital Punishment, 2011—Statistical Tables*, Snell notes that no women were executed during 2012. According to the DPIC, in "Execution List 2013" (2013, http://www.deathpenaltyinfo.org/execution-list-2013), as of October 2013 one woman, Kimberly McCarthy, had been

TABLE 6.12

Number of persons executed, by jurisdiction, 1930–2012 and 1977–2012

	Executed 1930–2012	Executed 1977–2012
U.S. total	**5,179**	**1,320**
Texas	789	492
Georgia	418	52
New York	329	0
North Carolina	306	43
California	305	13
Florida	244	74
Ohio	221	49
South Carolina	205	43
Virginia	201	109
Alabama	190	55
Mississippi	175	21
Oklahoma	162	102
Louisiana	161	28
Pennsylvania	155	3
Arkansas	145	27
Missouri	130	68
Kentucky	106	3
Illinois	102	12
Tennessee	99	6
New Jersey	74	0
Maryland	73	5
Arizona	72	34
Indiana	61	20
Washington	52	5
Colorado	48	1
Nevada	41	12
District of Columbia	40	0
West Virginia	40	0
Federal system	36	3
Delaware	28	16
Massachusetts	27	0
Connecticut	22	1
Utah	21	7
Oregon	20	2
Iowa	18	0
Kansas	15	0
Montana	9	3
New Mexico	9	1
Wyoming	8	1
Nebraska	7	3
Idaho	6	3
South Dakota	4	3
Vermont	4	0
New Hampshire	1	0
Alaska	0	0
District of Columbia	0	0
Hawaii	0	0
Maine	0	0
Michigan	0	0
Minnesota	0	0
North Dakota	0	0
Rhode Island	0	0
Wisconsin	0	0

Note: Statistics on executions under civil authority have been collected by the federal government annually since 1930. These data exclude 160 executions carried out by military authorities between 1930 and 1961.

SOURCE: Adapted from Tracy L. Snell, "Table 14. Number of Persons Executed, by Jurisdiction, 1930–2011" and "Figure 5. Advance Count of Executions, January 1, 2012–December 31, 2012," in *Capital Punishment, 2011—Statistical Tables*, U.S. Department of Justice, Office of Justice Programs, Bureau of Justice Statistics, July 16, 2013, http://www.bjs.gov/content/pub/pdf/cp11st.pdf (accessed September 3, 2013)

executed during 2013. McCarthy was executed in Texas for stabbing and beating to death her elderly neighbor, Dorothy Booth, during a 1997 robbery. McCarthy was suspected, but not convicted, of committing two other murders.

FIGURE 6.5

Executions per year, 1977–2012

SOURCE: Adapted from Tracy L. Snell, "Prisoners Executed under Civil Authority in the United States, by Year, Region, and Jurisdiction, 1977–2012," in *Prisoners Executed*, U.S. Department of Justice, Office of Justice Programs, Bureau of Justice Statistics, March 11, 2013, http://www.bjs.gov/content/data/exest.csv (accessed September 3, 2013)

FIGURE 6.6

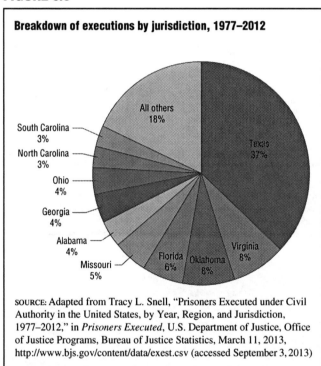

Breakdown of executions by jurisdiction, 1977–2012

SOURCE: Adapted from Tracy L. Snell, "Prisoners Executed under Civil Authority in the United States, by Year, Region, and Jurisdiction, 1977–2012," in *Prisoners Executed*, U.S. Department of Justice, Office of Justice Programs, Bureau of Justice Statistics, March 11, 2013, http://www.bjs.gov/content/data/exest.csv (accessed September 3, 2013)

FIGURE 6.7

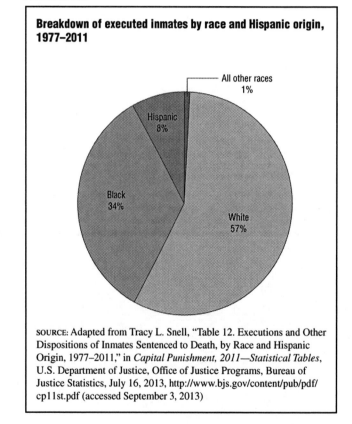

Breakdown of executed inmates by race and Hispanic origin, 1977–2011

SOURCE: Adapted from Tracy L. Snell, "Table 12. Executions and Other Dispositions of Inmates Sentenced to Death, by Race and Hispanic Origin, 1977–2011," in *Capital Punishment, 2011—Statistical Tables*, U.S. Department of Justice, Office of Justice Programs, Bureau of Justice Statistics, July 16, 2013, http://www.bjs.gov/content/pub/pdf/cp11st.pdf (accessed September 3, 2013)

Race and Ethnicity

Figure 6.7 shows the racial and ethnic makeup of the 1,277 prisoners executed between 1977 and 2011. More than half (57%) of those executed were white, while slightly more than a third (34%) were African American. Eight percent of the total executed were Hispanic. Other races accounted for 1%.

Method of Execution

As shown in Table 6.13, among the 1,320 prisoners executed between 1977 and 2012, 1,146 (86.8%)

received lethal injection, followed by electrocution (157, or 11.9%). Eleven executions were carried out by lethal gas, three by hanging, and three by firing squad. Texas, the state with the largest number of prisoners executed, used lethal injection in all 492 cases. Virginia executed 79 inmates by lethal injection and 30 inmates by electrocution. Oklahoma put to death 102 prisoners, all by lethal injection.

TABLE 6.13

Executions, by jurisdiction and method, 1977–2012

	Number executed	Lethal injection	Electrocution	Lethal gas	Hanging	Firing squad
U.S. total	**1,320**	**1,146**	**157**	**11**	**3**	**3**
Federal	3	3	0	0	0	0
Alabama	55	31	24	0	0	0
Arizona	34	32	0	2	0	0
Arkansas	27	26	1	0	0	0
California	13	11	0	2	0	0
Colorado	1	1	0	0	0	0
Connecticut	1	1	0	0	0	0
Delaware	16	15	0	0	1	0
Florida	74	30	44	0	0	0
Georgia	52	29	23	0	0	0
Idaho	3	3	0	0	0	0
Illinois	12	12	0	0	0	0
Indiana	20	17	3	0	0	0
Kentucky	3	2	1	0	0	0
Louisiana	28	8	20	0	0	0
Maryland	5	5	0	0	0	0
Mississippi	21	17	0	4	0	0
Missouri	68	68	0	0	0	0
Montana	3	3	0	0	0	0
Nebraska	3	0	3	0	0	0
Nevada	12	11	0	1	0	0
New Mexico	1	1	0	0	0	0
North Carolina	43	41	0	2	0	0
Ohio	49	49	0	0	0	0
Oklahoma	102	102	0	0	0	0
Oregon	2	2	0	0	0	0
Pennsylvania	3	3	0	0	0	0
South Carolina	43	36	7	0	0	0
South Dakota	3	3	0	0	0	0
Tennessee	6	5	1	0	0	0
Texas	492	492	0	0	0	0
Utah	7	4	0	0	0	3
Virginia	109	79	30	0	0	0
Washington	5	3	0	0	2	0
Wyoming	1	1	0	0	0	0

Note: In 1972, the U.S. Supreme Court invalidated capital punishment statutes in several states (*Furman v. Georgia*, 408 U.S. 238 (1972)), effecting a moratorium on executions. Executions resumed in 1977 when the Supreme Court found that revisions to several state statutes had effectively addressed the issues previously held unconstitutional (*Gregg v. Georgia*, 428 U.S. 153 (1976) and its companion cases).

SOURCE: Adapted from Tracy L. Snell, "Table 13. Executions, by Jurisdiction and Method, 1977–2011" and "Figure 5. Advance Count of Executions, January 1, 2012–December 31, 2012," in *Capital Punishment, 2011—Statistical Tables*, U.S. Department of Justice, Office of Justice Programs, Bureau of Justice Statistics, July 16, 2013, http://www.bjs.gov/content/pub/pdf/cp11st.pdf (accessed September 3, 2013)

CHAPTER 7
ISSUES OF FAIRNESS

In February 1967 the President's Commission on Law Enforcement and Administration of Justice published the report *The Challenge of Crime in a Free Society* (http://www.ncjrs.gov/pdffiles1/nij/42.pdf), which examined in detail many aspects of the nation's criminal justice system. In regards to capital punishment, the commission concluded, "Finally there is evidence that the imposition of the death sentence and the exercise of dispensing power by the courts and the executive follow discriminatory patterns. The death sentence is disproportionately imposed and carried out on the poor, the Negro, and the members of unpopular groups." This statement was quoted by Justice William O. Douglas (1898–1980) of the U.S. Supreme Court in his concurring opinion in *Furman v. Georgia* (408 U.S. 238 [1972]), in which the court ruled that capital punishment was unconstitutional. As described in Chapter 1, this landmark decision resulted in major reforms in state laws in an effort to create a more uniform death penalty system that eliminates arbitrary and discriminatory factors in capital sentencing.

In the 21st century there are still many concerns about the fairness with which the death penalty is applied in the United States. Capital punishment opponents raise fairness challenges that avoid emotionally charged arguments about the moral rightness or wrongness of capital punishment to focus on more legally definable issues, such as discrimination and the denial of legal rights. An enduring idea of U.S. jurisprudence (the philosophy of law) is that "justice is blind." In other words, the merits of a criminal case should be decided without regard to the race, ethnicity, or economic status of the accused. Death penalty opponents argue that death sentences are applied unfairly and provide evidence of geographical and racial bias and poor legal representation. These factors, they suggest, prove that the U.S. capital punishment system is flawed and should be eliminated. Death penalty advo-

cates counter that the judicial process contains adequate safeguards to ensure that defendants receive fair trials. They believe that if any discrepancies do exist in capital convictions and sentences, they should be remedied by applying the death penalty more often, not less often.

GEOGRAPHICAL DISPARITIES

Capital punishment is supposed to be applied in a uniform manner across the jurisdictions in which it is allowed. Statistics, however, indicate that there are huge geographical differences in the numbers of death sentences that are imposed and carried out.

Differences between Death Penalty States

As shown in Table 7.1, between 1973 and 2011, 8,300 inmates were sentenced to death under the federal and state judicial systems. Nearly half (48%) were sentenced in only five states:

- Texas (1,057, or 12.7% of the total)
- Florida (1,005, or 12.1%)
- California (962, or 11.6%)
- North Carolina (535, or 6.4%)
- Alabama (429, or 5.2%)

Likewise, Table 7.1 shows that nearly two-thirds (64.3%) of the 1,277 executions conducted between 1973 and 2011 were concentrated in only a handful of states:

- Texas (477 or 37.4% of the total)
- Virginia (109 or 8.5%)
- Oklahoma (96 or 7.5%)
- Florida (71 or 5.6%)
- Missouri (68 or 5.3%)

TABLE 7.1

Total number sentenced to death and executed, 1973–2011 and total number on death row at year end 2011, by jurisdiction

Jurisdiction	Total sentenced to death, 1973–2011	Number of removals, 1973–2011 Executed	Under sentence of death, 12/31/11
U.S. total	8,300	1,277	3,082
Federal	69	3	56
Alabama	429	55	196
Arizona	302	28	130
Arkansas	113	27	39
California	962	13	705
Colorado	22	1	3
Connecticut	14	1	10
Delaware	59	15	18
Florida	1,005	71	393
Georgia	323	52	96
Idaho	42	2	13
Illinois	307	12	0
Indiana	100	20	12
Kansas	13	0	9
Kentucky	83	3	34
Louisiana	244	28	87
Maryland	53	5	5
Massachusetts	4	0	0
Mississippi	193	15	57
Missouri	182	68	46
Montana	15	3	2
Nebraska	33	3	11
Nevada	152	12	81
New Hampshire	1	0	1
New Jersey	52	0	0
New Mexico	28	1	2
New York	10	0	0
North Carolina	535	43	158
Ohio	412	46	142
Oklahoma	350	96	63
Oregon	63	2	36
Pennsylvania	405	3	207
Rhode Island	2	0	0
South Carolina	205	43	52
South Dakota	6	1	4
Tennessee	225	6	87
Texas	1,057	477	301
Utah	27	7	8
Virginia	152	109	9
Washington	39	5	8
Wyoming	12	1	1
Percent of inmates sentenced to death, 1973–2011	100%	15.4%	37.1%

Note: In 1972, the U.S. Supreme Court invalidated capital punishment statutes in several states (*Furman v. Georgia*, 408 U.S. 238 (1972)), effecting a moratorium on executions. Executions resumed in 1977 when the Supreme Court found that revisions to several state statutes had effectively addressed the issues previously held unconstitutional (*Gregg v. Georgia*, 428 U.S. 153 (1976)) and its companion cases). Some inmates executed since 1977 or currently under sentence of death were sentenced prior to 1977. For persons sentenced to death more than once, the numbers are based on the most recent death sentence.

SOURCE: Adapted from Tracy L. Snell, "Table 17. Number Sentenced to Death and Number of Removals, by Jurisdiction and Reason for Removal, 1973–2011," in *Capital Punishment, 2011—Statistical Tables*, U.S. Department of Justice, Office of Justice Programs, Bureau of Justice Statistics, July 16, 2013, http://www.bjs.gov/content/pub/pdf/cp11st.pdf (accessed September 3, 2013)

TABLE 7.2

Persons under sentence of death, by jurisdiction and race, December 31, 2011

Region and jurisdiction	Prisoners under sentence of death, 12/31/11 Total[a]	White[b]	Black[b]
U.S. total	3,082	1,703	1,288
Federal[c]	56	28	27
State	3,026	1,675	1,261
Northeast	**218**	**81**	**128**
Connecticut	10	4	6
New Hampshire	1	0	1
New York	0	0	0
Pennsylvania	207	77	121
Midwest	**224**	**121**	**99**
Illinois	0	0	0
Indiana	12	9	3
Kansas	9	6	3
Missouri	46	26	20
Nebraska	11	7	2
Ohio	142	69	71
South Dakota	4	4	0
South	**1,595**	**853**	**717**
Alabama	196	99	96
Arkansas	39	14	24
Delaware	18	7	11
Florida	393	246	145
Georgia	96	50	46
Kentucky	34	29	5
Louisiana	87	31	55
Maryland	5	1	4
Mississippi	57	24	32
North Carolina	158	67	83
Oklahoma	63	33	26
South Carolina	52	22	30
Tennessee	87	49	36
Texas	301	176	120
Virginia	9	5	4
West	**989**	**620**	**317**
Arizona	130	100	17
California	705	413	257
Colorado	3	0	3
Idaho	13	13	0
Montana	2	2	0
Nevada	81	48	32
New Mexico	2	2	0
Oregon	36	30	4
Utah	8	6	1
Washington	8	5	3
Wyoming	1	1	0

[a]Includes American Indians, Alaska Natives, Asians, Native Hawaiians, other Pacific Islanders, and Hispanic inmates for whom no other race was identified.
[b]Counts of white and black inmates include persons of Hispanic or Latino origin, which may differ from other tables in this report.
[c]Excludes persons held under Armed Forces jurisdiction with a military death sentence for murder.

SOURCE: Adapted from Tracy L. Snell, "Table 4. Prisoners under Sentence of Death, by Region, Jurisdiction, and Race, 2010 and 2011," in *Capital Punishment, 2011—Statistical Tables*, U.S. Department of Justice, Office of Justice Programs, Bureau of Justice Statistics, July 16, 2013, http://www.bjs.gov/content/pub/pdf/cp11st.pdf (accessed September 3, 2013)

The South had more inmates on state death row than any other region as of December 31, 2011. (See Table 7.2.) Of the 3,026 prisoners under state sentence of death at that time, more than half (1,595, or 52.7% of the total) were in southern states. The remainder were located in the West (989 or 32.73%), the Midwest (224 or 7.4%), and the Northeast (218 or 7.2%).

Death penalty opponents often point to these differences between states (and between regions) as proof that

TABLE 7.3

Homicide rate by region and state, 2010

Murder and nonnegligent manslaughter

Area	Rate per 100,000[a]
United States total[b, c]	**4.8**
Northeast	**4.2**
New England	2.9
Connecticut	3.6
Maine	1.8
Massachusetts	3.2
New Hampshire	1.0
Rhode Island	2.8
Vermont	1.1
Middle Atlantic	4.6
New Jersey	4.2
New York	4.5
Pennsylvania	5.2
Midwest[b]	**4.4**
East North Central[b]	4.7
Illinois[b]	5.5
Indiana	4.5
Michigan	5.7
Ohio	4.1
Wisconsin	2.7
West North Central	3.6
Iowa	1.3
Kansas	3.5
Minnesota	1.8
Missouri	7.0
Nebraska	3.0
North Dakota	1.5
South Dakota	2.8
South[c]	**5.6**
South Atlantic[c]	5.6
Delaware	5.3
District of Columbia[c]	21.9
Florida	5.2
Georgia	5.8
Maryland	7.4
North Carolina	5.0
South Carolina	6.1
Virginia	4.6
West Virginia	3.3
East South Central	5.6
Alabama	5.7
Kentucky	4.3
Mississippi	7.0
Tennessee	5.6
West South Central	5.8
Arkansas	4.7
Louisiana	11.2
Oklahoma	5.2
Texas	5.0
West[b]	**4.2**
Mountain	4.2
Arizona	6.4
Colorado	2.4
Idaho	1.3
Montana	2.6
Nevada	5.9
New Mexico	6.9
Utah	1.9
Wyoming	1.4
Pacific[b]	4.2
Alaska	4.4
California	4.9
Hawaii	1.8
Oregon[b]	2.4
Washington	2.3

TABLE 7.3

Homicide rate by region and state, 2010 [CONTINUED]

Murder and nonnegligent manslaughter

[a]Based on U.S. Census Bureau provisional population estimates as of July 1, 2010.
[b]Because of changes in the state's reporting practices, figures are not comparable to previous years' data.
[c]Includes offenses reported by the Zoological Police and the Metro Transit Police.

SOURCE: Adapted from "Table 4. Crime in the United States by Region, Geographic Division, and State, 2009–2010," in *Crime in the United States 2010*, U.S. Department of Justice, Federal Bureau of Investigation, September 2010, http://www.fbi.gov/about-us/cjis/ucr/crime-in-the-u.s/2010/crime-in-the-u.s.-2010/tables/10tbl04.xls (accessed September 3, 2013)

capital punishment is applied inconsistently and unfairly. In particular, the large death sentencing and execution rates in southern states are often seen as indicators of lingering racial bias against African Americans, as will be explained later in this chapter. Critics counter that legitimate factors can account for varying death penalty rates between states and between regions. These include variations in the laws that make defendants eligible for a death sentence and differing murder rates. Capital offenses under state and federal laws are described in Chapter 5, as are the aggravating and mitigating factors that juries consider when deciding whether or not to impose capital punishment. Table 7.3 shows homicide rates (i.e., number of homicides per 100,000 population) by jurisdiction for 2010. The overall rate for the United States was 4.8 homicides per 100,000 population. The rates by jurisdiction varied considerably from a low of 1 in New Hampshire to 21.9 in the District of Columbia. The South had the highest regional rate at 5.6 homicides per 100,000 population, followed by the Midwest (4.4), the Northeast (4.2), and the West (4.2).

Public opinion also plays a major role in geographic differences in death penalty application, with some states and regions showing greater willingness than others to use capital punishment. Chapter 9 presents the results of polls regarding support for and opposition to the death penalty. There are notable differences based on demographic factors such as gender, age, educational level, political affiliation, and religious affiliation.

Political affiliation is particularly relevant to the discussion of geographical disparities, because of the substantial differences between Republicans and Democrats on the issue of capital punishment. For example, Lydia Saad of the Gallup Organization indicates in *U.S. Death Penalty Support Stable at 63%* (January 9, 2013, http://www.gallup.com/poll/159770/death-penalty-support-stable.aspx) that overall support for the death penalty among adults stood at 63%, according to a December 2012 poll. Support by Republicans was 80%, compared with only 51% among Democrats. Three-quarters (75%)

of respondents with a conservative ideology favored capital punishment, compared with only 47% of those with a liberal ideology.

Table 7.4 summarizes Gallup poll results for 2012 on a state-by-state basis by political party affiliation (and/or "leaning" toward a political party) and ideology. Republicans and conservatives tend to dominate states in the Southeast, Midwest, and interior West, the same states in which capital punishment is most active. By contrast, Democrats and liberals are more heavily concentrated in the Northeast and on the West Coast. States in these regions conduct few to no executions. California, a state generally known for its liberal politics, did have the largest death row population in the country in 2011, but as shown in Table 5.6 in Chapter 5 it executed a mere 1% of its condemned inmates between 1973 and 2011.

A National Study

In "Explaining Death Row's Population and Racial Composition" (*Journal of Empirical Legal Studies*, vol.

TABLE 7.4

Poll results indicating political party affiliation and ideology by state, 2012

	Presidential job approval		Party identification		Democratic advantage	Ideology			Conservative advantage
	Obama approval	Obama disapproval	Republican/lean	Democrat/lean		Conservative	Moderate	Liberal	
Alabama	36.9	57.3	50.3	35.7	−14.6	50.6	32.0	14.6	36.0
Alaska	31.4	58.3	46.5	34.3	−12.2	37.4	42.7	16.1	21.3
Arizona	44.3	48.3	44.0	40.5	−3.5	39.4	37.3	19.9	19.5
Arkansas	37.2	54.1	42.2	40.8	−1.4	45.3	33.5	18.6	26.7
California	54.2	36.5	33.5	48.4	14.9	33.2	36.1	26.9	6.3
Colorado	46.0	46.7	43.7	41.3	−2.4	39.2	34.2	23.5	15.7
Connecticut	55.6	38.3	33.9	50.9	17.0	30.2	37.8	28.4	1.8
Delaware	56.1	37.5	34.1	50.0	15.9	34.7	34.3	28.4	6.3
District of Columbia	82.4	11.3	13.3	77.4	64.1	20.5	35.3	40.8	−20.3
Florida	48.1	44.6	40.2	44.7	4.5	38.8	35.9	21.6	17.2
Georgia	45.6	47.8	45.1	40.4	−4.7	43.8	35.1	18.0	25.8
Hawaii	64.2	32.2	29.6	53.6	24.0	31.9	37.1	27.7	4.2
Idaho	34.2	57.6	56.0	28.4	−27.6	47.1	32.6	17.0	30.1
Illinois	52.3	40.8	33.7	50.4	16.7	35.1	37.4	24.6	10.5
Indiana	40.8	51.7	44.2	39.9	−4.3	43.4	33.9	20.0	23.4
Iowa	49.5	45.1	40.3	44.6	4.3	40.3	37.3	20.1	20.2
Kansas	38.1	53.8	51.1	34.8	−16.3	41.7	35.7	20.1	21.6
Kentucky	39.3	54.1	42.9	44.4	1.5	41.0	35.3	21.0	20.0
Louisiana	41.7	49.8	43.0	41.7	−1.3	45.6	34.8	15.2	30.4
Maine	49.8	42.8	37.7	45.9	8.2	36.3	35.4	25.0	11.3
Maryland	58.2	36.1	32.4	55.5	23.1	32.1	38.3	26.9	5.2
Massachusetts	56.0	38.3	32.4	52.4	20.0	28.3	38.1	30.5	−2.2
Michigan	51.2	42.1	36.1	48.4	12.3	35.7	38.0	23.3	12.4
Minnesota	50.4	42.5	37.3	48.6	11.3	35.7	36.1	25.5	10.2
Mississippi	44.4	51.0	46.5	41.4	−5.1	48.2	32.9	15.4	32.8
Missouri	40.6	51.7	43.8	40.2	−3.6	41.5	34.4	20.9	20.6
Montana	37.5	56.2	49.8	36.4	−13.4	43.6	37.6	16.9	26.7
Nation	48.0	46.0	40.7	44.9	4.2	38.4	35.8	22.5	15.9
Nebraska	37.0	55.4	50.8	33.9	−16.9	45.3	33.2	19.6	25.7
Nevada	46.3	46.8	42.5	40.5	−2.0	37.1	37.8	21.5	15.6
New Hampshire	46.2	47.3	42.3	42.7	0.4	36.4	35.5	25.4	11.0
New Jersey	55.3	37.7	35.2	48.3	13.1	32.0	37.6	26.5	5.5
New Mexico	47.2	45.1	39.4	46.4	7.0	38.8	34.0	23.3	15.5
New York	57.9	34.2	30.3	52.4	22.1	31.7	35.9	27.7	4.0
North Carolina	46.6	46.3	41.8	44.7	2.9	41.2	35.3	20.3	20.9
North Dakota	32.9	57.9	50.7	32.2	−18.5	48.6	33.9	14.7	33.9
Ohio	46.8	46.1	39.4	44.9	5.5	37.7	39.5	19.6	18.1
Oklahoma	35.2	56.7	48.3	38.5	−9.8	47.3	31.9	17.8	29.5
Oregon	47.1	45.7	39.3	46.5	7.2	33.0	35.1	29.3	3.7
Pennsylvania	47.0	46.7	40.2	46.4	6.2	38.1	35.8	22.9	15.2
Rhode Island	57.7	34.4	28.4	51.5	23.1	27.8	41.5	28.3	−0.5
South Carolina	44.2	49.7	47.0	39.6	−7.4	43.7	36.2	17.1	26.6
South Dakota	42.2	51.8	45.3	40.4	−4.9	41.6	35.8	19.9	21.7
Tennessee	39.1	53.9	44.6	39.8	−4.8	44.2	34.6	17.9	26.3
Texas	44.0	46.6	42.7	38.2	−4.5	42.6	34.4	19.4	23.2
Utah	27.9	65.6	62.3	25.6	−36.7	48.0	33.4	16.2	31.8
Vermont	59.1	34.6	33.0	49.9	16.9	31.0	37.4	29.2	1.8
Virginia	45.9	47.8	43.4	42.0	−1.4	38.8	37.3	20.4	18.4
Washington	51.3	42.0	37.3	47.1	9.8	32.9	36.0	28.3	4.6
West Virginia	32.6	60.1	42.1	44.8	2.7	43.9	33.3	18.7	25.2
Wisconsin	49.7	43.2	41.4	45.5	4.1	40.6	34.3	22.1	18.5
Wyoming	28.5	60.8	56.8	26.8	−30.0	48.6	34.1	13.3	35.3

SOURCE: "U.S. State Political Data, 2012," in *State of the States*, The Gallup Organization, 2013, http://www.gallup.com/poll/125066/State-States.aspx (accessed September 28, 2013). Copyright © 2013 Gallup, Inc. All rights reserved. The content is used with permission; however, Gallup retains all rights of republication.

1, no. 1, March 2004), John Blume, Theodore Eisenberg, and Martin T. Wells compare 23 years of death row statistics to state murder rates. They find that between 1977 and 1999 the number of death row inmates in most states, including those with a reputation for sending a high number of defendants to death row, was nearly proportional to the number of murders in that state.

Overall, the number of inmates on death row in each state was between 0.4% (Colorado) and 6% (Nevada) of murders in that state, and the mean (average) "death sentencing rate" among all states was 2.2%. Despite having the highest number of executions per year, Texas came in below this average with a death row to murder ratio of 2%. Although Texas juries sentenced 776 people to death row, a total of 37,879 murders had been committed during the study period. Florida, which had a total death row population of 735 inmates, had experienced 21,837 murders and a death sentencing rate of 3.4%. By contrast, Nevada had 124 death row inmates, but only 2,072 murders, giving the state a death sentencing rate three times that of Texas. California, Maryland, New Mexico, Virginia, and Washington all had death sentencing rates below 1.5%.

To explain the discrepancy between states, Blume, Eisenberg, and Wells look at the states' statutes, politics, and other factors that might influence sentencing rates. They find that death sentencing rates were nearly twice as high in states in which a judge handed out the sentence as opposed to a jury (4.1% versus 2.1%). State statutes also made a big difference. States with relatively open-ended statutes, which allowed a jury to base their verdicts on subjective standards, such as the heinousness of the murder, had sentencing rates of 2.7%. Sentencing rates dropped to 1.9% in states in which specific crimes, such as the murder of a pregnant woman or police officer, automatically warranted the death sentence.

Differences within Death Penalty States

State capital cases are prosecuted at the local level, that is, by county or city prosecutors, and are decided by juries made up of local residents. During a criminal trial these decision makers typically reflect the attitudes about crime and punishment that are prominent in their local areas. Thus, death penalty sentencing rates can (and do) vary significantly between local jurisdictions within a state.

In "The Geography of the Death Penalty" (October 17, 2010, http://www.unc.edu/~fbaum/Innocence/NC/Baumgartner-geography-of-capital-punishment-oct-17-2010.pdf), Frank R. Baumgartner of the University of North Carolina presents geographical data regarding the 1,229 executions that were conducted in the United States between 1977 and October 2010. He states that, out of the 3,146 total counties in death penalty states, only 454

counties delivered capital punishment sentences. Furthermore, only 14 counties accounted for nearly one-third (30%) of the national execution total. Harris County in southeastern Texas was the undisputed death penalty capital of the nation; Houston is the county seat of Harris County. According to Baumgartner, Harris County was responsible for 115 (9%) of the total executions between 1977 and October 2010, followed by Dallas County, Texas (44 executions), Oklahoma County, Oklahoma (36 executions), Tarrant County, Texas (34 executions), and Bexar County, Texas (31 executions). In "County of Conviction for Offenders on Death Row" (http://www.tdcj.state.tx.us/stat/dr_county_conviction_offenders.html), the Texas Department of Corrections provides a breakdown of inmates on death row in the state by county of conviction. Of the 274 inmates on the state's death row as of October 2013, 98 inmates (36%, the largest portion) had been convicted in Harris County.

Phillip Reese provides in "See Where Murderers Most Often Get the Death Penalty" (SacBee.com, March 21, 2011) a map showing large disparities between California counties regarding death sentences that were handed out per 100 homicide arrests between 2000 and 2009. (It should be noted that not all homicide arrests end in homicide convictions, and not all homicides are capital cases.) Reese includes excerpts from an interview that was conducted in 2009 with Rod Pacheco, the former district attorney of Riverside County, a county with one of the highest death sentence rates in the state. Between 2000 and 2009 Riverside County had 752 homicide arrests and handed out 28 death sentences. By contrast, San Francisco County had 288 homicide arrests and no death sentences. Pacheco noted, "The people here have a very different view of public safety than the people in San Francisco."

Death penalty opponents point to county disparities in death sentences as evidence that capital punishment is applied unevenly and unfairly. Critics disagree, noting that county death sentencing rates vary based on differing murder rates, financial resources (death penalty cases are more expensive to prosecute than noncapital homicides), and local attitudes about crime and punishment.

Differences between Federal Judicial Districts

Table 5.10 in Chapter 5 lists dozens of capital offenses that are prosecuted at the federal level. A federal death penalty trial is typically conducted in the federal judicial district in which the crime occurred. As of October 2013, the country was divided into 94 federal judicial districts. Like the nation's counties, these federal judicial districts show large geographic disparities in death sentencing. In "The Racial Geography of the Federal Death Penalty" (*Washington Law Review*, vol. 85, no. 3, 2010), G. Ben Cohen and Robert J. Smith present data indicating that six of the districts accounted for a third of all 460 death-authorized cases dating back to 1988. Similarly, just seven of the districts accounted for about 40% of the 57 inmates on federal death row as of August 2010. Cohen and Smith suggest that the discrepancy cannot be explained by differences in murder rates between jurisdictions, noting that "while there is no shortage of death-eligible murders in the United States each year, the number of murders in a particular location bears little relationship to the number of defendants from that jurisdiction who are sentenced to death federally." Instead, they believe the discrepancy is directly related to the racial demographics of the federal judicial districts, as explained in the next section.

RACIAL BIAS IN THE DEATH PENALTY?

One of the most contentious and long-standing issues within the death penalty debate is the role of race. As noted earlier in *The Challenge of Crime in a Free Society*, the President's Commission on Law Enforcement and Administration of Justice found in 1967 that capital punishment was "disproportionately imposed" and was more often carried out on African Americans than whites. The U.S. Supreme Court decision in *Furman v. Georgia* (1972) forced jurisdictions around the country to make their death penalty systems more equitable. Even capital punishment opponents agree that, overall, the reforms have substantially reduced bias based on the race of the defendant.

Some analysts, however, claim that a different racial bias is evident in death penalty statistics—that defendants who kill white victims are more likely to get the death penalty than defendants who kill African American victims. Another contentious issue relates to the jury selection process. Death penalty opponents claim that prosecutors routinely dismiss nonwhites from jury pools to increase their chances of obtaining death sentences. Public opinion polls do show that whites favor capital punishment at much higher levels than do African Americans. All these factors combine to arouse suspicions that death penalty decisions are tainted by racial considerations. Death penalty supporters, however, contend that the laws provide safeguards against such bias and that alleged racial disparities in capital sentencing can be explained by other factors.

Race and Public Opinion about the Death Penalty

As noted earlier, public support for capital punishment varies based on demographic factors. Saad indicates in *U.S. Death Penalty Support Stable at 63%* that in December 2012 nearly two-thirds (63%) of respondents were in favor of the death penalty for a person convicted of murder. Support was much higher among whites (68%) than among nonwhites (49%). Similar differences of opinion are evident in polling results compiled by the

Pew Research Center. In *Continued Majority Support for Death Penalty* (January 6, 2012, http://www.people-press.org/files/legacy-pdf/1-6-12%20Death%20penalty%20 release.pdf), Pew researchers note that a poll conducted in November 2011 found that 62% of respondents overall favored capital punishment for murderers. Support was much higher among whites (68%) than among African Americans (40%). Hispanics were nearly evenly split on the issue, with 52% favoring the death penalty. The racial divide was also evident among Protestants. Although 77% of white evangelical Protestants favored the death penalty, only 40% of African American Protestants did likewise.

Race and Homicide Statistics

Detailed homicide statistics are collected by the DOJ's Bureau of Justice Statistics (BJS). As of the October 2013 the most recent comprehensive report on the subject was *Homicide Trends in the United States, 1980–2008* (http://www.bjs.gov/content/pub/pdf/htus8008.pdf), which was published in November 2011 by Alexia Cooper and Erica L. Smith of the BJS. African Americans were disproportionately represented among homicide offenders and victims between 1980 and 2008. As shown in Table 7.5, African Americans constituted 47.4% of homicide victims and 52.5% of homicide offenders during this period even though they made up only about 12.6% of the U.S. population. Whites accounted for 50.3% of victims and 45.3% of offenders.

Table 7.5 also shows that 27.8 African Americans were victimized by homicide for every 100,000 African Americans in the U.S. population, a rate more than six times that of whites (4.5). African Americans were homicide offenders at more than seven times the rate of whites (34.4 versus 4.5) between 1980 and 2008. The annual homicide victimization and offending rates for African Americans and whites are shown in Figure 7.1 and Figure 7.2, respectively. In 2008 the homicide victimization rate for African Americans (19.6 per 100,000) was six times higher than that for whites (3.3). The homicide offending rate in 2008 was seven times higher for African Americans (24.7) than for whites (3.4).

Cooper and Smith indicate that the vast majority of homicides committed between 1980 and 2008 were intraracial: 84% of white victims were murdered by whites and 93% of African American victims were murdered by African Americans. Cases of "black-on-white" and "white-on-black" homicide were relatively uncommon as shown in Figure 7.3.

A similar pattern is apparent in 2010 data reported by the Federal Bureau of Investigation (FBI) in *Crime in the United States* (September 2011, http://www.fbi.gov/about-us/cjis/ucr/crime-in-the-u.s/2010/crime-in-the-u.s.-2010/tables/10shrtbl06.xls). The FBI indicates that racial

TABLE 7.5

Homicide victims and offenders by race, 1980–2008

	Percent of—			Rate per 100,000	
	Victims	Offenders	Population	Victims	Offenders
Total	100%	100%	100%	7.4	8.3
Race					
White	50.3%	45.3%	82.9%	4.5	4.5
Black	47.4	52.5	12.6	27.8	34.4
Other*	2.3	2.2	4.4	3.8	4.1

*Other race includes American Indians, Native Alaskans, Asians, Native Hawaiians, and other Pacific Islanders.

SOURCE: Adapted from Alexia Cooper and Erica L. Smith, "Table 1. Victims and Offenders, by Demographic Group, 1980–2008," in *Homicide Trends in the United States, 1980–2008*, U.S. Department of Justice, Office of Justice Programs, Bureau of Justice Statistics, November 2011, http://www.bjs.gov/content/pub/pdf/htus8008.pdf (accessed September 3, 2013)

FIGURE 7.1

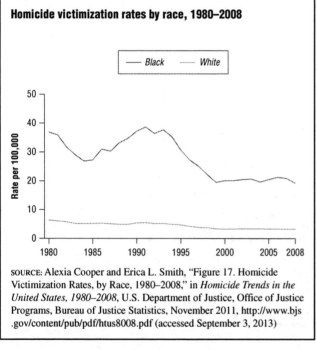

Homicide victimization rates by race, 1980–2008

SOURCE: Alexia Cooper and Erica L. Smith, "Figure 17. Homicide Victimization Rates, by Race, 1980–2008," in *Homicide Trends in the United States, 1980–2008*, U.S. Department of Justice, Office of Justice Programs, Bureau of Justice Statistics, November 2011, http://www.bjs.gov/content/pub/pdf/htus8008.pdf (accessed September 3, 2013)

FIGURE 7.2

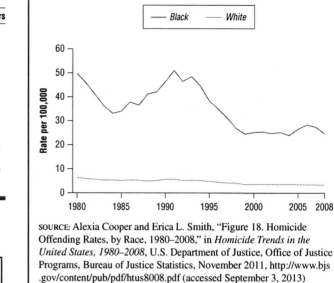

Homicide offending rates by race, 1980–2008

SOURCE: Alexia Cooper and Erica L. Smith, "Figure 18. Homicide Offending Rates, by Race, 1980–2008," in *Homicide Trends in the United States, 1980–2008*, U.S. Department of Justice, Office of Justice Programs, Bureau of Justice Statistics, November 2011, http://www.bjs .gov/content/pub/pdf/htus8008.pdf (accessed September 3, 2013)

FIGURE 7.3

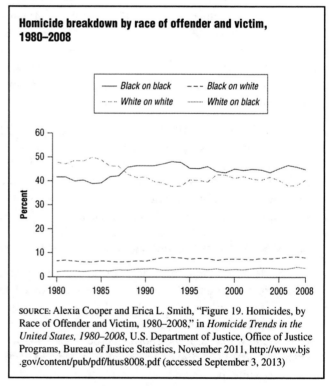

Homicide breakdown by race of offender and victim, 1980–2008

SOURCE: Alexia Cooper and Erica L. Smith, "Figure 19. Homicides, by Race of Offender and Victim, 1980–2008," in *Homicide Trends in the United States, 1980–2008*, U.S. Department of Justice, Office of Justice Programs, Bureau of Justice Statistics, November 2011, http://www.bjs .gov/content/pub/pdf/htus8008.pdf (accessed September 3, 2013)

information was known for 6,226 murder cases in 2010 involving a single offender and a single victim. Of the 3,327 white victims, the vast majority (2,777, or 83.5%) were killed by white offenders. Likewise, of the 2,720 African American victims, 2,459 (or 90.4%) were killed by African American offenders.

Racial Makeup of Death Row and Executed Inmates

Table 7.6 shows a racial breakdown of all prisoners sentenced to death between 1977 and 2011. Of the total 7,958 inmates, 3,842 (or 48.3%) were non-Hispanic whites and 3,264 (or 41%) were non-Hispanic African Americans. Table 6.6 in Chapter 6 provides racial and geographical information for the 3,082 prisoners on death

row as of December 31, 2011. There were 1,703 whites (55.3% of total) and 1,288 African Americans (41.8% of total) on death row.

According to Deborah Fins, in *Death Row U.S.A.: Winter 2013* (January 1, 2013, http://www.naacpldf.org/files/publications/DRUSA_Winter_2013.pdf), there were

TABLE 7.6

Racial breakdown of inmates sentenced to death, 1977–2011

Race/Hispanic origin	Total under sentence of death, 1977–2011[a]
Total	**7,958**
White[b]	3,842
Black[b]	3,264
Hispanic	725
All other races[b, c]	127

[a]Includes 5 persons sentenced to death prior to 1977 who were still under sentence of death on December 31, 2011; 374 persons sentenced to death prior to 1977 whose death sentence was removed between 1977 and December 31, 2011; and 7,579 persons sentenced to death between 1977 and 2011.
[b]Excludes persons of Hispanic or Latino origin.
[c]Includes American Indians, Alaska Natives, Asians, Native Hawaiians, and other Pacific Islanders.
Note: In 1972, the U.S. Supreme Court invalidated capital punishment statutes in several states (*Furman v. Georgia*, 408 U.S. 238 (1972)), effecting a moratorium on executions. Executions resumed in 1977 when the Supreme Court found that revisions to several state statutes had effectively addressed the issues previously held unconstitutional (*Gregg v. Georgia*, 428 U.S. 153 (1976) and its companion cases).

SOURCE: Adapted from Tracy L. Snell, "Table 12. Executions and Other Dispositions of Inmates Sentenced to Death, by Race and Hispanic Origin, 1977–2011," in *Capital Punishment, 2011—Statistical Tables*, U.S. Department of Justice, Office of Justice Programs, Bureau of Justice Statistics, July 16, 2013, http://www.bjs.gov/content/pub/pdf/cp11st.pdf (accessed September 3, 2013)

TABLE 7.7

Executions, by year, race, and Hispanic origin, 1977–2011

Year	All executions	White[a]	Black[a]	Hispanic	All other races[a, b]
Total	**1,277**	**722**	**440**	**101**	**14**
1977	1	1	0	0	0
1979	2	2	0	0	0
1981	1	1	0	0	0
1982	2	1	1	0	0
1983	5	4	1	0	0
1984	21	13	8	0	0
1985	18	9	7	2	0
1986	18	9	7	2	0
1987	25	11	11	3	0
1988	11	6	5	0	0
1989	16	6	8	2	0
1990	23	16	7	0	0
1991	14	6	7	1	0
1992	31	17	11	2	1
1993	38	19	14	4	1
1994	31	19	11	1	0
1995	56	31	22	2	1
1996	45	29	14	2	0
1997	74	41	26	5	2
1998	68	40	18	8	2
1999	98	53	33	9	3
2000	85	43	35	6	1
2001	66	45	17	3	1
2002	71	47	18	6	0
2003	65	41	20	3	1
2004	59	36	19	3	1
2005	60	38	19	3	0
2006	53	25	20	8	0
2007	42	22	14	6	0
2008	37	17	17	3	0
2009	52	24	21	7	0
2010	46	28	13	5	0
2011	43	22	16	5	0

[a]Excludes persons of Hispanic or Latino origin.
[b]Includes American Indians, Alaska Natives, Asians, Native Hawaiians, and other Pacific Islanders.
Note: In 1972, the U.S. Supreme Court invalidated capital punishment statutes in several states (*Furman v. Georgia*, 408 U.S. 238 (1972)), effecting a moratorium on executions. Executions resumed in 1977 when the Supreme Court found that revisions to several state statutes had effectively addressed the issues previously held unconstitutional (*Gregg v. Georgia*, 428 U.S. 153 (1976) and its companion cases).

SOURCE: Tracy L. Snell, "Table 11. Number of Inmates Executed, by Race, 1977–2011," in *Capital Punishment, 2011—Statistical Tables*, U.S. Department of Justice, Office of Justice Programs, Bureau of Justice Statistics, July 16, 2013, http://www.bjs.gov/content/pub/pdf/cp11st.pdf (accessed September 3, 2013)

3,125 inmates on death row as of January 1, 2013. Fins reports that 1,351 of the inmates (43.2% of the total) were white and 1,309 (41.9% of the total) were African American. Another 387 inmates (12.4% of the total) were classified as Latino/Latina, 44 (1.4% of the total) were believed to be Asian American, and 33 (1%) were Native American. The race of one inmate was unknown.

Table 7.7 shows BJS statistics regarding the racial makeup of prisoners executed between 1977 and 2011. Of the 1,277 inmates executed during this period, 722 (56.5% of the total) were white and 440 (34.5% of the total) were African American. Another 101 of the inmates, or 7.9% of the total, were Hispanic.

Race of Executed Prisoners' Victims

The BJS does not provide statistics on the racial makeup of the victims of executed prisoners. These data are difficult to collect and verify and may not be available for all victims. Some private organizations, however, do provide estimates. Fins reports that between 1977 and January 1, 2013, 76.4% of executed inmates had victimized a white person while 15.1% had victimized an African American. An additional 25 defendants were executed for murdering multiple victims of different races. An examination of the defendant-victim racial combination reveals that between 1977 and January 1, 2013, 52.1% of cases involved a white defendant and a white victim, 20.2% of cases involved an African American defendant and a white victim, 11.3% of cases involved an African American defendant and an African American victim, and 1.4% of cases involved a white defendant and an African American victim.

The Death Penalty Information Center (DPIC) notes in "Facts about the Death Penalty" (September 27, 2013, http://www.deathpenaltyinfo.org/documents/FactSheet.pdf) that as of September 27, 2013, 76% of victims in death penalty cases were white, 15% were African American, 7% were Hispanic, and 3% were of other races.

Racial Bias Allegations in State Capital Cases

Table 7.8 lists studies in which researchers claim to have found evidence of bias in state capital cases based on victim race. In some cases the bias is quite marked. For example, the 1983 and 1985 publications written by David C. Baldus et al. are collectively known as "the Baldus study," which is described in detail in Chapter 4. Baldus et al. found that murderers of white victims were 4.3 times more likely to receive the death penalty than murderers of African American victims. Other studies also point to a race-of-victim bias. For example, in *The Application of Indiana's Capital Sentencing Law: Findings of the Indiana Criminal Law Study Commission* (January 10, 2002, http://www.in.gov/cji/files/law_book.pdf), researchers note "if race plays a role in sentencing outcomes in Indiana, the race of the victim alone may play a more important role than the race of the offender or the interaction between victim and offender race."

Reports have also been published in which analysts examine data across several jurisdictions or review the findings of multiple studies concerning racial bias in state capital cases.

The U.S. General Accounting Office Review (1990)

The U.S. General Accounting Office (GAO; now the U.S. Government Accountability Office), in *Death Penalty Sentencing: Research Indicates Pattern of Racial Disparities* (February 1990, http://archive.gao.gov/t2pbat11/140845.pdf), reviewed 28 studies on race and the death penalty that had been published as of 1990. The GAO reported that "in 82% of the studies, the race of the victim was found to influence the likelihood of being charged with capital murder or receiving the death penalty." The GAO found that when the victim was white, the defendant (whether white or African American), was more likely to get a death sentence.

The GAO added that in the small number of horrendous murders, death sentences were more likely to be imposed, regardless of race. Nevertheless, when the offender killed a person while robbing the person or when the murderer had a previous record, the race of the victim played a role. The GAO also explained that for crimes of passion, the convicted person (regardless of race) rarely received the death penalty.

Baldus and Woodworth Review (2003)

In 2003 David C. Baldus and George Woodworth reviewed the results of multiple studies examining race in capital cases in "Race Discrimination in the Administration of the Death Penalty: An Overview of the Empirical Evidence with Special Emphasis on the Post-1990 Research" (*Criminal Law Bulletin*, vol. 39, 2003).

TABLE 7.8

Statistical studies showing a race-of-victim bias in capital cases

Study title	Author(s)	Publisher(s)/sponsor(s)	Publication date	Jurisdiction	Data time period
Comparative Review of Death Sentences: An Empirical Study of the Georgia Experience	David C. Baldus, Charles A. Pulanski Jr., and George Woodworth	Journal of Criminal Law and Criminology	1983	Georgia	1970s
Monitoring and Evaluating Contemporary Death Sentencing Systems: Lessons from Georgia	David C. Baldus, Charles A. Pulanski Jr., and George Woodworth	University of California Davis Law Review	1985	Georgia	1970s
Race and the Death Penalty in Kentucky Murder Trials, 1976–1991: A Study of Racial Bias as a Factor in Capital Sentencing	Thomas J. Keil and Gennaro F. Vito	Northern Kentucky Law Review (Study commissioned by the Kentucky legislature)	1993	Kentucky	1976–1991
Capital Punishment in Missouri: Examining the Issue of Racial Disparity	Jonathan R. Sorensen and Donald H. Wallace	Behavioral Sciences & the Law	1995	Missouri	1977–1991
Racial Discrimination and the Death Penalty in the Post-Furman Era: An Empirical and Legal Analysis with Recent Findings from Philadelphia	David C. Baldus, et al.	Cornell Law Review	1998	Philadelphia, Pennsylvania	1983–1994
The Use of Peremptory Challenges In Capital Murder Trials: A Legal And Empirical Analysis	David C. Baldus, et al.	University of Pennsylvania Journal of Constitutional Law	2001	Philadelphia, Pennsylvania	1981–1997
Race and the Death Penalty in North Carolina—An Empirical Analysis: 1993–1997	Isaac Unah and John Charles Boger	University of North Carolina	2001	North Carolina	1993–1997
The Application of Indiana's Capital Sentencing Law: Findings of the Indiana Criminal Law Study Commission	Kathryn Janeway	Indiana Criminal Justice Institute (Study requested by state governor and legislature)	2002	Indiana	1993–2001
An Empirical Analysis of Maryland's Death Sentencing System with Respect to the Influence of Race and Legal Jurisdiction	Raymond Paternoster et al.	University of Maryland (Study commissioned by the state of Maryland) Santa Clara Law Review	2003	Maryland	1978–1999
The Impact of Legally Inappropriate Factors on Death Sentencing for California Homicides, 1990–99	Glenn L. Pierce and Michael L. Radelet		2005	California	1990–1999
Death Penalty Unequal; Capital Cases Hard for Smaller Counties; and Two Killers: One Spared	Andrew Welsh-Huggins; Kate Roberts; and John Seewer	Ohio Associated Press	2005	Ohio	1981–2002

SOURCE: Created by Kim Masters Evans for Gale, 2013

They also wrote about their findings in "Race Discrimination and the Death Penalty: An Empirical and Legal Overview" (James R. Acker, Robert M. Bohm, and Charles S. Lanier, editors, *America's Experiment with Capital Punishment: Reflections on the Past, Present, and Future of the Ultimate Penal Sanction*, 2003). Baldus and Woodworth reviewed 18 studies conducted between 1991 and 2003 that assess race effects in death penalty cases in Arizona; California; Connecticut; the federal system; Florida; Illinois; Indiana; Kentucky; Maryland; Missouri; Nebraska; New Jersey; North Carolina; Philadelphia, Pennsylvania; South Carolina; Texas; and Virginia. Overall, they conclude the following:

- Two studies showed "no race effects at all": Nebraska and New Jersey

- Three studies showed effects based both on the race of the victims and the defendants: Connecticut, the federal system, and Philadelphia, Pennsylvania

- Two studies showed racial disparities only for cases involving African American defendants and white victims: Kentucky and Maryland

- Twelve studies showed effects based on the race of the victims, but not on the race of the defendants: Arizona, California, Florida, Illinois, Indiana, Maryland (two studies), Missouri, North Carolina, South Carolina, Texas, and Virginia

A 2004 Multistate Analysis

In the 2004 study "Explaining Death Row's Population and Racial Composition," Blume, Eisenberg, and Wells compared the race of death row inmates to the race of all inmates arrested for murder for 1977 through 1999. Nationwide, African Americans committed 51.5% of the murders over this period, but made up only 41.3% of the inmates on death row. The researchers analyzed data from seven states—Georgia, Indiana, Maryland, Nevada, Pennsylvania, South Carolina, and Virginia—to determine why these percentages did not match.

Generally, what Blume, Eisenberg, and Wells found was that juries gave the death sentence to a far smaller percentage of African American murderers when the victim was also African American, rather than white. In South Carolina, for instance, only 0.3% of African Americans who killed African Americans received the death penalty, whereas 6.8% of African Americans who murdered whites were sentenced to death. Because 94% of the African American homicide victims they studied had been killed by African Americans, the percentage of African Americans on death row tended to be lower than the percentage of African American murderers. Even though the researchers speculated that racism may have affected the percentages, they also believed that African American juries in communities with a great deal of

"black-on-black" crime were less likely to hand out death sentences.

State Legislative Actions

The 14th Amendment to the U.S. Constitution says in part that no state can "deny to any person within its jurisdiction the equal protection of the laws." Some analysts claim that studies showing racial bias in death penalty cases prove that capital punishment violates the equal protection clause. In 1987, however, the U.S. Supreme Court made this claim very difficult to pursue with its decision in *McClesky v. Kemp* (481 U.S. 279 [1987]), which is described in Chapter 4. In *Final Report of the Pennsylvania Supreme Court Committee on Racial and Gender Bias in the Justice System* (March 3, 2003, http://www.pa-interbranchcommission.com/_pdfs/Final Report.pdf), the Pennsylvania Supreme Court Committee on Racial and Gender Bias in the Justice System notes that "under federal constitutional doctrine, as defined principally by the United States Supreme Court's opinion in *McCleskey v. Kemp*, traditional statistically-based evidentiary paths to prove discrimination have been closed. The McCleskey court, however, suggested that legislative action was required if such evidence was to be considered."

Since 1987 legislatures in two states, Kentucky in 1998 and North Carolina in 2009, have passed Racial Justice Acts that supporters hoped would open the door for the use of statistical information to demonstrate equal protection problems with capital punishment. However, the actual effects of these laws have been blunted, and North Carolina repealed its Racial Justice Act in 2013.

Michael Hewlett indicates in "N.C., Ky. Diverge on Racial Justice" (JournalNow.com, December 25, 2011) that the Kentucky law is considered very restrictive in scope. It does not apply to persons who were already under sentence of death when the law was passed in 1998. In addition, death row defendants can only raise claims before trial. Hewlett notes, "They also have to prove by clear and convincing evidence that racial bias played a role in their individual case, which limits the use of statewide statistics." In *Evaluating Fairness and Accuracy in State Death Penalty Systems: The Kentucky Death Penalty Assessment Report* (December 2011, http://www.americanbar.org/content/dam/aba/administrative/death_penalty_moratorium/final_ky_report.authcheckdam.pdf), the American Bar Association (ABA) complains that the Kentucky Racial Justice Act "appears to have a number of restrictions limiting its effectiveness at identifying and remedying racial discrimination in the administration of the death penalty." Neither Hewlett nor the ABA knew of a case successfully raised under Kentucky's Racial Justice Act.

In 2009 North Carolina passed legislation allowing death row inmates the right to use state and county prosecutorial statistics to prove that racial bias was a factor in their death penalty conviction, thus gaining the right to have a sentence converted to life imprisonment. In *State of North Carolina v. Marcus Reymond Robinson* (April 20, 2012, http://www.deathpenaltyinfo.org/docu ments/RobinsonRJAOrder.pdf), a North Carolina court notes that the law allowed any of three grounds for making such a claim:

- Evidence that defendants of a particular race were more likely to be charged with a capital crime, or have a death sentence imposed, than defendants of other races

- Evidence that those who had victimized people of a particular race were more likely to be charged with a capital crime, or have a death sentence imposed, than those who victimized people of other races

- Evidence that race played a significant role in decisions about which people to strike (exclude) from the pool of potential jurors

The law was controversial and immediately came under attack by opponents. Criticism of the law grew in intensity during 2012, when four of North Carolina's death row inmates—Marcus Robinson, Tilmon Golphin, Christina Walters, and Quintel Augustine—had their sentences reduced to life in prison without chance of parole. All four of their commutations were based on evidence that race was a significant factor in decisions to exercise peremptory strikes during jury selection at their original trials. The jury selection process and its racial controversies are explained later in this chapter.

Michael Biesecker states in "NC Judge Commutes 3 Deaths Sentences; Cites Bias" (Associated Press, December 13, 2012) that Golphin, Walters, and Augustine "were among the most notorious killers on North Carolina's death row. Two had killed law enforcement officers." Golphin was on death row for the 1997 murders of Ed Lowry (a state trooper) and David Hathcock (a sheriff's deputy). Walters was sentenced to death for kidnapping and killing two women, Tracy Rose Lambert and Susan Raye Moore, and wounding a third, Debra Cheeseborough, during a gang initiation ritual in 1998. Augustine was on death row for killing Roy Turner Jr. (a police officer) in 2001. Robinson, the first of the four inmates to obtain a sentence reduction, had been sentenced to death for murdering 17-year-old Erik Tornblom during a robbery in 1991.

The Racial Justice Act was repealed in June 2013. In "North Carolina Repeals Law Allowing Racial Bias Claim in Death Penalty Challenges" (NYTimes.com, June 5, 2013), Kim Severson explains that "conservatives have been chipping away at the Racial Justice Act

since its inception four years ago. In 2012, the legislature severely limited how statistics could be used and put a stronger burden of proof on the inmate making the appeal." The election of a Republican governor in late 2012, replacing the Democrat who had signed the act into law, opened the door to repeal. According to Severson, during its existence "nearly everyone facing execution" in North Carolina had filed a claim under the law. Those behind the repeal effort felt that the law was deeply flawed. Severson quotes Representative Tim Moore, "It tries to put a carte blanche solution on the problem. A white supremacist who murdered an African-American could argue he was a victim of racism if blacks were on the jury."

In 2013 prosecutors appealed Robinson's revised sentence to the North Carolina Supreme Court. In "Racial Justice Act Case Heads to NC Supreme Court" (CharlotteObserver.com, August 13, 2013), Anne Blythe reports that the court has allowed interested parties to file amicus curiae briefs in the case. Amicus curiae is a Latin phrase that means "friend of the court." Amicus curiae parties are not directly involved in a particular case but have an interest in its outcome, usually because of broader civil rights or constitutional issues. According to Blythe, parties indicating their support for Robinson's reduced sentence under the Racial Justice Act include "former senior military officials, families of murder victims from across North Carolina, potential jurors who contend they 'were denied a voice in capital decision-making because of their race,' professors and social scientists, and the N.C. Advocates for Justice, a nonprofit, nonpartisan association." As of October 2013, the North Carolina Supreme Court had not heard the case.

Death Penalty Advocates Speak about Alleged Race-of-Victim Bias

The Criminal Justice Legal Foundation (CJLF) is a California-based group that supports capital punishment. Kent S. Scheidegger of the CJLF points out in "Rebutting the Myths about Race and the Death Penalty" (*Ohio State Journal of Criminal Law*, vol. 10, no. 1, 2012) that the statistical models used in the 1980s-era Baldus study were found to be flawed by the federal district court that heard the *McCleskey v. Kemp* case before it was ultimately appealed to the Supreme Court. The latter assumed that the study was valid, although it rejected the claim that it proved bias against McCleskey.

Scheidegger argues that many of the studies that appear to show a race-of-victim bias fail to take into account key factors that affect death penalty sentencing decisions: the strength of the evidence in the case, the heinousness of the crime, the criminal status of the victim (e.g., the murder of a fellow drug dealer versus the murder of an innocent victim), and the jurisdiction. Jurisdictional factors, in particular, are cited by death penalty advocates as the main cause of perceived race-of-victim bias.

Scheidegger points to polls showing that capital punishment receives higher support from whites than from African Americans. Thus, the death penalty is applied less often in predominantly African American jurisdictions, even though these areas have large numbers of African American murder victims. Scheidegger states, "Naturally, a jurisdiction with a large black population elects a prosecutor who seeks the death penalty more selectively, and those are the jurisdictions where most of the black-victim homicides occur."

Charles Lane notes in *Stay of Execution: Saving the Death Penalty* (2010) that "above all, prosecutors do not seek the death penalty unless they think they can actually persuade a jury to impose it. In jurisdictions with large African American populations, where most black-on-black crime occurs, persuading a jury to sentence a defendant to death is relatively difficult."

REMEDYING A RACIAL BIAS? In February 2006 the U.S. Senate Committee on the Judiciary Subcommittee on the Constitution, Civil Rights, and Human Rights conducted the hearing "An Examination of the Death Penalty in the United States." One of the scholars who testified was John McAdams of Marquette University (http://www.judiciary.senate.gov/hearings/testimony.cf m?id=e655f9e2809e5476862f735da10e0680&wit_id= e655f9e2809e5476862f735da10e0680-2-1). McAdams noted that death penalty opponents often play "the race card" in debates over capital punishment. He acknowledged that studies do show "a huge bias" against African American victims of homicide. He testified, "This is clearly unjust, but it leaves open the question of whether the injustice should be remedied by executing nobody at all, or rather executing more offenders who have murdered black people."

Scheidegger presents a similar argument, noting "if the death penalty is imposed less often when the victim is black, that means that there are perpetrators in black-victim cases who should have been sentenced to death but were not."

Racial Issues Related to Jury Selection

A contentious racial issue in the death penalty debate involves jury selection. A venire is a pool of prospective jurors, who are typically selected at random using voter registration records or similar databases of local residents. In state capital cases the venire is usually drawn from the county in which the crime occurred and in which the trial will be held. In federal capital cases the venire is drawn from the judicial district in which the crime occurred and in which the trial will be held. As noted earlier, the United States is divided into 94 federal judicial districts. Thus, each district may include many counties that are spread over a large geographical area.

Prior to the start of a criminal trial, the judge, the prosecutor, and the lawyer for the defendant can interview potential jurors and strike (dismiss) individuals from serving on the jury. There are two types of dismissals: dismissals for cause and peremptory strikes. Dismissals for cause can be made by the judge or the attorneys (with the judge's approval) for specific allowable reasons, for example, a potential juror is related to the victim. Attorneys (not judges) make peremptory strikes, which are dismissals for which no reason has to be given to the court. Peremptory strikes are allowed in both federal and state capital trials.

In "Three Strikes and You're Out? Critics Seek Juror-Dismissal Cap" (WSJ.com, March 5, 2009), Nathan Koppel explains that lawyers for the prosecution and defense are allowed an unlimited number of challenges for cause, but are limited under state statute as to the number of peremptory strikes they can make per venire. According to Koppel, in 2009 that number ranged from six in Ohio, to 20 in California and New York, to 25 in Connecticut.

ARE PEREMPTORY STRIKES MISUSED? Peremptory strikes are forbidden by law to be based on the race or sex of the potential juror. The race provision stems from a U.S. Supreme Court decision in *Batson v. Kentucky* (476 U.S. 79 [1986]), in which the court ruled that discriminatory jury selection is unconstitutional. However, critics claim that prosecutors often use peremptory strikes to eliminate African Americans from capital case juries because African Americans are known to have lower public support for the death penalty than whites.

The Equal Justice Institute (EJI), a nonprofit legal organization in Alabama, alleges in *Illegal Racial Discrimination in Jury Selection: A Continuing Legacy* (August 2010, http://eji.org/eji/files/EJI%20Ra ce%20and%20Jury%20Report.pdf) that African Americans are purposely struck by prosecutors from many juries, particularly in the South and especially in capital cases. The organization says it examined jury selection practices in Alabama, Arkansas, Florida, Georgia, Louisiana, Mississippi, South Carolina, and Tennessee and found "shocking evidence of racial discrimination" in all these states. For example, in rural Houston County, Alabama, the EJI claims that prosecutors used peremptory strikes to dismiss 80% of African American potential jurors from venires between 2005 and 2009. *Batson v. Kentucky* allows defense lawyers to object to prosecutors' peremptory strikes. The prosecutors must then provide to the court "race-neutral" explanations for the strikes to stand. The EJI presents dozens of reasons that were used by prosecutors as excuses to strike African Americans from juries, including low intelligence, lack

of education, wearing eyeglasses, chewing gum, marital status, age, being unemployed, having a child out of wedlock, looking like a drug dealer, having dyed red hair, and living in a high-crime neighborhood.

Since 2009 EJI lawyers have attempted to obtain new trials for two Alabama death row inmates, Jason Michael Sharp and Earl Jerome McGahee, by arguing on appeal that African American jurors were improperly struck from their original trial juries. Sharp, who is white, was convicted for the 1999 rape and murder of Tracy Lynn Morris, a white woman. In the press release "Alabama Death Row Prisoner Wins New Trial from Appeals Court Due to Illegal Racial Discrimination in Jury Selection" (February 25, 2011, http://eji.org/node/509), the EJI notes that seven African Americans were struck from Sharp's venire for lacking "sophistication." In 2011 an appeals court rejected this reason as "historically suspect" and further stated that "the record does not support any of the State's strikes for this reason." However, Brian Lawson reports in "Alabama Appeals Court Reverses Its 2011 Decision That Granted Convicted Murderer Jason Sharp a New Trial" (AL.com, March 23, 2012) that the following year the court reversed its decision after the state attorney general's office asked that it reexamine the prosecution's reasons for striking African Americans from the venire. In August 2013 the Alabama Supreme Court refused to grant Sharp a new trial.

McGahee, an African American, is under sentence of death for the 1985 murders of Connie Brown and Cassandra Lee, also African Americans. The EJI explains in "EJI Wins Relief for Earl McGahee" (March 5, 2009, http://eji.org/node/284) that all of the African Americans were struck from McGahee's venire by the prosecutor for "low intelligence." Prosecutors claimed this was evidenced by the fact that the potential jurors were unemployed or held blue-collar jobs. An appeals court, however, found that whites who were unemployed were not struck from the venire. In March 2009 the U.S. Court of Appeals for the 11th Circuit ordered a new trial for McGahee, citing illegal discrimination in the use of peremptory challenges. As of October 2013, no further information could be located regarding McGahee's case; his name, however, did appear on a listing of death row inmates kept by the Alabama Department of Corrections (http://www.doc.state.al.us/DeathRow.aspx).

RACIAL ISSUES RELATED TO FEDERAL JURIES. Claims of racial bias in jury selection are not limited to state capital cases. Similar claims are also made about federal death penalty cases. As noted earlier, Cohen and Smith have documented significant geographic disparities in federal capital sentences dating from 1988 to 2010 indicating that only a few federal judicial districts account for significant numbers of federal inmates on death row. Cohen and Smith also allege that African Americans were disproportionately sentenced to death in these districts due to federal jury selection processes.

Federal venires are drawn from the district at large, rather than from a single county. Thus, African American defendants who might not be sentenced to death by a mostly African American jury from their local city or county can end up with a mostly white jury that is drawn from the entire district. Cohen and Smith indicate that the highest death sentencing rates are in districts largely made up of an African American–majority city or county that is surrounded by white-majority counties, such as New Orleans, Louisiana, in the Eastern District of Louisiana; St. Louis, Missouri, in the Eastern District of Missouri; Richmond, Virginia, in the Eastern District of Virginia; and Prince George's County in the District of Maryland. Twelve of the 57 inmates on the federal death row as of 2010 were prosecuted in these four districts and all were African American. Cohen and Smith complain that "federal prosecutors are able to dilute minority-concentrated populations (obtaining far whiter jury pools) simply by prosecuting the same case in federal rather than state court." They also claim that data indicate death sentences have been infrequently given in districts that contain large minority populations or those in which the population demographics are similar throughout the district.

LEGAL REPRESENTATION: QUESTIONS ABOUT QUALITY

The Sixth Amendment to the U.S. Constitution guarantees the "assistance of counsel for . . . defense" in federal criminal prosecution. In *Gideon v. Wainwright* (372 U.S. 335 [1963]), the U.S. Supreme Court extended the right to counsel to state criminal prosecution of indigent (poor) people who are charged with felonies. In *Argersinger v. Hamlin* (407 U.S. 25 [1972]), the high court held that poor people who are charged with any crime that carries a sentence of imprisonment have the right to counsel.

The court later ruled in *Strickland v. Washington* (466 U.S. 688 [1984]) that the lawyers provided for poor defendants must abide by certain professional standards in criminal cases. Some of these standards include demonstrating loyalty to the client, avoiding conflicts of interest, keeping the defendant informed of important developments in the trial, and conducting reasonable factual and legal investigations that may aid the client's case.

Indigent Capital Defense in State Trials

States vary in their methods of fulfilling *Gideon*. Some states have undertaken the establishment and funding of an indigent defense system, whereas others have passed the responsibility on to individual counties.

Across the United States different jurisdictions use one or a combination of three systems to provide counsel to poor defendants. The first system used by some jurisdictions has public defenders, who are usually government employees. Under the second system, the court-assigned counsel system, a judge appoints private lawyers to represent the poor. A third system involves contract lawyers who bid for the job of providing indigent defense.

Court-assigned lawyers belong to a list of private lawyers who accept clients on a case-by-case basis. In jurisdictions that employ these lawyers, judges appoint lawyers from a list of private bar members and determine their pay. In most cases the pay is low.

A PHILADELPHIA CHALLENGE. In "Court-Appointed Death Penalty Lawyers Want More $$$" (Philly.com, April 6, 2011), Joseph A. Slobodzian reports that in April 2011 a group of court-appointed capital defense lawyers in Philadelphia, Pennsylvania, filed a petition in court against Philadelphia County protesting its pay structure. The petitioners alleged that the county "pays its court-appointed attorneys less to prepare a capital case than any remotely comparable jurisdiction in the country." According to Slobodzian, the county's pay schedule includes flat fees of $1,333 for pretrial preparation and $2,000 for the trial. By comparison, a private attorney in the Philadelphia area can charge as much as $50,000 to defend a murder case. Slobodzian notes in "Pennsylvania Supreme Court urged to Consider How Philadelphia Pays Death-Penalty Lawyers" (Philly.com, June 9, 2011) that in June 2011 the petitioners asked the Pennsylvania Supreme Court to hear the case after their petition was twice rejected by a lower court. Slobodzian indicates in "Phila. Courts Increase Pay for Capital Defense" (Philly.com, February 29, 2012) that low pay for court-appointed_lawyers was seen a "major factor" in 69 capital cases from Philadelphia having been reversed or remanded by appeals courts due to serious mistakes by defense lawyers. Slobodzian reports that in early 2012 the Philadelphia court system "dramatically increased" fees for court-appointed attorneys and took other steps to increase the number of attorneys available in hopes of reducing a backlog of capital cases awaiting trial and improving the quality of representation for indigent defendants.

A STUDY OF HARRIS COUNTY, TEXAS. As noted earlier, Harris County, Texas, prosecuted 115 (9%) of the 1,229 total executions that were carried out in the United States between 1977 and October 2010. In "Legal Disparities in the Capital of Capital Punishment" (*Journal of Criminal Law and Criminology*, vol. 99, no. 3, Spring 2009), Scott Phillips of the University of Denver examines the legal representation received by 504 defendants who were indicted for capital murder in Harris County between 1992 and 1999. Phillips notes that at that time

Harris County was the largest metropolitan area in the country using a court-appointed system, rather than a public defender office. Of the 504 cases examined, the vast majority (369, or 73%) featured court-appointed lawyers. Hired lawyers represented only 31 (6%) of the defendants. The remaining 104 defendants used a mixture of court-appointed and hired lawyers throughout their legal proceedings. Phillips finds that the defendants with hired lawyers were approximately 20 times more likely to be acquitted than the other defendants. He notes that "the relationship between legal counsel and acquittals is troubling. It does not seem plausible to conclude that defendants who hired counsel were actually twenty times more likely to be innocent." Rather, Phillips believes this discrepancy is due in large part to problems that are inherent to the county's court-appointed lawyer system:

- Flat-fee payments rather than hourly payments discourage appointed lawyers from spending large amounts of time on a particular case.

- A judge has to approve the hiring of any specialists, such as investigators or expert witnesses, and can limit the funding for them. Phillips notes that judges can be reluctant to spend funds on such specialists for fear of being perceived as sympathetic to defendants and "soft on crime."

- Judges appoint attorneys to handle cases. The lawyers vying for these positions can experience a conflict of interest between representing their clients aggressively in court (which risks antagonizing the judge) and maintaining a positive relationship with the judge to obtain additional appointments in the future.

- The judges also face a conflict of interest in that they are supposed to ensure that indigent defendants receive adequate representation, but are under funding pressures from the county government and political pressures to be tough on crime so they can be reelected.

- Political and personal factors can affect judges' appointment decisions, meaning that lawyers can be appointed to cases for reasons other than their legal skills or trial experience.

Phillips recommended that Harris County replace its court-appointment system with a capital defender office. In 2010 Harris County created a public defender office (http://harriscountypublicdefender.org/), which began accepting cases in February 2011. However, clients are assigned to the public defender office by judges, who also have the discretion to assign clients to private attorneys instead. Furthermore, as of October 2013 the office did not handle capital cases.

Ineffective Counsel?

Death penalty opponents claim that some lawyers who have defended capital cases were inexperienced, ill-trained, or incompetent. They point to cases in which the defense lawyers fell asleep during trial, drank to excess the night before, or even showed up in the courtroom intoxicated. They also cite well-publicized cases of inmates who have been exonerated as a result of college students finding evidence that defense lawyers had failed to uncover.

In "In Pursuit of the Public Good: Lawyers Who Care" (April 9, 2001, http://www.supremecourt.gov/publicinfo/speeches/viewspeeches.aspx?Filename=sp_04-09-01a.html), Justice Ruth Bader Ginsburg (1933–) of the U.S. Supreme Court expresses her concerns about proper representation in capital cases. She states, "I have yet to see a death case, among the dozens coming to the Supreme Court on eve of execution petitions, in which the defendant was well represented at trial.... Public funding for the legal representation of poor people in the United States is hardly generous. In capital cases, state systems for affording representation to indigent defendants vary from adequate to meager."

The ABA provides in "*Gideon*'s Broken Promise: America's Continuing Quest for Equal Justice" (December 2004, http://www.americanbar.org/) some insight into why poor defendants may receive inadequate counsel. The ABA analyzed the indigent defense system in 22 states and found that lawyers who took on poor defendants received low pay and that judges tended to be lax about legal protocols to clear overcrowded dockets. In addition, the ABA complained that indigent defense systems lacked the basic accountability and oversight needed to ensure decent legal representation or to correct these problems.

To remedy some of the problems inherent in death penalty trials, Congress passed and President George W. Bush (1946–) signed the Innocence Protection Act of 2004. This act launched a program in which state governments received grants from the federal government to improve the quality of legal representation for poor defendants in state capital cases. To receive such a grant, a state's capital defense system had to meet a number of requirements, which included establishing minimum standards for defense attorneys and monitoring the performance of these attorneys. The Innocence Protection Act expired in 2009 and was not reauthorized by Congress. In 2013 the U.S. senator Patrick Leahy (1940–; D-VT) introduced the Justice for All Reauthorization Act of 2013, which would reestablish the grants to states with capital cases. As of October 2013, the legislation had not been passed.

The GAO describes in *Indigent Defense: DOJ Could Increase Awareness of Eligible Funding and Better Determine the Extent to Which Funds Help Support This Purpose* (May 2012, http://www.gao.gov/assets/600/590736.pdf) DOJ grants that provided funding to states for general indigent defense in fiscal years (FY) 2005 through 2010. (The federal fiscal year extends from October 1 through September 30.) One of the programs, the Capital Case Litigation Initiative, specifically designated funds for capital cases; total funding, however, was split between the prosecutorial side and the defense side. A total of $2.5 million was allocated to the initiative in FY 2010.

In a 2012 address to the ABA (February 4, 2012, http://www.justice.gov/iso/opa/ag/speeches/2012/ag-speech-120204.html), the U.S. attorney general Eric Holder Jr. (1951–) acknowledged problems with the nation's indigent defense system overall, noting that "across the country, public defender offices and other indigent defense providers are underfunded and understaffed. Too often, when legal representation is available to the poor, it's rendered less effective by insufficient resources, overwhelming caseloads, and inadequate oversight."

CHAPTER 8
EXONERATIONS AND MORATORIUMS

Since the 1990s dozens of inmates who were once on death row have been exonerated, meaning that the original capital charges against them were dropped, they were retried and acquitted (found not guilty), or they were pardoned based on new evidence of innocence. Exonerations are heralded by death penalty opponents as proof that the U.S. capital punishment system is flawed and should be abandoned. Death penalty advocates argue that the importance of exonerations is exaggerated, but that their occurrence proves that the capital justice system protects the rights of the accused. Nevertheless, exonerations and other concerns about the capital punishment system have spurred several states to cease conducting executions, at least temporarily. These temporary moratoriums allow officials time to reexamine their capital punishment systems and determine if there are systematic problems in their administration.

OVERTURNING CAPITAL CASES

Capital cases begin with a trial in which the guilt of the defendant is assessed. Defendants found guilty are then subject to a hearing at which their sentences are determined. As explained in Chapter 5, state death penalty convictions are subject to a lengthy appeals process that begins with an automatic direct appeal to a state's highest court. During the direct appeal a court reviews the original trial court records for constitutional or legal errors. If the direct appeals are not successful, the defendant can pursue what is called the state appeals process, followed by the federal appeals process. The state and federal appeals processes are collectively known as post-conviction review. At any point during a direct appeal or post-conviction review, if a court finds a problem that rises above what is called "harmless error," it can overturn the defendant's conviction or sentence. Alternatively, it can remand (send back) the case to a lower court for reconsideration.

The prosecutor decides whether or not to retry defendants who have had their convictions overturned. Charges may be dropped (dismissed) if the prosecutor does not believe the case against the defendant is strong enough to persuade a new jury of guilt. The decision not to retry might be based on errors uncovered during appeal, witnesses who have died or changed their minds about the case since it was originally tried, or other evidentiary problems. When a capital defendant is retried, he or she might be found guilty again or might be acquitted (i.e., found not guilty) by the new jury. Defendants convicted on retrial might or might not be given the death penalty during their sentencing hearings.

EXONERATIONS

The Death Penalty Information Center (DPIC) is opposed to capital punishment. In "Innocence: List of Those Freed from Death Row" (2013, http://www.deathpenaltyinfo.org/innocence-list-those-freed-death-row), the DPIC lists the names of 142 people that it says were exonerated between 1973 and 2012 (as of October 11, 2013). The so-called Innocence List is often touted by death penalty opponents as proof that the U.S. capital punishment system is flawed. People are added to the DPIC list in one of two ways: when their conviction is overturned and they are acquitted on retrial or all charges are dropped; or when they receive a pardon because of new evidence of innocence.

It is important to note that the Innocence List is not limited solely to inmates who were on death row at the time of their exoneration. The list also includes people originally sentenced to death who had been resentenced (e.g., to life in prison). Thus, it is most correct to say that those on the Innocence List were on death row at some point prior to their exoneration, as opposed to claiming that everyone on the list was freed directly from death row.

Table 8.1 lists the exonerated inmates along with their races, the states in which they were convicted, and information about their cases. Overall, 89 had charges against them dismissed, 46 were acquitted on retrial, and seven were pardoned. Eighteen of the inmates were exonerated based on DNA evidence. The earliest conviction dates back to 1963, and is one of four convictions from the 1960s. Another 30 convictions are from the 1970s, 67 from the 1980s, 37 from the 1990s, and four from the first decade of the 21st century. The first exoneration listed occurred in 1973 and was one of 14 exonerations during the 1970s. Another 25 exonerations occurred during the 1980s, 43 during the 1990s, 55 during the first decade of the 21st century, and five during the 2010s (as of September 2013).

In total, 26 states had exonerations between 1973 and October 2013. (See Table 8.1.) Florida had 24 exonerations, the most of any state. It was followed by Illinois (20), Texas (12), Oklahoma (10), and Louisiana (9). The amount of time that elapsed between conviction and exoneration ranged from one year to 33 years. Overall, the average amount of time that passed between conviction and exoneration was 9.8 years.

Of the inmates reported exonerated, 71 were African American and 57 were white. (See Table 8.1.) Twelve were Hispanic and two were classified as "other" races.

David Keaton: The First Exoneree

David Keaton (1952–), a Florida teenager who was convicted of murder in 1971, was the first person exonerated from death row in the modern era. His legal history is detailed by the Florida Commission on Capital Cases in *Case Histories: A Review of 24 Individuals Released from Death Row* (September 10, 2002, http://www.floridacapitalcases.state.fl.us/Publications/innocentsproject.pdf). Keaton was convicted of felony murder for the shooting of Thomas Revels during an armed robbery at a grocery store in Tallahassee in 1970. Keaton and four other men, known as the "Quincy Five," were indicted for the crime. Keaton was not accused of being the triggerman and initially he confessed to being involved in the robbery, but he later recanted. In 1971 Keaton was convicted and sentenced to death, based on his own confession and the testimony of eyewitnesses who placed him at the scene. The following year his sentence was converted to life in prison following the U.S. Supreme Court's finding in *Furman v. Georgia* (408 U.S. 238 [1972]) that the death penalty, as then practiced, was unconstitutional.

Meanwhile, three other men were arrested for the murder of Revels based on fingerprint evidence and the testimony of an informant. In 1973 the Florida Supreme Court ordered a new trial for Keaton; the prosecutor, however, decided not to retry the case. In "The Stigma Is Always There" (TampaBay.com, July 4, 1999), Sydney P. Freedberg notes that the prosecutor claimed the original witnesses were too ill to testify at the retrial. However, Freedberg points out a number of problems with the original case against Keaton, including "threats and lies" that were used by sheriff's deputies to gain his confession (which did not even match the known facts) and a disreputable polygraph tester. Plus, Keaton, an African American, was convicted by an all-white jury. At the time of his exoneration for murder, Keaton was also serving a 20-year prison sentence for a separate robbery. He was released from prison in 1979 at the age of 27 years.

Kirk Bloodsworth: The First Exoneree Freed by DNA Evidence

Kirk Bloodsworth (1960–) was the first person exonerated from death row based on DNA evidence that proved his innocence. He was convicted in 1984 of raping and murdering nine-year-old Dawn Hamilton in Maryland. Details about the Bloodsworth case can be found on the website of the Center on Wrongful Conviction (CWC) at the Northwestern University School of Law (http://www.law.northwestern.edu/legalclinic/wrongfulconvictions/exonerations/md/kirk-bloodsworth.html). According to the CWC, five eyewitnesses identified Bloodsworth as being with the victim on the day of the murder or at the scene where the crime later occurred. In addition, the prosecution claimed that shoe prints on Hamilton's body corresponded with shoes owned by Bloodsworth. He was convicted and given a death sentence in March 1985. The following year his conviction was overturned by the Maryland Court of Appeals because the prosecution had withheld potentially exculpatory evidence (evidence that is favorable to the defendant) from the defense. Bloodsworth was retried, found guilty, and sentenced to two life terms in prison. In 1988 that sentence was upheld on appeal. From his prison cell, Bloodsworth obtained court approval for DNA testing of crime scene evidence, and the DNA samples were found not to match Bloodsworth. He was released from prison in 1993, and the following year he was formally pardoned by the Maryland governor William D. Schaefer (1921–2011). In 2003 more DNA testing identified a man named Kimberly Shay Ruffner (1958–) as the perpetrator in Hamilton's murder. The following year Ruffner pleaded guilty to the murder and was sentenced to life in prison.

Since his release from prison Bloodsworth has become a vocal activist who speaks and writes about problems with the criminal justice system. In September 2008 Bloodsworth testified before the Maryland Commission on Capital Punishment (http://www.goccp.maryland.gov/capital-punishment/documents/transcript-sep-5.doc) saying, "I'm living proof that Maryland's capital

TABLE 8.1

Inmates previously on death row who have been exonerated as of September 30, 2013

[The list includes cases in which the release occurred 1973 or later]

NR[a]	Name	State	Race	Convicted	Exonerated	Years between	Reasons	DNA[b]
1	David Keaton	FL	B	1971	1973	2	Charges dismissed	
2	Samuel A. Poole	NC	B	1973	1974	1	Charges dismissed	
3	Wilbert Lee	FL	B	1963	1975	12	Pardoned	
4	Freddie Pitts	FL	B	1963	1975	12	Pardoned	
5	James Creamer	GA	W	1973	1975	2	Charges dismissed	
6	Christopher Spicer	NC	B	1973	1975	2	Acquitted	
7	Thomas Gladish	NM	W	1974	1976	2	Charges dismissed	
8	Richard Greer	NM	W	1974	1976	2	Charges dismissed	
9	Ronald Keine	NM	W	1974	1976	2	Charges dismissed	
10	Clarence Smith	NM	W	1974	1976	2	Charges dismissed	
11	Delbert Tibbs	FL	B	1974	1977	3	Charges dismissed	
12	Earl Charles	GA	B	1975	1978	3	Charges dismissed	
13	Jonathan Treadway	AZ	W	1975	1978	3	Acquitted	
14	Gary Beeman	OH	W	1976	1979	3	Acquitted	
15	Jerry Banks	GA	B	1975	1980	5	Charges dismissed	
16	Larry Hicks	IN	B	1978	1980	2	Acquitted	
17	Charles Ray Giddens	OK	B	1978	1981	3	Charges dismissed	
18	Michael Linder	SC	W	1979	1981	2	Acquitted	
19	Johnny Ross	LA	B	1975	1981	6	Charges dismissed	
20	Ernest (Shujaa) Graham	CA	B	1976	1981	5	Acquitted	
21	Annibal Jaramillo	FL	L	1981	1982	1	Charges dismissed	
22	Lawyer Johnson	MA	B	1971	1982	11	Charges dismissed	
23	Larry Fisher	MS	W	1984	1985	1	Acquitted	
24	Anthony Brown	FL	B	1983	1986	3	Acquitted	
25	Neil Ferber	PA	W	1982	1986	4	Charges dismissed	
26	Clifford Henry Bowen	OK	W	1981	1986	5	Charges dismissed	
27	Joseph Green Brown	FL	B	1974	1987	13	Charges dismissed	
28	Perry Cobb	IL	B	1979	1987	8	Acquitted	
29	Darby (Williams) Tillis	IL	B	1979	1987	8	Acquitted	
30	Vernon McManus	TX	W	1977	1987	10	Charges dismissed	
31	Anthony Ray Peek	FL	B	1978	1987	9	Acquitted	
32	Juan Ramos	FL	L	1983	1987	4	Acquitted	
33	Robert Wallace	GA	B	1980	1987	7	Acquitted	
34	Richard Neal Jones	OK	W	1983	1987	4	Acquitted	
35	Willie Brown	FL	B	1983	1988	5	Charges dismissed	
36	Larry Troy	FL	B	1983	1988	5	Charges dismissed	
37	Randall Dale Adams	TX	W	1977	1989	12	Charges dismissed	
38	Robert Cox	FL	W	1988	1989	1	Charges dismissed	
39	James Richardson	FL	B	1968	1989	21	Charges dismissed	
40	Clarence Brandley	TX	B	1981	1990	9	Charges dismissed	
41	John C. Skelton	TX	W	1983	1990	7	Acquitted	
42	Dale Johnston	OH	W	1984	1990	6	Charges dismissed	
43	Jimmy Lee Mathers	AZ	W	1987	1990	3	Acquitted	
44	Gary Nelson	GA	B	1980	1991	11	Charges dismissed	
45	Bradley P. Scott	FL	W	1988	1991	3	Acquitted	
46	Charles Smith	IN	B	1983	1991	8	Acquitted	
47	Jay C. Smith	PA	W	1986	1992	6	Acquitted	
48	Kirk Bloodsworth	MD	W	1984	1993	9	Charges dismissed	Yes
49	Federico M. Macias	TX	L	1984	1993	9	Charges dismissed	
50	Walter McMillian	AL	B	1988	1993	5	Charges dismissed	
51	Gregory R. Wilhoit	OK	W	1987	1993	6	Acquitted	
52	James Robison	AZ	W	1977	1993	16	Acquitted	
53	Muneer Deeb	TX	O	1985	1993	8	Acquitted	
54	Andrew Golden	FL	W	1991	1994	3	Charges dismissed	
55	Adolph Munson	OK	B	1985	1995	10	Acquitted	
56	Robert Charles Cruz	AZ	L	1981	1995	14	Acquitted	
57	Rolando Cruz	IL	L	1985	1995	10	Acquitted	Yes
58	Alejandro Hernandez	IL	L	1985	1995	10	Charges dismissed	Yes
59	Sabrina Butler	MS	B	1990	1995	5	Acquitted	
60	Joseph Burrows	IL	W	1989	1996	7	Charges dismissed	
61	Verneal Jimerson	IL	B	1985	1996	11	Charges dismissed	Yes
62	Dennis Williams	IL	B	1979	1996	17	Charges dismissed	Yes
63	Roberto Miranda	NV	L	1982	1996	14	Charges dismissed	
64	Gary Gauger	IL	W	1993	1996	3	Charges dismissed	
65	Troy Lee Jones	CA	B	1982	1996	14	Charges dismissed	
66	Carl Lawson	IL	B	1990	1996	6	Acquitted	
67	David Wayne Grannis	AZ	W	1991	1996	5	Charges dismissed	
68	Ricardo Aldape Guerra	TX	L	1982	1997	15	Charges dismissed	
69	Benjamin Harris	WA	B	1985	1997	12	Charges dismissed	
70	Robert Hayes	FL	B	1991	1997	6	Acquitted	

TABLE 8.1

Inmates previously on death row who have been exonerated as of September 30, 2013 [CONTINUED]

[The list includes cases in which the release occurred 1973 or later]

NR[a]	Name	State	Race	Convicted	Exonerated	Years between	Reasons	DNA[b]
71	Christopher McCrimmon	AZ	B	1993	1997	4	Acquitted	
72	Randal Padgett	AL	W	1992	1997	5	Acquitted	
73	Robert Lee Miller, Jr.	OK	B	1988	1998	10	Charges dismissed	Yes
74	Curtis Kyles	LA	B	1984	1998	14	Charges dismissed	
75	Shareef Cousin	LA	B	1996	1999	3	Charges dismissed	
76	Anthony Porter	IL	B	1983	1999	16	Charges dismissed	
77	Steven Smith	IL	B	1985	1999	14	Acquitted	
78	Ronald Williamson	OK	W	1988	1999	11	Charges dismissed	Yes
79	Ronald Jones	IL	B	1989	1999	10	Charges dismissed	Yes
80	Clarence Dexter, Jr.	MO	W	1991	1999	8	Charges dismissed	
81	Warren Douglas Manning	SC	B	1989	1999	10	Acquitted	
82	Alfred Rivera	NC	L	1997	1999	2	Charges dismissed	
83	Steve Manning	IL	W	1993	2000	7	Charges dismissed	
84	Eric Clemmons	MO	B	1987	2000	13	Acquitted	
85	Joseph Nahume Green	FL	B	1993	2000	7	Charges dismissed	
86	Earl Washington	VA	B	1984	2000	16	Pardoned	Yes
87	William Nieves	PA	L	1994	2000	6	Acquitted	
88	Frank Lee Smith—died prior to exoneration	FL	B	1986	2000**	14	Charges dismissed	Yes
89	Michael Graham	LA	W	1987	2000	13	Charges dismissed	
90	Albert Burrell	LA	W	1987	2000	13	Charges dismissed	
91	Oscar Lee Morris	CA	B	1983	2000	17	Charges dismissed	
92	Peter Limone	MA	W	1968	2001	33	Charges dismissed	
93	Gary Drinkard	AL	W	1995	2001	6	Charges dismissed	
94	Joaquin Jose Martinez	FL	L	1997	2001	4	Acquitted	
95	Jeremy Sheets	NE	W	1997	2001	4	Charges dismissed	
96	Charles Fain	ID	W	1983	2001	18	Charges dismissed	Yes
97	Juan Roberto Melendez	FL	L	1984	2002	18	Charges dismissed	
98	Ray Krone	AZ	W	1992	2002	10	Charges dismissed	Yes
99	Thomas Kimbell, Jr.	PA	W	1998	2002	4	Acquitted	
100	Larry Osborne	KY	W	1999	2002	3	Charges dismissed	
101	Aaron Patterson	IL	B	1986	2003	17	Pardoned	
102	Madison Hobley	IL	B	1987	2003	16	Pardoned	
103	Leroy Orange	IL	B	1984	2003	19	Pardoned	
104	Stanley Howard	IL	B	1987	2003	16	Pardoned	
105	Rudolph Holton	FL	B	1986	2003	16	Charges dismissed	
106	Lemuel Prion	AZ	W	1999	2003	4	Charges dismissed	
107	Wesley Quick	AL	W	1997	2003	6	Acquitted	
108	John Thompson	LA	B	1985	2003	18	Acquitted	
109	Timothy Howard	OH	B	1976	2003	26	Charges dismissed	
110	Gary Lamar James	OH	B	1976	2003	26	Charges dismissed	
111	Joseph Amrine	MO	B	1986	2003	17	Charges dismissed	
112	Nicholas Yarris	PA	W	1982	2003	21	Charges dismissed	Yes
113	Alan Gell	NC	W	1998	2004	6	Acquitted	
114	Gordon Steidl	IL	W	1987	2004	17	Charges dismissed	
115	Laurence Adams	MA	B	1974	2004	30	Charges dismissed	
116	Dan L. Bright	LA	B	1996	2004	8	Charges dismissed	
117	Ryan Matthews	LA	B	1999	2004	5	Charges dismissed	Yes
118	Ernest Ray Willis	TX	W	1987	2004	17	Charges dismissed	
119	Derrick Jamison	OH	B	1985	2005	20	Charges dismissed	
120	Harold Wilson	PA	B	1989	2005	16	Acquitted	
121	John Ballard	FL	W	2003	2006	3	Acquitted	
122	Curtis McCarty	OK	W	1986	2007	21	Charges dismissed	Yes
123	Michael McCormick	TN	W	1987	2007	20	Acquitted	
124	Jonathon Hoffman	NC	B	1995	2007	12	Charges dismissed	
125	Kennedy Brewer	MS	B	1995	2008	13	Charges dismissed	Yes
126	Glen Chapman	NC	B	1994	2008	14	Charges dismissed	
127	Levon Jones	NC	B	1993	2008	15	Charges dismissed	
128	Michael Blair	TX	O	1994	2008	14	Charges dismissed	Yes
129	Nathson Fields	IL	B	1986	2009	23	Acquitted	
130	Paul House	TN	W	1986	2009	23	Charges dismissed	
131	Daniel Wade Moore	AL	W	2002	2009	7	Acquitted	
132	Ronald Kitchen	IL	B	1988	2009	21	Charges dismissed	
133	Herman Lindsey	FL	B	2006	2009	3	Acquitted	
134	Michael Toney	TX	W	1999	2009	10	Charges dismissed	
135	Yancy Douglas	OK	B	1995	2009	14	Charges dismissed	
136	Paris Powell	OK	B	1997	2009	12	Charges dismissed	
137	Robert Springsteen	TX	W	2001	2009	8	Charges dismissed	
138	Anthony Graves	TX	B	1994	2010	16	Charges dismissed	
139	Gussie Vann	TN	W	1994	2011	17	Charges dismissed	
140	Joe D'Ambrosio	OH	W	1989	2012	23	Charges dismissed	

TABLE 8.1

Inmates previously on death row who have been exonerated as of September 30, 2013 [CONTINUED]

[The list includes cases in which the release occurred 1973 or later]

NR[a]	Name	State	Race	Convicted	Exonerated	Years between	Reasons	DNA[b]
141	Damon Thibodeaux	LA	W	1997	2012	15	Charges dismissed	Yes
142	Seth Penalver	FL	W	1999	2012	13	Acquitted	

[a]The list is ordered by the year of the inmate's release. Occainaly new cases of earlier releases are discovered. Thus, the number assigned to a person above may differ from his or her number in various published Death Penalty Information Center (DPIC) reports.
[b]DPIC refers to the Innocence Project's (Cardozo Law School, NY) criteria for whether a post-conviction exoneration was the result of DNA testing.
Notes: James Bo Cochran (AL) and Timothy Hennis (NC) were originally on this list but are excluded following further research and developments. Average number of years between being sentenced to death and exoneration is 9.8 years. Number of cases in which DNA played a substantial factor in establishing innocence is 18.
The Innocence Project requires that both 1) DNA testing played a role in the defendant's reversal and 2) the results of the testing were central to the inmate's defense and to the identity of the perpetrator.

SOURCE: "The Innocence List," in *Innocence: List of Those Freed From Death Row*, Death Penalty Information Center, 2013, http://www.deathpenaltyinfo.org/innocence-list-those-freed-death-row (accessed September 30, 2013)

punishment system is broken. And I'm living proof that Maryland gets it wrong." In early 2009 Maryland legislators voted to limit capital cases to only those in which DNA evidence, videotaped confessions, or videotape linking the defendant to the murder are available. In 2013 the state abolished the death penalty going forward, but those sentenced prior to the change in the law remained on death row. The state of Maryland paid $300,000 to Bloodsworth to compensate him for lost income during his years in prison.

A 2012 Exoneration

As of September 2013, the most recent exoneration reported by the DPIC occurred in December 2012, when the Florida inmate Seth Penalver was acquitted of the murder charges against him. Details about the case are included in "The National Registry of Exonerations" (http://www.law.umich.edu/special/exoneration/pages/casedetail.aspx?caseid=4084), which is maintained by the University of Michigan Law School and the CWC. Penalver and Pablo Ibar were alleged to be two men caught on videotape in 1994 at the home of Casimir Sucharski. Sucharski and two guests, Sharon Anderson and Marie Rogers, were shot and killed by the intruders. The videotape was of poor quality, and there was no physical evidence linking Penalver and Ibar to the crime. The prosecutor relied in great part on witnesses who told investigators that the two men depicted in the video appeared to be Penalver and Ibar. However, these witnesses gave conflicting testimony during the 1998 trial, and the jury could not reach a unanimous decision, which is required for capital convictions in Florida. (The jury was 10–2 in favor of conviction.) A mistrial was declared.

At his second trial in 1999 Penalver was found guilty and sentenced to death. Ibar, retried separately in 2000, was also convicted and sentenced to death. Subsequently, Ibar's attorney uncovered prosecution documents that were favorable to Penalver's case, because they indicated that the witnesses only identified Penalver as one of the men in the video after "considerable pressure" from the police. In addition, it was learned that a witness had received a reward from a private group called Crime Stoppers for identifying Penalver, even though the prosecutor said during the original trial that no rewards were given. The Florida Supreme Court upheld Ibar's conviction, but overturned Penalver's conviction. Penalver was retried in 2012 and acquitted by a jury. In "Jury Finds Penalver Not Guilty in Casey's Nickelodeon Triple Murder Case" (Sun-Sentinel.com, December 21, 2012), Rafael Olmeda quotes prosecutor Chuck Morton as saying after the verdict, "We are still confident that the defendant was one of the two men captured on the video."

The Innocence List Disputed

Death penalty advocates are critical of the DPIC's Innocence List, claiming that it exaggerates the number of exonerations and mischaracterizes them. In 2000 the DPIC reported the 100th addition to the list, an event that was widely publicized in the media. In response, Ramesh Ponnuru attacked the list in "Bad List: A Suspect Roll of Death Row 'Innocents'" (NationalReview.com, September 16, 2002). Ponnuru claimed that most of the exonerations resulted from legal technicalities, rather than from actual innocence. He recounted the violent criminal records of some of the exonerees and the formidable evidence introduced at trial against them. He described legal motions and maneuvers that ultimately resulted in the reversal of their sentences. He complained that "the list leads people to think that innocence has been proven when the most that can be said is that the legal system cannot establish guilt beyond a reasonable doubt."

Ponnuru argued that approximately 32 of the 102 exonerees on the list at that time could truly be regarded as innocent. He noted that more than 7,000 people had been on death row since 1973; thus, the percentage of actual innocence cases was extremely low.

In *Critique of DPIC List ("Innocence: Freed from Death Row")* (2002, http://www.prodeathpenalty.com/DPIC.htm), Ward A. Campbell, the supervising deputy attorney general in California, investigated the 102 cases of exonerated death row inmates on the DPIC list at that time. He concluded that at least 68 of the 102 inmates on the list should not have been included. Campbell found that "many defendants on the List were not 'actually innocent'" Some defendants had pleaded guilty to lesser charges and had their sentences commuted. Campbell noted that "an acquittal because the prosecution has not proven guilt beyond a reasonable doubt does not mean that the defendant did not actually commit the crime."

In June 2002 the Florida Commission on Capital Cases released *Case Histories: A Review of 24 Individuals Released from Death Row*, which listed the results of its investigation into 24 cases on the DPIC list. The commission concluded, "Of these 24 inmates, none were found 'innocent,' even when acquitted, because no such verdict exists. A defendant is found guilty or not guilty, never innocent. The guilt of only four defendants, however, was subsequently doubted by the prosecuting office or the Governor and Cabinet members.... An analysis of the remaining 20 inmates can be divided into three categories that account for their releases: (1) seven cases were remanded due to evidence issues, (2) an additional seven were remanded in light of witness issues, and (3) the remaining six were remanded as a result of issues involving court officials."

QUESTIONS ABOUT LEGAL ERRORS IN DEATH PENALTY CASES

As shown in Table 6.10 in Chapter 6, 8,300 persons were sentenced to death between 1973 and 2011. Courts removed 3,059 individuals from death row over that same period: 522 because an appeal or higher court overturned the relevant death penalty statute or law, 863 because the individual's conviction was overturned, and 1,674 because the individual's death penalty was overturned. (See Table 6.1 in Chapter 6.) Overturned capital convictions and sentences are troubling because they indicate that appeals courts found procedural errors or other serious problems that occurred during the original trials.

Liebman Study

James S. Liebman, Jeffrey Fagan, and Valerie West conducted the first study of its kind, a statistical study of modern U.S. capital appeals, for the U.S. Senate Committee on the Judiciary. The study, called *A Broken System: Error Rates in Capital Cases, 1973–1995* (June 12, 2000, http://www2.law.columbia.edu/instructional services/liebman/liebman_final.pdf), examined 5,760

death penalty sentences that had been imposed in the United States between 1973 and 1995.

On direct appeal, the state high courts reviewed 4,578 death penalty cases. Liebman, Fagan, and West found that 1,885 (or 41% of the total) were overturned due to "serious" errors. Many of the cases that were upheld upon direct appeal went to the second level, which is called state appeals. At least 10% of these cases were overturned. Fifty-three cases that were upheld at this level went to the third appeal level, federal appeals. According to Liebman, Fagan, and West, 40% of these cases were overturned. Overall, the researchers concluded that for every 100 capital cases reviewed by appeals courts in 28 states from 1973 through 1995, 68% were overturned due to "serious" errors.

Liebman, Fagan, and West found that "82% of the people whose capital judgments were overturned by state post-conviction courts due to serious error were found to deserve a sentence less than death when the errors were cured on retrial; 7% were found to be innocent of the capital crime."

THE LIEBMAN STUDY IS CRITICIZED. Appearing before the Senate Committee on the Judiciary hearing on "Reducing the Risk of Executing the Innocent: The Report of the Illinois Governor's Commission on Capital Punishment" (June 12, 2002, http://www.gpo.gov/fdsys/pkg/CHRG-107shrg86544/html/CHRG-107shrg86544.htm), Senator Strom Thurmond (1902–2003; R-SC) warned:

> A Columbia University report known as the Liebman study is often cited as proof that capital punishment in this country is deeply flawed. This study ... alleged that from 1973 to 1995, 70% of death penalty convictions were reversed on appeal. The implication is that 70% of the time, innocent people were sentenced to death. This study should be viewed carefully because during the period addressed by this study, the Supreme Court issued a series of retroactive rules that nullified a number of verdicts. These reversals were not based on the actual innocence of defendants, but rather were based on procedural rules.

As shown in Table 6.1 in Chapter 6, during the 1970s more than 400 inmates were removed from death row due to the court system striking down state death penalty statutes then in effect as unconstitutional. Chapters 2, 3, and 4 describe many of the U.S. Supreme Court decisions made during the 1970s and 1980s that these precipitated removals from death row.

Latzer Study

In "Capital Appeals Revisited" (*Judicature*, vol. 84, no. 2, September–October 2000), Barry Latzer and James N. G. Cauthen noted that their reexamination of the Liebman study found that about one-fourth (27%), and not two-thirds (68%), of capital convictions were reversed between 1973 and 1995. Latzer and Cauthen stated that the Liebman study did not differentiate between reversals of convictions and reversals of death sentences.

Latzer and Cauthen conducted their own investigation, covering the period 1990 to 1999, using reversal data in 26 of the states studied by Liebman and his colleagues. Latzer and Cauthen wanted more recent data of the death penalty system that would provide more complete reversal rate differences.

Latzer and Cauthen found that of the 837 death penalty reversals in state-level direct appeal or post-conviction review, 61% were sentence reversals and 39% were conviction reversals. Using the Liebman study's conclusion that five out of 10 capital judgments were reversed at either the direct-appeal phase or the post-conviction review phase, Latzer and Cauthen applied this finding to their study and concluded that, of the five reversals, three were sentence reversals and two were conviction reversals.

Latzer and Cauthen also investigated reversals at the federal level, the third stage of death penalty judgment review, using data from the U.S. Court of Appeals for the Ninth Circuit, the largest of the circuit courts. Of the 29 capital cases reversed by the court during the 10-year period, 21 (72.4%) were sentence reversals and eight (27.7%) were conviction reversals. This was consistent with their findings regarding direct-appeal and post-conviction sentence reversals at the state level. Using the Liebman study's finding that 68 out of 100 capital judgments were reversed, Latzer and Cauthen concluded, "If 68 of 100 capital decisions are reversed after direct, post-conviction, and federal habeas corpus review, and 39 percent of these are conviction reversals, then convictions in 26.52 (39 percent of 68) of 100 capital decisions are reversed."

FORENSIC SCIENCE

Forensic science is the application of scientific knowledge to legal problems. In the modern era the criminal justice system relies heavily on forensic science to reveal the guilt (or innocence) of suspects. Examples include fingerprint analysis, firearms testing, DNA testing, autopsies, arson and explosives investigations, and analysis of bloodstains, handwriting, bite marks, and so on. DNA testing, in particular, plays a major role in capital case investigations. DNA, which stores the genetic code of the human body, is found in saliva, skin tissue, bones, blood, semen, vaginal secretions, and the root of hair.

The science of DNA testing is improving rapidly. When DNA testing was first used in criminal trials starting in the mid-1980s, DNA samples had to be not only fresh but also contain thousands of cells. As DNA tech-

nology has become more sophisticated, scientists are able to test a single cell for DNA patterns that can link suspects to hair or body fluids found on a victim.

Post-conviction DNA Testing

Before DNA testing became available as proof of identity, the U.S. Supreme Court held the view that U.S. appellate courts could not reverse a murder conviction based on newly discovered post-trial evidence. In *Herrera v. Collins* (506 U.S. 390 [1993]), the Supreme Court ruled that newly discovered evidence does not constitute grounds for a federal habeas relief if there is no evidence of a constitutional violation occurring during state criminal proceedings. (In this case, Leonel Torres Herrera [1947–1993] alleged 10 years after his initial trial that he was innocent of a double murder, presenting evidence that his brother, who had since died, had committed the crime.) However, the National Commission on the Future of DNA Evidence stated in *Postconviction DNA Testing: Recommendations for Handling* (September 1999, https://www.ncjrs.gov/txtfiles1/nij/177626.txt) that with the availability of DNA testing, "the possibility of demonstrating actual innocence has moved from the realm of theory to the actual."

A CIVIL RIGHTS ISSUE? In March 2011 the U.S. Supreme Court issued a stay of execution in a case in which a Texas death row inmate, Henry "Hank" Skinner, alleged that the state violated his civil rights when it refused to conduct post-conviction DNA testing of certain physical evidence that had been collected at the crime scene. Skinner was convicted and sentenced to death in 1995 for the 1993 murders of his girlfriend, Twila Busby, and her two adult sons, Randy Busby and Elwin Caler. The four shared the same residence. Twila Busby was bludgeoned and stabbed to death, and her two sons were stabbed to death. At the original trial the prosecution presented fingerprint and DNA results for some, but not all, of the physical evidence that had been collected at the crime scene. In particular, the untested items included a bloodied ax handle, knives, the victims' fingernail clippings, and vaginal swabs taken from Busby. Skinner was found by police soon after the murders in a closet at the residence; his clothes were smeared with the victims' blood. Other physical evidence also linked him to the crime. He admitted that he was in the house at the time of the murders, but claimed that he did not commit the murders because he was passed out after ingesting a large amount of alcohol and codeine.

Throughout his appeals process Skinner sought unsuccessfully to force the state to test the evidence that was not previously tested. In 2001 the Texas legislature passed a rule allowing for post-conviction DNA testing under limited circumstances. Skinner was unable to qualify under this rule. When he exhausted the last of his appeals, he was scheduled to be executed on March 24, 2010. After Skinner finished his "last meal" and minutes before his execution was to take place, the U.S. Supreme Court issued a temporary stay of execution so it could consider whether or not to hear his civil rights claim, which had been denied by an appeals court. Nearly a year later, on March 6, 2011, the Supreme Court overturned the appeals court's decision and remanded the case (returned it to the lower court). In May 2011 the appeals court remanded the decision back to the district court that had originally heard (and denied) Skinner's civil rights claim.

In "Skinner's Lawyer, AG Disagree over DNA Results" (TexasTribune.org, August 29 2013), Brandi Grissom indicates that as of August 2013 DNA testing had been conducted on previously untested evidence in the case; however, the prosecution and defense attorneys disagree on the implications of the results. As of October 2013, Skinner had not been retried.

In June 2011 Governor Perry signed into law a bill that modified the Texas Code of Criminal Procedure to greatly expand defendant access to post-conviction testing of biological evidence that is collected at crime scenes.

Innocent Men Executed?

As noted earlier, the DPIC claims that more than 140 people who were once on death row had been exonerated between 1973 and September 2013. Since the turn of the 21st century two executions have taken place in which serious concerns arose either before or after the executions about the innocence of the condemned men.

CAMERON WILLINGHAM. The validity of forensic science techniques, specifically arson investigations, has taken center stage in the debate over the possible innocence of a man who was executed in Texas in 2004. Cameron Todd Willingham (1968–2004) was executed for setting a house fire that killed his three young children in 1991. His conviction rested largely on expert testimony from the state fire marshal that the fire had been deliberately set. Willingham maintained that the fire started while he was sleeping. Steve Mills and Maurice Possley describe in "Man Executed on Disproved Forensics" (ChicagoTribune.com, December 9, 2004) the findings of several arson investigators who were hired by the *Chicago Tribune* to review the trial evidence. All of the investigators disputed the original finding that the fire was definitely arson.

In 2008 the Innocence Project, an organization dedicated to securing exonerations of death row inmates through DNA testing, filed a formal complaint regarding the Willingham case with the Texas Forensic Science Commission (TFSC; http://www.fsc.state.tx.us/), which had been created in 2005 by the Texas legislature. In

August 2009 a private company hired by the TFSC issued a scathing report criticizing the lack of scientific methods that were employed by the original fire investigators. A copy of the report, *Analysis of the Fire Investigation Methods and Procedures Used in the Criminal Arson Cases against Ernest Ray Willis and Cameron Todd Willingham* (August 17, 2009, http://www.deathpenaltyinfo .org/documents/BeylerArsonRpt082509.pdf), has been made public by the DPIC. The report details numerous shortcomings in the original investigation and describes subsequent development of fire science standards by the National Fire Protection Association (NFPA). The report concludes, "The investigators had poor understandings of fire science and failed to acknowledge or apply the contemporaneous understanding of the limitations of fire indicators. Their methodologies did not comport with the scientific method or the process of elimination. A finding of arson could not be sustained based upon the standard of care expressed by NFPA 921, or the standard of care expressed by fire investigation texts and papers in the period 1980–1992."

The controversial case continued to develop in late 2009, when Governor Perry replaced the chairman Sam Bassett and three other members of the TFSC just days before a scheduled hearing on the Willingham case at which the commission planned to review the report. Perry's critics suggested that the commission appointments were politically motivated and were a preemptive move that was designed to stall inquiry into the Willingham execution. Perry defended his decision not to stay the execution in 2004, stating that Willingham's death sentence had been upheld at every level of the Texas court system and that reports challenging forensic testimony amounted to little more than opinions. According to James C. McKinley Jr., in "Controversy Builds in Texas over an Execution" (NYTimes.com, October 19, 2009), Perry said, "Willingham was a monster.... Here's a guy who murdered his three children.... Person after person has stood up and testified to the facts in this case."

In April 2011 the TFSC issued its final report on the Willingham case and an arson case from the 1980s involving the defendant Ernest Ray Willis. In *Report of the Texas Forensic Science Commission: Willingham/ Willis Investigation* (http://www.fsc.state.tx.us/docu ments/FINAL.pdf), the TFSC makes no direct findings about the guilt or innocence of Willingham, but it does review testimony given by the chief arson investigator during the trial about specific clues that led him to believe the fire was deliberately set. The commission critiques these statements and finds fault with them in light of the improvements made in fire science since that time. The TFSC notes that "there was no uniform standard of practice for state or local fire investigators in the early 1990's in Texas or elsewhere in the United States."

The commission also presents an August 2010 letter it received from the Texas State Fire Marshal's Office in which the latter stated that "in reviewing documents and standards in place then and now, we stand by the original investigator's report and conclusions." The commission complains, "This appears to be an untenable [incapable of being defended] position in light of advances in fire science." However, the TFSC does not directly criticize the original investigator, noting that "in light of the jurisdictional issues discussed above and related litigation concerns, the Commission declines to issue any finding regarding negligence or professional misconduct."

Death penalty opponents hailed the TFSC report as proof that improper arson science was used to convict and execute Willingham. However, critics disputed this interpretation. In July 2011 the Texas attorney general Greg Wayne Abbott (1957–; http://www.fsc.state.tx.us/documents/11.pdf) issued an opinion stating that the commission could not consider evidence "that was tested or offered into evidence" prior to September 1, 2005, the date the TFSC was created. He also limited the TFSC's authority to investigate testing facilities and certain fields of forensic analysis. Abbott's opinion was seen by death penalty opponents as a political ploy to stifle any further investigation into the Willingham case. In the editorial "Forensic Science Commission Still Has Work to Do" (Chron.com, August 14, 2011), Barry Scheck, the co-director of the Innocence Project, accuses Abbott and the state's fire marshal of "protecting themselves and shielding Gov. Rick Perry from potential criticism and political backlash stemming from the fact that a man was allowed to be executed even though his conviction was based on flawed and outdated science."

TROY DAVIS. In 1991 Troy Davis was convicted in Georgia for the 1989 murder of Mark MacPhail, an off-duty police officer. The case was unusual in that there was essentially no physical evidence tying Davis to the crime and the murder weapon was never found. Instead, his conviction was based almost entirely on the testimony of seven witnesses to the crime and two people who said Davis confessed to them after the murder. In the years following his conviction, Davis's lawyers obtained affidavits (sworn statements) from five of the witnesses and the two people alleging that Davis confessed to them, in which they recanted (withdrew) parts or all of their original testimony. The lawyers argued unsuccessfully during the appeals process that these recantations offered evidence of Davis's innocence. Publicity about Davis's case garnered him many supporters including human rights organizations, such as the National Association for the Advancement of Colored People and Amnesty International, and prominent public figures, such as former president Jimmy Carter (1924–) and former U.S. representative Bob Barr (1948–; R-GA). All advocated

for a new hearing to consider Davis's post-conviction innocence claims.

In "Davis Ruling Raises New Death-Penalty Questions" (Time.com, August 18, 2009), David Von Drehle reports that Davis's case was complicated by the 1996 passage of the Antiterrorism and Effective Death Penalty Act, which placed new restrictions on federal habeas corpus appeals for state and federal death row inmates. As noted in Chapter 5, a death row inmate who has exhausted all state appeals can file a petition for a federal habeas corpus review on grounds of violation of his or her constitutional rights. According to Von Drehle, the new law essentially limits inmates to one set of appeals at the federal level. Because Davis had already had a federal appeal, his subsequent attempts to obtain a rehearing in federal courts were denied.

In 2007 Davis was scheduled to be executed when he received a temporary stay of execution from the Georgia State Board of Pardons and Paroles. Von Drehle notes that the board "conducted a detailed examination of the new evidence," but was not convinced of his innocence. Davis's lawyers appealed to the Georgia Supreme Court and a federal court, but were again rebuffed. It should be noted that recantations are treated suspiciously by courts because they indicate witnesses have likely lied under oath. As Von Drehle explains, "The Davis case became a morass of contradictory statements from addled witnesses, many of whom were either lying then or are lying now—or maybe both." In 2008 Davis's lawyers petitioned the U.S. Supreme Court to force a federal court to hear the innocence claims. In 2009 the U.S. Supreme Court agreed. In *In Re Troy Anthony Davis* (555 U.S. ___), a federal court was ordered to "receive testimony and make findings of fact as to whether evidence that could not have been obtained at the time of trial clearly establishes petitioner's innocence."

Von Drehle states that the decision was highly controversial because it basically undermined the intent of the 1996 law. Ordinarily, nine Supreme Court justices take part in the court's decisions. In the Davis ruling, only three justices concurred in the decision, while two dissented. Another three justices mysteriously neither concurred nor dissented. A ninth justice had recently been installed on the court and took no part in the proceedings. The concurring justices stated that "the substantial risk of putting an innocent man to death clearly provides an adequate justification for holding an evidentiary hearing." The dissenting justices complained that "the allegedly new evidence we shunt off to be examined by the District Court has already been considered (and rejected) multiple times. Davis's postconviction 'actual-innocence' claim is not new. Most of the evidence on which it is based is almost a decade old. A State Supreme Court, a State Board of Pardons and Paroles, and a

Federal Court of Appeals have all considered the evidence Davis now presents and found it lacking."

In 2010 Davis received his long-sought hearing in federal court. However, the U.S. District Court for the Southern District of Georgia rejected Davis's "actual-innocence" claim. In *In Re Troy Anthony Davis* (No. CV409-130), Judge William Moore (1940–) recounted the testimony that was presented during the original trial and examined in detail the recanted statements. He noted that "Mr. Davis's new evidence does not change the balance of proof from trial. Of his seven 'recantations,' only one is a meaningful, credible recantation.... The value of that recantation is diminished because it only confirms that which was obvious at trial—that its author was testifying falsely.... Four of the remaining six recantations are either not credible or not true recantations and would be disregarded.... The remaining two recantations were presented under the most suspicious of circumstances, with Mr. Davis intentionally preventing the validity of the recantation from being challenged in open court through cross-examination." Some of the recanting witnesses claimed the police had coerced or pressured them during the original trial to identify Davis as the killer. Moore disputed these claims, noting that none of the recanting witnesses were absolute in their original identification of Davis as the killer. For example, Antoine Williams originally testified that he was 60% certain in his identification. Moore noted that "Mr. Williams's statements were far from ideal and if the State was to coerce testimony, it surely would have coerced testimony more favorable [to its case] than that actually provided by Mr. Williams."

The judge also criticized Davis's lawyers for not requesting a subpoena (a formal notice to appear before a court) to force the state's key witness during the original trial, Sylvester "Red" Coles, to testify at the hearing. Coles was standing near Davis when the murder occurred and has subsequently been claimed by some recanting witnesses and new witnesses to have been the actual killer. Moore discounted this "hearsay" testimony because Coles was not present for cross-examination. Likewise, Davis's lawyers did not call two of the recanting witnesses to testify at the hearing, but merely presented their written affidavits to the court. Thus, these two witnesses could not be cross-examined. Moore noted that "affidavit evidence is viewed with great suspicion and has diminished value." The judge concluded, "Ultimately, while Mr. Davis's new evidence casts some additional, minimal doubt on his conviction, it is largely smoke and mirrors. The vast majority of the evidence at trial remains intact, and the new evidence is largely not credible or lacking in probative [proof-supplying] value." The court rejected Davis's innocence claims.

The court's decision spurred the state of Georgia to set a September 2011 execution date for Davis. The U.S. Supreme Court refused to hear additional motions filed by his lawyers, and the Georgia State Board of Pardons and Paroles denied him clemency. As described earlier, Davis garnered much public support during his long fight against his death sentence. As his execution neared, his case received widespread media attention. Hundreds of thousands of supporters, including many celebrities and well-known public figures, signed petitions on his behalf and called for Davis to be pardoned. Nevertheless, he was executed on September 21, 2011. In his last words, Davis reportedly reiterated his innocence. The execution was widely condemned in the press. Former President Carter (September 22, 2011, http://www.cartercenter.org/news/pr/davis-092211.html) remarked, "If one of our fellow citizens can be executed with so much doubt surrounding his guilt, then the death penalty system in our country is unjust and outdated." However, according to the article "Ex DA: Doubt, Recantations 'Manufactured' in Troy Davis Case" (September 21, 2011, http://www.11alive.com/news/article/206167/40/Ex-DA-Doubt-recantations-manufactured-in-Troy-Davis-case), Spencer Lawton, the original prosecutor, argues that the public doubts about Davis's guilt were "manufactured" by death penalty opponents via the much-publicized recantations, which he says were coaxed out of the witnesses years after the murder by Davis's defense team and by supporters from Amnesty International.

MORATORIUMS

Table 8.2 shows the number of executions conducted by jurisdiction and the year of the last execution from 1977 through 2012 for the jurisdictions that had death row inmates as of 2013. Note that New Mexico (2009), Connecticut (2012), and Maryland (2013) have outlawed capital punishment for future cases, but already condemned inmates remain on their death rows.

Since the turn of the 21st century a number of measures have been put in place in death penalty states to remedy perceived problems in their capital punishment systems. These measures include moratoriums (suspensions) in executions. Moratoriums fall into two types: de jure and de facto. The term *de jure* means "by right." A de jure moratorium is a moratorium imposed by law. The term *de facto* means "in reality" or "actually." A de facto moratorium on executions means that executions are legally permissible, but are on hold for some other reason.

States with de Jure Moratoriums

As of October 2013, there was no legal means to carry out capital punishment in the District of Columbia or in 18 states: Alaska, Connecticut, Hawaii, Illinois, Iowa, Maine, Maryland, Massachusetts, Michigan (excluding treason), Minnesota, New Jersey, New Mexico, New York, North Dakota, Rhode Island, Vermont

TABLE 8.2

States with death row inmates as of 2013 and execution history, 1977–2012

State	Number of executions (1977–2012)	Last execution year (1977–2012)
Alabama	55	2011
Arizona	34	2012
Arkansas	27	2005
California	13	2006
Colorado	1	1997
Connecticut	1	2005
Delaware	16	2012
Florida	74	2012
Georgia	52	2011
Idaho	3	2012
Indiana	20	2009
Kansas	0	—
Kentucky	3	2008
Louisiana	28	2010
Maryland	5	2005
Mississippi	21	2012
Missouri	68	2011
Montana	3	2006
Nebraska	3	1997
Nevada	12	2006
New Hampshire	0	—
New Mexico	1	2001
North Carolina	43	2006
Ohio	49	2012
Oklahoma	102	2012
Oregon	2	1997
Pennsylvania	3	1999
South Carolina	43	2011
South Dakota	3	2012
Tennessee	6	2009
Texas	492	2012
Utah	7	2010
Virginia	109	2011
Washington	5	2010
Wyoming	1	1992
U.S. government	3	2003
U.S. military	0	—

SOURCE: Adapted from Tracy L. Snell, "Prisoners Executed under Civil Authority in the United States, by Year, Region, and Jurisdiction, 1977–2012," in *Prisoners Executed*, U.S. Department of Justice, Office of Justice Programs, Bureau of Justice Statistics, March 11, 2013, http://www.bjs.gov/content/data/exest.csv (accessed September 3, 2013)

(excluding treason), West Virginia, and Wisconsin. As described in Chapter 1, most of these states and the District of Columbia outlawed capital punishment many years ago. As of 2013, five states had abolished the death penalty through their statutes during the 21st century: New Jersey (2007), New Mexico (2009; future cases only), Illinois (2011), Connecticut (2012; future cases only), and Maryland (2013; future cases only).

NEW JERSEY. In December 2007 New Jersey officially abolished the death penalty. According to Keith B. Richburg, in "N.J. Approves Abolition of Death Penalty; Corzine to Sign" (WashingtonPost.com, December 14, 2007), the New Jersey law replaced the death penalty with a sentence of life in prison without the possibility of parole. New Jersey had eight inmates on death row at the time the law went into effect.

NEW MEXICO. In March 2009 the New Mexico governor Bill Richardson (1957–), a Democrat, signed into law a bill that repealed the state's death penalty and replaced it with a sentence of life in prison with no chance for parole. The article "New Mexico Governor Repeals Death Penalty in State" (CNN.com, March 18, 2009) reports that in a statement Richardson noted how there had been over 130 exonerations from death row in the preceding 10 years and said, "Regardless of my personal opinion about the death penalty, I do not have confidence in the criminal justice system as it currently operates to be the final arbiter when it comes to who lives and who dies for their crime."

The repeal did not affect New Mexico's existing death row population. In *Death Row U.S.A.: Winter 2013* (January 1, 2013, http://www.naacpldf.org/files/publications/DRUSA_Winter_2013.pdf), Deborah Fins lists two inmates under sentence of death in the state as of January 1, 2013.

ILLINOIS. On January 31, 2000, Illinois became the first state in the modern death penalty era to declare a moratorium on the death penalty. Governor George Ryan (1934–), a Republican and death penalty supporter, suspended all executions because he believed the state's death penalty system was "fraught with errors." On January 10, 2003, the day before leaving office, Governor Ryan pardoned four inmates who had been on death row in Illinois for at least 12 years. The governor claimed the men were innocent of the murders for which they had been convicted. He found that the police had tortured the men into making false confessions. Three of the men were released. The fourth inmate remained in prison because of a separate conviction. The following day Governor Ryan commuted 167 death sentences to life imprisonment without the possibility of parole, emptying death row.

After Ryan left office, the de facto moratorium he had imposed ended and new individuals received death sentences in Illinois. However, in March 2011 Governor Pat Quinn (1948–), a Democrat, signed a bill that eliminated the death penalty in the state. He also commuted the sentences of the state's 15 death row inmates to life in prison without the possibility of parole.

CONNECTICUT. In April 2012 the Connecticut governor Dannel Malloy (1955–), a Democrat, signed a law repealing capital punishment in the state for future cases. In "Connecticut Becomes 17th State to Abolish Death Penalty" (CNN.com, April 25, 2012), David Ariosto notes that the governor cited the "unworkability" of the state's death penalty process and the very low number of executions (only two) that had been carried out in Connecticut since the 1950s. Both persons executed were volunteers, meaning that they purposely skipped allowable appeals in order to hasten their own executions. Ariosto quotes Malloy as complaining that "the people of this state pay for appeal after appeal, and then watch time and again as defendants are marched in front of the cameras, giving them a platform of public attention they don't deserve."

Individuals already on Connecticut's death row at the time the law was enacted remained under sentence of death. According to Fins, Connecticut had 11 inmates under sentence of death as of January 1, 2013.

MARYLAND. In 2013 Maryland became the 18th state to abolish capital punishment after Governor Martin O'Malley (1963–), a Democrat, signed into law a repeal that is prospective (i.e., affecting future cases only.) Ian Simpson indicates in "Maryland Becomes Latest U.S. State to Abolish Death Penalty" (Reuters.com, May 2, 2013) that the governor gave multiple reasons for his decision, including concerns about racial bias, high costs, the irreversibility of the death penalty, and lack of confidence that capital punishment is a deterrent. According to Fins, Maryland had five inmates under sentence of death as of January 1, 2013.

Death Penalty States with Long-Standing de Facto Moratoriums

Two states with death penalty statutes on the books in 2013, Kansas and New Hampshire, had not executed anyone in over 45 years. (See Table 8.2.)

KANSAS. The last executions in Kansas were in June 1965. It was not until 1994 that the state reinstated the death penalty following the nationwide moratorium triggered by the U.S. Supreme Court's decision in *Furman v. Georgia*. However, as of October 2013 no one had been executed in Kansas under the new statute. For more than a decade the state's new death penalty law was subject to court challenges regarding its constitutionality. The issue was settled by the U.S. Supreme Court in 2006 in *Kansas v. Marsh* (548 U.S. 163) in which the new law was upheld. Fins notes that Kansas had 10 inmates on death row as of January 1, 2013.

NEW HAMPSHIRE. New Hampshire has not executed anyone since July 1939. Two death sentences handed out during the 1950s were later overturned by courts. In December 2008 a New Hampshire jury sentenced Michael Addison (1980–) to death for killing a police officer. According to Fins, Addison was the sole inmate on New Hampshire's death row as of January 1, 2013.

Death Penalty States with Recent de Facto Moratoriums

During the second decade of the 21st century two states, Oregon and Colorado, implemented de facto moratoriums on capital punishment by executive decree.

In 2011 the Oregon governor John Kitzhaber (1947–), a Democrat, granted a temporary reprieve to the condemned inmate Gary Haugen just weeks before his scheduled execution. According to Helen Jung, in "John Kitzhaber Moratorium on Death Penalty Leaves Inmate Gary Haugen and Oregon Lawmakers Wondering What's Next" (OregonLive.com, December 5, 2011), Haugen was on death row for beating to death fellow inmate David Polin in 2003. Haugen killed Polin while serving a life sentence with the possibility of parole for beating Mary Archer to death in 1981. Jung notes that Haugen abandoned his death penalty appeals to hasten his own execution. In an unusual move, Kitzhaber issued the reprieve for Haugen (who did not want it) and declared a moratorium on capital punishment during his remaining time in office, that is, through January 2015. Kitzhaber also expressed support for a law change repealing the death penalty in Oregon. Haugen fought the reprieve in court, but in 2013 it was upheld by the Oregon Supreme Court in *Gary D. Haugen v. Kitzhaber* (SC S060761).

In 2013 the Colorado governor John Hickenlooper (1952–), a Democrat, signed an executive order granting a temporary reprieve to the death row inmate Nathan J. Dunlap. Dunlap was convicted in 1996 of shooting to death four people—Sylvia Crowell, Benjamin Grant, Margaret Kohlberg, and Colleen O'Connor—during a 1993 robbery at a Chuck E. Cheese restaurant. A fifth victim, Bobby Stephens, survived the attack. Dunlap was nearing exhaustion of his appeals when Hickenlooper granted the reprieve. In the statement "Gov. Hickenlooper Grants Temporary Reprieve of Death Sentence" (http://www.colorado.gov/), the governor cited a number of problems with the state's capital punishment system, including lack of fairness, difficulties with obtaining lethal injection drugs, and the national and international trend toward abolishing the death penalty.

Since 2000 several other death penalty states have ceased carrying out executions due to lethal injection protocol and/or drug acquisition problems. (The issues are described in detail in Chapter 5.) The U.S. Supreme Court's decision in September 2007 to hear a case concerning the constitutionality of Kentucky's lethal injection protocol triggered a de facto moratorium on executions around the country. In *Baze v. Rees* (553 U.S. ___ [2008]), the nation's highest court upheld that protocol. Some states resumed executions immediately; however, other states continued to reexamine and sometimes adjust their lethal injection protocols to ensure their constitutionality. One major example is California.

In December 2006 a federal judge in California ruled in *Morales v. Tilton* (No. C 06 219 JF RS) that the state's lethal injection protocol was unconstitutional. The judge complained that the protocol "lacks both reliability and transparency" and results in "undue and unnecessary risk of an Eighth Amendment violation." The state began constructing a new execution chamber and developing new lethal injection protocols. Fins notes that as of January 1, 2013, California's death row contained 727 inmates, the largest number of any state. As of October 2013, a de facto moratorium remained in effect in California.

CHAPTER 9
PUBLIC ATTITUDES TOWARD CAPITAL PUNISHMENT

Like all statistics, those contained in public opinion polls should be viewed cautiously. The way a question is phrased can influence the respondents' answers. Many other factors may also influence a response in ways that are often difficult to determine. Respondents might never have thought of the issue until asked, or they might be giving the pollster the answer they think the pollster wants to hear. Organizations that survey opinions do not claim absolute accuracy. Their findings are approximate snapshots of the attitudes of the nation at a given time.

THE MORALITY OF CAPITAL PUNISHMENT

The Gallup Organization conducts an annual values and beliefs poll in which it measures Americans' views about various moral issues. In May 2013 respondents were asked about 17 particular issues that were deemed important to society. As shown in Table 9.1, nearly two-thirds (62%) of those asked rated the death penalty as morally acceptable. It was the fifth-most morally accept-able issue to Americans out of the 17 being polled, after birth control, divorce, an unmarried woman having a baby, gambling, and sex between an unmarried man and woman. Capital punishment was considered more morally acceptable than many other controversial issues, including doctor-assisted suicide and abortion.

Table 9.2 shows that the moral acceptability of cap-ital punishment in Gallup's May 2013 poll was virtually unchanged from that indicated in polls dating back to May 2001, when 63% of respondents found the death penalty morally acceptable. Over this period 58% to 71% of respondents rated the death penalty as morally accept-able, whereas 22% to 34% deemed it morally wrong. Small percentages (4% to 7%) said the moral accept-ability of the death penalty depends on the situation.

In Table 9.3 the Gallup Organization provides a breakdown by age group of the moral acceptability rat-ings obtained in its May 2013 poll. The moral issues are ranked by the difference between the percentage of respondents aged 18 to 34 years rating an issue morally acceptable and those aged 55 years and older giving the same opinion. Overall, the largest difference between the two age groups was on the subject of pornography. Whereas 49% of those aged 18 to 34 years deemed it to be morally acceptable, only 19% of those aged 55 years and older agreed, for a difference of 30 percentage points. Overall, there were 13 moral issues that the younger age group deemed to be more morally acceptable than did the oldest age group. At the other end of the spectrum lie issues that people aged 55 years and older deemed to be more morally acceptable than did people aged 18 to 34 years. Only five issues fell into this category, including the death penalty with a six percentage point difference. Actually a larger divide on this issue was found between the youngest age group and the middle age group (i.e., respondents aged 35 to 54 years old). Sixty-six percent of the respondents in the middle age group said the death penalty is morally acceptable, compared with 57% of respondents in the youngest age group. Thus, the data indicate that capital punishment enjoys less moral sup-port among respondents aged 18 to 34 years old than it does among older respondents.

SUPPORT FOR THE DEATH PENALTY
Gallup Polling

According to Gallup poll results from 1936, about three out of five (59%) respondents favored the death penalty at that time for a person convicted of murder. (See Figure 9.1.) This was the first time the Gallup Organization polled Americans regarding their attitudes toward the death penalty for murder. For the next three decades support for capital punishment fluctuated, drop-ping to its lowest point in 1966 (42%). This was a period of civil rights and anti–Vietnam War (1954–1975) marches and the peace movement. It was also the only

TABLE 9.1

Public opinion on the moral acceptability of various issues, May 2013

NEXT, I'M GOING TO READ YOU A LIST OF ISSUES. REGARDLESS OF WHETHER OR NOT YOU THINK IT SHOULD BE LEGAL, FOR EACH ONE, PLEASE TELL ME WHETHER YOU PERSONALLY BELIEVE THAT IN GENERAL IT IS MORALLY ACCEPTABLE OR MORALLY WRONG. HOW ABOUT—[RANDOM ORDER]?

	Morally acceptable	Morally wrong
	%	%
Birth control	91	6
Divorce	68	24
An unmarried woman having a baby*	67	26
Gambling	64	31
Sex between an unmarried man and woman	63	33
The death penalty	62	31
Medical research using stem cells obtained from human embryos	60	32
Having a baby outside of marriage*	60	36
Buying and wearing clothing made of animal fur	59	36
Gay or lesbian relations	59	38
Medical testing on animals	56	39
Doctor-assisted suicide	45	49
Abortion	42	49
Cloning animals	34	60
Sex between teenagers	32	63
Pornography	31	66
Suicide	16	77
Polygamy, when a married person has more than one spouse at the same time	14	83
Cloning humans	13	83
Married men and women having an affair	6	91

*Asked of a half sample.

SOURCE: Frank Newport and Igor Himelfarb, "Next I'm going to read you a list of issues. Regardless of whether or not you think it should be legal, for each one, please tell me whether you personally believe that in general it is morally acceptable or morally wrong. How about—[Random Order]?" in *In U.S., Record-High Say Gay, Lesbian Relations Morally OK*, The Gallup Organization, May 20, 2013, http://www.gallup.com/poll/162689/record-high-say-gay-lesbian-relations-morally.aspx (accessed September 3, 2013). Copyright © 2013 Gallup, Inc. All rights reserved. The content is used with permission; however, Gallup retains all rights of republication.

time in the period of record that those who opposed capital punishment (47%) outnumbered those who favored it. Starting in early 1972 support for capital punishment steadily increased, peaking at 80% in 1994. Between 2000 and 2012 support hovered from 61% to 70%. In 2012 Gallup found that 63% of Americans favored the death penalty for people convicted of murder.

DEMOGRAPHIC DIFFERENCES. In *U.S. Death Penalty Support Stable at 63%* (January 9, 2013, http://www.gallup.com/poll/159770/death-penalty-support-stable.aspx), Lydia Saad of the Gallup Organization breaks down Gallup's 2012 polling data on capital punishment by demographic factors. Table 9.4 shows differences by gender, age, region, and education level. Support for the death penalty was higher among men (67% approval) than it was among women (59% approval). There were also differences between age groups with 67% of respondents aged 55 and older expressing support compared with 62% of respondents aged 35 to 54 years

and 61% of respondents aged 18 to 34 years. In other words, support for the death penalty increased with age. On a regional basis, persons in the South (68%) most highly supported capital punishment followed by persons in the Midwest (66%), the West (60%), and the East (54%). There were noticeable differences of opinion on the issue based on education level. Two-thirds (68%) of respondents that had not attended college favored the death penalty, compared with 66% of those who had some college background, 57% of those who had graduated with undergraduate degrees, and 50% of those who were postgraduates. Thus, support for the death penalty decreased with increasing education level.

According to Saad, Gallup's 2012 poll found that two-thirds of Catholics and Protestants supported capital punishment. At least 60% of respondents indicated support for the death penalty no matter how often they attended religious services. The lowest support for capital punishment (56%) was from persons with no religious preference or affiliation. This group includes atheists (those who do not believe in a deity) and agnostics (those who neither believe nor disbelieve in a deity). Interestingly, Saad notes that support for the death penalty was much higher among respondents who personally owned guns (80%) than among those who did not personally own guns (56%).

Gallup found that the largest demographic divide on capital punishment in 2012 was based on political affiliation and ideology. As shown in Table 9.5, three-fourths (75%) of conservatives favored the death penalty, compared with 60% of moderates and 47% of liberals. There was a 28 percentage point difference between conservatives and liberals on the issue. Likewise, 80% of Republicans supported capital punishment, compared with 65% of Independents and 51% of Democrats. There was a 29 percentage point difference between Republicans and Democrats on the issue. Figure 9.2 shows support for the death penalty from 2001 through 2012 Gallup polls broken down by political affiliation. Republicans consistently expressed higher levels of support (73% to 84%) than did Independents (58% to 67%) or Democrats (45% to 65%). The largest divide in opinion occurred in 2009 when there was a 34 percentage point difference between Republicans (82% in favor) and Democrats (48% in favor).

As explained in Chapter 7, application of the death penalty across the country and across individual states varies considerably, and much of this geographical disparity is believed linked to differences in political affiliation and ideology.

Gallup does not provide a breakdown for its 2013 capital punishment poll by respondent race. Such data, however, are available for 2011 and earlier years. In *In*

TABLE 9.2

Public opinion on the morality of the death penalty, selected years 2001–13

NEXT, I'M GOING TO READ YOU A LIST OF ISSUES. REGARDLESS OF WHETHER OR NOT YOU THINK IT SHOULD BE LEGAL, FOR EACH ONE, PLEASE TELL ME WHETHER YOU PERSONALLY BELIEVE THAT IN GENERAL IT IS MORALLY ACCEPTABLE OR MORALLY WRONG. HOW ABOUT THE DEATH PENALTY?

	Morally acceptable	Morally wrong	Depends on situation (vol.)	Not a moral issue (vol.)	No opinion
	%	%	%	%	%
2013 May 2–7	62	31	5	*	2
2012 May 3–6	58	34	6	*	1
2011 May 5–8	65	28	5	*	2
2010 May 3–6	65	26	7	—	2
2009 May 7–10	62	30	6	*	2
2008 May 8–11	62	30	5	*	3
2007 May 10–13	66	27	5	*	2
2006 May 8–11	71	22	5	*	2
2005 May 2–5	70	25	4	*	1
2004 May 2–4	65	28	4	1	2
2003 May 5–7	64	31	4	—	1
2002 May 6–9	65	28	5	*	2
2001 May 10–14	63	27	7	1	2

*Less than 0.5%.
(vol.) = Volunteered response.

SOURCE: "Next I'm going to read you a list of issues. Regardless of whether or not you think it should be legal, for each one, please tell me whether you personally believe that in general it is morally acceptable or morally wrong. How about the death penalty?" in *Death Penalty*, The Gallup Organization, 2013, http://www.gallup.com/poll/1606/Death-Penalty.aspx (accessed October 2, 2013). Copyright © 2013 Gallup, Inc. All rights reserved. The content is used with permission; however, Gallup retains all rights of republication.

TABLE 9.3

Public opinion on the moral acceptability of various issues, by age group, May 2013

NEXT, I'M GOING TO READ YOU A LIST OF ISSUES. REGARDLESS OF WHETHER OR NOT YOU THINK IT SHOULD BE LEGAL, FOR EACH ONE, PLEASE TELL ME WHETHER YOU PERSONALLY BELIEVE THAT IN GENERAL IT IS MORALLY ACCEPTABLE OR MORALLY WRONG.

% morally acceptable

	18 to 34 years	35 to 54 years	55 and older	Net support among 18–34 vs. 55+
	%	%	%	
Pornography	49	28	19	+30
Sex between teenagers	48	30	22	+26
Gay or lesbian relations	74	54	51	+23
Sex between an unmarried man and woman	72	63	56	+16
Having a baby outside of marriage	71	67	57	+14
Polygamy	19	15	8	+11
Abortion	48	40	38	+10
Cloning humans	19	11	9	+10
Cloning animals	37	35	32	+5
Gambling	66	65	62	+4
Doctor-assisted suicide	46	47	43	+3
Suicide	17	15	16	+1
Married men and women having an affair	7	6	6	+1
Divorce	68	66	69	−1
Buying and wearing clothes made of animal fur	58	61	59	−1
Medical research using stem cells from human embryos	58	59	63	−5
The death penalty	57	66	63	−6
Medical testing on animals	47	60	61	−14

Ranked by net support among 18- to 34-year-olds vs. those aged 55 and older.

SOURCE: Joy Wilke and Lydia Saad, "Americans' Views on the Morality of Major Societal Issues," in *Older Americans' Moral Attitudes Changing*, The Gallup Organization, June 3, 2013, http://www.gallup.com/poll/162881/older-americans-moral-attitudes-changing.aspx (accessed September 3, 2013). Copyright © 2013 Gallup, Inc. All rights reserved. The content is used with permission; however, Gallup retains all rights of republication.

U.S., Support for Death Penalty Falls to 39-Year Low (October 13, 2011, http://www.gallup.com/poll/150089/Support-Death-Penalty-Falls-Year-Low.aspx), Frank New-

port of the Gallup Organization indicates that polling conducted in October 2011 found death penalty support among whites at 68%, compared with 41% among

FIGURE 9.1

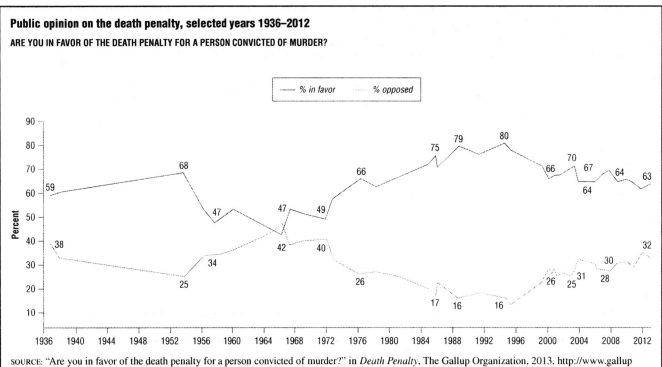

Public opinion on the death penalty, selected years 1936–2012

ARE YOU IN FAVOR OF THE DEATH PENALTY FOR A PERSON CONVICTED OF MURDER?

— % in favor   ⋯⋯ % opposed

SOURCE: "Are you in favor of the death penalty for a person convicted of murder?" in *Death Penalty*, The Gallup Organization, 2013, http://www.gallup .com/poll/1606/Death-Penalty.aspx (accessed October 2, 2013). Copyright © 2013 Gallup, Inc. All rights reserved. The content is used with permission; however, Gallup retains all rights of republication.

TABLE 9.4

Public opinion on the death penalty by gender, age, region, and education level, December 2012

	Favor	Oppose
	%	%
Men	67	28
Women	59	35
18 to 34 years	61	35
35 to 54 years	62	32
55 and older	67	27
East	54	40
Midwest	66	31
South	68	25
West	60	33
Postgraduate	50	45
College graduate only	57	40
Some college	66	30
No college	68	24

SOURCE: Lydia Saad, "U.S. Adult Support for the Death Penalty by Demographic and Regional Groups," in *U.S. Death Penalty Support Stable at 63%*, The Gallup Organization, January 9, 2013, http://www.gallup.com/poll/ 159770/death-penalty-support-stable.aspx (accessed September 3, 2013). Copyright © 2013 Gallup, Inc. All rights reserved. The content is used with permission; however, Gallup retains all rights of republication.

TABLE 9.5

Public opinion on the death penalty by political party and ideology, December 2012

	Favor	Oppose
	%	%
Conservative	75	18
Moderate	60	34
Liberal	47	50
Republican	80	15
Independent	65	32
Democrat	51	42

SOURCE: Lydia Saad, "U.S. Adult Support for the Death Penalty by Ideology and Party ID," in *U.S. Death Penalty Support Stable at 63%*, The Gallup Organization, January 9, 2013, http://www.gallup.com/poll/159770/death-penalty-support-stable.aspx (accessed September 3, 2013). Copyright © 2013 Gallup, Inc. All rights reserved. The content is used with permission; however, Gallup retains all rights of republication.

nonwhites. This is a difference of 27 percentage points. Figure 9.3 shows opinion trends for African Americans and whites from 1972 through 2007. Support for capital punishment among whites was greater than support among African Americans by 23 to 33 percentage points across the entire period.

DEATH PENALTY VERSUS LIFE SENTENCE. In some Gallup surveys, pollsters have asked respondents to choose between the death penalty and life imprisonment with "absolutely no possibility of parole" as the "better penalty for murder." As reported in "Death Penalty" (November 19, 2013, http://www.gallup.com/poll/1606/ Death-Penalty.aspx), when this question was asked in 2010 respondents were split nearly equally, with 49% choosing the death penalty option and 46% choosing the life imprisonment option.

FIGURE 9.2

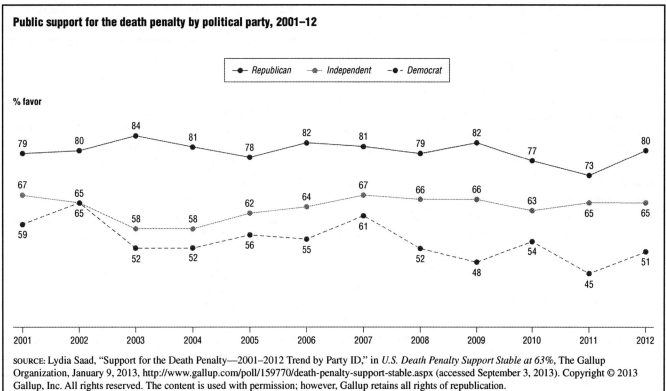

Public support for the death penalty by political party, 2001–12

━●━ Republican   ⋯⊙⋯ Independent   ─●─ Democrat

% favor

Republican: 79, 80, 84, 81, 78, 82, 81, 79, 82, 77, 73, 80

Independent: 67, 65, 58, 58, 62, 64, 67, 66, 66, 63, 65, 65

Democrat: 59, 65, 52, 52, 56, 55, 61, 52, 48, 54, 45, 51

2001   2002   2003   2004   2005   2006   2007   2008   2009   2010   2011   2012

FIGURE 9.3

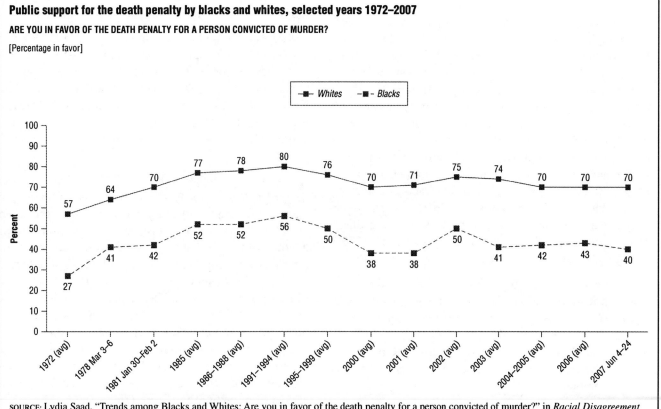

Public support for the death penalty by blacks and whites, selected years 1972–2007

ARE YOU IN FAVOR OF THE DEATH PENALTY FOR A PERSON CONVICTED OF MURDER?

[Percentage in favor]

━■━ Whites   ─■─ Blacks

Whites: 57, 64, 70, 77, 78, 80, 76, 70, 71, 75, 74, 70, 70, 70

Blacks: 27, 41, 42, 52, 52, 56, 50, 38, 38, 50, 41, 42, 43, 40

1972 (avg), 1978 Mar 3–6, 1981 Jan 30–Feb 2, 1985 (avg), 1986–1988 (avg), 1991–1994 (avg), 1995–1999 (avg), 2000 (avg), 2001 (avg), 2002 (avg), 2003 (avg), 2004–2005 (avg), 2006 (avg), 2007 Jun 4–24

Rasmussen Reports Polling

Rasmussen Reports is a media company that conducts public opinion polling. In "59% Favor Death Penalty" (March 25, 2013, http://www.rasmussenreports.com/public_content/politics/general_politics/march_2013/59_favor_death_penalty), the company notes it conducted a poll in March 2013 and found that 59% of respondents favored the death penalty, 24% opposed it, and 17% were undecided. The survey results were somewhat similar to those obtained by Rasmussen in July 2012. In "66% Say Colorado Shooter Suspect Should Get Death Penalty" (July 27, 2012, http://www.rasmussenreports.com/public_content/politics/current_events/gun_control/66_say_colorado_shooter_suspect_should_get_death_penalty), Rasmussen notes that at that time 67% of respondents indicated support for capital punishment and 25% opposed it.

Pew Research Center Polling

The Pew Research Center conducts polling on various issues. In "Continued Majority Support for Death Penalty" (January 6, 2012, http://www.people-press.org/files/legacy-pdf/1-6-12%20Death%20penalty%20release.pdf), Pew indicates that it first quizzed Americans about their support for the death penalty in 1996. At that time 78% of respondents favored capital punishment for persons convicted of murder. By 2011 the percentage had dropped to 62%.

Pew found divisions of opinion on the issue between demographic groups during its November 2011 polling. For example, respondents aged 18 to 29 years showed less support (59%) for capital punishment than did respondents aged 30 to 49 years (64% in favor) or those aged 50 to 64 years (65% in favor). Respondents aged 65 years and older were the least likely to favor the death penalty (56% in favor). Education level also affected results. Nearly two-thirds (65%) of those with some college education or less supported the death penalty, compared with 53% of those with an undergraduate degree or more education. There was some difference based on religious affiliation. Protestants (67%) were more likely than Catholics (59%) or unaffiliated respondents (57%) to support capital punishment.

The widest divides found by Pew were based on race and political affiliation. Support among non-Hispanic whites (68%) was much higher than that among Hispanics (52%) and non-Hispanic African Americans (40%). Likewise, 84% of conservative Republicans favored the death penalty compared with only 40% of liberal Democrats.

Angus Reid Public Opinion Polling

In "Support for Death Penalty in U.S. Surges after Boston Bombings" (April 29, 2013, http://www.angusreidglobal.com/wp-content/uploads/2013/04/2013.04.29_Death_USA.pdf), Angus Reid Public Opinion, a polling firm, reports the results of an online poll it conducted in April 2013, shortly after the Boston Marathon bombing attack. In this poll, 78% of respondents supported "the possibility of prosecutors relying on the death penalty for murder cases." Sixteen percent of respondents were opposed and 5% were not sure. Support for capital punishment was highest in the South (80% support) and among Republicans (86% support). It was lowest in the Northeast (75% support) and among Democrats (72%).

REASONS FOR SUPPORTING OR OPPOSING THE DEATH PENALTY

Angus Reid Public Opinion, in its April 2013 online poll, asked respondents why they either supported or opposed the death penalty. Note that more than one answer was accepted from each respondent; thus, the totals sum to more than 100%. Overall, 78% of total respondents indicated support for capital punishment. The most popular reason was "a convicted murderer has taken a life, so the death penalty fits the crime." This answer was cited by two-thirds (68%) of death penalty supporters. Roughly half (52%) mentioned that capital punishment "saves taxpayers money" compared with keeping murderers in prison. The same percentage cited the deterrent effect the death penalty has on potential murders as a reason they support capital punishment.

Angus Reid Public Opinion also asked the 16% of its respondents who opposed the death penalty to specify why they opposed it. Most (71%) of them chose "a person may be wrongly convicted, and then executed." Nearly half (44%) cited moral concerns as their reasoning, noting that "even if a convicted murderer has taken a life, it is wrong to take the murderer's own life as punishment."

In its November 2011 poll, Pew Research also quizzed poll participants about their reasons for supporting or opposing the death penalty. (Again, respondents could give more than one answer to the question.) Among the 62% of people that favored capital punishment at that time the most popular reason for doing so was that the death penalty was a "deserved/appropriate punishment." More than half (53%) of death penalty supporters cited this reason. Fifteen percent cited the costs associated with life in prison and/or prison overcrowding as a reason they supported capital punishment. Percentages ranging from 1% to 8% supported the death penalty for other reasons, including its deterrent effect (6%) and because it prevents people from committing more crimes (5%).

Among the 31% of overall respondents that opposed capital punishment in 2011, the most popular reasons were that "it's wrong/immoral to kill someone/not our right" and "justice system imperfect/could execute wrong person." Each of these reasons was cited by 27% of death penalty opponents. Sixteen percent said they had religious reasons or that "judgment should be left to God." Percentages ranging from 1% to 10% opposed the death penalty for other reasons, including 3% who said they do not believe capital punishment has a deterring effect and 10% who felt that "person needs to pay/life sentence more appropriate."

In *Death Penalty*, Gallup notes that in May 2003 (the most recent poll in which this question was asked) respondents were asked to give their reasons for supporting or opposing the death penalty. At that time, 64% of respondents believed that the death penalty was the appropriate punishment for murder. These capital punishment supporters were asked why they favor the death penalty for convicted murderers. Most of the responses reflect a philosophical, moral, or religious basis of reasoning. Thirty-seven percent gave their reason as "an eye for an eye/they took a life/fits the crime." Another 13% said "they deserve it," whereas 5% cited biblical beliefs. Four percent stated that the death penalty would "serve justice," and 3% considered it a "fair punishment." Together, these morality-based responses accounted for 62% of all responses.

A minority of people who supported capital punishment in May 2003 did so because of practical consider-ations. Eleven percent said the death penalty saves tax-payers' money. Another 11% thought that putting a murderer to death would set an example so that others would not commit similar crimes; 7% responded that the death penalty prevents murderers from killing again; 2% each said that capital punishment helps the victims' families or believed that prisoners could not be rehabilitated. One percent each noted that prisoners given life sentences do not always spend life in prison or said that capital punishment relieves prison overcrowding. In total, just over a third (35%) of the reasons given for supporting the death penalty appear to be based on issues of practicality, rather than on morality.

Interestingly enough, death penalty opponents also rely heavily on moral reasoning to support their position. In May 2003, 32% of respondents in the Gallup poll expressed opposition to capital punishment. Nearly half (46%) of opponents said it is "wrong to take a life." A quarter feared that some innocent suspects may be "wrongly convicted." Another 13% cited their religious beliefs or noted that "punishment should be left to God," and 5% said that murderers "need to pay/suffer longer/think about their crime" (presumably by serving long prison sentences). By contrast, 5% said that there is a possibility of rehabilitation, and 4% opposed the death penalty because of "unfair application."

CHAPTER 10

CAPITAL PUNISHMENT AROUND THE WORLD

Capital punishment is practiced by only a few dozen countries around the world. As a result, the United States receives fierce criticism from many nations for its position on the death penalty. In addition, the United States increasingly faces legal challenges in its attempt to prosecute and execute foreign nationals for capital offenses.

UNITED NATIONS RESOLUTIONS

The United Nations' (UN) position on capital punishment is a compromise among those countries that want it completely abolished, those that want it limited to serious offenses, and those that want it left up to each country to decide. In 1946, just after the end of World War II (1939–1945), the UN General Assembly gathered to draft a bill of human rights for all UN member nations to follow. From the beginning, the death penalty was a topic of contention, and in 1948, when the assembly released the International Bill of Human Rights, there was no mention of the death penalty. After nine years of debate, the General Assembly included a statement on the death penalty in the International Covenant on Civil and Political Rights, which was later added to the International Bill of Human Rights. On December 16, 1966, the General Assembly adopted the covenant in Resolution 2200 (http://www.un-documents.net/iccpr.htm). Article 6 of the covenant states:

1. Every human being has the inherent right to life. This right shall be protected by law. No one shall be arbitrarily deprived of his life.

2. In countries which have not abolished the death penalty, sentence of death may be imposed only for the most serious crimes in accordance with the law in force at the time of the commission of the crime and not contrary to the provisions of the present Covenant and to the Convention on the Prevention and Punishment of the Crime of Genocide [systematic killing of a

racial, political, or cultural group]. This penalty can only be carried out pursuant to a final judgement rendered by a competent court.

3. When deprivation of life constitutes the crime of genocide, it is understood that nothing in this article shall authorize any State Party to the present Covenant to derogate [turn away] in any way from any obligation assumed under the provisions of the Convention on the Prevention and Punishment of the Crime of Genocide.

4. Anyone sentenced to death shall have the right to seek pardon or commutation of the sentence [replacement of the death sentence with a lesser sentence]. Amnesty, pardon or commutation of the sentence of death may be granted in all cases.

5. Sentence of death shall not be imposed for crimes committed by persons below eighteen years of age and shall not be carried out on pregnant women.

6. Nothing in this article shall be invoked to delay or to prevent the abolition of capital punishment by any State Party to the present Covenant.

The General Assembly has dealt with the death penalty in several other documents and meetings. Among them is Resolution 2393 (November 26, 1968, http://daccess-dds-ny.un.org/doc/RESOLUTION/GEN/NR0/243/53/IMG/NR024353.pdf?OpenElement), which specifies the following legal safeguards that should be offered to condemned prisoners by countries with capital punishment:

1. A person condemned to death shall not be deprived of the right to appeal to a higher judicial authority or, as the case may be, to petition for pardon or reprieve;

2. A death sentence shall not be carried out until the procedures of appeal or, as the case may be, of petition for pardon or reprieve have been terminated;

3. Special attention [should] be given in the case of indigent [poor] persons by the provision of adequate legal assistance at all stages of the proceedings.

Since that time the General Assembly has more explicitly appealed for an end to capital punishment throughout the world. For example, Resolution 2857 (December 20, 1971, http://daccess-dds-ny.un.org/doc/RESOLUTION/GEN/NR0/328/73/IMG/NR032873.pdf?OpenElement) observes that "in order fully to guarantee the right to life, provided for in Article 3 of the Universal Declaration of Human Rights [a section of the International Bill of Human Rights], the main objective to be pursued is that of progressively restricting the number of offences for which capital punishment may be imposed, with a view to the desirability of abolishing this punishment in all countries."

The UN Economic and Social Council Resolution 1574 of May 20, 1971, made a similar declaration. In 1984 the Economic and Social Council then adopted the Safeguards Guaranteeing Protection of the Rights of Those Facing the Death Penalty (http://www.ohchr.org/EN/ProfessionalInterest/Pages/DeathPenalty.aspx). It reiterated many of the UN's earlier statements on capital punishment, and also stated that "capital punishment may be imposed only when the guilt of the person charged is based upon clear and convincing evidence leaving no room for an alternative explanation of the facts." Over the succeeding years, resolutions emanating from the General Assembly and the Economic and Social Council continued to call for the abolition of the death penalty.

On December 15, 1989, the General Assembly, under Resolution 44/128 (http://www.un.org/Depts/dhl/resguide/r44.htm), adopted the Second Optional Protocol to the International Covenant on Civil and Political Rights, aiming at the Abolition of the Death Penalty (referred to here as the Death Penalty Protocol). A nation that signs the Death Penalty Protocol pledges that it will not execute anyone under its jurisdiction and that it will "take all necessary steps to abolish the death penalty within its jurisdiction." The only exception is "the application of the death penalty in time of war pursuant to a conviction for a most serious crime of a military nature committed during wartime," and even in this situation a nation that wishes to carry out such executions must have taken special steps when first agreeing to the treaty.

As of October 2013, the UN reported that 78 nations were parties to the Death Penalty Protocol (http://treaties.un.org/Pages/ViewDetails.aspx?src=TREATY&mtdsg_no=IV-12&chapter=4&lang=en), meaning that they had agreed to be legally bound by its terms. Another four countries had signed the treaty, indicating their intention to become parties to the Death Penalty Protocol, but had not yet acceded the treaty (i.e., taken the additional steps necessary to become party to the treaty). These nations were not legally bound by the treaty but were nevertheless obliged to avoid acts that would go against the treaty. The United States was not a party to the Death Penalty Protocol as of October 2013, nor had it signed it.

Push for a Moratorium

On December 18, 2000, the UN secretary general Kofi Annan (1938–) issued a statement (http://www.unhchr.ch/huricane/huricane.nsf/view01/0CFC538C82EBB17FC12569BA002BE9A6?opendocument) noting that he had received a petition signed by more than 3 million people from 130 countries appealing for an end to executions. The secretary general issued a personal appeal for a worldwide moratorium on the death penalty, noting that the taking of life as punishment for crime is "too absolute, too irreversible, for one human being to inflict it on another, even when backed by legal process."

Since April 1997 the UN Human Rights Council (formerly the UN Commission on Human Rights) has adopted several resolutions calling for a moratorium on executions and an eventual abolition of the death penalty. The United States has consistently voted against these resolutions. During its 2002 session the Human Rights Council, in Resolution 2002/77 (http://www.unhchr.ch/Huridocda/Huridoca.nsf/0/e93443efabf7a6c4c1256bab00500ef6?Opendocument), asked countries with the death penalty "to ensure that... the death penalty is not imposed for non-violent acts such as financial crimes, non-violent religious practice or expression of conscience and sexual relations between consenting adults." The part of the resolution referring to sexual relations between consenting adults resulted from the potential execution of a Nigerian woman who became pregnant while divorced. She was convicted of adultery and, in 2002, was sentenced to die by stoning. The man who fathered the child claimed innocence, brought in three men to corroborate his claim as required by law, and was released. The woman was acquitted in 2003.

The Human Rights Council adopted Resolution 2003/67 on April 24, 2003. For the first time, the council asked countries that retained capital punishment not to extend the application of the death penalty to offenses to which it does not currently apply. It also admonished those countries to inform the public of any scheduled execution and to abstain from holding public executions and inhuman forms of executions, such as stoning. The UN also called on death penalty countries not to impose the death sentence on mothers with dependent children.

On December 18, 2007, the UN General Assembly (http://www.un.org/News/Press/docs/2007/ga10678.doc.htm)

adopted Resolution 62/149 by a vote of 104 to 54, with 29 abstentions, calling for a worldwide moratorium on the use of the death penalty. The United States was among the nations that voted against the resolution. The General Assembly has reaffirmed its call for the moratorium several times since then, including in December 2012 through passage of Resolution 67/176 (http://www.un.org/en/ga/search/view_doc.asp?symbol=A/RES/67/176) by a vote of 111 to 41 with 34 abstentions (http://www.un.org/News/Press/docs//2012/ga11331.doc.htm). The United States also voted against this resolution. The resolutions are nonbinding. That is, they are suggestions or requests, not issuances of international law.

THE INTERNATIONAL STATUS OF CAPITAL PUNISHMENT

Amnesty International (2013, http://www.amnesty.org/en/death-penalty) is a private human rights organization that calls the death penalty "the ultimate denial of human rights." Amnesty International maintains information on capital punishment throughout the world. The organization refers to countries that retain and use the death penalty as retentionist countries; those that no longer use the death penalty are called abolitionist countries.

Retentionist Countries

As of 2012, 58 countries and territories retained and used the death penalty as a possible punishment for ordinary crimes. (See Table 10.1.) Ordinary crimes are crimes that are committed during peacetime. Ordinary crimes that can lead to the death penalty include murder, rape, and, in some countries, robbery or embezzlement of large sums of money. By contrast exceptional crimes are military crimes that are committed during exceptional times, mainly wartime. Examples are treason, spying, or desertion (leaving the armed services without permission).

Amnesty International notes in *Death Sentences and Executions, 2012* (April 9, 2013, http://www.amnesty.org/en/library/info/ACT50/001/2013/en) that only 21 of the retentionist countries were known to have carried out executions in 2012. The organization estimates that at least 682 people were executed in 2012. This number does not include the thousands of people Amnesty International believed were executed in China that year. China's government does not disclose exact figures on how many people are executed there. Amnesty International estimates that excluding China, the nine countries with the most executions in 2012 were Iran (314+), Iraq (129+), Saudi Arabia (79+), the United States (43), Yemen (28+), Sudan (19+), Afghanistan (14), Gambia (9), and Japan (7). The organization also reports that 58 countries imposed a total of at least 1,722 death sentences in 2012. In total, at least 23,386 people around the world

TABLE 10.1

Countries and territories that retain the death penalty for ordinary crimes, 2012

Afghanistan	Kuwait
Antigua and Barbuda	Lebanon
Bahamas	Lesotho
Bahrain	Libya
Bangladesh	Malaysia
Barbados	Nigeria
Belarus	North Korea
Belize	Oman
Botswana	Pakistan
Chad	Palestinian Authority
China	Qatar
Comoros	Saint Kitts and Nevis
Democratic Republic of the Congo	Saint Lucia
Cuba	Saint Vincent and the Grenadines
Dominica	Saudi Arabia
Egypt	Singapore
Equatorial Guinea	Somalia
Ethiopia	South Sudan
Gambia	Sudan
Guatemala	Syria
Guinea	Taiwan
Guyana	Thailand
India	Trinidad and Tobago
Indonesia	Uganda
Iran	United Arab Emirates
Iraq	United States of America
Jamaica	Viet Nam
Japan	Yemen
Jordan	Zimbabwe

SOURCE: Adapted from "Retentionist," in *Abolitionist and Retentionist Countries*, Amnesty International, 2013, http://www.amnesty.org/en/death-penalty/abolitionist-and-retentionist-countries (accessed October 2, 2013)

were believed by Amnesty International to be under sentence of death at yearend 2012.

Abolitionist Countries

Amnesty International reports that in 2012, 97 countries around the world were abolitionist for all crimes. (See Table 10.2.) Since 1976, when the United States reinstated the death penalty after a nine-year moratorium, many countries have stopped imposing capital punishment. Belgium, the United Kingdom, and Greece, the last three west European democracies to have the death sentence, abolished it for all crimes in 1996, 1998, and 2004, respectively. In reality, Belgium has not executed any prisoner since 1950. The last execution in the United Kingdom occurred in 1964. In 2002 Yugoslavia (now Serbia and Montenegro) and Cyprus abolished the death penalty for all crimes. Armenia shut down its death penalty system in 2003. Bhutan, Samoa, Senegal, and Turkey abolished the death penalty for all crimes in 2004, and Mexico abolished the death penalty for all crimes in 2005. They were followed by the Philippines in 2006; Albania, the Cook Islands, Kyrgyzstan, and Rwanda in 2007; Argentina and Uzbekistan in 2008; Burundi and Togo in 2009; Gabon in 2010; and Latvia in 2012.

Amnesty International indicates that in 2012, eight countries did not impose the death penalty for ordinary crimes committed during peacetime, although they may impose it for exceptional crimes. (See Table 10.3.) Since 2000 two countries, Chile (2001) and Kazakhstan (2007), have joined this group.

A list of all countries that have abolished the death penalty since 1976, for ordinary crimes or for all crimes, is provided by year in Table 10.4.

ABOLITIONIST IN PRACTICE COUNTRIES. Table 10.5 is a list of the 35 countries that Amnesty International considered to be abolitionist in practice in 2012. These countries had death penalty laws for crimes such as murder but had not carried out an execution for several years. Some of these nations had not executed anyone for the past 50 years or more. Others had made an international commitment not to impose the death sentence.

FOCUS ON CHINA

As noted earlier, Amnesty International estimates that China executed at least 1,000 people in 2012. Human rights groups claim that China executes more people each year than all the other death penalty nations combined. The Chinese government does not publish statistics on death sentences or executions. In *Death Sentences and Executions, 2012*, Amnesty International notes that Chinese law allows the death penalty for crimes other than murder, including drug and financial crimes. In addition, there are no provisions under Chinese law for death row prisoners to seek or obtain pardons or commutations of their sentences. Nevertheless, the organization notes some encouraging developments in China, including steps to reduce use of capital punishment and to provide greater legal safeguards in death penalty cases. These include "publishing key judgements from the Supreme People's Court with a view to clarifying norms of the application of the death penalty." Changes to China's criminal law that went into effect in January 2013 include reforms such as requiring the recording or videotaping of interrogations in capital cases. In another positive step, during 2013 China announced that it was implementing a voluntary organ donation program in the country "to phase out reliance on organs removed from executed prisoners."

Amnesty International notes that Chinese officials claim that since 2007 the country has halved the number of executions it carries out annually; lack of data, however, prevent the organization from verifying the claim.

THE UNITED STATES CONFLICTS WITH THE INTERNATIONAL COMMUNITY

As shown in Table 1.1 in Chapter 1, 32 U.S. states, the federal government, and the military had enforceable

TABLE 10.2

Countries that are abolitionist for all crimes, 2012

Albania	Haiti	Portugal
Andorra	Holy See	Romania
Angola	Honduras	Rwanda
Argentina	Hungary	Samoa
Armenia	Iceland	San Marino
Australia	Ireland	Sao Tome and Principe
Austria	Italy	Senegal
Azerbaijan	Kiribati	Serbia (including Kosovo)
Belgium	Kyrgyzstan	Seychelles
Bhutan	Latvia	Slovakia
Bosnia-Herzegovina	Liechtenstein	Slovenia
Bulgaria	Lithuania	Solomon Islands
Burundi	Luxembourg	South Africa
Cambodia	Macedonia	Spain
Canada	Malta	Sweden
Cape Verde	Marshall Islands	Switzerland
Colombia	Mauritius	Timor-Leste
Cook Islands	Mexico	Togo
Costa Rica	Micronesia	Turkey
Cote D'Ivoire	Moldova	Turkmenistan
Croatia	Monaco	Tuvalu
Cyprus	Montenegro	Ukraine
Czech Republic	Mozambique	United Kingdom
Denmark	Namibia	Uruguay
Djibouti	Nepal	Uzbekistan
Dominican Republic	Netherlands	Vanuatu
Ecuador	New Zealand	Venezuela
Estonia	Nicaragua	
Finland	Niue	
France	Norway	
Gabon	Palau	
Georgia	Panama	
Germany	Paraguay	
Greece	Philippines	
Guinea-Bissau	Poland	

Note: Countries whose laws do not provide for the death penalty for any crime.

SOURCE: Adapted from "Abolitionist for All Crimes," in *Abolitionist and Retentionist Countries*, Amnesty International, 2013, http://www.amnesty.org/en/death-penalty/abolitionist-and-retentionist-countries (accessed October 2, 2013)

TABLE 10.3

Countries that are abolitionist for ordinary crimes only, 2012

Bolivia
Brazil
Chile
El Salvador
Fiji
Israel
Kazakhstan
Peru

Note: Countries whose laws provide for the death penalty only for exceptional crimes such as crimes under military law or crimes committed in exceptional circumstances.

SOURCE: Adapted from "Abolitionist for Ordinary Crimes Only," in *Abolitionist and Retentionist Countries*, Amnesty International, 2013, http://www.amnesty.org/en/death-penalty/abolitionist-and-retentionist-countries (accessed October 2, 2013)

death penalty laws as of 2013. The majority of other countries in the world have abolished capital punishment. As a result, the United States often faces intense criticism and complicated legal challenges from other nations over

TABLE 10.4

Countries that have abolished the death penalty since 1976

1976: **Portugal** abolished the death penalty for all crimes.

1978: **Denmark** abolished the death penalty for all crimes.

1979: **Luxembourg, Nicaragua** and **Norway** abolished the death penalty for all crimes. **Brazil, Fiji** and **Peru** abolished the death penalty for ordinary crimes.

1981: **France** and **Cape Verde** abolished the death penalty for all crimes.

1982: The **Netherlands** abolished the death penalty for all crimes.

1983: **Cyprus** and **El Salvador** abolished the death penalty for ordinary crimes.

1984: **Argentina** abolished the death penalty for ordinary crimes.

1985: **Australia** abolished the death penalty for all crimes.

1987: **Haiti, Liechtenstein** and the **German Democratic Republic**[a] abolished the death penalty for all crimes.

1989: **Cambodia, New Zealand, Romania** and **Slovenia**[b] abolished the death penalty for all crimes.

1990: **Andorra, Croatia**[b], the **Czech and Slovak Federal Republic**[c], **Hungary, Ireland, Mozambique, Namibia** and **Sao Tomé and Príncipe** abolished the death penalty for all crimes.

1992: **Angola, Paraguay** and **Switzerland** abolished the death penalty for all crimes.

1993: **Guninea-Bissau, Hong Kong**[d] and **Seychelles** abolished the death penalty for all crimes.

1994: **Italy** abolished the death penalty for all crimes.

1995: **Djibouti, Mauritius, Moldova** and **Spain** abolished the death penalty for all crimes.

1996: **Belgium** abolished the death penalty for all crimes.

1997: **Georgia, Nepal, Poland** and **South Africa** abolished the death penalty for all crimes. **Bolivia** abolished the death penalty for ordinary crimes.

1998: **Azerbaijan, Bulgaria, Canada, Estonia, Lithuania** and the **United Kingdom** abolished the death penalty for all crimes.

1999: **East Timor, Turkmenistan** and **Ukraine** abolished the death penalty for all crimes. **Latvia**[e] abolished the death penalty for ordinary crimes.

2000: **Cote D'Ivoire** and **Malta** abolished the death penalty for all crimes. **Albania**[f] abolished the death penalty for ordinary crimes.

2001: **Bosnia-Herzegovina**[g] abolished the death penalty for all crimes. **Chile** abolished the death penalty for ordinary crimes.

2002: **Cyprus** and **Yugoslavia** (now two states **Serbia** and **Montenegro**[i] abolished the death penalty for all crimes.

2003: **Armenia** abolished the death penalty for all crimes.

2004: **Bhutan, Greece, Samoa, Senegal** and **Turkey** abolished the death penalty for all crimes.

2005: **Liberia**[h] and **Mexico** abolished the death penalty for all crimes.

2006: **Philippines** abolished the death penalty for all crimes.

2007: **Albania**[f], **Cook Islands, Kyrgyzstan** and **Rwanda** abolished the death penalty for all crimes. **Kazakhstan** abolished the death penalty for ordinary crimes.

2008: **Uzbekistan** and **Argentina** abolished the death penalty for all crimes.

2009: **Burundi** and **Togo** abolished the death penalty for all crimes.

2010: **Gabon** abolished the death penalty for all crimes.

2012: **Latvia** abolished the death penalty for all crimes.

[a]In 1990 the German Democratic Republic became unified with the Federal Republic of Germany, where the death penalty had been abolished in 1949.
[b]Slovenia and Croatia abolished the death penalty while they were still republics of the Socialist Federal Republic of Yugoslavia. The two republics became independent in 1991.
[c]In 1993 the Czech and Slovak Federal Republic divided into two states, the Czech Republic and Slovakia.
[d]In 1997 Hong Kong was returned to Chinese rule as a special administrative region of China. Since then Hong Kong has remained abolitionist.
[e]In 1999 the Latvian parliament voted to ratify Protocol No. 6 to the European Convention on Human Rights, abolishing the death penalty for peacetime offences.
[f]In 2007 Albania ratified Protocol No. 13 to the European Convention on Human Rights, abolishing the death penalty in all circumstances. In 2000 it had ratified Protocol No. 6 to the European Convention on Human Rights, abolishing the death penalty for peacetime offences.
[g]In 2001 Bosnia-Herzegovina ratified the Second Optional Protocol to the International Covenant on Civil and Political Rights, abolishing the death penalty for all crimes.
[h]In 2005 Liberia ratified the Second Optional Protocol to the International Covenant on Civil and Political Rights, abolishing the death penalty for all crimes.
[i]Montenegro had already abolished the death penalty in 2002 when it was part of a state union with Serbia. It became an independent member state of the United Nations on 28 June 2006. Its ratification of Protocol No. 13 to the European Convention on Human Rights, abolishing the death penalty in all circumstances, came into effect on 6 June 2006.

SOURCE: Adapted from "Countries That Have Abolished the Death Penalty since 1976," in *Abolitionist and Retentionist Countries*, Amnesty International, 2013, http://www.amnesty.org/en/death-penalty/abolitionist-and-retentionist-countries (accessed October 2, 2013)

its continued use of the death penalty. In 2012 the U.S. Department of State published *Why Does the U.S. Have Capital Punishment?* (http://photos.state.gov/libraries/amgov/133183/english/P_You_Asked_WhyCapitalPunishment_English.pdf) as an outreach document regarding the thorny issue. The report is written by David Garland of New York University. Garland notes that "in countries where the death penalty has been removed from the law books, it was repealed by national governments imposing top-down reform because they decided the death penalty was no longer necessary or legitimate. In many cases, repeal was carried out even if a majority of citizens continued to support capital punishment. That the death penalty has been abolished throughout most of the western world (and in many other nations) but not in the United States speaks not to differences in popular attitudes—heinous murderers are unpopular everywhere—but to differences in political institutions."

Garland explains that there are really 52 legislative systems in the United States including federal law, military law, and the differing laws of the 50 states. He points

TABLE 10.5

Countries that are abolitionist in practice, 2012

Algeria	Madagascar	South Korea
Benin	Malawi	Sri Lanka
Brunei	Maldives	Suriname
Burkina Faso	Mali	Swaziland
Cameroon	Mauritania	Tajikistan
Central African Republic	Mongolia	Tanzania
Congo (Republic of)	Morocco	Tonga
Eritrea	Myanmar	Tunisia
Ghana	Nauru	Zambia
Grenada	Niger	
Kenya	Papua New Guinea	
Laos	Russian Federation*	
Liberia	Sierra Leone	

*The Russian Federation introduced a moratorium on executions in August 1996. However, executions were carried out between 1996 and 1999 in the Chechen Republic.

Note: Countries which retain the death penalty for ordinary crimes such as murder but can be considered abolitionist in practice in that they have not executed anyone during the past 10 years and are believed to have a policy or established practice of not carrying out executions. The list also includes countries which have made an international commitment not to use the death penalty.

SOURCE: Adapted from "Abolitionist in Practice," in *Abolitionist and Retentionist Countries*, Amnesty International, 2013, http://www.amnesty.org/en/death-penalty/abolitionist-and-retentionist-countries (accessed October 2, 2013)

out that "the U.S. political system makes it more difficult for elected officials to disregard the preferences of the majority of their citizens than is the case elsewhere."

Garland's assertion that popular support for the death penalty existed in some countries even as they abolished capital punishment is supported by Andrew Hammel in his book *Ending the Death Penalty: The European Experience in Global Perspective* (2010). Hammel—a death penalty opponent—was a law professor at a German university when he wrote his book, but during the 1990s he worked as a defense lawyer for Texas defendants in capital cases. Hammel states that abolishment of capital punishment in west European democracies was achieved through top-down legislative action rather than through grassroots (bottom-up) activism. He explains the European model for abolition as follows:

> First, there is an ingrained human desire to inflict retribution or revenge on those who commit serious crimes. Second, this predisposition to seek revenge will lead a majority of ordinary citizens to favor the death penalty for murder and it is very difficult to change their views. Third, persons with higher levels of formal education think about crime and punishment differently than members of the general public and are thus less likely to favor the death penalty. The fourth thesis—which follows from the previous three—is that if capital punishment is to be abolished, it must be abolished by educated elites.

Opinion polls conducted during the early 2010s indicate popular support for the death penalty lingers in some countries that have abolished it. For example, in "Three-in-Five Canadians Would Bring Back Death Penalty" (March 20, 2013, http://www.angusreidglobal.com/wp-content/uploads/2013/03/2013.03.20_Death_CAN.pdf), the polling company Angus Reid indicates that in 2013 its online survey of a representative sample of 1,514 Canadian adults found that 63% supported reinstating capital punishment. The death penalty was abolished nationally in Canada in 1976. Likewise, Angus Reid reports in "Most Britons Support Reinstating the Death Penalty for Murder" (August 23, 2011, http://www.angusreidglobal.com/wp-content/uploads/2011/08/2011.08.23_Death_BRI.pdf) that 65% of respondents in its 2011 online poll of 2,039 adults in Great Britain supported reinstating the death penalty. Great Britain abolished capital punishment for murder in 1969, and in 1973 joined the European Union, which forbids capital punishment.

Richard Dieter is the director of the Death Penalty Information Center, an organization that is opposed to capital punishment. In "The Death Penalty and Human Rights: U.S. Death Penalty and International Law" (April 2008, http://www.deathpenaltyinfo.org/Oxfordpaper.pdf), Dieter notes that abolitionist movements in Europe and other countries around the world have been rooted in concerns over human rights. However, he notes that Americans focus on "civil rights" and "constitutional rights" and tend to think of human rights issues only in terms of other countries. Dieter states, "The notion that the death penalty should be abandoned because it is a violation of human rights would not reverberate with many Americans."

Human Rights Criticisms

The UN Human Rights Council conducts periodic reviews of the human rights records of all 192 member states of the UN. In November 2010 the United States underwent its first-ever review. The results are detailed in *Working Group on the Universal Periodic Review: United States of America* (January 4, 2011, http://www.ohchr.org/EN/HRBodies/UPR/PAGES/USSession9.aspx). The representatives of more than 80 nations provided input about the United States' human rights record. Hundreds of statements and recommendations involving the death penalty were made by countries from around the world, including some of the United States' closest allies. For example, the United Kingdom representative expressed concern "that the death penalty could sometimes be administered in a discriminatory manner and encouraged the United States to address those systemic issues." Other nations also expressed concern about the United States' use of capital punishment, including Australia, Belgium, Cyprus, Denmark, Ireland, Italy, the Netherlands, New Zealand, and Sweden.

The review resulted in 228 recommendations to the United States to improve its human rights practices. More than 20 of the recommendations involved the death penalty; many nations called for the United States to issue a moratorium on executions or to restrict the number of crimes that are subject to the death penalty as a first step toward abolishing capital punishment. France recommended that the United States "undertake studies to determine the factors of racial disparity in the application of the death penalty [and] to prepare effective strategies aimed at ending possible discriminatory practices." Sweden recommended that the United States ensure that its death penalty "complies with minimum standards under international law" and introduce a national moratorium on capital punishment. Cuba and Ireland recommended that capital punishment be abolished for the mentally ill.

In March 2011 the U.S. Department of State responded to the report with *U.S. Response to UN Human Rights Council Working Group Report* (http://www.state.gov/j/drl/upr/157986.htm). With so many recommendations to address, the Department of State simply divided its responses into three broad categories indicating various levels of support. France's recommendation was included under the category "The following enjoy our support"; however, no further information was given about what that support entails. The recommendations from Sweden, Cuba, and Ireland enjoyed "support, in part" in that the United States promised to ensure that its implementation of the death penalty complies with its international obligations. However, the Department of State noted that recommendations involving abolishing capital punishment for "all persons with any mental illness" or putting a moratorium on the death penalty "do not enjoy our support."

Executing Foreign Nationals

The Death Penalty Information Center reports in "Foreign Nationals and the Death Penalty in the US" (July 2013, http://www.deathpenaltyinfo.org/foreign-nationals-and-death-penalty-us) that 143 foreign nationals were awaiting execution in the United States as of July 2, 2013. Approximately 42.7% (61) were Mexican. The vast majority of foreign nationals under the sentence of death were in California (60), Texas (23), and Florida (23).

Under Article 36 of the Vienna Convention on Consular Relations (VCCR), local U.S. law enforcement officials are required to notify detained foreigners "without delay" of their right to consult with the consulate of their home country. The United States ratified (formally approved and sanctioned) this international agreement and an Optional Protocol to the VCCR in 1969. The Optional Protocol provided that the International Court of Justice (ICJ; the UN's highest court) would have the authority to decide when VCCR rights have been violated. Capital punishment opponents claim that the

United States has a poor record of informing foreign nationals under arrest of their rights under the VCCR.

During the 1990s Paraguay and Germany brought suits against the United States before the ICJ regarding pending executions in Virginia and Arizona, respectively. In both cases the ICJ ruled that the executions should be stayed (postponed) pending further analysis. However, both condemned men—Angel Francisco Breard (1966–1998) of Paraguay and Walter LaGrand (1962–1999) of Germany—were executed for murder. The U.S. Supreme Court refused to intervene in Breard's case, noting in *Breard v. Greene* (523 U.S. 371 [1998]) that because he had failed to exercise his VCCR rights at the state level, he could not raise a claim of violation on federal habeas review.

MEXICO SUES THE UNITED STATES. In 2003 the ICJ was asked to settle another case involving the United States and consular notification. Mexico sued the United States for allegedly violating the VCCR with respect to 54 Mexican nationals on death row in U.S. prisons. The ICJ ordered that the pending executions of three of the inmates be stayed until it could make a final ruling in the case. In 2004 the ICJ (http://www.icj-cij.org/docket/files/128/8188.pdf) found that the United States had violated sections of the VCCR by not informing the 54 Mexicans on death row of their right to notify their government about their detention. The court did not annul the convictions and sentences as Mexico had requested, but it did rule that the United States must review and reconsider the Mexican nationals' convictions and sentences.

José E. Medellin (1975–2008) was one of the 54 Mexicans on death row. Texas jurors sentenced him to death for participating in the 1993 rape and murder of two teenage girls: Elizabeth Pena (aged 16) and Jennifer Ertman (aged 14). The Mexican consular office did not learn of or have the opportunity to help Medellin with his legal defense until 1997, after Medellin had exhausted most of his appeals. When the ICJ decision regarding Mexican nationals was handed down, Medellin appealed once again to the U.S. Court of Appeals for the Fifth Circuit, claiming that he did not receive adequate counsel and that he was not allowed to contact the Mexican consulate after his indictment. The federal appellate court ruled against Medellin. The court cited *Breard v. Greene*, which stated that the issues addressed by the VCCR had to be considered in the state courts before they could be addressed in federal court. Because Medellin had already gone through his appeals on the state level, he had no recourse. Medellin appealed to the U.S. Supreme Court, and in December 2004 the court agreed to hear his case and to reassess its position on the VCCR and ICJ rulings.

Just before the oral arguments in the Medellin case, President George W. Bush (1946–) signed an executive order in February 2005 demanding that the appropriate

U.S. state courts review the sentences and convictions of the 54 Mexicans on death row without applying the procedural default rule discussed in *Breard v. Greene.* By issuing this order, the president in essence tried to force the courts to comply with the ICJ ruling regarding the Mexicans. In light of the executive order, the U.S. Supreme Court dismissed Medellin's case, and it was sent back to the state courts for review.

According to Linda Greenhouse, in "Supreme Court to Hear Appeal of Mexican Death Row Inmate" (NYTimes.com, May 1, 2007), the Texas Court of Criminal Appeals subsequently accused Bush of "intrusive" meddling in the state's court system and refused to comply with the president's order. In response, the Bush administration urged the U.S. Supreme Court to overturn the Texas court's decision. In March 2008 the U.S. Supreme Court ruled in *Medellin v. Texas* (No. 06-984) that the VCCR was not binding on state courts because it had not been enacted into law by Congress. In August 2008 Medellin was executed by the state of Texas.

THE UNITED STATES WITHDRAWS FROM THE OPTIONAL PROTOCOL TO THE VCCR. In March 2005 President Bush pulled the United States out of the Optional Protocol to the VCCR, which had been in place for 30 years. Charles Lane indicates in "U.S. Quits Pact Used in Capital Cases" (WashingtonPost.com, March 10, 2005) that the administration no longer wanted the U.S. court system to be influenced by the ICJ with regard to executing foreign nationals. It should be noted, however, that this action did not end U.S. obligations under the VCCR to inform foreign arrestees about their consular rights.

ANOTHER EXECUTION. In 2011 the VCCR debate arose again after the state of Texas set an execution date of July 7, 2011, for another Mexican citizen involved in Mexico's 2003 lawsuit against the United States. Humberto Leal Garcia Jr. (1973–2011) was sentenced to death for murdering a 16-year-old girl, Adria Sauceda, in 1994. The administration of Barack Obama (1961–) petitioned the U.S. Supreme Court to delay the execution while Congress considered VCCR-related legislation that had been proposed earlier in the year by the U.S. senator Patrick Leahy (1940–; D-VT). According to the press release "Leahy Renews Effort to Bring U.S. into Compliance with International Consular Notification Treaty" (http://leahy.senate.gov/press/press_releases/release/?id=5f4b8b0e-d975-4aa7-94d5-8860de1a6bc0), the Consular Notification Compliance Act would allow federal courts to review the cases of all foreign nationals on death row who were not granted their consular rights under the VCCR at the time of their arrests. It would also "clarify for future cases that courts must ensure that all foreign nationals charged with a capital offense are informed of their right to contact their consulate." The press release notes that U.S. noncompliance with the VCCR has repercussions to Americans traveling abroad, stating that "it would also be completely unacceptable to us if our citizens were treated in this manner."

In a 5–4 opinion issued on July 7, 2011, the U.S. Supreme Court declined to stay Leal's execution, and he was executed hours later. In *Humberto Leal v. Texas* (564 U. S. ___), the court stated, "We are doubtful that it is ever appropriate to stay a lower court judgment in light of unenacted legislation. Our task is to rule on what the law is, not what it might eventually be." As of October 2013, the Consular Notification Compliance Act had not been passed by Congress.

Extradition Complications

An increasing number of countries refuse to extradite (surrender for trial) criminals to the United States who might face the death penalty. In 2005 the German government refused to extradite Mohammed Ali Hamadi (1964–) to the United States out of fear that Hamadi would face the death penalty for his role in killing a U.S. Navy diver during a 1985 airplane hijacking. Hamadi served 19 years of a life sentence in Germany for the hijacking before being paroled in 2005 and deported to his native Lebanon. The Lebanese government has refused to turn him over to U.S. authorities. As of October 2013, Hamadi was on the Federal Bureau of Investigation's "Most Wanted Terrorists" list (http://www.fbi.gov/wanted/wanted_terrorists/@@wanted-group-listing), and a reward of up to $5 million was offered for information leading to his capture.

In 2007 U.S. authorities filed an extradition request for the accused drug-cartel leader Benjamin Arellano-Félix (1952–), who had been in custody in Mexico since 2002. His brother Francisco Javier Arellano-Félix (1969–) was captured by the U.S. Coast Guard while in international waters in 2006. Both men were accused of operating a violent drug smuggling ring and committing multiple crimes that are subject to the death penalty under U.S. law. In November 2007 Francisco Javier received a life sentence without parole after a plea bargain deal was reached that eliminated the death penalty as an option in exchange for his guilty plea. In April 2011 Mexico extradited Benjamin to the United States. Adriana Gomez Licon and Elliot Spagat note in "Mexico Extradites Reputed Drug Lord Arellano Felix" (Associated Press, April 30, 2011) that Benjamin was indicted in 1986 in the United States for engaging in "widespread violence" along the U.S.-Mexican border. In 2008, however, he was charged with racketeering, a noncapital crime. According to Licon and Spagat, this was done by U.S. officials "in an effort to increase their chances of winning extradition from Mexico, which opposes the death penalty." In February 2012 Benjamin Arellano-Félix made a plea bargain with the federal government that resulted in a 25-year jail sentence for racketeering and money laundering.

CHAPTER 11
THE DEBATE: CAPITAL PUNISHMENT SHOULD BE MAINTAINED

FROM THE TESTIMONY OF LEWIS K. SMITH, DISTRICT ATTORNEY OF POWELL COUNTY, MONTANA, BEFORE THE HOUSE COMMITTEE ON JUDICIARY, MONTANA LEGISLATURE, REGARDING HOUSE BILL 370, ABOLISH DEATH PENALTY AND REPLACE WITH LIFE IN PRISON WITHOUT PAROLE. FEBRUARY 14, 2013

My name is Lewis K. Smith and I am currently the Powell County Attorney located in Deer Lodge, Montana. Our office prosecutes crimes which occur in Powell County as well as the Montana State Prison. My Deputy and I have both participated in the capital punishment training provided by the Attorney General's Office. During my six plus years in office we have had two homicides inside the prison and two homicides which occurred outside within the community. Three of those are currently pending and I will not comment directly on them for that reason. I also have found that you cannot lump all people into various categories and be accurate. Different punishments work for different people and figuring what does or does not motivate people can be very difficult and some people have nothing which will motivate them.

The prison cases present a special problem as some of the people who commit violent crimes in the prison are facing long sentences or life sentences. When dealing with these people we often hear "you can do what you want to me, and it doesn't matter, cause I'm never getting out." The death penalty provides the only punishment left that we can impose upon those offenders, if they have committed certain crimes. There is little disincentive in another life or lengthy prison sentence for someone who already will never see the outside under his current sentences. We deal with that problem regularly on offenses ranging from Aggravated Assault and Assault with a Weapon to Deliberate Homicide.

... Two years ago John Connor testified on this subject that following the 1991 riots, better training of staff at MSP [Montana State Prison] reduced homicides to zero. However, in the last two years we have two more. Correctional Officers and staff are still trained to the same standards as before. However, inmates cannot be kept completely segregated twenty-four hours a day. Sooner or later an inmate needs mental health counseling, medical treatment and he will be in contact with staff or someone simply makes a mistake and someone may have to pay with their life. The last two homicides happened in the High Side security area of the prison, but not in the Maximum Security unit. Shaun Morrison was being reintegrated back down through classification to try to mainstream him. He was doing well until someone stole his $10 earbuds and he went into his cell to confront him and ended up cutting him, stomping his throat and choking him until he was dead. Shaun is a danger to anyone he comes in contact with because you do not know what will set him off. Weighing the life of a person who is doing their job and trying to be a good member of society, against that of a person who has no regard for human life, I believe the choice is clear.

The Montana Correctional Officers at the Montana State Prison and other prison facilities in the State face a very difficult job and are the people we ask to deal with the some of the worst among us on a daily basis. The majority of the Correctional Officers my Deputy and I have dealt with wanted to know why Morrison, who was convicted at trial last fall and with whom they have to deal daily, was not getting the death penalty. They saw him as a person who was a continuing danger to themselves, their co-workers and other inmates as he could not control his behaviors and took pride in spitting on staff and assaulting other inmates. They see him as a person who exhibited no hint of remorse at taking the life of another inmate and threatens to do the same to other inmates and officers as well. We seriously considered the death penalty for Morrison, however, under the current system for the death penalty we determined that

Morrison was not a proper case for the death penalty and we did not seek it. That in no way lessened the correctional officers and staffs' concern in having to deal with him. Even though we can cage people up, we cannot eliminate their access to others at some time.

Finally, it is not just people in prison who commit heinous crimes which endanger all of our safety in our communities and the prisons. Study the aggravating factors and the mitigating factors in the statutes on the death penalty and then ask yourself whether or not the persons who commit those types of crimes should not be considered to forfeit their lives for what they have done to others. Fixing the death penalty is not done by eliminating it, it is done by shortening the time frame. Look at the systems used in other states where the average time for carrying out the sentence is much shorter. The appeal side of the death penalty is where you can cut the cost of the death penalty. (http://leg.mt.gov/bills/2013/Minutes/House/Exhibits/juh33a17.pdf)

FROM THE TESTIMONY OF DON KLEINE, DISTRICT ATTORNEY OF DOUGLAS COUNTY, NEBRASKA, APPEARING ON BEHALF OF THE NEBRASKA COUNTY ATTORNEYS ASSOCIATION BEFORE THE COMMITTEE ON JUDICIARY, NEBRASKA LEGISLATURE, REGARDING LEGISLATIVE BILL 543 WHICH PROPOSES REPEAL OF THE DEATH PENALTY. MARCH 13, 2013.

We feel that in certain unique circumstances in the state of Nebraska, that we need to have this ultimate punishment on certain unique cases. Certainly I can talk about my experience in that regard. I've tried probably as many first-degree murder cases as anybody has in the state in my 28 years as a prosecutor. Two of those cases, the jury and the three-judge panel found that the defendant deserved the death penalty, and these people are on death row. Both of those individuals killed children; one killed two children. Arthur Lee Gales killed Latara Chandler, raped and strangled her, and then killed her little brother, Tramar. And then Roy Ellis killed Amber Harris. In both of those cases, they had a pretty significant history also.

So it's not something that I know prosecutors in Nebraska use as any kind of a tool. It's not used in . . . and I think there's some statements . . . that there have been some misstatements made. It's not used in an interrogation process; it can't be used in that regard. Our interrogations at this time are all videotaped. You can't interrogate somebody and make them an offer to get them to say something. It makes it an improper statement or admission by the defendant. I'd be happy to answer any questions.

The cost factor one of the senators brought up I think is an interesting factor. I think it's . . . certainly the penalty isn't something that's going to be litigated on a continuous basis historically, if somebody is sentenced to life without parole. But to say that there's not going to be a lot of costs involved in somebody who gets sentenced to life without parole is a little disingenuous. Certainly the person is going to appeal every issue that they can, and rightfully so, with regard to that sentence also and they're going to go back on constitutional issues about their counsel also, about having ineffective assistance of counsel, which always seems to be the manner in which defendants then, you know, continue to litigate their case even after they've been convicted. (http://www.legislature.ne.gov/FloorDocs/103/PDF/Transcripts/Judiciary/2013-03-13.pdf)

FROM THE TESTIMONY OF KEVIN KANE, CHIEF STATE'S ATTORNEY, STATE OF CONNECTICUT, BEFORE THE JUDICIARY COMMITTEE, CONNECTICUT GENERAL ASSEMBLY, REGARDING BILL NO. 280, AN ACT REVISING THE PENALTY FOR CAPITAL FELONIES. MARCH 14, 2012.

There are people who believe that the punishment should fit the crime and there are crimes that are so horrendous that the death penalty is reasonable and appropriate for the state to carry out. You've decided that in the past. Historically, you've had that in the past. Historically, you've executed people for a variety reasons, one of which is a deterrent. There was a time when—to maximize that effect they executed people in public. Not only executed them but tortured them, disemboweled them, beheaded them, whatever, in public with crowds watching. I'm sure that was a terrific deterrent. And maybe that was necessary in those days—and maybe that was necessary in those day.

We've certainly advanced. We've advanced a lot when—in deciding whether or not to—how to carry out the death penalty and we've done it in a much more humane way. There's no torture. Is it good? Did it (inaudible) those crimes that they punished? You can understand why the victims of the families, the public, the people in the neighborhood thought that these crimes were horrendous. Michael Ross raped and murdered two—two young women in Windham—in Windham County, four in New London County. Raped three of them, murdered all four of them. Two in New York, one somewhere else and I'm not too sure how many others there were. There are a couple I wonder about to this day. We don't know, maybe somebody else did it, maybe he did. Those crimes were cruel, heinous.

We have what I think is the best death penalty statute in the whole state—whole country, probably whole world. It's narrow. It's focused. It's focused on the worst crimes. People are saying—or criticizing it by saying very few people are executed. Well, it was intended to be one in which very few people would be executed. It should be one in which results in very few executions and it has resulted in very few executions. We have to proof, as you know, not only a certain limited capitol felony—what is a capital felony? There are certain murders that are capital felonies. We have to proof aggravating factors beyond a reasonable doubt, both beyond a reasonable doubt.

Our discretion to seek the death penalty is narrow, guided and focused and we have to proof certain elements beyond a reasonable doubt. On the other hand, our discretion to be lenient under the constitution has to be unlimited. We have to have unlimited discretion to seek—to decide not to seek the death penalty. And have right now we're confronted with situations where people, defense attorneys will come in and argue with us not to seek the death penalty. We know what's going to happen when we decide not to. They're going to use it against—later on to say we're arbitrary. Nevertheless, I think the state's attorney have been very, very responsible in thinking this out and have not sought the death penalty in many cases.

...

One of the things we see when we talk about time and money we see in the cases that have been tried, those cases, the evidence of guilt is overwhelming. I've seen cases over the years that have some very good and courageous defense attorneys come in and ask me to bargain, agree to come off the death penalty if they plead guilty. I said no. They plead guilty. And we're planning to go trial and ask the jury to find a mitigating factors. And one of those mitigating factors was the evidence of their guilty plea, that it was a straight guilty plea where they admitted to all the facts of the crime and they admitted that they were guilty. It wasn't an Alford plea. It wasn't a nolo contendere plea. It was a straightforward, honest, open guilty plea in which they fully took responsibility for their actions, fully took it. And then argued that that should be a mitigating factor. You don't see that anymore.

One of the reasons I don't think you see that anymore is because the defense attorneys are hoping that they can somehow get the trial judge to make a mistake during the guilt phase and have an appeal. That's in those cases. You don't see that in other murder cases. You litigate—we all assess the—we all predict what the likelihood of a jury—what the jury will do when they hear a given case, make that prediction and they advise their clients what to do and there are those cases where you disagree or the client just won't plead guilty and you go to trial on those. That's not happening in death penalty cases today.

The reason that is often given and I've heard it over the years and I've heard some very good respectful representatives say this is that the death penalty is unworkable. Those people that say that tend to be opposed to the death penalty for a variety of reasons, but that the idea that the death penalty is unworkable is an excuse and it's not an excuse for which you accept or even think about because you can make it workable. (http://cga.ct.gov/2012/juddata/chr/2012JUD00314-R001100-CHR.htm)

FROM THE TESTIMONY OF KIMBERLY SUNDQUIST BEFORE THE JUDICIARY COMMITTEE, CONNECTICUT GENERAL ASSEMBLY, REGARDING BILL NO. 280, AN ACT REVISING THE PENALTY FOR CAPITAL FELONIES. MARCH 14, 2012.

For the record, I'm the former president for Survivors of Homicide, a position I held for three years following the tragic murder of my beloved Uncle Jerry Timmons Barnette on September 11th, 2003. My position regarding this bill in no way reflects the position of SOH since we as a whole do not take a position on the death penalty. My words today are of my own opinion regarding this matter.

Because my uncle's case ended without justice served, I've made it my mission to fight for those who should be considered yet are far more often forgotten throughout the process.

...

If we keep the death penalty we're able to use it to save taxpayers money and allow them to plea for 60—for a 60-year life sentence with no chance of being released. If you repeal the death penalty, then death row will not exist, this will mean criminals, even the most heinous ones, will have many more liberties while in jail. Death row requires inmates to remain in their cell for 23 hours per day. Until jail is treated as such, I will continue to oppose all bills that will allow them any sort of freedom.

One option you should consider would be to limit the appeals lawyers for the convicted are allowed to file. This procedure is a tactic to delay the inevitable while making a mockery of our entire current injustice system.

This abuse of the appellate process can cause $100,000 or more before the case can even get to trial which most—of which most are denied. The reason those advocating for appeal can say it costs more to execute a prisoner is because of the abuse of the system and because this allows the sentence to be delayed, thus costing more in food, medical supplies, doctor visits, staff and other resources. By limiting appeals it can be said that once criminals have exhausted their legal rights to appeal, the sentence will be carried out.

...

It is a fact that some of the very elected officials who claim that the death penalty should not be used by our state in the name of justice claim that very victory when Osama Bin Laden was killed in reaction to the 2001 terrorist attacks. The difference in the cases are vast and I see that you cannot compare apples and oranges. However, if justice should never be followed by death of an offender with taxpayer dollars, then those same lawmakers should have condemned the actions by our brave military that day and would have preferred to see the terrorist brought to justice while he sits in a jail cell.

...

In closing I would like to add that we are victims, we are not heard from enough in cases that surround our loved ones. We are fearful of the world around us. Our bodies may still be here but the act that took our loved ones away from us, it's as if we were also murdered because we are not the same people we were one hour before the act took place. We know our loved ones watch over us and it's us who suffer. This sort of loss is unbearable. You wonder if you could have changed the end result or wonder if in their dying moments they cried out for you. They stay with us for the rest of our lives. We don't look for revenge, we look for the justice promised to us. Rather than repealing the act of justice—an act of justice, instead look at ways we can make it stronger and more effective. Look at the ways lawyers are allowed to abuse our system and put an end to those tactics. Allow victims to voice opinions about how they would like to proceed. Don't allow terrorism to be accepted in any way, shape or form. (http://cga.ct.gov/2012/juddata/chr/2012JUD00314-R001100-CHR.htm)

FROM THE TESTIMONY OF ROBERT BLECKER, PROFESSOR OF LAW, NEW YORK LAW SCHOOL, BEFORE THE COMMITTEE ON JUDICIARY, CONNECTICUT GENERAL ASSEMBLY, REGARDING SENATE BILL 1035, AN ACT REVISING THE PENALTY FOR CAPITAL FELONIES TO REPEAL THE DEATH PENALTY AND SUBSTITUTE LIFE IMPRISONMENT WITHOUT THE POSSIBILITY OF RELEASE AS THE AUTHORIZED SENTENCE FOR PERSONS CONVICTED OF CERTAIN MURDERS, MARCH 7, 2011

Killing Killers: A Like Kind Response

Early witnesses disparaged retributive support for the death penalty as vestigial hypocrisy. We debase and degrade ourselves by resorting to the same conduct that we condemn for those who kill. Killing because someone else has killed was not consistent with the mores of a civilized society. We cannot teach respect for life by taking life. Or as former Warden Mary Wolff testified to this committee, by killing the heinous killer, we "follow in the footsteps of the criminal." But this well-worn argument—that we debase life by taking life—if it proves anything, proves too much. When we imprison kidnappers, do we thereby debase liberty? When we impose fines on thieves, do we debase property? Punishment acts as a like kind response—inflicting justified pain upon a person who earlier inflicted unjustified pain (so, too, of course celebration—returning pleasure for past pleasure). Thus the basic retributive measure—like for like—"as he has done, so shall it be done to him"; "giving a person a taste of her own medicine"; "fighting fire with fire"—satisfies at a primal level. Reciprocity is not hypocrisy.

Two years ago, in your earlier hearings, witnesses disparaged retribution as a synonym for vengeance. Those who insist on equating retribution with revenge must recognize deterrence for what it is. Because if retribution is pure revenge, then deterrence is pure terrorism, as Hobbes—the first and greatest modern utilitarian—said in disparaging retribution and proposing deterrence: "The ayme of punishment is not revenge but terror." Now, we've come to appreciate that deterrence is not pure terror. You should also appreciate that retribution is not pure revenge.

Although they stem from a common desire to inflict pain on the source of pain, revenge may be limitless and misdirected at the undeserving, as with collective punishment. Retribution, however, must be limited and proportional—no more (or less) than what's deserved.

Retribution provides the basis for limiting punishment as well as for affirming it. We retributive advocates of the death penalty are as concerned that those who do not deserve it do not get it, as we are that those who do, do.

Abolitionists who reject retribution—who do not feel the urge to punish, or do feel it but suppress that feeling of righteous indignation as irrational and shameful—cannot really grasp what moves us retributivists. Most retributive death penalty supporters, then, define the "worst of the worst" as deserving to die for the extreme harms they cause (rape-murder, mass-murder, child-murder, torture-murder) along with the attitude with which they cause it—sadistically or with a depraved callousness.

According to Immanuel Kant's classic retributivism, we impose punishment as an abstract duty without any emotion. By punishing, we dignify the transgressor, acknowledging the free will that produced the crime. More persistent and popular than Kant's retributivism from an abstract sense of duty, emotive/intuitive retributivism has deeper roots.

Abolitionist critics of retribution insist that emotion may never properly move us individually or collectively. They sympathize with the anger of the victims' friends or family, but insist that no humane person would want to act out of that anger. Emotive retributivists' urge to punish, however, stems directly from a projected empathy with the victim's suffering. "Our heart, as it adopts and beats time to his grief," declared Adam Smith in *A Theory of Moral Sentiments*, the first great work of modern retributive psychology. Haunted by the victim's suffering, retributive death penalty supporters cannot forget or forgive the victim's fate: "We feel that resentment which we imagine he ought to feel, and which he would feel if in his cold and lifeless body there remained any consciousness of what passes upon earth," Smith further explained. "His blood...calls aloud."

Jennifer Hawke-Petit's blood calls aloud. Hayley Petit's blood calls aloud. Michaela's too.

Embracing human dignity as our primary value, emotive retributivists since Adam Smith emphasize "a humanity that is more generous and comprehensive," "opposing to the emotions of compassion which we feel for a particular" criminal, "a more enlarged compassion which we feel for mankind."

Financial Costs of the Death Penalty

The death penalty enhances costs from investigation to appeal. Public Defender's offices estimate that abolishing capital punishment would save money. Departments of Corrections estimate that eliminating the death penalty would save $1 million per death row prisoner over each inmate's lifetime.

The vast majority of criminal cases result in plea bargains which not only save time, effort, and costs of trial and appeal, but also protect against an unpredictable and errant jury ignoring the evidence and acquitting a sympathetic accused. In return for pleading guilty, criminals almost always receive lesser charges or lighter sentences.

Without a death penalty as a threat, what would move an aggravated murderer to waive trial and appeal, and accept life without parole? Perhaps, in a rare case, remorse. Overwhelmingly, however, first degree murderers plead guilty and accept life without parole only to avoid the death penalty. Each such guilty plea saves the people hundreds of thousands of dollars.

Emotional and Psychological Costs of the Death Penalty

Before committee and commission such as this, family members of murder victims testify about the devastating emotional costs of the death penalty. Survivors testify to the pain of being forced to relive the trauma of their loved ones' murders during prolonged appeals. Victims' families talk of the frustration of wanting and waiting for their loved ones' killers to die. Much of the victims' family bitterness and frustration came from the false promise of justice. The system would never deliver on its promise—endless stays and reversals.

Psychologists can testify to the adverse effects of executions on judges, jurors, correctional staff, journalists, clergy and spiritual advisors, as well as the families of the condemned. These intangible emotional and psychological costs must also be taken into consideration in weighing the costs of the death penalty, abolitionists insist.

But if non-quantifiable emotional costs *do* count, then how about the cost of not doing justice? In some cases, abolishing the death penalty—retributively, the only proportional punishment—abolishes justice. If you abolish the death penalty, how about the cost to parents who realize their child's rapist murderer now lives in prison playing basketball or watching the Huskies play on a color TV? What does it cost to contemplate the person who tortured your child to death now in art class or lying on a prison bed, lost in a good book? (http://www.cga.ct.gov/2011/JUDdata/Tmy/2011SB-01035-R000307-Professor%20Robert%20Blecker-TMY.PDF)

FROM THE STATEMENT OF JUSTICE CLARENCE THOMAS, CONCURRING, IN *THOMPSON V. MCNEIL* (556 U.S. ___), U.S. SUPREME COURT, MARCH 9, 2009

I also disagree with JUSTICE STEVENS that other aspects of the criminal justice system in this country require the fresh examination of the costs and benefits of retaining the death penalty that he seeks.... For example, JUSTICE STEVENS criticizes the "dehumanizing effects" of the manner in which petitioner has been confined,...but he never pauses to consider whether there is a legitimate penological reason for keeping certain inmates in restrictive confinement.... Indeed, the disastrous consequences of this Court's recent foray into prison management,...should have suppressed any urge to second-guess these difficult institutional decisions....

JUSTICE STEVENS also points to the 129 death row inmates that have been "exonerated" since 1973.... These inmates may have been freed from prison, but that does not necessarily mean that they were declared innocent of the crime for which they were convicted.... Many were merely the beneficiaries of "this Court's Byzantine death penalty jurisprudence."...Moreover, by citing these statistics, JUSTICE STEVENS implies "that the death penalty can only be just in a system that does not permit error."...But no criminal justice system operates without error. There is no constitutional basis for prohibiting Florida "from authorizing the death penalty, even in our imperfect system." ...

Finally, JUSTICE STEVENS altogether refuses to take into consideration the gruesome nature of the crimes that legitimately lead States to authorize the death penalty and juries to impose it.

The facts of this case illustrate the point. On March 30, 1976, petitioner and his codefendant were in a motel room with the victim and another woman. They instructed the women to contact their families to obtain money. The victim made the mistake of promising that she could obtain $200 to $300; she was able to secure only $25. Enraged, petitioner's codefendant ordered her into the bedroom, removed his chain belt, forced her to undress, and began hitting her in the face while petitioner beat her with the belt. They then rammed a chair leg into her vagina, tearing its inner wall and causing internal bleeding; they repeated the process with a nightstick. Petitioner and his codefendant then tortured her with lit cigarettes and lighters and forced her to eat her sanitary napkin and to lick spilt beer off the floor. All the while, they continued to beat her with the chain belt, the club, and the chair leg. They stopped the attack once to force the victim to again call her mother to ask for money. After the call, petitioner and his codefendant resumed the torture until the victim died.... Three juries recommended that petitioner receive the death penalty for this heinous murder, and petitioner has received judicial review of his sentence on at least 17 occasions. The decision to sentence petitioner to death is not "'the product of habit and inattention rather than an acceptable deliberative process.'"... It represents the considered judgment of the people of Florida that a death sentence, which is expressly contemplated by the Constitution, ... is warranted in this case. It is the crime—and not the punishment imposed by the jury or the delay in petitioner's execution—that was "unacceptably cruel." (http://www.supremecourt.gov/opinions/08pdf/08-7369Thomas.pdf)

CHAPTER 12
THE DEBATE: CAPITAL PUNISHMENT SHOULD BE ABOLISHED

FROM THE TESTIMONY OF STANLEY L. GARNETT, DISTRICT ATTORNEY OF THE 20TH JUDICIAL DISTRICT, BOULDER COUNTY, COLORADO, BEFORE THE HOUSE JUDICIARY COMMITTEE, COLORADO GENERAL ASSEMBLY, REGARDING HOUSE BILL 13-1264 TO REPEAL THE DEATH PENALTY AS A SENTENCING OPTION FOR CLASS 1 FELONY OFFENSES COMMITTED ON OR AFTER JULY 1, 2013. MARCH 19, 2013.

I am here today to testify in favor of House Bill 13-1264 to replace the death penalty in Colorado with mandatory life without parole. As many of you know, I published a guest opinion in December of 2012, which has been widely circulated, identifying practical problems with the death penalty in Colorado. To save time, I have attached copies of this guest opinion to this written version of my testimony.

I approach this issue as a person with the responsibility to manage and run a prosecutor's office. I am a pragmatic person and my position on the death penalty is pragmatic; my view is that, for three basic reasons, the death penalty is not a practical tool for law enforcement in Colorado.

First there is the expense, which is several million dollars at least (more than the entire annual operating budget for my office), for any case in which the death penalty is sought, all of which must be funded by state and local governments.

The next is the amount of time involved in a death penalty case. Every murder case that has occurred within my first term has been taken to verdict and sentence within one year of the murder. Every prosecutor knows that prompt resolution is in the interest of the family of the victim, especially in a case involving a violent death. One of the major problems with the death penalty is that it takes years to resolve the case, years which can take an

extreme emotional toll on the grieving families of the victim by failing to provide closure.

The final concern I noted in the guest opinion is the randomness of the death penalty. Because it is sought in only a tiny fraction of cases, it is by definition random. Nothing illustrates this like the fact that all of the men on Colorado's death row are from the same county and went to the same high school. In the nearly 140 years since statehood, Boulder County has never had a death sentence handed down, and yet Boulder County has one of the lowest crime rates generally (and homicide rates specifically) of any comparable county in the U.S.

Those are the practical problems with the death penalty that lead me to support House Bill 13-1264 and that I explain in the attached guest opinion.

In response to my guest opinion, a number of folks have made arguments in support of the death penalty and I anticipate that most of them will testify here this afternoon. I take most seriously those arguments that are put forth by other elected prosecutors. These are my colleagues whom I respect and agree with on many issues and their views are honorable. However, I disagree with their conclusions on the repeal of the death penalty. Let me tell you why.

The arguments in favor of the death penalty are essentially three fold. First, there is the argument that "these are very bad people," or as Greg Dobbs said in his *Denver Post* opinion piece that was published on Sunday, that they are "pieces of scum." The fundamental problem with this argument is that it is beside the point. As prosecutors we deal with many, many very bad people, many of whom have done unspeakable things to other human beings. The question is not whether these people are bad, or even if they are hypothetically deserving of execution. The question is whether a system can be devised to execute only those truly deserving of death; a system that is fair, efficient, consistent, not influenced by race or other improper factors and that doesn't create undue collateral problems or pragmatic nightmares. Our history has shown that such a perfect system is not possible and that endlessly tinkering with a system devised by human beings to make it absolutely flawless is fruitless. As Justice Blackmun said in his famous 1994 dissent, trying to get the procedure for the death penalty exactly right is nothing more than "tinkering with the machinery of death" and, I suggest, is a hopeless exercise and unseemly for a civilized society.

The second argument I've heard in favor of the death penalty from elected prosecutors, and one that I'm sure you will hear this afternoon because it is one the Colorado Attorney General himself has made, is that the death penalty is justified from the point of view of what they call "societal self-defense." This is an argument that concedes that very, very few defendants are truly worthy of the death penalty, but maintains that there are a certain number of defendants who commit terrorist acts and other very serious murders whom society must be able to execute to be able to protect itself. The fundamental problem with such an argument is that there is no credible evidence that the existence of the death penalty is a deterrent to specific acts of violence. Because modern prisons are very secure and virtually escape proof, the idea that certain very bad people need to be killed to be able to protect society is, I believe, facetious; trying to devise a statute that would do so is, again, pointless "tinkering with death." This legislature has better things to do.

And the final argument I've heard, and I anticipate you will hear from elected prosecutors this afternoon, is that having the death penalty on the books is necessary to assure that pleas of guilty to first degree murder with life without parole sentences can be obtained on tough cases. This justification surprises me because there are so many practical and ethical problems with this position. Every prosecutor agrees that it is an inappropriate use of the death penalty to threaten it to coerce a guilty plea; doing so is both unethical and immoral.

I note, in closing, that this debate is not new; repealing the death penalty has been discussed many times in Colorado's history. It was once repealed in the late 19th century and my association, Colorado District Attorneys' Council (CDAC) formerly supported its repeal in 1965, (though CDAC remains neutral this year.)

Colorado has a fair and effective justice system. The death penalty is not a practical or important part of it and it should be repealed.(http://www.leg.state.co.us/CLICS/CLICS2013A/commsumm.nsf/b4a3962433b52fa787256e5f00670a71/a0ac48e1169e256c87257b33005d08f0/$FILE/13HseJud0319AttachA.pdf)

FROM THE TESTIMONY OF JIM CUNNINGHAM, EXECUTIVE DIRECTOR OF THE NEBRASKA CATHOLIC BISHOPS CONFERENCE BEFORE THE COMMITTEE ON JUDICIARY, NEBRASKA LEGISLATURE, REGARDING LEGISLATIVE BILL (LB) 543 WHICH PROPOSES REPEAL OF THE DEATH PENALTY. MARCH 13, 2013.

What we have suggested in the past is that a legitimate test for use of the death penalty is whether or not it's absolutely necessary; that is, are there absolutely no other means by which to defend society from an unjust aggressor. And in analyzing this question, the late Pope John Paul II himself responded from a global perspective that the cases of absolute necessity are extremely rare, if not practically not existent.

We urge you, as policymakers, to consider LB543 from within this framework. We think a proper response to the test of whether the death penalty is absolutely necessary is unambiguously, no, of course not. The death penalty fails the test. In this modern era, this technologically sophisticated age, means of punishment and protection other than the death penalty are available and sufficient. The conditions necessary to justify using this means of last resort do not exist. Let's get rid of it. What's more, in this culture, which too frequently resorts to death and violence as a response to social problems, using the death penalty when there is no absolute necessity for doing so diminishes society even more and contributes even more to the growing disrespect for the dignity and value of every human life.

The death penalty offers the tragic illusion that society can defend life by taking life. We understand and respect that many people have legitimate concerns and fears about the frequency of violence and heinous crimes in their communities. Legislators and society as a whole need to do all they can to deter and respond promptly to this violence that undermines a stable society. Moreover, the needs of victims and their loved ones must be addressed. Society must strive for ways to support them, compensate them, and help them heal. Nonetheless, much of the support for capital punishment, we believe, stems from a desire for revenge or a desperate attempt to balance the terrible damage wrought by a capital crime, and such feelings are understandable in the face of brutal and senseless violence inflicted upon innocent people. Just retribution is a legitimate desire. Nonetheless, it cannot be truly achieved under the veil of vengeance and its own form of violence. We urge a response that meets evil with justice worthy of our best nature as human beings, enlightened by faith and the possibility of redemption and forgiveness.

All Nebraskans personally and collectively face the challenge of rejecting a culture of death and embracing a culture of life. This means overcoming all ways in which killing isproposed as a solution. (http://www.legislature.ne.gov/FloorDocs/103/PDF/Transcripts/Judiciary/2013-03-13.pdf)

FROM THE TESTIMONY OF SUSAN O. STOREY, CHIEF PUBLIC DEFENDER, STATE OF CONNECTICUT, BEFORE THE JUDICIARY COMMITTEE, CONNECTICUT GENERAL ASSEMBLY, REGARDING BILL NO. 280, AN ACT REVISING THE PENALTY FOR CAPITAL FELONIES. MARCH 14, 2012.

Death penalty cases are complex and prone to a high rate of legal error. Conviction of a capital offense is only the first step in the process of seeking a death sentence. In a separate penalty phase, the prosecution must prove at least one aggravating factor. Then the jury considers the aggravating and mitigating factors to decide whether circumstances concerning the crime or aspects of the defendant's character and background suggest that a sentence of life without the possibility of release is the appropriate sentence rather than death. Those who call for the death penalty in particular cases based solely on the facts of the crime have no understanding of the more complex legal framework that governs how juries must decide whether one who has been found guilty of a capital offense should receive a death sentence.

The consideration of mitigation, sometimes criticized as focusing more on the defendant than the victims, is constitutionally mandated by the United States Supreme Court. Any State that chooses to authorize the death penalty must operate within this constitutional framework. Its purpose is to provide the sentencing process with some form of rational guidance. Because jurors in a capital case act as the conscience of the community in deciding whether or not the government may take the life of one of its citizens, they are constitutionally required to consider anything about the circumstances of the crime or the individual as a person in deciding whether death is the appropriate punishment. Any State that attempts to short circuit this process will have its death sentences overturned in federal court.

It is extraordinarily difficult for any State to get the process right. The complexity of the legal framework and the constantly evolving requirements announced by the United States Supreme Court mean that lengthy appellate and post-conviction review and repeated retrials are the norm in any State that seeks to carry out the death penalty in a fair and constitutional manner. A chart attached to this written testimony gives summaries of a selection of court decisions reversing death sentences in other States in just the past year. These decisions provide a sense of the reasons for reversal that may arise in Connecticut cases, including on federal court review of cases in which the Connecticut Supreme Court has upheld a death sentence.

Attempting to truncate the appellate and post-conviction review of death sentences sacrifices accuracy and fairness. Death penalty supporters sometimes suggest that we look to states like Virginia and Texas as models for how Connecticut might shorten the time between a death sentence and an execution. The rate of reversing death sentences in those states is far below the national average. This suggests that they may have a higher tolerance for error and are willing to sacrifice accuracy and fairness by moving cases more quickly so that executions are carried out without a full review of the legal errors in the case.

Connecticut's own history of wrongful convictions shows that a single appeal does not suffice to protect those who are innocent. Four individuals who served lengthy prison terms before being exonerated had their convictions upheld by the Connecticut Supreme Court years before they were released. Had these men been sentenced to death, they may well have faced execution despite their innocence. In death penalty cases, where the results are irreversible, thorough and painstaking review of death sentences through direct appeal and state and federal habeas review is simply a necessary part of a system that even aspires to be fair and nondiscriminatory and to avoid the wrongful execution of innocent persons. (http://www.ct.gov/ocpd/lib/ocpd/bills2012/280_death_penalty_sos.pdf)

FROM THE TESTIMONY OF ANNE STONE BEFORE THE JUDICIARY COMMITTEE, CONNECTICUT GENERAL ASSEMBLY, REGARDING BILL NO. 280, AN ACT REVISING THE PENALTY FOR CAPITAL FELONIES. MARCH 14, 2012.

Our son, Ralph, was brutally stabbed to death during a robbery in his condominium in Washington, D.C.

We learned of his murder shortly before midnight in July of 1997 and by morning we were on a flight to D.C. The police response was horrifyingly inadequate as we were directed to the wrong police station. When we found our way to the correct police station there was no one available to talk with us. Not until late in the evening did a detective come to where we were staying to give us details of the murder.

In the end, Ralph's murder was never solved and was labeled a cold case, one of those cases all but forgotten by society but for us the case will always be remembered and it is very difficult not having more information about what happened to our son or some legal finality and accountability.

Right now in Connecticut, it is estimated that there are nearly 900 cold cases that could be investigated because there is a living witness or suspect—or suspect but there are only 16 to 20 cases being actively investigated by the prosecutor's cold case unit.

The State's Chief Prosecutor has said there simply are not enough resources to fully investigate all the cases. A year ago the cold case unit had 22 inspectors and now only has 13 with budget shortfalls threatening even fewer first personnel will be able to work on the many cold cases in Connecticut. It breaks my heart to know there are so many families like ours living with uncertainty and wishing that someone in authority would care enough to pay attention to our cases not to mention how alarming it is that there are maybe 900 murderers loose on the street.

Then I think about the death penalty. The notion of the death penalty never brought my family any solace. In fact, we were relieved to learn that Washington, D.C. doesn't even have the death penalty because we knew what a rollercoaster ride the process would be for our family. But we spend millions of dollars every year to keep the death penalty while 900 families like mine are left without answers.

This doesn't make any sense to me at all. Of course hard decisions have to be made when resources are finite. But to spend millions on a death penalty system that affects a handful of cases while hundreds of families are desperate for answers seems like the wrong cherished choice for Connecticut victims. I hope the legislature will take the important step of repealing the death penalty so we stop squandering resources that could be put to much better use. Thank you. (http://cga.ct.gov/2012/juddata/chr/2012JUD00314-R001100-CHR.htm)

THE TESTIMONY OF RAY KRONE BEFORE THE COMMITTEE ON JUDICIARY, CONNECTICUT GENERAL ASSEMBLY, REGARDING SENATE BILL 1035, AN ACT REVISING THE PENALTY FOR CAPITAL FELONIES TO REPEAL THE DEATH PENALTY AND SUBSTITUTE LIFE IMPRISONMENT WITHOUT THE POSSIBILITY OF RELEASE AS THE AUTHORIZED SENTENCE FOR PERSONS CONVICTED OF CERTAIN MURDERS, MARCH 7, 2011

My name is Ray Krone, I am the 100th death row inmate in America freed due to my innocence. Today I'm the Director of Training and Communications for a group called Witness to Innocence, which is consisted solely of death row survivors, people that were sentenced to death for something they didn't do.

I'm from a small agriculture town in southern Pennsylvania. I was in a church choir, was an acolyte, I played Little League baseball, Pee Wee football, did good in high school, graduated, enlisted for six years in the U.S. Air Force. When I got out of the Air Force in Phoenix, Arizona, I got a job at the U.S. Post Office, bought my own home, living the American dream, if you will. I've

been an honest citizen, no record, not even traffic violations.

One day I was questioned about a murder of a local bar maid at a bar that I played darts at, that I played on their volleyball team for. Within two days I was arrested for that murder based on testimony from the local medical examiner who said a mark on the body matched my teeth. Just seven months after that murder I was sitting trial with the court-appointed attorney that was granted $5,000 to defend me. Of course, I had nothing to worry about. I didn't do anything. I was sure. I believed in the system. I actually supported the death penalty.

After the three and a half day trial, I was convicted and sentenced to death because I didn't show remorse. How do you show remorse for a crime you didn't commit? And so I went to death row and was there for three years.

My case was overturned because the prosecutor withheld evidence. I got a new trial. By the second trial my family realized this was serious, and they mortgaged their home, cashed in their retirement funds. Friends of my high school took up donations, and churches took up donations. My second cousin spent more than $100,000 on legal fees. I had a luxury few on death row have: I was able to hire my own attorney. My second trial lasted six and a half weeks. Over 30 experts testified, 500 exhibits were introduced. And after that six and a half weeks I was again found guilty because the jury said it was too hard for them to understand the DNA, and they believed the bite mark expert by the prosecutor. However, this time the judge ruled that there was a residual doubt in my guilt. He sat there for six and a half weeks and listened to all the testimony; he wasn't sure I did it. He said this case will haunt him for the rest of his life. And so he sentenced me to 25 to life instead sending me back to death row.

As horrible as death row was, I tell you—prison is worse. When I was on death row I saw people taken off and executed. There was nobody kicking and screaming saying I want to live. I don't want to die. You make peace with dying. It was easier to die than to live in prison. It was easier to be killed because you no longer have to think about your consequences of what you've done. The ultimate punishment is sitting everyday in prison knowing you're never going to get out. It's your fault. You deserved it.

Thankfully, in 2001, the legislature in Arizona passed legislation allowing inmates to request DNA testing on the evidence that had not previously been tested if it might have bearing on their innocence. I was one of the first cases that filed for post-conviction relief—to have testing done on the victim's pants and underwear that had never been tested. It was always available and stored in a police evidence locker in that courtroom, but had never been tested. DNA testing was done from the victims' pants and from her underwear. That DNA matched on both those sources and it was not mine and it was not the victim's. So that DNA was taken and plugged into the nationwide DNA data bank and it did come back with a match to a man who had a history of sexual assault against women and children, a man who was on parole at the time of this murder and lived right behind the bar where the murder took place.

I was lucky to have this DNA evidence. DNA evidence is available in only about 15% of murders. Even after DNA showed this man was the offender and I was innocent, I still had to fight to be released. Once a man is convicted of a crime, it is tremendously difficult to exonerate him. But eventually, after 10 years, three months, and eight days, I was released to reunite with my family and my friends, start my life all over again at the age of 45 and wondering why did this happen? What was the point? I was perfectly happy being a mailman. I certainly expected to retire in my mid-fifties after 30 years of serving in our government. Instead, now I find myself sometimes having to testify and relive that nightmare for me, and not just for me, but for what my family went through.

But for those innocent people like me, and there's a multitude of them. We still had a chance at life, a chance to be released, a chance to be reunited with our family. I know that Connecticut has a fine criminal justice system. But mistakes happen for all sorts of reasons. It happened to me, I assure you, wrongful convictions can happen to anyone. Thank you. (http://www.cga.ct.gov/2011/JUDdata/Tmy/2011SB-01035-R000307-Ray%20Krone-TMY.PDF)

FROM THE STATEMENT OF JUSTICE JOHN PAUL STEVENS IN *THOMPSON V. MCNEIL* (556 U.S. ___), U.S. SUPREME COURT, MARCH 9, 2009

Last term, in my opinion in *Baze v. Rees*, 553 U. S. ___ (2008), I suggested that the "time for a dispassionate, impartial comparison of the enormous costs that death penalty litigation imposes on society with the benefits that it produces has surely arrived." ... This petition for certiorari describes costs that merit consideration in any such study.

In June 1976, having been advised by counsel that he would not receive the death penalty if he accepted responsibility for his crime, petitioner pleaded guilty to a capital offense. The advice was erroneous, and he was sentenced to death. Since that time, two state-court judgments have set aside his death sentence.... At a third penalty hearing—after petitioner presented mitigation evidence about his limited mental capacity and dysfunctional childhood that had previously been barred—five

members of the advisory jury voted against a death sentence, but the court again imposed a sentence of death.

Thirty-two years have passed since petitioner was first sentenced to death. In prior cases, both JUSTICE BREYER and I have noted that substantially delayed executions arguably violate the Eighth Amendment's prohibition against cruel and unusual punishment.... Petitioner's case involves a longer delay than any of those earlier cases.

As he awaits execution, petitioner has endured especially severe conditions of confinement, spending up to 23 hours per day in isolation in a 6- by 9-foot cell. Two death warrants have been signed against him and stayed only shortly before he was scheduled to be put to death. The dehumanizing effects of such treatment are undeniable. See *People v. Anderson*, 6 Cal. 3d 628, 649, 493 P. 2d 880, 894 (1972) ("[T]he process of carrying out a verdict of death is often so degrading and brutalizing to the human spirit as to constitute psychological torture"); *Furman v. Georgia*, 408 U. S. 238, 288 (1972) ... ("[T]he prospect of pending execution exacts a frightful toll during the inevitable long wait between the imposition of sentence and the actual infliction of death"). Moreover, as I explained in *Lackey* [*Lackey v. Texas*, 514 U.S. 1045 (1995)], delaying an execution does not further public purposes of retribution and deterrence but only diminishes whatever possible benefit society might receive from petitioner's death. It would therefore be appropriate to conclude that a punishment of death after significant delay is "so totally without penological justification that it results in the gratuitous infliction of suffering." ...

While the length of petitioner's confinement under sentence of death is extraordinary, the concerns his case raises are not unique. Clarence Allen Lackey had spent 17 years on death row when this Court reviewed his petition for certiorari. Today, condemned inmates await execution for an average of nearly 13 years.... To my mind, this figure underscores the fundamental inhumanity and unworkability of the death penalty as it is administered in the United States.

Some respond that delays in carrying out executions are the result of this Court's insistence on excessive process. But delays have multiple causes, including "the States' failure to apply constitutionally sufficient procedures at the time of initial [conviction or] sentencing." ... The reversible error rate in capital trials is staggering. More than 30 percent of death verdicts imposed between 1973 and 2000 have been overturned, and 129 inmates sentenced to death during that time have been exonerated, often more than a decade after they were convicted. Judicial process takes time, but the error rate in capital cases illustrates its necessity. We are duty bound to "insure that every safeguard is observed" when "a defendant's life is at stake." ...

In sum, our experience during the past three decades has demonstrated that delays in state-sponsored killings are inescapable and that executing defendants after such delays is unacceptably cruel. This inevitable cruelty, coupled with the diminished justification for carrying out an execution after the lapse of so much time, reinforces my opinion that contemporary decisions "to retain the death penalty as a part of our law are the product of habit and inattention rather than an acceptable deliberative process." (http://www.supremecourt.gov/opinions/08pdf/08-7369Stevens.pdf)

IMPORTANT NAMES AND ADDRESSES

American Bar Association
Criminal Justice Section
1050 Connecticut Avenue, NW, Suite 400
Washington, DC 20036
(202) 662-1000
FAX: (202) 662-1501
E-mail: crimjustice@americanbar.org
URL: http://www.abanet.org/crimjust/
home.html/

American Civil Liberties Union
125 Broad St., 18th Floor
New York, NY 10004
(212) 549-2500
URL: http://www.aclu.org/

Amnesty International U.S.A.
5 Penn Plaza
New York, NY 10001
(212) 633-4254
FAX: (212) 627-1451
E-mail: aimember@aiusa.org
URL: http://www.amnestyusa.org/

Bureau of Justice Statistics
U.S. Department of Justice
810 Seventh St., NW
Washington, DC 20531
(202) 307-0765
E-mail: askbjs@usdoj.gov
URL: http://www.ojp.usdoj.gov/bjs

Center on Wrongful Convictions
Bluhm Legal Clinic
Northwestern University School of Law
375 E. Chicago Ave.
Chicago, IL 60611
(312) 503-2391
FAX: (312) 503-8977
E-mail: cwc@law.northwestern.edu
URL: http://www.law.northwestern.edu/cwc/

Constitution Project
1200 18th St., NW, Ste. 1000
Washington, DC 20036
(202) 580-6920
FAX: (202) 580-6929

E-mail: info@constitutionproject.org
URL: http://www.constitutionproject.org/

Criminal Justice Legal Foundation
2131 L Street
Sacramento, CA 95816
(916) 446-0345
URL: http://www.cjlf.org/

Death Penalty Information Center
1015 18th St., NW, Ste. 704
Washington, DC 20036
(202) 289-2275
FAX: (202) 289-7336
E-mail: dpic@deathpenaltyinfo.org
URL: http://www.deathpenaltyinfo.org/

Equal Justice Initiative
122 Commerce St.
Montgomery, AL 36104
(334) 269-1803
FAX: (334) 269-1806
E-mail: contact_us@eji.org
URL: http://eji.org/eji/

Federal Bureau of Investigation
J. Edgar Hoover Bldg.
935 Pennsylvania Ave., NW
Washington, DC 20535-0001
(202) 324-3000
URL: http://www.fbi.gov/

Federal Bureau of Prisons
320 First St., NW
Washington, DC 20534
(202) 307-3198
E-mail: info@bop.gov
URL: http://www.bop.gov/

Innocence Project
40 Worth St., Ste. 701
New York, NY 10013
(212) 364-5340
E-mail: info@innocenceproject.org
URL: http://www.innocenceproject.org/

Innocence Project Clinic
University of Virginia School of Law
580 Massie Rd.
Charlottesville, VA 22903
(434) 924-7354
E-mail: lawcomm@virginia.edu
URL: http://www.law.virginia.edu/html/
academics/practical/innocenceclinic.htm

Murder Victims' Families
for Reconciliation
405 Morson Street
Raleigh, NC 27601
(877) 896-4702
E-mail: info@mvfr.org
URL: http://www.mvfr.org/

NAACP Legal Defense and Educational
Fund
40 Rector St., Fifth Floor
New York, NY 10006
(212) 965-2200
URL: http://www.naacpldf.org/

National Association of Criminal Defense
Lawyers
1660 L St., NW, 12th Floor
Washington, DC 20036
(202) 872-8600
FAX: (202) 872-8690
E-mail: assist@nacdl.com
URL: http://www.nacdl.org/

National Center for Victims of Crime
2000 M St., NW, Ste. 480
Washington, DC 20036
(202) 467-8700
FAX: (202) 467-8701
URL: http://www.ncvc.org/

National Coalition to Abolish the
Death Penalty
1620 L Street, NW, Ste. 250
Washington, DC 20036
(202) 331-4090
E-mail: admin-info@ncadp.org
URL: http://www.ncadp.org/

National District Attorneys Association
99 Canal Center Plaza, Ste. 330
Alexandria, VA 22314
(703) 549-9222
FAX: (703) 836-3195
URL: http://www.ndaa.org/

**Office of the United Nations High
Commissioner for Human Rights**
Palais des Nations, CH-1211
Geneva 10 Switzerland
(011-41) 22-917-9220
E-mail: InfoDesk@ohchr.org
URL: http://www.ohchr.org/EN/Pages/
WelcomePage.aspx/

U.S. Commission on Civil Rights
1331 Pennsylvania Ave., NW, Suite 1150
Washington, DC 20425
(202) 376-7700
URL: http://www.usccr.gov/

U.S. Department of Justice
950 Pennsylvania Ave. NW
Washington, DC 20530-0001
(202) 514-2000
E-mail: askdoj@usdoj.gov
URL: http://www.usdoj.gov/

U.S. Government Accountability Office
441 G St., NW
Washington, DC 20548
(202) 512-3000
E-mail: contact@gao.gov
URL: http://www.gao.gov/

**U.S. House of Representatives Committee
on the Judiciary**
2138 Rayburn House Office Bldg.
Washington, DC 20515
(202) 225-3951
URL: http://judiciary.house.gov/

U.S. Senate Committee on the Judiciary
224 Dirksen Senate Office Bldg.
Washington, DC 20510
(202) 224-7703
FAX: (202) 224-9516
URL: http://judiciary.senate.gov/

**U.S. Sentencing Commission
Office of Public Affairs**
1 Columbus Circle, NE, Ste. 2-500
Washington, DC 20002-8002
(202) 502-4500
E-mail: pubaffairs@ussc.gov
URL: http://www.ussc.gov/

U.S. Supreme Court
1 First St., NE
Washington, DC 20543
(202) 479-3000
URL: http://www.supremecourtus.gov/

RESOURCES

Numerous federal and state agencies, courts, legislative bodies, committees, and commissions served as resources for this book. The Bureau of Justice Statistics (BJS) within the U.S. Department of Justice collects statistics on death row inmates as part of its National Prisoner Statistics. Since 1993 the BJS has prepared the annual bulletin *Capital Punishment*, which provides an overview of capital punishment in the United States. Bulletins published through 2006 include much historical data. The Federal Bureau of Investigation collects and publishes crime data through its annual *Uniform Crime Report* and *Crime in the United States*.

Information about the current status of death row inmates was obtained from the websites of state departments of corrections and the federal Bureau of Prisons. Legal opinions from state courts, federal district courts, and the U.S. Supreme Court were an invaluable resource in preparation of this book. In addition, public hearings held by state legislatures provided records of testimony given by many stakeholders—both for and against capital punishment. Other government sources included the reports of committees and commissions that were tasked by various states and the federal government to examine contentious issues related to the death penalty, such as costs, the appeals process, and racial discrimination and other fairness issues. Offices established and/or funded by the government to provide legal assistance to inmates charged in capital cases also provided useful information.

Prominent law schools around the country publish journal articles and news releases concerning death penalty cases and the legal issues involved in them. Several schools host or sponsor organizations or student clinics that are dedicated to clearing wrongfully convicted death row inmates. Examples include the Center on Wrongful Convictions at the Northwestern University School of Law, the Innocence Project at the Benjamin N. Cardozo School of Law at Yeshiva University, and the Innocence

Project Clinic at Virginia Law School. All of these sources were consulted.

The Death Penalty Information Center (DPIC) is a nonprofit organization that provides the media and the general public with information and analysis regarding capital punishment. The DPIC, which is against the death penalty, serves as a resource for those working on this issue. Its reports and graphics on capital punishment were used in preparing this book. The National Coalition to Abolish the Death Penalty maintains an up-to-date list of news stories from the media regarding the death penalty.

The National Association for the Advancement of Colored People's Legal Defense and Educational Fund (LDF) maintains statistics on capital punishment and is strongly opposed to the death penalty. The LDF publishes *Death Row U.S.A.*, a periodic compilation of capital punishment statistics and information, including the names, gender, and race of all those who have been executed or are currently on death row. Gender and racial information on the victims of those executed is also provided. Data from this publication were helpful in preparing this book.

Other private organizations consulted for this book include the American Bar Association, the American Board of Anesthesiology, the American Civil Liberties Union, the American Medical Association, Amnesty International, the Criminal Justice Legal Foundation, the Equal Justice Initiative, Murder Victims' Families for Reconciliation, the National Center of Victims of Crime, Pro-Death Penalty.com, and the Urban Institute.

Major media sources consulted for this book include ABC News, the Associated Press, the BBC, CBS News, CNN, Fox News, NBC News, Reuters News Service, and newspapers, such as the *New York Times*. Polls taken by Angus Reid Public Opinion, the Gallup Organization, the Pew Research Center, and Rasmussen Reports were also used in preparing this book.

INDEX

Page references in italics refer to photographs. References with the letter t following them indicate the presence of a table. The letter f indicates a figure. If more than one table or figure appears on a particular page, the exact item number for the table or figure being referenced is provided.

A

ABA (American Bar Association), 92, 97
Abbott, Greg Wayne, 107
Abell Foundation, 79
"Abolitionist and Retentionist Countries" (Amnesty International), 14
Abolitionist countries, 121–122
Abolitionist movement, 3–4
Acker, James R., 91–92
Addison, Michael, 110
Advocates, death penalty
  numbers supporting death penalty, 111–114
  on race-of-victim bias, 93–95
AEDPA. *See* Antiterrorism and Effective Death Penalty Act
African Americans
  biased strikes in jury selection, 47–48
  death penalty rate of, 88
  homicide rates of, 88–89
  jury strikes of, 94–95
  race as factor in capital cases, 45–47
  support for death penalty among, 114
Age
  of inmates on death row, 69–70
  of juveniles sentenced to death, 37–40
  moral acceptability of various issues by, 113(t9.3)
  opinion on capital punishment and, 111
  public attitudes on death penalty by, 114(t9.4)
  support for death penalty and, 112, 116
Aggravating factors
  capital case, 50
  death penalty, 5

Alabama
  judge sentencing in, 21–22
  recent death penalty legislation, 52
  trial judge sentencing in, 53
Alabama, Beck v., 17–18
Alabama, Harris v., 21, 53
Alabama, Rudolph v., 5
Alabama, Swain v., 47
"Alabama Appeals Court Reverses Its 2011 Decision That Granted Convicted Murderer Jason Sharp a New Trial" (Lawson), 95
"Alabama Death Row Prisoner Wins New Trial from Appeals Court Due to Illegal Racial Discrimination in Jury Selection" (EJI), 95
Aldridge, Joyce, 9–10
Alfred P. Murrah Federal Building, 65
Allen, Nancy, 38
American Bar Association (ABA), 92, 97
American League to Abolish Capital Punishment, 4
American Society for the Abolition of Capital Punishment, 4
Amicus curiae, 93
Amnesty International
  "Abolitionist and Retentionist Countries," 14
  on abolitionist countries, 121–122
  on China, 122
  Death Sentences and Executions, 14, 121
  on retentionist countries, 121
Analysis of the Fire Investigation Methods and Procedures Used in the Criminal Arson Cases against Ernest Ray Willis and Cameron Todd Willingham (TFSC), 106
Anderson, People v., 137
Anderson, Sharon, 103
Angus Reid Public Opinion, 116, 124
Annan, Kofi, 120
Anti–death penalty movement, 4–5

Anti-Drug Abuse Act
  allowance for death penalty in, 7
  ban of execution of mentally retarded, 41–42
  habeas corpus reviews and, 28
Antiterrorism and Effective Death Penalty Act (AEDPA)
  challenging, 31–33
  enactment of, 65
  federal habeas corpus, restrictions on, 107
Appeals
  based on new evidence, 29–31
  capital cases, post-conviction counsel, 54–55
  capital cases, state processes of, 53–54
  federal, restriction on, 32–33
  process, described, 99
  process, quickening of, 56, 57–58
  process for capital cases, 5, 54f
  protraction of, 54–55
The Application of Indiana's Capital Sentencing Law: Findings of the Indiana Criminal Law Study Commission (Indiana Criminal Law Study Commission), 91
Apprendi v. New Jersey, 22
Araujo Torres, Lourdes Yesenia, 51
Archer, Mary, 110
Arellano-Félix, Benjamin, 126
Arellano-Félix, Francisco, 126
Argersinger v. Hamlin, 95
Ariosto, David, 109
Arizona
  sentencing in, 22–23
  Tison v. Arizona, 27
Arizona, Ring v., 22
Arizona, Tison v., 27
Arizona, Walton v., 22
Armstrong, Jeanette, 26
Armstrong, Sampson, 26

overview of, 99–100

Penalver, Seth, 103

"Explaining Death Row's Population and Racial Composition" (Blume, Eisenberg, & Wells), 86–87, 92

Extradition, 126

F

"Facts about the Death Penalty" (DPIC), 90

Fagan, Jeffrey, 104

Fairness

  executions by year/race/Hispanic origin, 90(*t7.7*)

  geographical disparities, 83–88

  homicide breakdown by race of offender/victim, 89(*f7.3*)

  homicide offending rates by race, 89(*f7.2*)

  homicide rate by region/state, 85*t*

  homicide victimization rates by race, 89(*f7.1*)

  homicide victims/offenders by race, 89*t*

  legal representation, quality of, 95–97

  numbers sentenced to death/executed/on death row, by jurisdiction, 84(*t7.1*)

  overview of, 83

  persons under sentence of death by jurisdiction/race, 84(*t7.2*)

  political party affiliation/ideology by state, 86*t*

  race-of-victim bias in capital cases, 91*t*

  racial bias, 88–95

  racial breakdown of inmates sentenced to death, 90(*t7.6*)

Faulkner, Elizabeth, 19

FBI (Federal Bureau of Investigation), 88–89

FDA (Food and Drug Administration), 33, 63

Federal Bureau of Investigation (FBI), 88–89

"Federal Death Row Prisoners" (DPIC), 65

"Federal Executions 1927–2003" (DPIC), 64–65

Feguer, Victor, 65

Fetal homicide, 51–52

"Fetal Homicide Laws" (National Conference of State Legislatures), 51

Fierro, David Rey, 33–34

Fierro v. Gomez, 33–34

"59% Favor Death Penalty" (Rasmussen Reports), 116

Final Report of the Death Penalty Subcommittee of the Committee on Public Defense (WSBA), 79

Final Report of the Pennsylvania Supreme Court Committee on Racial and Gender Bias in the Justice System (Pennsylvania Supreme Court Committee on Racial and Gender Bias in the Justice System), 92

Final Report on HB 520, Chapter 284, Laws of 2009 (Commission to Study the Death Penalty in New Hampshire), 79

Fins, Deborah

  Death Row U.S.A.: Winter 2013, 67, 109

  on inmates on death row, numbers of, 73

  prisoners on death row by state, 110

  on race of death row inmates, 89–90

  on race of executed prisoners' victims, 90

Florida

  judge sentencing in, 20–21

  prisoners on death row, 56

  recent death penalty legislation, 52–53

  Timely Justice Act, 58

  trial judge sentencing in, 53

Florida, Enmund v., 26

Florida, Foster v., 35

Florida, Proffitt v., 16–17

Florida, Spaziano v., 20–21, 53

Florida Commission on Capital Cases, 100, 104

Food and Drug Administration (FDA), 33, 63

Ford, Alvin Bernard, 40

Ford v. Wainwright, 8, 40–41

Foreign nationals, 125–126

"Foreign Nationals and the Death Penalty in the US" (DPIC), 125

Forensic science

  DNA testing, post-conviction, 105–106

  execution of innocent, 106–108

  role in exonerations, 105

"Forensic Science Commission Still Has Work to Do" (Scheck), 107

"Fort Hood Shooter Sentenced to Death Penalty" (NPR), 66

Foster, Charles Kenneth, 35

Foster, Kenneth, 50–51

Foster v. Florida, 35

14th Amendment

  biased strikes in jury selection, 47–48

  description of, 92

  federal habeas corpus review, 54

  Furman v. Georgia, Supreme Court ruling on, 5

  jury sentencing and, 22

Franklin, Benjamin, 3

Freedberg, Sydney P., 100

Furman v. Georgia

  Eighth Amendment and, 49

  Stevens, John Paul, on, 137

  Supreme Court dissenting opinions on, 16

  Supreme Court majority opinions on, 15–16

  Supreme Court ruling on, 5

G

Gales, Arthur Lee, 128

Gallup Organization

  "Death Penalty," 114, 117

  on political party affiliation by state, 86

polling of on support for death penalty, 111–114

on public attitudes toward capital punishment, 111

U.S. Death Penalty Support Stable at 63%, 1

GAO (U.S. Government Accountability Office), 91, 97

Garland, David, 123–124

Garnett, Stanley, L., 133–134

Gary D. Haugen v. Kitzhaber, 110

Garza, Juan Raul, 65

Garza, Robert Gene, 51

Gas, lethal, 33–34

Gender

  of inmates on death row, 69

  public attitudes on death penalty by, 114(*t9.4*)

  support for death penalty and, 112

Geographical disparities

  death penalty states, differences between, 83–86

  death penalty states, differences within, 87

  federal judicial districts, differences between, 87–88

  national study on, 86–87

  overview of, 83

"Geography of the Death Penalty" (Baumgartner), 87

Georgia

  ban on execution of mentally retarded people, 7

  confidentiality for execution participants, law enacting, 63

Georgia, Coker v., 25

Georgia, Furman v.

  Eighth Amendment and, 49

  Stevens, John Paul, on, 137

Georgia, Gregg v.

  automatic direct appeal and, 53

  Supreme Court's decision on, 16–17

Georgia v. McCollum, 47

Germany, extradition refusal of, 126

Giarratano, Joseph M., 28

Giarratano, Murray v.

  post-conviction counsel, 54

  Supreme Court's ruling on, 28

Gideon v. Wainwright, 95

"Gideon's Broken Promise: America's Continuing Quest for Equal Justice" (ABA), 97

Gilmore, Gary, 5, 15

Ginsburg, Ruth Bader

  Atkins v. Virginia, opinion on, 43

  "In Pursuit of the Public Good: Lawyers Who Care," 97

  Ring v. Arizona, opinion on, 22

Godinez v. Moran, 44

Goldberg, Arthur J., 5

Golphin, Tilmon, 93

Gomez, Fierro v., 33–34
Gomez, James, 33–34
Gould, Jon B., 78–79
"Governor Allows Fetal Homicide Bill to Become Law" (Soptelean), 51
Grant, Benjamin, 110
Gray, Ronald, 66
Great Britain, 124
Great Recession, 11
Greeley, Horace, 4
Green, Frank, 58
Greenawalt, Randy, 27
Greene, Breard v., 125–126
Greenhouse, Linda, 126
Greenman, Lisa, 78–79
Gregg v. Georgia
    automatic direct appeal and, 53
    Supreme Court's decision on, 16–17
Grissom, Brandi, 106
Guns, 112

H

Habeas corpus
    federal relief, AEDPA and, 31
    procedure, description of, 53–54
    reviews, execution delays by federal judges and, 28–29
Hamadi, Mohammed Ali, 126
Hamilton, Dawn, 9–10, 100
Hamlin, Argersinger v., 95
Hammel, Andrew, 124
Handspike, Joseph, 63
Hanging, 33
A Hanging in Detroit: Stephen Gifford Simmons and the Last Execution under Michigan Law (Chardavoyne), 3
Harberts, Laura Lynn, 20–21
Harmless error
    appeals process and, 53
    description of, 99
Harris, Amber, 128
Harris, Daniel Marcus, 23
Harris, Isaiah, 21
Harris, Louise, 21–22
Harris, Pulley v., 23
Harris, Robert Alton, 23, 33–34
Harris County, Texas
    court-appointed lawyers in, 96
    death sentence rates of, 87
Harris v. Alabama, 21, 53
Hasan, Nidal Malik, 66
Hathcock, David, 93
Haugen, Gary, 110
Hearings, federal evidentiary, 32
Heckler v. Chaney, 33
Hellams, Susan, 8
Hendrickson, Barbara, 33
Herrera, Leonel Torres, 29, 105
Herrera v. Collins, 29–30, 105

Hewlett, Michael, 92
Hickenlooper, John, 110
Hill, Clarence E., 34–35
Hill, Warren Lee, 63
Hill v. McDonough, 35
Hispanics
    on death row, numbers of, 70
    executions by Hispanic origin, 90(t7.7)
Hitchcock v. Dugger, 37
Hokanson, Terri Lynn, 28
Holder, Eric, 62, 97
Homicide
    breakdown by race of offender/victim, 89(f7.3)
    decline of, death sentence declines and, 73–74
    offending rates by race, 89(f7.2)
    rate, capital punishment connection with, 6–7
    rate, number of executions and, 9(f1.4)
    rate by region/state, 85t
    rates of, 85
    victimization rates by race, 89(f7.1)
    victims/offenders by race, 89t
Homicide Trends in the United States, 1980–2008 (Cooper & Smith), 88
"Hospira Statement Regarding Pentothal (Sodium Thiopental) Market Exit" (Hospira), 62
House, Paul, 30
House v. Bell, 30–31
Huddleston, Jack, 39
Human rights, 124–125
Humberto Leal v. Texas, 126
Hybrid sentencing systems, 53

I

Ibar, Pablo, 103
Illegal Racial Discrimination in Jury Selection: A Continuing Legacy (EJI), 94–95
Illinois
    death penalty, abolition of in, 11
    moratorium on death penalty, 109
Illinois, Witherspoon v., 18
Illyankoff, Walter, 40
"In Pursuit of the Public Good: Lawyers Who Care" (Ginsburg), 97
In Re Troy Anthony Davis, 107–108
In U.S., Support for Death Penalty Falls to 39-Year Low (Newport), 113–114
Indigent Defense: DOJ Could Increase Awareness of Eligible Funding and Better Determine the Extent to Which Funds Help Support This Purpose (GAO), 97
"Information on Defendants Who Were Executed since 1976 and Designated as 'Volunteers'" (DPIC), 59

Inmates
    on death row, 68–69
    on death row, numbers of, 87
    death row, with sentence/conviction overturned, 72
    death row/executed, racial makeup of, 89–90
    numbers put to death after moratorium, 6
    under sentence of death, numbers of, 2
    sentenced to death, racial breakdown of, 90(t7.6)
    See also Prisoners
Innocence List
    description of, 99
    disputed, 103–104
"Innocence: List of Those Freed from Death Row" (DPIC), 99
Innocence Project, 106
Innocence Protection Act
    indigent defendants and, 97
    passing of, 10
Insane
    ban on execution of, 7
    execution of, Supreme Court's opinion on, 40–41
    stabilized on drugs, execution of, 41
International Bill of Human Rights, 119
Iowa
    abolition of death penalty in, 4
    de Jure moratorium in, 108
Ivester, Sally, 35

J

James City, Virginia, 2
Jamestown, Virginia, 2
Jensen, Max, 5
Jersey, Apprendi v. New, 22
Jindal, Bobby, 25
"John Kitzhaber Moratorium on Death Penalty Leaves Inmate Gary Haugen and Oregon Lawmakers Wondering What's Next" (Jung), 110
John Paul II, Pope, 134
Johnson, Dorsie Lee, Jr., 39–40
Johnson, Penry v., 42
Johnson v. Texas, 39–40
Jolly, David, 62
Jones, Louis, Jr., 65
Judge, James, 27
Judge, Margene, 27
Judges
    death sentence rates by, 87
    federal, execution delays by, 28–29
    judicial override, 53
    sentencing by, 20–22
Judicial districts, federal
    death sentence rate disparities among, 87–88
    racial bias in, 94

New Mexico, 11, 109

"New Mexico Governor Repeals Death Penalty in State" (CNN.com), 109

New York (state), 6

Newport, Frank, 113–114

Nicklasson, Allen, 63

19th century, 4

"N.J. Approves Abolition of Death Penalty; Corzine to Sign" (Richburg), 109

NJDPSC (New Jersey Death Penalty Study Commission), 79

Nonhomicide crimes, 50–51

Norris, Singleton v., 41

North Carolina

  death penalty, proper imposition of in, 16–17

  on racial bias in capital cases, 93

  Racial Justice Act of, 92–93

North Carolina, Woodson v., 16–17

"North Carolina Repeals Law Allowing Racial Bias Claim in Death Penalty Challenges" (Severson), 93

O

Obama, Barack

  on death penalty for child rape, 25

  delay of execution of Mexican national, 126

O'Connor, Colleen, 110

O'Connor, Sandra Day

  Atkins v. Virginia, opinion on, 43

  on death penalty for minors, 38

  Enmund v. Florida, opinion on, 26

  execution of mentally retarded, opinion on, 40

  Penry v. Lynaugh, opinion on, 42

  Ring v. Arizona, opinion on, 22

  Tison v. Arizona, opinion on, 27

Office of Defender Services (ODS), 78

Ohio

  child rape, death penalty for in, 51–52

  mitigating circumstances, judicial consideration in, 37

  one-drug protocol in, 62

  recent death penalty legislation, 52

Ohio, Lockett v.

  mitigating circumstances and, 37

  Supreme Court's decision on, 18

Ohio, Powers v., 47

Ohio Department of Rehabilitation and Correction

  "Capital Punishment in Ohio," 62

  use of pentobarbital, 62

Oklahoma

  bombing of Alfred P. Murrah Federal Building, 65

  recent death penalty legislation, 53

Oklahoma, Thompson v., 38

Olmeda, Rafael, 103

Opinion. *See* Public attitudes

Opponents, death penalty

  international criticism, 119

  reasons for opposition, 116–117

Optional Protocol

  description of, 125

  U.S. withdrawal from, 126

Ordinary crimes. *See* Common crimes

Oregon

  de facto moratorium in, 110

  death penalty in, 6

Owens, Albert, 11

P

Pacheco, Rod, 87

Pardon, 59

Parole information, 20

Patel, Marilyn Hall, 34

"Path to Execution Swifter, More Certain in Va." (Green), 58

Patterson, James Earl, 9–10

Patton, Paul E., 39

Payne, Pervis Tyrone, 44–45

Payne v. Tennessee, 44–45

Pena, Elizabeth, 125

Penalver, Seth, 103

Pennsylvania Supreme Court Committee on Racial and Gender Bias in the Justice System, 92

"Pennsylvania Supreme Court Urged to Consider How Philadelphia Pays Death-Penalty Lawyers" (Slobodzian), 96

Penry, Johnny Paul

  execution of mentally retarded, 41–42

  resentencing of, 43

Penry v. Johnson, 42

Penry v. Lynaugh

  on execution of mentally retarded, 7

  Supreme Court's ruling on, 41–42

Pentobarbital, 62

People v. Anderson, 137

Peremptory strikes

  biased in jury selection, 47–48

  description of, 94

  misuse of, 94–95

  in North Carolina, 93

Perry, Rick

  Foster, Kenneth, clemency granting, 51

  post-conviction testing bill, signing of, 106

  Texas Forensic Science Commission, appointments to, 106

Pew Research Center, 116

Pharmacy compounding, 63

"Pharmacy Compounding" (FDA), 63

"Phila. Courts Increase Pay for Capital Defense" (Slobodzian), 96

Philadelphia, Pennsylvania, 96

Phillips, Scott, 96

Pleau, Jason W., 65

Plymouth Colony, Massachusetts, 8

Polin, David, 110

Political party

  affiliation/ideology by state, 86*t*

  geographical disparities in death sentence and, 85–86

  public attitudes on death penalty by, 114(*t*9.5)

  support for death penalty by, 112, 116, 115(*f*9.2)

Ponnuru, Ramesh, 103–104

Poore, Barbel, 38

Possley, Maurice, 106

Post-conviction counsel, 54–55

Postconviction DNA Testing: Recommendations for Handling (National Commission on the Future of DNA Evidence), 105

"Post-conviction Proceedings in Capital Cases" (Emas), 54

Post-conviction review, 99

Powell, Lewis F., Jr.

  Booth v. Maryland, opinion on, 44

  on constitutionality of death penalty, 16

  McCleskey v. Kemp, opinion on, 46

Powers v. Ohio, 47

President's Commission on Law Enforcement and Administration of Justice, 83, 88

Prisoners

  on death row by jurisdiction/year of sentencing, 57*t*

  on death row/time on death row, 56(*t*5.4)

  time on death row, 55–56

  See also Inmates

Prisons, earliest U.S., 3

ProDeath Penalty.com, 58

Proffitt v. Florida, 16–17

Prohibition

  abolitionist movement during, 4

  homicide rate during, 6–7

Provenzano, Thomas, 34

Provenzano v. Moore, 34

Public attitudes

  about death penalty, race and, 88

  on death penalty, 1936–2012, 114*f*

  on death penalty by gender/age/region/education level, 114(*t*9.4)

  on death penalty by political party/ideology, 114(*t*9.5)

  death penalty support/opposition, reasons for, 116–117

  geographical disparities in death sentence and, 85

  on moral acceptability of various issues, 112*t*

  on moral acceptability of various issues, by age group, 113(*t*9.3)

  morality of capital punishment, 111

  on morality of death penalty, 113(*t*9.2)

  support for death penalty, 111–114, 116

support for death penalty by blacks/
    whites, 115(f9.2)
support for death penalty by political
    party, 115(f9.2)
Public defenders, 96
Pulanski, Charles A., Jr., 45–46
Pulley v. Harris, 23

Q

Quijano, Walter, 47
Quincy Five, 100
Quinn, Pat, 109

R

"Race Discrimination and the Death
    Penalty: An Empirical and Legal
    Overview" (Acker, Bohm, & Lanier),
    91–92
"Race Discrimination in the Administration
    of the Death Penalty: An Overview of
    the Empirical Evidence with Special
    Emphasis on the Post-1990 Research"
    (Baldus & Woodworth), 91–92
Race/ethnicity
    Baldus/Woodworth review on racial
        bias, 91–92
    bias in death penalty cases, 10
    bias in state capital cases, 90–91
    capital cases and, 45
    death penalty, race/public opinion
        about, 88
    death penalty, racial bias in, 88
    death row/executed inmates, racial
        makeup of, 89–90
    executed prisoners' victims, race of, 90
    executions by, 90(t7.7)
    future dangerousness and, 47
    GAO review of death penalty
        sentencing, 91
    homicide offending rates by, 89(f7.2)
    homicide victimization rates by, 89(f7.1)
    homicide victims/offenders by, 89t
    of inmates on death row, 69
    jury selection, racial issues related to,
        94–95
    multistate analysis, 92
    of offender/victim, homicide by, 89(f7.3)
    persons under death sentence by,
        84(t7.2)
    of prisoners executed, 81
    race/homicide statistics, 88–89
    race-of-victim bias, death penalty
        advocates on, 93–95
    race-of-victim bias in capital cases, 91t
    racial attitudes, limits to consideration
        of, 45–47
    state legislative actions, 92–94
    support for death penalty and, 112–114,
        116
"The Racial Geography of the Federal
    Death Penalty" (Cohen & Smith), 87–88

"Racial Justice Act Case Heads to NC
    Supreme Court" (Blythe), 93
Racial Justice Acts, 92–93
Randa, Laura E.
    on abolitionist stance on public
        executions, 4
    *Society's Final Solution: A History and
        Discussion of the Death Penalty*, 2
Rape
    of adult women/kidnapping, 25
    child, 25
Rasmussen Reports, 116
Reasoned choice, 44
"Rebutting the Myths about Race and the
    Death Penalty" (Scheidegger), 93–94
"Recent Legislative Activity" (DPIC), 52
Reckless indifference, 26
"Reducing the Risk of Executing the
    Innocent: The Report of the Illinois
    Governor's Commission on Capital
    Punishment" (Thurmond), 104
Rees, Baze v.
    on constitutionality of Kentucky's
        3-drug protocol, 61
    state moratoriums resulting from, 110
    Stevens, John Paul, on, 137–138
    Supreme Court's ruling on, 35
Reese, Phillip, 87
Regions
    with most death sentences, 83–85
    public attitudes on death penalty by,
        114(t9.4)
    support for death penalty and, 112
Rehnquist, William H.
    on constitutionality of death penalty, 16
    execution of insane, opinion on, 40
    execution of mentally retarded, opinion
        on, 40
    Herrera v. Collins, opinion on, 29
    Lockhart v. McCree, opinion on, 19
    Murray v. Giarratano, opinion on, 28
    Ring v. Arizona, opinion on, 22
    Wainwright v. Witt, opinion on, 18
Reid, Willie, 44
Religion, 112, 116
*Report of the Texas Forensic Science
    Commission: Willingham/ Willis
    Investigation* (TFSC), 106–107
*Report to the Committee on Defender
    Services, Judicial Conference of the
    United States: Update on the Cost and
    Quality of Defense Representation in
    Federal Death Penalty Cases* (Gould
    & Greenman), 78–79
Reprieve, 59
Resolutions, United Nations, 119–120
Retentionist countries, 121
Revels, Thomas, 100
Reversals. *See* Exonerations
Rhodes, Russell, 43

"R.I. Aims to Block Death-Penalty Trial"
    (Valencia), 65
Richard, Martin, 52
Richardson, Bill, 109
Richburg, Keith B., 109
Ring, Timothy Stuart, 22
Ring v. Arizona, 22
Riverside County, California, 87
Roberts v. Louisiana, 16–17
Robinson, Marcus, 93
*Robinson, State of North Carolina v.
    Marcus Reymond*, 93
Rogers, Marie, 103
Roman, John, 79
Roper, Donald, 8
Roper v. Simmons, 8, 39
Rosenberg, Ethel, 64
Rosenberg, Julius, 64
Ross, Michael, 128
Rucker, David, 29
Rudolph v. Alabama, 5
Ruffner, Kimberly Shay, 100
Ruggles, Kimberly Anne, 66
Ruiz, Alejandro Gilbert, 33–34
Rumbo, Thomas, 65
Rush, Benjamin, 3–4
Ryan, George, 59, 109

S

Saad, Lydia
    on demographic factors in death penalty
        support, 112
    on support for death penalty, 1, 88
Sack, Kevin, 61–62
Safeguards Guaranteeing Protection of the
    Rights of Those Facing the Death
    Penalty, 120
Saldano, Victor, 47
Saldano v. Texas, 47
Sametz, Lynn, 8
Sauceda, Adria, 126
Sawyer v. Whitley, 30
Scalia, Antonin
    Atkins v. Virginia, opinion on, 43
    on death penalty for minors, 38
    execution of mentally retarded, opinion
        on, 40
    Hitchcock v. Dugger, opinion on, 37
    Ring v. Arizona, opinion on, 22
Schaefer, William D., 100
Scheck, Barry, 107
Scheideggar, Kent, 63, 93–94
Schlatt, Frank, 45
Schlup, Lloyd E., Jr., 30
Schlup v. Delo, 30
Schriro v. Summerlin, 23
Schwartz, John, 62
Schwarzenegger, Arnold, 11
Science, forensic. *See* Forensic science

U.S. Government Accountability Office (GAO), 91, 97
U.S. military, death penalty laws of, 65–66
"The U.S. Military Death Penalty" (DPIC), 66
"U.S. Quits Pact Used in Capital Cases" (Lane), 126
U.S. Response to UN Human Rights Council Working Group Report (U.S. Department of State), 125
U.S. Senate Committee on the Judiciary Subcommittee on the Constitution, Civil Rights, and Human Rights, 94
U.S. Supreme Court
  AEDPA, challenging, 31–33
  anti–capital punishment jurors, exclusion of, 18–19
  capital punishment for minors, ending, 37–40
  competency standard, 43–44
  criminal intent, 26–27
  death penalty, circumstances found not to warrant, 25
  death penalty, proper imposition of, 16–17
  death penalty constitutionality, 15–16
  death row, extended stays on, 35–36
  decisions involving the death penalty, 6*t*
  effective counsel, right to, 27–29
  execution, methods of, 33–35
  insanity, execution and, 40–41
  on judge sentencing, 20–22
  jurors' lesser charge consideration, 17–18
  on jurors' responsibility for death sentence, 19–20
  jury selection, biased peremptory strikes in, 47–48
  on jury sentencing, 22–23
  mental retardation, execution and, 41–43
  mitigating circumstances, 37
  new evidence, appeals based on, 29–31
  race issue in capital cases, 45–47
  on sentencing procedures, 23
  Skinner, Henry, stay of execution, 106
  Trop v. Dulles, 5
  victim impact statements, 44–45
  on withholding parole information from jury, 20
USA Patriot Act, 65
USA Patriot Act Improvement and Reauthorization Act, 65
Uttecht v. Brown, 18

V

Valencia, Milton J., 65
Vandervoort, Linda, 43
Vasquez Beltran, Dantizene Lizeth, 51
Venires
  bias in, 94
  federal, racial bias in, 95
Victim impact statements, 44–45
Victims, race of executed prisoners, 90
Vienna Convention on Consular Relations (VCCR), 125–126
Violent Crime Control and Law Enforcement Act, 65
Virginia
  colonial, death sentence in, 2
  death penalty process, efficiency of, 58
  DNA evidence, executions based on, 8–9
  efficiency of death penalty process in, 58
  execution of mentally retarded in, 43
  racial bias in capital cases, 45
  state-paid counsel in, 28
  suppressed evidence in, 32
Virginia, Atkins v., 8, 39, 43
Volunteers, execution of, 59

W

Wainwright, Ford v., 8, 40–41
Wainwright, Gideon v., 95
Wainwright v. Witt, 18
Walker, Douglas, 48
Walters, Christina, 93
Walton v. Arizona, 22
Washa, Holly, 18
Washington, Strickland v., 31, 95
Washington State Bar Association (WSBA), 79
Wells, Martin T.
  on death penalty/murder statistics, 92
  "Explaining Death Row's Population and Racial Composition," 86–87
West, Valerie, 104
White, Byron R.
  on constitutionality of death penalty, 16
  execution of mentally retarded, opinion on, 40
  Turner v. Murray, opinion on, 45
Whitley, Kyles v., 31
Whitley, Sawyer v., 30
Why Does the U.S. Have Capital Punishment? (Garland), 123–124
"Why So Long? Explaining Processing Time in Capital Appeals" (Cauthen & Latzer), 56
Wicklund, Ranae, 33
Wicklund, Shannah, 33

Wiggins, Kevin Eugene, 27–28
Wiggins v. Smith, 27–28
Wilkins, Heath, 38
Wilkins v. Missouri, 37–40
Williams, Antoine, 108
Williams, Carol J., 59
Williams, Michael Wayne, 32–33
Williams, Stanley "Tookie," 11
Williams, Terry, 31–32
Williams v. Taylor, 32
Willingham, Cameron Todd, 106–107
Willis, Ernest Ray, 106–107
Wilson, George, 34
Witherspoon v. Illinois, 18
Witness to Innocence, 136
Witnesses, state executions, 63–64
Witt, Wainwright v., 18
Wolff, Mary, 130
Women
  on death row, numbers of, 70
  executed in U.S., 80
Wood, Campbell v., 33
Woodson v. North Carolina, 16–17
Woodworth, George
  "Comparative Review of Death Sentences: An Empirical Study of the Georgia Experience," 45–46
  "Race Discrimination in the Administration of the Death Penalty: An Overview of the Empirical Evidence with Special Emphasis on the Post-1990 Research," 91–92
Working Group on the Universal Periodic Review: United States of America (UN Human Rights Council), 124–125
World. *See* Capital punishment, worldwide
Wright, Cheryl Renee, 59
Wright, Myra, 63
Writ of certiorari, 53
WSBA (Washington State Bar Association), 79

Y

Yang, Tasi-Shai, 11
Yang, Yen-I, 11
"Year That States Adopted Life without Parole (LWOP) Sentencing" (DPIC), 10
York, Mary Lou, 41
Yowell, Carol, 63
Yowell, John, 63
Yowell, Michael, 63

Z

Zezima, Katie, 62